ANALYZING DEVIANCE

The Dorsey Series in Sociology

Advisory Editor
Robin M. Williams, Jr.
Cornell University

Consulting Editor
Charles M. Bonjean
The University of Texas at Austin

ANALYZING DEVIANCE

James D. Orcutt
Florida State University

1983

THE DORSEY PRESS
Homewood, Illinois 60430

© THE DORSEY PRESS, 1983

All rights reserved. No part of this publication may be reproduced, stored in a retrieval system, or transmitted, in any form or by any means, electronic, mechanical, photocopying, recording, or otherwise, without the prior written permission of the publisher.

ISBN 0-256-02303-4
Library of Congress Catalog Card No. 82-73403
Printed in the United States of America

1 2 3 4 5 6 7 8 9 0 ML 0 9 8 7 6 5 4 3

Preface

Textbooks sometimes bear little resemblance to the professional literature in the same area of study. This is certainly true in the sociology of deviance. In my own experience of a decade of teaching and research on deviance, I have encountered a rather frustrating gap between materials published for student audiences and the actual scholarship presented in journals, monographs, and professional meetings. This book represents an attempt to bridge that gap.

No single conceptual perspective or theoretical position dominates this volume. Neither is it tied to any particular research tradition or methodology. In these respects, at least, this book is faithful to contemporary scholarship on deviance and social control. The sociological literature in this area is animated by diverse theoretical viewpoints, alternative research strategies, and numerous other points of controversy. What I have tried to do in the following pages is provide a clear, systematic, and balanced introduction to the different approaches that sociologists have taken toward these issues. To this end, the book is organized according to a relatively simple twofold scheme that has proven very useful in my own undergraduate and graduate courses. On the one hand, I distinguish between "normative" and "relativistic" perspectives on deviance. Although often expressed in other terms, this distinction should be familiar to most instructors as a division between the older sociological focus on norm-violating behavior and the more recent conceptual emphasis on societal reactions to deviance. On the other hand, I introduce a cross-cutting distinction between the macro- and micro-levels of analysis in sociological inquiry into deviance. Combining these two dimensions, then, yields four distinct approaches to the study of deviance.

Each approach is carefully developed and illustrated in Chapter 1. Following a general discussion of the historical background of the sociology of deviance and some of its central concerns and issues in Chapters 2 and 3, the remainder of the book is divided into four parts corresponding to these analytical approaches. The first chapter in each part reviews the major theoretical contributions to the approach. A second chapter turns to empirical implications of the approach and features three research illustrations drawn from leading sociological journals. In each case, the opening research illustration is a classic study of deviance or social control while the other two articles are more recent investigations of key problems in research on crime, mental disorder, and other forms of deviance. A concluding section to these chapters summarizes recent empirical evidence bearing on important theoretical questions raised by each approach to deviance.

The difficult task of researching and writing this book was eased considerably by a Developing Scholar Award granted by Florida State University. I am grateful for the advice and support of many students and colleagues, but I especially want to acknowledge the dedicated effort of my graduate assistant, Susan Jaquith. Two good friends (and good sociologists), Al Bayer and Candy West, gave me encouragement when I really needed it. I also want to thank the reviewers for The Dorsey Press who provided helpful comments on the manuscript, Sheldon Ekland-Olson, University of Texas, Austin; Charles E. Frazier, University of Florida, Gainesville; and consulting editors Charles Bonjean and Robin Williams. Finally, at the end as in the beginning, my gratitude to Mary and Michelle goes beyond words.

James D. Orcutt

Contents

1. **Sociological points of view** 2

    The diversity of deviant phenomena. Sociological definitions of deviance. The normative perspective on deviance: *Describing the characteristics of deviants. Explaining the causes of deviant behavior. A macro-normative theory of deviance: Merton's anomie theory. A micro-normative theory of deviance: Sutherland's differential association theory.* The relativistic perspective on deviance: *Describing the nature of definitional processes. Understanding the sources and implications of reactions to deviance. A micro-relativistic theory of deviance: Becker's labeling theory. A macro-relativistic theory of deviance: Quinney's theory of the social reality of crime.* Analyzing deviance: An overview: *An overview of sociological approaches to deviance. An overview of the book.*

2. **Early development of the field of deviance** 30

    Early conceptions of social problems and deviance: *The social pathology period. The social disorganization period.* The normative period and deviant behavior: *The emergence of the normative perspective. Cumulative development of the sociology of deviant behavior.* The relativistic period and deviance.

3. **Central issues in the study of deviance: Definitions, descriptions, theories, and values** 52

    The issue of defining deviance. The issue of describing deviance. The issue of theorizing about deviance. The issue of values in the study of deviance.

ix

4. **The macro-normative approach: Anomie and subculture theory** 66

   Theoretical traditions in the normative perspective. The anomie tradition: *Durkheim's classic contribution. Merton's theory of social structure and anomie. Later developments in the anomie tradition.* The subcultural tradition: *Cohen and the culture of the delinquent gang. Cloward and Ohlin: Illegitimate opportunities. Other contributions to the subcultural tradition.*

5. **Research on rates of deviant behavior** 86

   Introductory comments on Hollingshead and Redlich's research, 88
   Research illustration 5–A: Social stratification and psychiatric disorders, August B. Hollingshead and Frederick C. Redlich, 91

   Introductory comments on Hindelang's research, 102
   Research illustration 5–B: Race and involvement in common law personal crimes, Michael J. Hindelang, 104

   Introductory comments on Erlanger's research, 128
   Research illustration 5–C: Is there a "subculture of violence" in the South? Howard S. Erlanger, 132

6. **The micro-normative approach: Social learning and control theory** 150

   The social learning tradition: *Sutherland's differential association theory. Criticisms and revisions of Sutherland's theory.* The control tradition: *Conformity as problematic. Hirschi's theory of the social bond. Earlier contributions to the control tradition.*

7. **Research on interpersonal relationships and deviant behavior** 166

   Introductory comments on Short and Strodtbeck's research, 169
   Research illustration 7–A: The response of gang leaders to status threats: An observation on group process and delinquent behavior, James F. Short, Jr., and Fred L. Strodtbeck, 172

   Introductory comments on Orcutt's research, 184
   Research illustration 7–B: Marijuana use and social relationships, James D. Orcutt, 185

   Introductory comments on Gove and Geerken's research, 204
   Research illustration 7–C: The effect of children and employment on the mental health of married men and women, Walter R. Gove and Michael R. Geerken, 207

8. **The micro-relativistic approach: Labeling theory** 222

   Intellectual foundations of the labeling tradition: *The influence of interactionist social psychology. Lemert: Societal reaction and secondary deviation.*

Becker, Kitsuse, and Erikson: The mainstream of labeling theory. Later developments in the labeling tradition.

9. **Research on interpersonal reactions to deviance** **244**

   Introductory comments on Rosenhan's research, 246
   Research illustration 9–A: On being sane in insane places, *David L. Rosenhan, 249*

   Introductory comments on Lundman's research, 269
   Research illustration 9–B: Routine police arrest practices: A commonweal perspective, *Richard J. Lundman, 272*

   Introductory comments on Steffensmeier and Terry's research, 288
   Research illustration 9–C: Deviance and respectability: An observational study of reactions to shoplifting, *Darrell J. Steffensmeier and Robert M. Terry, 291*

10. **The macro-relativistic approach: Interest group and neo-Marxist conflict theory** **310**

    Intellectual foundations of the conflict tradition: *Marx and class conflict. Other sources of the conflict tradition.* Interest group conflict theories: *Gusfield and status politics. Later work on interest group conflict.* Neo-Marxist conflict theories: *Taylor, Walton, and Young: The new criminology. Radical criticism in the United States. Recent trends in neo-Marxist theory.*

11. **Research on societal definitions and reactions to deviance** **336**

    Introductory comments on Chambliss' research, 338
    Research illustration 11–A: A sociological analysis of the law of vagrancy, *William J. Chambliss, 340*

    Introductory comments on Morgan's research, 355
    Research illustration 11–B: The legislation of drug law: Economic crisis and social control, *Patricia A. Morgan, 358*

    Introductory comments on Galliher and Walker's research, 371
    Research illustration 11–C: The puzzle of the social origins of the Marihuana Tax Act of 1937, *John F. Galliher and Allynn Walker, 372*

References **389**

Name index **407**

Subject index **415**

ANALYZING DEVIANCE

Sociological points of view

1

This book is about two topics that share the name *deviance*. One of these topics will be various *social phenomena* that sociologists study as instances of deviance. The other topic is the *sociological field* of deviance itself. There was a time not so long ago when textbooks on deviance could pass over the latter topic rather quickly. Despite some theoretical differences of opinion, sociologists appeared to agree among themselves about what deviance is and how it should be studied. Since there seemed to be a general consensus on these basic questions, sociologists did not worry a great deal about the nature of their field as they went about their normal business of studying deviant phenomena.

Sociologists and textbooks in the area of deviance can no longer afford this luxury. The keynote of recent sociological work on deviance is controversy. The questions of what deviance is and how it should be studied are now the subject of intense debates between sociologists. While these controversies have generated a good deal of intellectual excitement within the field of deviance, they are also likely to confuse anyone else who wants to know what the sociology of deviance is all about. When the study of *deviant phenomena* means entirely different things to different sociologists, it would be unwise if not impossible to pursue that topic without first analyzing the sociologists themselves and their differing points of view on the subject matter of their field.

THE DIVERSITY OF DEVIANT PHENOMENA

What is deviance? This question is a good place to begin an analysis of the sociological field of deviance and the phenomena it investigates. You can probably give numerous examples of people or behavior that strike you as immoral, weird, evil, illegal, sick, or, in a word, deviant. Your answers might be similar to those obtained in a survey by J. L. Simmons, in which he asked a sample of 180 persons in 1965 to "list those things or types of persons whom you regard as deviant." Table 1–1 shows the responses given by 10 percent or more of Simmons' sample. In addition to this list of the "top 14" deviants, a few of Simmons' respondents also placed such persons as career women, junior executives, girls who wear makeup, and know-it-all professors in the category of "deviant."

Many of the responses obtained in Simmons' study refer to major

Table 1–1
Most frequent responses by a public sample to the question "what is deviant?"

Response	Percent mentioning
Homosexuals	49
Drug addicts	47
Alcoholics	46
Prostitutes	27
Murderers	22
Criminals	18
Lesbians	13
Juvenile delinquents	13
Beatniks	12
Mentally ill	12
Perverts	12
Communists	10
Atheists	10
Political extremists	10

Source: Adapted from J. L. Simmons, "Public Stereotypes of Deviants," *Social Problems* 13 (Fall 1965), p. 224.

forms of deviant phenomena that capture a great deal of public attention and have been the subject of intensive investigation by sociologists in the field of deviance. Other answers to Simmons' question refer to phenomena that neither you nor most other people would define as deviant. For instance, you would probably be unlikely to consider girls who wear makeup as deviant (but how would you evaluate the person who gave such an answer?).

What should impress you most about the findings of Simmons' study is the incredible *diversity* of the social phenomena that people classify as deviant. Social definitions of deviance not only vary markedly across different segments of the general public but they also change across time. How many of us today, only a few years since Simmons' study, would include beatniks or atheists in our top 14? How many of us would place homosexuals, drug addicts, or alcoholics at the very top of our lists of deviants? Further research of the kind conducted by Simmons would be required for an adequate answer to these questions, but an informed guess would be that some important changes have occurred in public definitions of these and other forms of deviance (see Thielbar & Feldman, 1978).

SOCIOLOGICAL DEFINITIONS OF DEVIANCE

If at this point you can appreciate the sheer diversity of phenomena that are considered deviant by the general public, you can also appreciate the difficulties confronting sociologists when they themselves attempt to answer the question "what is deviance?" Sociological efforts to define deviance are less concerned with particular kinds of deviance than they are with what all forms of deviance have in common. What sociologists seek in a definition of deviance is an abstract concept that can be applied to deviant phenomena *in general*.

The choice of definitions for central concepts is extremely important in any area of scientific study, and the field of deviance is no exception. The choice of a certain definition of deviance amounts to a decision to study those phenomena that fit under the definition and to ignore phenomena excluded by the definition. In other words, a definition of deviance defines the boundaries of this field of study.

Not only do conceptual definitions direct scientific attention to particular phenomena but they also limit attention to only selected aspects of those phenomena. Since the empirical world—that reality we observe through our senses—is infinitely complex, any empirical phenomenon can be viewed in any number of ways. Concepts simplify the task of studying the empirical world by restricting attention to particular, selected features of phenomena that scientists agree are most useful for scientific purposes. Concepts represent mutual agreements among scientists to look at certain phenomena in certain ways.

Conceptual definitions, being agreements to adopt a particular perspective on reality, are not true or false. However, these agreements are hardly arbitrary. Depending on the scientific problem at hand, some definitions will be more useful than others. For instance, many geneticists have agreed to define and classify human "races" according to the distribution of various blood proteins in different human populations. This concept of race has proven useful for investigating various biological problems relating to human inheritance. Such a definition of race is useless to sociologists involved in the study of race relations. Instead, sociologists define race in terms of social distinctions made between groups of people in various societies that may have little or no relationship to biological inheritance, but have great significance for understanding racial prejudice and discrimination. Needless to say, geneticists have not found sociological definitions of race to be particularly useful in their work.

Returning to our initial concern, "what is deviance?," we can now refine this question to ask "which way of defining deviance is most useful for its study?" Sociologists simply do not agree among themselves on a conceptual answer to this basic question. In fact, disagreement over the utility of competing sociological definitions of deviance lies at the heart of much of the controversy in the contemporary field of deviance.

Although sociologists have proposed a number of different definitions of deviance, many of these differences are minor and represent little more than variations on a broader conceptual theme. Most of the disagreement over the concept of deviance appears to boil down to a choice between two alternative definitions: a *normative* definition versus a *relativistic* definition of deviance. The normative definition is the older of these two sociological conceptualizations. According to this definition, *deviance refers to behavior that violates social norms or to persons that engage in such behavior*. Only in the past two decades has this traditional definition of deviance been seriously challenged by sociologists who favor the relativistic alternative. According to the relativistic definition, *deviance refers to behavior or persons that are defined as deviant by social audiences*. This definition is termed *relativistic* because it views persons or their behavior as deviant *only relative to* the way other people react to them.

You might wonder why the distinction between these two definitions is a source of considerable controversy between sociologists in the field of deviance. Although differences in the wording of these definitions may seem subtle and of little consequence, each conceptualization focuses attention on quite different aspects of deviant phenomena. The normative definition narrows in on persons who engage in norm-violating behavior. The relativistic definition emphasizes not the deviants themselves but the social audiences that define them as deviant. These two conceptualizations also raise different questions for research and theorizing on deviance. The normative definition suggests the importance of identifying who breaks norms and explaining why they commit deviant acts. The relativistic definition, on the other hand, indicates a need for research and theory on how social audiences go about defining others as deviant. Simmons' (1965) study of public definitions of deviance is a good example of the kind of research inspired by a relativistic definition.

Thus, the normative-relativistic distinction refers to much more than a mere disagreement over words. These terms identify two distinct *perspectives* for the study of deviant phenomena. Although sociologists within the normative perspective and those within the relativistic perspective sometimes go their separate ways studying different research problems, their divergent points of view on the same phenomena often bring them into direct disagreement with one another. Their competing descriptions and competing explanations of empirical events have generated a good deal of intellectual excitement and controversy in the field of deviance.

Most of this book will be devoted to a review and analysis of theories and research within these two sociological perspectives on deviance. No attempt will be made to resolve once and for all the major controversies between these two perspectives. Resolution of conflict within the field of deviance seems neither to be possible nor desirable at the present time. However, the positions of each perspective on various issues will be examined critically, and we will assess the relative usefulness of the two definitions of deviance for the study of certain empirical problems. Now that you have been introduced to these two sides of the sociological point of view on deviance, we can begin to take a closer look at what each side has to offer.

THE NORMATIVE PERSPECTIVE ON DEVIANCE

In its definition of deviance, the normative perspective offers sociologists a straightforward formula for reducing the bewildering diversity of deviant phenomena to a common denominator. The concept of norm violation appears to be a simple, objective criterion for determining what is deviant and what is not. The normative definition of deviance is especially appealing to many sociologists because it is based on one of the most familiar terms in their scientific vocabulary, *social norms*. This term refers to *rules or expectations for behavior that are shared by members of a group or society*. The concept of social norm has been honored by a long tradition of sociological theory and research that views *consensus* as a basic fact of organized social life. According to this sociological tradition, consensus or shared agreement exists in all organized groups and societies about what behaviors are appropriate and expected of members. This consensus is expressed through social norms—shared rules that channel behavior in various areas of social life into orderly and predictable patterns. Sometimes, of course, behavior deviates from these normative patterns. Such behavior, according to the normative definition, is deviant behavior; and deviants are those people who violate the normative consensus of organized society.

Some of the different kinds of social norms that sociologists study and deviants violate are suggested by the responses from Simmons' (1965) study in Table 1–1. Murderers have broken a very *general* social norm that applies to nearly all members of society and refers to expected behavior in virtually all situations: Thou shalt not kill! This is also an example of a *legal* norm that has been formally enshrined into law. Criminals are another category of deviants who have violated legal norms. However, it is not illegal to be an alcoholic in American society. This is an example of a deviant whose behavior violates a general *moral norm* relating to appropriate patterns of alcohol use. Similarly, atheists who speak their convictions violate a general moral norm of many social groups: Thou shalt believe in God! Other social norms are very *specific* and consist of expectations for the behavior of only certain people in certain situations. Students, for instance, can be defined as juvenile delinquents for violating the specific legal norm that Thou shalt not play hooky from school! Finally, it should be pointed out that some of the answers obtained by Simmons, such as girls who wear makeup or know-it-all professors, do not refer to violations of widely shared norms. Therefore, according to the normative definition of deviance, people who behave in these ways would not be considered deviant (and many of us can rest easier!).

One of the principal merits of the normative definition is its apparent objectivity. Social norms are characteristics of groups and societies that can be identified through empirical research. Norms can be inferred from observations of the characteristic patterns of behavior in a group or society. Or, norms can be determined directly by asking people what rules and expectations for behavior they share with other members of their group or society. Thus, objective, scientific research, instead of the personal values of the social scientist, determines the standards used to define deviant behavior.

In practice, however, sociologists within the normative perspective usually bypass the study of social norms and move directly to the study of norm violators. In so doing, the normative perspective often relies on the legal norms specified by the criminal law or on the scientific standards used in other fields such as psychiatry as guidelines for identifying deviance. But, more typically, many forms of deviance appear to be so obviously in violation of important moral norms that there is little reason to question the applicability of the normative definition of deviance.

When we read in the newspaper about cases where a number of people have been slain by a gunman or where school children have been assaulted by a child molester, we don't pause to wonder whether these behaviors violate social norms. These are cases where *deviance is objectively given by the very nature of the acts themselves* (Rubington & Weinberg, 1978). It seems unimportant and even strange to ask "what norms have been violated here?" Instead, we ask "who could do such a thing?" Or "why do they do it?" These last two questions are the very issues that are of greatest concern to the normative perspective on deviance.

This is not to imply that sociologists in the normative perspective are motivated by sensationalism in their studies of deviance. Most forms of deviance studied by this perspective are much less dramatic than mass murder or child molestation. Rather, these cases illustrate why the attention of the normative perspective focuses directly on deviants rather than on the social norms they violate. Certain forms of behavior appear, by their very nature, to be inherently and objectively deviant. By virtue of engaging in such behavior, the deviant also seems to stand out as a person who is inherently and objectively different from the rest of us. This way of looking at deviants and their behavior leads naturally into the two basic analytical problems of the normative perspective on deviance: *describing* the characteristics of deviants (who could do such a thing?) and *explaining* the causes of deviant behavior (why do they do it?).

Describing the characteristics of deviants

When a newspaper reporter investigates a particular case where someone has violated an important social norm and asks "who could do such a thing?," he or she is typically seeking a different kind of description than would a sociologist who is describing the characteristics of deviants. Reporters tend to focus on the unique and unusual characteristics of individual deviants. Sociologists in the normative perspective, on the other hand, usually have little interest in specific details about individual deviants. Instead, the efforts of these sociologists are primarily directed toward the description of general characteristics that are useful in distinguishing most deviants from most nondeviants. For the normative perspective, then, the question of who is deviant is not directed at any particular individual but at the distinguishing characteristics of deviants in general.

Much of the descriptive work conducted by sociologists in the normative perspective has been based on data taken from the official records of agencies that deal with deviants, such as law enforcement statistics or the admissions records of psychiatric hospitals. These records, of course, are based on large numbers of cases where important norms have been violated and would appear to be a good source of general information on the characteristics of deviants. Information from these records is often used to compare deviants to nondeviants on such variables as occupation, race, or area of residence. The distinguishing characteristics of deviants can be described by noting which characteristics show up with greater frequency in the official records than in the general population. For instance, persons who are in low-status occupations, who are black, or who live in slum areas of cities are overrepresented in arrest statistics (Clinard & Meier, 1979) and in first admissions to psychiatric hospitals (Rose & Staub, 1955; Eaton, 1980).

Although the normative perspective has for years relied on official records as a major source of descriptive data, these sociologists have also had to find ways of getting around the limitations of *secondary* data that were originally gathered for nonsociological purposes. Thus, sociologists sometimes conduct interviews or administer questionnaires to deviants in order to gather *primary* data that are directly relevant to sociological purposes. Sometimes this research is conducted on people who are known to have violated social norms, such as prisoners or mental patients. Other research is based on more general samples where people are classified as deviant according to their self-reported involvement in norm-violating behavior in answer to questions during the interview or on the questionnaire. All of these techniques for gathering primary data, which are generally known as *survey techniques*, make it possible to measure and describe characteristics that are important to sociologists rather than to official agencies.

Whether based on official records or on survey data, the accumulated results of descriptive research are used by the normative perspective to derive *empirical generalizations*—statements describing general differences between the characteristics of deviants and nondeviants on certain social variables. In this way, sociologists arrive at very general answers to the question "who could do such a thing?" An empirical generalization about *who* is deviant does not by itself give sociologists an answer to the question of *why* such persons engage in deviant behavior. However, descriptions of deviants do provide important clues in the search for theoretical explanations of deviant behavior within the normative perspective.

Explaining the causes of deviant behavior

The normative definition of deviance sorts social behavior into two categories: conforming behavior and norm-violating behavior. Faced with a choice between these two alternatives, most people in most situations will conform. At least this is the assumption made by the normative perspective on deviance. Behavior that conforms to norms shared by members of organized society is expected and rewarded. Thus, conformity is unproblematic, both to sociologists in the normative perspective and to members of society. The problems arise when behavior goes against the heavy odds in favor of conformity. Some people do choose to behave in ways that violate expectations and run the risk of punishment by organized society. Why do they do it? What causes these people to make such a "bad" choice of behaviors?

In attempting to answer these questions, sociologists in the normative perspective usually do not see the deviant's choice as a free one. Deviant behavior is usually explained as a forced choice determined by factors that cause the deviant to act differently from the rest of us.

The central problem of this perspective is to develop theories that state, in very general terms, exactly what those determining factors are.

Sociologists, of course, are not the only scientists interested in the explanation of deviant behavior. Psychiatrists, psychologists, and biologists also share an interest in this problem. However, theories of deviant behavior in those disciplines tend to emphasize different determining factors than do sociological explanations. Nonsociological theories tend to locate the causes of deviant behavior *within* the deviant individual. These theories view deviant behavior as a product of pathology or deficiencies in the personality or biological constitution of the deviant. Sociological theories of deviant behavior, on the other hand, locate the causes of deviant behavior in the *social environment* of the deviant. Sociologists look to distinctive features of the deviant's social relationships or to pressures and disorganizing influences in society for factors which produce deviant behavior. Where other scientific theories focus on kinds of *people* to explain various forms of deviant behavior, sociological theories focus on kinds of *environments* (Reasons, 1975). Thus, when sociologists attempt to describe the general characteristics of deviants, they are searching for clues to the kinds of environmental factors that force people into deviant behavior.

This search for important environmental factors in deviant behavior is not conducted at random but is guided by theoretical concepts that define selected aspects of the social environment as being particularly worthy of sociological attention. Like concepts of deviance, concepts referring to the social environment are defined by agreement among sociologists. And here, too, disagreements arise about which concepts are most useful for the purpose of explaining deviant behavior. While not as controversial as the conceptual conflict that separates general perspectives on deviance, different conceptions of the social environment do form the basis for important divisions between theoretical approaches to deviant behavior *within* the normative perspective.

One of the most important divisions between theoretical approaches within the normative perspective is based on differences in the *level of analysis* that characterizes various conceptions of the social environment. Some normative theories of deviant behavior are concerned with a *macro* level of analysis whereas others are directed at a *micro* level of analysis. Macro-level theories of deviant behavior are based on concepts that focus on very large-scale features of the social environment and attempt to explain broad patterns of variation in deviant behavior. Social class, community, or social institution are some examples of concepts that are used in macro-level theories to deal with large-scale features of the social environment. Micro-level theories, on the other hand, employ concepts that look at small-scale features of the social environment, such as face-to-face relationships and group influences on the individual. Micro-level theories of deviant behavior attempt to analyze the impact of the deviant's immediate social environment upon his or her behavior.

This classification of theoretical approaches according to conceptual levels of analysis is helpful in understanding sociological explanations of deviant behavior within the normative perspective. While two theories might both fall within the normative perspective by virtue of the common way they define deviance, their explanations of deviant behavior may be quite dissimilar since they focus on phenomena at different levels of analysis. As we shall see later, the macro-micro distinction can also be applied to theoretical approaches within the relativistic perspective on deviance.

Before turning to the relativistic perspective, however, we should briefly consider two particular examples of normative theories that attempt to relate causes in the social environment to deviant behavior. One of these is the major *macro-normative* theory of deviant behavior, Robert K. Merton's (1957) *anomie* theory. The other is the most important *micro-normative* theory, Edwin H. Sutherland's (1947) *differential association* theory. Although a number of theories can be classified as macro normative or as micro normative, Merton and Sutherland are the best-known examples of theorists that use these respective approaches to the explanation of deviant behavior.

A macro-normative theory of deviance: Merton's anomie theory

First presented in 1938, Merton's anomie theory of deviant behavior played a major part in the development of the field of deviance and continues to influence the work of many contemporary sociologists. No other theory so well exemplifies the macro-normative approach to the analysis of deviance. Merton makes it clear that he is interested in broad patterns of norm-violating behavior rather than in the behavior of individual deviants (1957: 132): "We look at variations in the *rates* of deviant behavior." Analysis of this macro-level problem requires macro-level concepts. Merton focuses on nothing less than the cultural goals, institutional norms, and social structures of *entire societies*.

Merton devotes most of his attention to American society and analyzes how people located in certain segments of this society are exposed to environmental pressures toward deviant behavior. All segments of American society are encouraged to strive for the cultural goal of material success; i.e., money and the prestigious goods it can buy. This society is characterized by a cultural environment "which places a high premium on economic affluence and social ascent for *all* its members" (1957: 146). So much emphasis is placed on the dominant goal of material success, in fact, that considerably less importance is assigned to the particular ways or means members of society use to attain this goal. Although institutionalized norms in American society specify that material success should be sought through certain legitimate means, such as a good education or a respectable job, it is the goal itself that *really* counts. Furthermore, people in *some* segments of this society do not have equal access to these legitimate channels to success. Specifically, the lower class in American society is confronted by restricted educational and occupational opportunities. In other words, the legitimate pathways to the common goal of material success are blocked in some locations in the social environment.

These broad-scale features of American society—overemphasis of the economic goal, underemphasis of the norms specifying legitimate means, and restricted access to those means in some segments of society—add up to a strong pressure toward deviant behavior. Members of society loosen their commitment to the institutional norms, a state of *anomie* or normlessness that is particularly acute in the lower class. The lower class is especially likely to adapt to these environmental conditions by choosing *illegitimate* means to achieve economic success. With little confidence in their chances of "making it" legitimately, members of the lower class turn to criminal and delinquent pathways to their economic goal. Merton defines this lower-class solution as *innovation*, since it involves the rejection of conventional means to the cultural goal in favor of "innovative," illegitimate means.

Although Merton discusses how environmental conditions in American society lead to other deviant adaptations in addition to innovation, his analysis of pressures toward crime and delinquency in the lower class provides a sufficient illustration for now of the macro-normative approach to deviance. Using this broad explanation of deviant behavior, Merton can account for an important empirical generalization mentioned earlier: that persons with low-status jobs, blacks, and slum dwellers have high arrest rates for criminal activities. All of these characteristics describe persons who are located conceptually in a lower-class environment, the *kind of social environment* that, according to anomie theory, is productive of criminal behavior. Thus, a general theory based on macro-level concepts is used to explain the social causes of a broad pattern of norm-violating behavior—class variations in crime rates. This is a classic example of how deviance is analyzed by the macro-normative approach.

② A micro-normative theory of deviance: Sutherland's differential association theory

Although Sutherland began work on a general explanation of criminal behavior in the 1920s, this first formal statement of differential association theory appeared in the 1939 edition of his textbook, *Principles of Criminology*. This theory, like anomie theory, has had a major impact on the sociological study of deviance, particularly among sociologists specializing in the study of criminal behavior. Although Merton and Sutherland share a common interest in the social causes of norm-violating behavior, their explanations of deviant behavior focus on quite different aspects of the social environment. As opposed to the attempt of anomie theory to explain broad variations in rates of deviant behavior in different segments of society, Sutherland explicitly points out that differential association theory "purports to explain the criminal and noncriminal behavior of individual persons" (Sutherland & Cressey, 1974: 77). Distinctly micro-level concepts are brought to bear on this problem. Sutherland focuses on the small-scale environment of the intimate personal group and analyzes how the attitudes and behavior of the deviant are influenced by processes of interpersonal communication.

The central explanatory principle of differential association theory is simple and straightforward: a person engages in criminal behavior "because of an excess of definitions favorable to violation of law over definitions unfavorable to violation of law" (Sutherland & Cressey, 1974: 75). All of us are members of intimate personal groups where we are exposed to definitions unfavorable to violation of law. In the family environment, for instance, we learn from our parents that we should respect and obey the law. However, most of us have also at some time been involved in groups where the law is defined in unfavorable terms. For example, some of your close friends might define laws prohibiting the use of certain drugs as unfair and might assure you that the chances of being caught for drug use are small. But, as Sutherland points out above, the mere fact that interpersonal communication in some groups exposes a person to unfavorable definitions of the law is not sufficient to produce criminal behavior. Criminal behavior results only when such definitions *exceed* noncriminal definitions that support the law. Thus, it is not the *absolute* amount of exposure to criminal patterns that is important; the *differential or ratio of associations* with criminal and noncriminal patterns is what provides the theoretical key to Sutherland's explanation of criminal behavior.

Sutherland goes into additional details of this criminal learning process, but this brief review of the basic elements of differential association theory highlights the main features of the micro-normative approach to deviance. It is clear that the concepts used in Sutherland's theory narrow in on smaller-scale aspects of the social environment than is the case with anomie theory. Instead of focusing on locations of large segments of society in a class structure, Sutherland deals with the location of individuals in various small group environments. The concepts used in differential association theory direct attention to individuals' definitions and attitudes toward the law rather than to the cultural goals and institutional norms of society in general. In short, Sutherland's micro-level analysis brings into focus details of the social environment that are blurred or missing in Merton's macro-level approach.

However, as Sutherland himself recognized (Sutherland & Cressey, 1974: 77), differential association theory can only indirectly account for broad empirical generalizations such as the relationships between occupation, race, area of residence, and criminal arrest rates. It can be argued that these general characteristics of deviants reflect high rates of exposure to groups where criminal learning occurs. But, differential association theory is more powerful in explaining generalizations derived from surveys and other research techniques where the linkages between group influences and individual behavior can be directly measured. For instance, a number of surveys have found that the best predictor of a student's own use of illegal drugs is the number of his or her friends who use the drug (Johnson, 1973; Kandel, 1980). Sutherland's theory is well suited to explain this kind of empirical generalization.

This discussion of the theoretical work of Merton and Sutherland has emphasized some important differences between the macro-normative and micro-normative approaches to deviance. However, a comparison of differences between these theoretical levels of analysis should not obscure the dominant theme that runs through all the theories within the normative perspective. Both Merton and Sutherland agree that the central problem for the sociological field of deviance is the analysis of persons and behavior that violate social norms. The significance of this common viewpoint on deviant phenomena will become clearer as we examine a conflicting point of view held by other sociologists—the relativistic perspective on deviance.

THE RELATIVISTIC PERSPECTIVE ON DEVIANCE

The relativistic perspective approaches the study of deviant phenomena with quite a different conception of the nature of social life than does the normative perspective. For sociologists within the relativistic perspective, *diversity*, not consensus, is the central fact of social life. Emphasizing the great complexity and diversity of people and behavior in modern industrialized societies, these sociologists argue that it is unrealistic to assume that social organization is based on a general normative consensus. People and groups often have *competing* or *conflicting* interests rather than *shared* interests and goals. Instead of being a product of consensus, organized social behavior may be an outcome of self-interested bargaining between opposing parties or of coercion of some people by others who are more powerful.

In addition, the relativistic perspective emphasizes that existing social arrangements are *always subject to change*. These sociologists argue that the static concept of "norm" tends to overlook dynamic aspects of social life. Most sociologists within the relativistic perspective do not deny that social rules and expectations guide behavior in many situations, but they view these behavioral guidelines as arrangements that have been created or worked out through *dynamic social processes*. On a micro level, social relationships are not rigidly determined by stable normative expectations. Rather, social relationships are formed and changed through *interactional processes* that have a spontaneous and dynamic character. Similarly, on a macro level, the class structure of society is not viewed as a fixed entity. The relativistic perspective analyzes society as an arena where *conflict processes*, shifting class relationships, and struggles for power are played out over time.

The relativistic perspective, with this dynamic and diversified conception of social life, is highly critical of the usefulness of the concept of social norm as a standard for defining deviance. If organized patterns of behavior are *not* based on widely shared, stable norms, then it becomes misleading to define behavior that departs from those patterns as "norm violations." In other words, the concept of norm is not useful in distinguishing deviant behavior from nondeviant behavior. Furthermore, if rules and guidelines for behavior are *created* in interpersonal or historical situations by dynamic social processes, then it is difficult, if not impossible, to specify *beforehand* the particular behaviors that will be appropriate or inappropriate in those situations. Finally, since persons or groups in society are often in competition or conflict with one another, they may likewise have competing or conflicting views about deviance. Therefore, answers to the question "what is deviant?" will depend very much on *who* you ask. This is precisely the point of Simmons' (1965) study that was discussed earlier. The diversity of the answers he received to his question reflects the diversity of *social audiences* in a complex and changing society.

In short, the relativistic perspective reaches the conclusion that neither the concept of social norm nor any other supposedly "objective" criterion is useful for defining deviance. This is an unsettling conclusion for it seems to leave us with no abstract standard—no common benchmark for deciding what is deviant and what is not. Fortunately, you already know the relativistic solution to this dilemma: deviance is simply whatever is defined as deviant by social audiences. This definition intentionally shys away from the "objective" viewpoint of sociologists looking at society from the outside and places the burden of defining deviance on the subjective viewpoints of social audiences within society. Instead of treating deviance as *objectively given* by the inherent nature of certain acts and actors, the relativistic definition treats deviance as *subjectively problematic*, as a phenomenon that is completely dependent on how social audiences define acts and actors (Rubington & Weinberg, 1978).

The relativistic definition calls attention to quite a different set of "deviant phenomena" and research problems than does the normative definition of deviance. Whereas the normative perspective attempts to describe the distinguishing characteristics of deviants, the relativistic perspective focuses on the social processes involved in audience definitions of deviance and reactions to persons who have been so defined. Rather than attempting to explain the kinds of environments that cause deviant behavior, the relativistic perspective attempts to understand the implications of audience reactions, both for persons who have been defined as deviant and for society in general. In other words, the relativistic perspective shifts the focus of the field of deviance from deviants and deviant behavior to social audiences and definitional processes.

Describing the nature of definitional processes

Since the central concept of the relativistic perspective is based on audience definitions of persons and behaviors as deviant, a major task for these sociologists is the description of the general processes involved in these definitional phenomena. In describing social processes, the relativistic perspective tends to avoid such terms as *characteristics* or *variables* that imply a certain state or condition of a phenomenon at a single point in time and refer instead to "stages" or "contingencies" involved in a process over time. One of the clearest examples of this style of description is John I. Kitsuse's (1962: 248) conception of deviance as an interactional process:

> deviance may be conceived as a process by which the members of a group, community, or society (1) interpret behavior as deviant, (2) define persons who so behave as a certain kind of deviant, and (3) accord them the treatment considered appropriate to such deviants.

Here, Kitsuse defines deviance relativistically as an *audience* definition and breaks this definitional process down into three sequential stages. Deviance researchers can and do attempt to describe important events and contingencies occurring at each separate stage of a process. For example, under what conditions will a certain act be interpreted as deviant? Are we as likely to define a close friend as deviant as we would be to define a stranger as deviant? However, the central problem for research in the relativistic perspective is to determine how these separate stages *fit together* as a single dynamic process over time. Using Kitsuse's process as an example, how does interaction between a deviant and a social audience progress from the stage of interpreting an act, through the stage of defining the deviant person, to the final stage of treating the person as a deviant?

Official records and survey research techniques are usually inappropriate for relativistic research on definitional processes. These sources of data can, at best, provide only very indirect measures of dynamic processes that occur in social situations. Therefore, descriptions of definitional processes are typically based on *direct observation* of social interaction between social audiences and the people they define as deviant. The sociologist who is present in such social situations can observe and record definitional processes as they unfold.

A study of police encounters with juveniles by Piliavin and Briar (1964) provides a good illustration of direct observational techniques. The researchers rode in police cars with juvenile officers during their regular patrol shifts. Whenever an officer stopped to question a juvenile on the street, the observers would record on a form such details of the encounter as the race and general appearance of the juvenile, the behavior of the juvenile toward the officer (e.g., cooperative versus uncooperative), and the way the officer treated the juvenile (e.g., arrest, reprimand, release, etc.). One of the major findings of this study was that juveniles who were uncooperative and disrespectful toward the officers were more likely to receive a severe reaction from the officer, such as arrest, than were cooperative juveniles. Piliavin and Briar were able to describe an interactional process where juveniles who were uncooperative were defined as "bad kids" by the officers, which, in turn, resulted in a severe outcome to the encounter. Using direct observation, this study provides an empirical description of Kitsuse's three-stage interactional process: interpretation of behavior as deviant, definition of the actor as deviant, and treatment considered appropriate to such deviants.

Whereas work such as Kitsuse's and Piliavin and Briar's focuses on micro-level interactional processes involved in audience definitions of deviance, other sociologists within the relativistic perspective are interested in the description of macro-level processes. Macro-level descriptive research by these sociologists usually focuses on long-term patterns of change in definitions of deviance as reflected in *historical documents*. Such documents might include legal codes, trial transcripts, or magazine articles written at various points in the past that shed light on historical trends in the definition and treatment of deviants. Relativistic sociologists also make use of accounts written by historians of specific incidents that reveal how societies have reacted to deviance at certain points in time. Unlike many historians, however, sociologists are less interested in the specific details of events recorded in historical documents than they are in describing general, macro-level patterns of change in the definition of deviance. From these patterns, sociologists seek insights into how reactions to deviance are related to *conflict processes* that operate over long periods of time. The vantage point of history makes it possible for sociologists to see how struggles for economic and political power or shifting conflicts between classes and cultural groups shape the way societies define and deal with deviance over time.

The description of definitional processes, whether based on direct observation or on historical documents, is a difficult task. Although sociologists have developed a variety of methods for describing relationships between variables, their ability to describe complex, dynamic social processes is much more limited. As a consequence, the relativistic perspective has been slow in developing a well-researched body of empirical generalizations that describes definitional processes. Nonetheless, crucial insights from observational and historical studies have contributed to theoretical work on the sources and implications of audience reactions to deviance.

Understanding the sources and implications of reactions to deviance

Differences between the relativistic perspective and the normative perspective are nowhere more apparent than in their contrasting approaches to deviance theory. We have already noted some important differences in the kinds of phenomena that are of theoretical interest in the two perspectives. Normative theories focus on deviants and deviant behavior; relativistic theories focus on audience definitions and reactions to deviance. However, even more basic differences can be found in the respective ways these perspectives deal with fundamental questions about the nature and goals of theoretical knowledge.

As we have seen, the normative perspective stresses an objective, scientific approach to theory. Above all, the normative perspective strives for "value-free" explanations of deviant phenomena—theories that are untainted by the personal values or political beliefs of the social scientist. In contrast, most relativistic sociologists take the position that deviance theory *cannot* and *should not* be value free. They argue that the normative perspective is far from value free in its theorizing about deviant behavior. By basing its research on official records and by taking official definitions of deviance as given, the normative perspective uncritically adopts the conservative values of the established agencies of social control. Taking this argument a step further, relativistic sociologists point out that *all* theories of deviance, either intentionally or unintentionally, are based on social values that influence the selection and conceptualization of theoretical problems.

Therefore, most sociologists in the relativistic perspective have no qualms about taking a "value-engaged" approach to theoretical work on deviance (Thio, 1973). If deviance theories are inevitably based on value positions, these sociologists feel it is best to make one's values explicit rather than hiding them behind the facade of value-free science. Thus, Howard Becker (1967), one of the major relativistic theorists, has phrased an explicit question for the field of deviance: "whose side are we on?" Becker answers this question by arguing that sociologists should side with the "underdogs" in society, persons who have been singled out and labeled as deviant by social control agencies.

Becker and many other relativistic sociologists who agree with his position believe that deviance theory should be oriented by *humanistic* values. Developing a theoretical tradition that is known as *labeling theory*, these sociologists have attempted to advance a sympathetic view of deviant persons by analyzing the dehumanizing impact of audience reactions upon them. Labeling theory can be classified as a *micro-relativistic* approach to deviance since it focuses primarily on the small-scale interactional processes through which individuals are labeled and punished as deviants.

Labeling theorists have been particularly interested in the implications of *formal* reactions to deviance, social control administered by law enforcement agencies or mental health professionals. Although persons may be brought to the attention of formal social control agencies by *informal* reactions in such groups as the family or co-workers, official labels applied by judges and psychiatrists are thought to have an especially profound impact on the deviant. Official labeling of a person as criminal or psychotic can lead to confinement in dehumanizing institutions such as prisons and asylums. Labeling theorists also point out that official, public labels *stigmatize* deviants by defining them as morally inferior beings who should be avoided and rejected by members of conventional society. Labeled as deviant by powerful agents of social control and treated as outcasts by conventional society, deviants may actually come to *see themselves as the thing they have been labeled*. By accepting society's definition of them as criminal or crazy, deviants may begin to engage in the criminal or crazy behaviors that are expected of someone who carries those labels. Ironically, the labeling process itself becomes a cause of deviant behavior. By identifying humanistically with labeled deviants and tracing the oppressive consequences of social control processes, micro-relativistic theories have attempted to understand these and other implications of audience reactions to deviance.

The other major theoretical tradition within the relativistic perspective, conflict theory, basically agrees with the humanistic orientation of labeling theory. Conflict theorists also side with the underdogs and are highly critical of official agencies of social control. However, these sociologists argue that deviance theory should not stop at the point of sympathizing with deviants and understanding the human implications of social control. Many conflict theorists believe that deviance theory should be oriented by *activist* values and should be used as a tool for *changing* the systems of social control that oppress deviants and other underdogs.

As a first step in bringing about radical social change, conflict theorists attempt to analyze and understand the underlying sources of society's definitions and reactions to deviance. Deviance theory must look beyond the micro-level interactional processes through which individual deviants are labeled and attempt to analyze the macro-level processes of class or cultural conflict through which labels are created. Therefore, conflict theorists have attempted to show how powerful interest groups influence the passage of laws that define as deviant the activities of opposing groups. For instance, laws against the organizing of labor unions can be seen as definitions of deviance that have been created to protect the economic interests of industrialists. Conflict theorists also analyze how conflict processes affect the enforcement of existing laws. To use another example from labor-industrial conflict, in the years immediately following the passage of the Sherman Anti-Trust Act of 1890, which was designed to limit the growth of industrial monopolies, this law was more frequently enforced against labor organizations than it was against big business (McCormick, 1977).

In general, conflict theory is a *macro-relativistic* approach that focuses on the definition and reaction to deviance as a political phenomenon. Looking to historical patterns of change in the law and social control for insights into conflict processes, these sociologists use large-scale concepts to analyze the structure of power in entire societies. Inspired by activist values, conflict theorists see a macro-level approach as necessary for understanding and changing the systems of political domination that shape a society's reactions to deviance.

As was the case with the normative perspective, a distinction between the macro and micro levels of analysis points out some important theoretical differences within the relativistic perspective on deviance. These differences will become clearer after taking a closer look at Becker's (1963) version of *labeling* theory and comparing it to one of the major conflict theories—Richard Quinney's (1975) theory of the *social reality of crime*.

A micro-relativistic theory of deviance: Becker's labeling theory

The beginnings of the relativistic perspective on deviance go back a number of years (Tannenbaum, 1938; Lemert, 1951). However, a serious challenge to the dominant normative perspective did not develop until the early 1960s, when three important micro-relativistic analyses of deviance were published. The best known of these theoretical statements is contained in Becker's book, *Outsiders* (1963; also see Kitsuse, 1962; Erikson, 1962). The term *labeling theory*, which is usually applied to all of these theoretical statements, comes from Becker's version of the relativistic definition of deviance (1963: 9):

> deviance is not a quality of the act the person commits, but rather a consequence of the application by others of rules and sanctions to an "offender." The deviant is one to whom that label has successfully been applied; deviant behavior is behavior that people so label.

Although Becker's book devotes some attention to macro-level problems, such as the influence of powerful interest groups on antimarijuana legislation, his greatest contribution is an insightful analysis of the micro-level implications of the labeling of individual deviants.

Becker argues that deviance theory should be concerned with dynamic interactional processes rather than cause-and-effect relationships between static variables (1963: 23): "all causes do not operate at the same time, and we need a model which takes into account the fact that patterns of behavior *develop* in an orderly sequence." He suggests the concept of "career" as a useful model for labeling theory. This concept is applied in *Outsiders* in an analysis of the steps and contingencies involved in the development of a *deviant career*—a stable pattern of deviant behavior which is an outcome of labeling processes.

Becker points out that many people occasionally commit nonconforming acts without becoming involved in a sustained pattern of deviant activity. The main reason for this is that most people do not get caught in their nonconformity and remain "secret deviants." One of the most important steps in the process of involvement in a deviant career, according to Becker, is "the experience of being caught and publicly labeled as deviant" (1963: 31). No matter who the person was before being labeled, others' reactions to this person now become focused on one overwhelming aspect of his or her identity—the label or deviant status of fairy, dope fiend, nut, etc.

As a result of these reactions, one of the next steps in the developing deviant career is that "one tends to be cut off . . . from participation in more conventional groups" (1963: 34). A person who has been labeled as a homosexual or a drug addict, for instance, may be denied employment in a "respectable" job and subsequently "drift into unconventional, marginal occupations where it does not make so much difference" to be this kind of deviant (1963: 34). In fact, the deviant may have no choice but to enter into the very kinds of pursuits typically expected of such a person—deviant activities.

The final stages of the deviant career come with the person's increasing involvement with others who have been similarly labeled in organized deviant groups. Membership in a deviant group confirms one's *self*-identity as the kind of deviant he or she has been labeled. In addition, members of such groups share a *deviant subculture*, "a set of perspectives and understandings about what the world is like and how to deal with it" (1963: 38). This subculture provides the deviant with rationalizations and justifications for further deviant activity. Thus, the deviant who eventually ends up in an organized deviant group and shares in its subculture "is more likely than ever before to continue in his ways" (1963: 39).

Becker's analysis gives us a dynamic account of how a person can be funneled into a deviant career by labeling processes. This is also a compellingly humanistic theory of deviance. We can identify and sympathize with the deviant who has been the victim of labeling processes, even to the extent of realizing that it could happen to any of us. In this and many other respects, Becker's micro-relativistic approach to deviance theory contrasts markedly with normative theories that emphasize in a detached, "objective" way the fundamental differences between deviants and nondeviants. If Becker makes us understand the *human* implications of reactions to deviance, then he has accomplished one of his major theoretical goals.

A macro-relativistic theory of deviance: Quinney's theory of the social reality of crime

Conflict theory is even more a child of the 1960s than is labeling theory. In the latter part of that decade, a number of sociologists began to develop macro-relativistic analyses of deviance that were in tune with the currents of social change and radical activism running through society at large. Quinney is foremost among those who have encouraged the growth of conflict theory within the field of deviance.

In his popular textbook, *The Social Reality of Crime* (1970), he introduced a systematic macro-relativistic theory of criminal deviance. This theory was slightly revised in the 1975 edition of Quinney's text to bring it more into line with a Marxist view of class relations in capitalist society (also see Quinney, 1977, 1979).

The theory of the social reality of crime consists of six statements. The first of these statements, which presents Quinney's definition of crime, is clearly relativistic in nature (1975: 37):

> I. The Official Definition of Crime: *Crime as a legal definition of human conduct is created by agents of the dominant class in a politically organized society.*

As opposed to Becker's micro-level focus on the labeling of individuals, Quinney's definition of crime takes a macro-level view of the social audiences that define criminal deviance with its reference to "agents of the dominant class." This definition sets the stage for a theoretical analysis of how broad-scale class conflict processes influence the legal structure of an entire society.

The influence of conflict processes on the formation and application of criminal definitions is pointed out explicitly in the next two statements in Quinney's theory (1975: 38):

> II. Formulating Definitions of Crime: *Definitions of crime are composed of behaviors that conflict with the interests of the dominant class.*
>
> III. Applying Definitions of Crime: *Definitions of crime are applied by the class that has the power to shape the enforcement and administration of criminal law.*

In these statements, the criminal law is seen as a *tool* that is used by a dominant class to maintain its advantageous position in conflicts with less powerful classes. The political nature of deviance is apparent not only in the passage of laws that protect the dominant class but also in the coercive application of those laws by official agents of social control.

The fourth statement in Quinney's theory is complex, but extremely interesting:

> IV. How Behavior Patterns Develop in Relation to Definitions of Crime: *Behavior patterns are structured in relation to definitions of crime, and within this context people engage in actions that have relative probabilities of being defined as criminal.*

With this statement, Quinney attempts to include micro-normative theories, such as differential association, and micro-relativistic theories, such as labeling theory, within his general theoretical framework on criminal deviance. As Quinney points out in his discussion of this statement (1975: 39), although class interests determine what the laws will be, the probability that certain people will *violate* these legal definitions depends on additional social factors. The actions that are most likely to be defined as criminal are performed by persons who have been exposed to group influences that support violation of the law (differential association) or who have become involved in deviant careers through labeling processes (labeling theory). Therefore, Quinney attempts to integrate several theories of deviance into his general theory of criminality.

In the fifth statement of his theory, Quinney returns to his main theme of class conflict (1975: 39):

> V. Constructing an Ideology of Crime: *An ideology of crime is constructed and diffused by the dominant class to secure its hegemony.*

Here, Quinney argues that a dominant class will not simply rely on direct coercion and official social control to maintain its superordinate position in class conflicts. A less obvious, but no less influential, means of maintaining control is to structure the way people think and talk about crime. Using the mass media and other forms of communication, the dominant class exposes the public to certain images or ideas that cause us to look at crime in ways that are favorable to the interests of the dominant class. Thus, when political leaders or the mass media speak of the "crime problem," they are referring to crime in the streets, lower-class crime, not crimes committed by the rich or powerful. This ideology shapes reality and creates a certain way of perceiving and reacting to crime as a phenomenon in the real world. In short, it defines the social reality of crime.

In the final statement of his theory, Quinney combines and summarizes his previous statements as follows (1975: 40):

> VI. Constructing the Social Reality of Crime: *The social reality of crime is constructed by the formulation and application of definitions of crime, the development of behavior patterns in relation to these definitions, and the construction of an ideology of crime.*

The thrust of this and the other statements in Quinney's theory is to achieve an understanding of the sources of audience definitions of and reactions to criminal deviance. Quinney's theory calls attention to important macro-level problems for the relativistic perspective that are beyond the scope of micro-level approaches such as labeling theory. However, like Becker, Quinney not only addresses his theory to scientific problems but to questions of values as well. In addition to the insights it provides into deviant phenomena, Quinney's theory can also be read as an activist critique of the class structure of American society that attempts to create an awareness of the need for radical changes in that society. Quinney and other conflict theorists use the macro-relativistic approach to reveal how inequities of social control are tied into fundamental inequities of the capitalist system. The activist values that inspire conflict theorists are evident in the concluding paragraph of Quinney's textbook (1975: 301):

> Only a vision that goes beyond the reform of the capitalist system can provide us with a humane existence and a world free of the authoritarian state. . . . Only with a critical philosophy of our present condition can we suggest a way out of our possible (neofascist) future.

ANALYZING DEVIANCE: AN OVERVIEW

An overview of sociological approaches to deviance

Having come this far, you should now realize why this chapter began by emphasizing the need to examine the sociological field of deviance before moving on to the conventional subject matter of deviance textbooks, the study of deviant phenomena. As we have seen, sociological viewpoints on this subject matter differ markedly. There is no single, agreed-upon way of looking at deviant phenomena in the contemporary field of deviance. Recognizing that many disagreements do exist among sociologists who study deviance, this chapter has attempted to introduce you to the major divisions in the field that give rise to these controversies.

Much of the controversy in the field of deviance stems from a fundamental difference in *perspective*. Sociologists who use a normative definition see deviant phenomena differently than those who use a relativistic definition. For instance, sociologists in the two perspectives can look at the same empirical generalization, such as a high arrest rate for lower-class persons, and come to quite different conclusions about what it represents. For sociologists in the normative perspective, this generalization shows that lower-class persons are particularly prone to engage in criminal behavior, a phenomenon that is caused by factors in the lower-class environment. To a relativistic sociologist, on the other hand, this generalization reflects a tendency for law enforcement agencies to define lower-class persons as criminals and to react accordingly by arresting them (Kitsuse and Cicourel, 1963). This phenomenon, a high rate of audience reaction to lower-class persons, can be analyzed as an outcome of a process of class conflict. This is only one example out of many that could be chosen to illustrate how sociologists within the two perspectives look at empirical reality from separate viewpoints that not only differ but frequently conflict.

However, differences between sociologists in the field of deviance do not end with the disagreement over definitions of deviance. Even among those sociologists who share a given perspective on deviant phenomena, important differences in their analytical approaches remain as an additional source of controversy. Normative sociologists who use a macro level of analysis in their theorizing and research take quite a different approach to norm-violating phenomena than do others who focus on a micro level of analysis. Still greater disagreement occurs within the relativistic perspective, where the debate between sociologists who conduct micro-level analyses of labeling processes and the macro-level advocates of conflict theory is fueled by differences in values as well as by differences in analytical approach.

Therefore, an adequate understanding of the sociological field of deviance and its controversial issues seems to require a classification of approaches based on two major criteria: (1) the *perspective* implied by a definition of deviance and (2) the *level of analysis* at which deviant phenomena are studied. This chapter has attempted to introduce you to the four major sociological approaches that result from the combination of two perspectives and two levels of analysis: (1) macro-normative; (2) micro-normative; (3) macro-relativistic; and (4) micro-relativistic. Table 1–2 presents an overview of this classification by summarizing the major characteristics of each approach.

As we noted earlier, concepts or classifications are tools used by scientists to simplify the task of studying the empirical world. So it is with this classification of sociological approaches to deviance. This classification simplifies a complex part of the empirical world—the sociological field of deviance. Throughout the remainder of this book, this framework will be used to assist your study of the phenomena with which we are concerned, sociological theories and research on deviance. At all times you should remember, however, that this classification, like all conceptual frameworks, oversimplifies reality for the sake of clarity. Therefore, we will discover many points of overlap between approaches that are rigidly distinguished in this conceptual scheme as we examine concrete examples of sociological work on deviance.

An overview of the book

This introductory chapter has touched briefly on some of the major works and central issues that have marked the development of the contemporary field of deviance. The next two chapters will fill out this general picture. In Chapter 2, we will examine the field from a historical perspective, paying particular attention to how early stages in the development of the sociology of deviance shaped its identity and many of its continuing problems. The current state of the central

Table 1–2
Classification of four major sociological approaches to the analysis of deviance

Characteristics of approaches	Perspective (definition of deviance) and level of analysis			
	Normative perspective (deviance as norm violation)		Relativistic perspective (deviance as audience definition)	
	Macro level of analysis	Micro level of analysis	Macro level of analysis	Micro level of analysis
1. General descriptive term for approach	Macro-normative	Micro-normative	Macro-relativistic	Micro-relativistic
2. Example of a theory using approach	Anomie theory	Differential association theory	Conflict theory	Labeling theory
3. Central theoretical goal of approach	Explain societal rates of deviant behavior	Explain deviant behavior of individuals	Understand societal sources of reactions to deviance	Understand individual implications of reactions to deviance
4. Nature and focus of theoretical concepts	Large-scale environmental variables	Small-scale environmental variables	Large-scale conflict processes	Small-scale interactional processes
5. Typical source of empirical data	Official records	Survey techniques	Historical documents	Direct observation
6. Orientation toward values	Scientific, value free	Scientific, value free	Activist, value engaged	Humanistic, value engaged

problems and controversies in the field will be the subject of Chapter 3. We will see that the normative and relativistic perspectives are divided on at least four crucial issues that we have only discussed in passing in this chapter.

The subsequent four chapters will focus specifically on theory and research within the normative perspective. Chapter 4 will expand upon our discussion of Merton to include other anomie and subcultural theorists who have contributed to the macro-normative approach. Chapter 5 will turn to the empirical side of that approach by presenting some exemplary cases of research on rates of deviant behavior. Chapter 6 will examine micro-normative theory, with the work of social learning theorists (such as Sutherland) being contrasted to the work of control theorists. Chapter 7 will illustrate how these theories can be applied in micro-level research on delinquency, marijuana use, and mental disorder.

The relativistic perspective will be featured in four chapters on labeling theory and some recent versions of conflict theory. An analysis of the works of Lemert, Becker, and other micro-relativistic theorists in Chapter 8 will be followed by some illustrations of observational research on social reactions to deviance in Chapter 9, ranging from an insider's view of mental institutions to an experimental study of shoppers' reactions to staged acts of shoplifting. Chapter 10 will introduce you to a distinction between interest group theory and neo-Marxist theory, and will discuss some recent developments in macro-relativistic theorizing on conflict and deviance. Finally, Chapter 11 will present some key illustrations of the historical research that this approach to deviance has inspired.

Early development of the field of deviance

2

Chapter 1 gave you a glimpse of some of the central sociological problems in the contemporary field of deviance. The controversial questions of how deviant phenomena can best be defined, described, and explained are key issues that will be explored more fully in the next chapter. Before digging deeper into those controversies, however, we should consider a question that may have occurred to you by now. Since sociologists currently disagree on many fundamental issues in the study of deviant phenomena, does it really make sense to talk about the sociology of deviance as a single field of study? Are there not several "sociologies" of deviance, each using different methods and different theories to analyze different phenomena?

Admittedly, one can easily get such an impression by looking only at the contemporary positions on these issues as we did in Chapter 1. What such a viewpoint fails to show, however, is the tradition of sociological inquiry from which these positions have evolved over time. By extending, criticizing, and building upon the earlier work of their colleagues, sociologists in the area of deviance have developed a field of study that is held together by mutual interest, if not by mutual agreement, in its central issues. In this chapter, then, we will see how this field acquired an identity (as well as several persisting problems) by reviewing some major developments and crises that occurred in the sociology of deviance during its formative years.

The historical development of sociological work on deviant phenomena can be broken down into four relatively distinct periods: (1) the *social pathology* period, (2) the *social disorganization* period, (3) the *normative* period, and (4) the *relativistic* period (cf. Rubington & Weinberg, 1981). A distinct, specialized field of deviance did not exist in American sociology during the social pathology and social disorganization periods, which date from the turn of the century to World War I and from the early 1920s to the middle 1930s, respectively. Instead, deviant phenomena were studied as only part of a more general area of sociological interest in urban social problems. The early conceptions of pathology and disorganization were applied to broad social issues such as urban poverty and community instability as well as to various forms of deviant behavior. Nonetheless, particularly during the social disorganization period, some important contributions by early sociologists set the stage for later, more specialized approaches to deviance.

The normative period dates from the time that Merton published his initial statement of anomie theory (1938) and Sutherland his first systematic version of differential association theory (1939). This period was dominated, of course, by the normative perspective and the issues it raised for the sociology of deviance. During this period, many sociologists began to identify deviant behavior as their area of specialization. Others concentrated on more specific kinds of norm violation and identified themselves as criminologists or psychiatric sociologists.

However, the field of deviance did not become firmly established as a distinct area within sociology until the relativistic period of the 1960s and 1970s. Labeling theory, especially, consolidated the study of deviant phenomena by emphasizing processes of audience definition and social control that are implicated in all forms of deviance. We will now take a more careful look at how the sociology of deviance eventually arrived at this most recent period in its development.

EARLY CONCEPTIONS OF SOCIAL PROBLEMS AND DEVIANCE

The social pathology period

Early American sociologists were preoccupied with solving the pressing social problems resulting from industrialization and immigration to urban areas around the turn of the century. In fact, sociology was founded on the hope that it could contribute to the amelioration or improvement of social problems. This value-engaged, amelioristic orientation of early sociologists in the United States was due as much to their social backgrounds as it was to the scholarly ideas on which they based their new discipline.

The first departments of sociology established in American universities during the 1890s were staffed by individuals who came from rural, religious backgrounds (Hinkle & Hinkle, 1954; Mills, 1942). Many early sociologists had begun their careers in the Protestant ministry. Persons from such backgrounds could not have been expected to adopt a neutral, detached view of the tragic social conditions that existed in the industrializing urban areas of the United States at the turn of the century. Taking academic positions at schools like the University of Chicago or Columbia University in New York City, they were directly confronted with an urban way of life that clashed drastically with the values and outlook of their rural, middle-class origins. Although appalled by the poverty, slums, and criminality they saw about them, these early sociologists also had a religious commitment to moral reform that gave them faith that these conditions could be changed. For them, sociology was to be a science dedicated to human progress and to the amelioration of the degrading conditions of urban life.

The personal views of these sociologists were reinforced and given direction by a variety of 19th-century philosophical and scientific ideas. The writings of Auguste Comte, a French philosopher who first coined the term *sociology*, had been influential in the United States throughout the latter half of the 1800s (Davis, 1980). Comte's conceptions of social science and society were an important source of intellectual inspiration for sociologists during the social pathology period.

Comte argued that civilization was constantly evolving in a progressive direction, a pattern of change that was especially apparent in the forward advance of scientific knowledge. He believed that knowledge in the physical and natural sciences had reached a stage of development where it would be possible to apply the combined resources of all the sciences to the study of society itself. This task would be carried out by sociology, the "Queen of the Sciences" as Comte grandly described it. By using scientific methods to discover the "natural laws" that determine the development of society, sociology would provide useful knowledge for increasing the rate of human progress. Although Comte's doctrine of *positivism*—that the laws of social science could be discovered by the same investigative methods used in the physical and natural sciences—would become a controversial issue among sociologists at a later date, it found a receptive audience in American sociology during the social pathology period.

Comte's conception of society as an *organism* also had some impact on early American sociologists. Using what is known as an *organismic analogy*, Comte proposed that society, like a biological organism, is an ordered, harmonious system of interrelated and interdependent parts. He emphasized that this social organism is more than merely the sum of its individual parts and must be studied as a whole (Coser, 1971: 9).

Although American sociologists during the social pathology period adopted an organismic conception of society, they rejected Comte's emphasis on *macro-level* analysis of the whole social organism. Instead, taking the progressive and generally harmonious organization of society for granted, they tended to concentrate their attention on the adjustment and adaptation of *individuals* within this organismic system. In this respect, these sociologists were more directly influenced by the ideas of Herbert Spencer, a 19th-century English social theorist, than they were by Comte (Hinkle & Hinkle, 1954: 4–7). Even though Spencer, like Comte, used the organismic analogy to describe social life, he argued that society is not greater than the sum of its individual members. For Spencer, the progressive evolutionary development of society is accomplished by the improvement and successful adaptation of individuals. Another implication of this argument, of course, is that social problems and disruptions of progress are due to the *failure of individuals to adapt to organized social life*.

From these personal and intellectual sources, early American sociologists fashioned their conception of social problems and deviance as *social pathology*. With the methods of positive science as their model for sociology and the organismic analogy as their model for society, these sociologists developed a clear and optimistic vision for their attack on the social problems of urban America. The following passage from an early textbook titled *Social Pathology* gives a glimpse of the lofty goals which inspired the advocates of this approach (Smith, 1911, cited in Rubington & Weinberg, 1981: 22–23):

> Pathology in social science has a certain parallel to pathology in medical science. As the study of physical disease is essential to the maintenance of physical health, so social health can never be securely grounded without a wider and more definite knowledge of social disease. . . . Social pathology would be a gloomy study indeed if its accurate knowledge of facts and principles did not indicate pathways out of social difficulties leading to a discovery of the means by which the social causes of disease can be removed, the weak individual be socially reinforced so that finally . . . the social body shall exist . . . radiant with health, in which there is not a living being which does not share in the general glow of wholesomeness and power.

While social pathologists such as Smith recognized the pathological influences of the undesirable environmental conditions of urban slums and poverty, the primary focus of these sociologists was on individual pathology and maladjustment. Viewing deviant behavior and social problems as products of individual defects, the theoretical speculations of the social pathologists amounted to a hodgepodge of biological, psychological, moral, and environmental factors that were held accountable for personal maladjustment. Similarly, the principal research technique used by these sociologists was case studies of deviant or impoverished individuals, which documented the influence of various pathological factors in their personal lives.

Whether due to the intellectual impact of Herbert Spencer or to the individualistic world view of the rural, Protestant background of the social pathologists, the sociological study of deviance in the United States began on a distinctly microscopic level of analysis. In contrast, early European sociologists tended to follow Comte's macroscopic approach to social organization and social problems. This tendency of American sociologists to focus on the causes and characteristics of individual deviants continues to be an important and controversial issue in the contemporary field of deviance.

The faith in progress and reform that inspired sociologists during the social pathology period was severely shaken by the violence and irrationality of World War I, which to them "symbolized a primitive stage of social evolution which modern man was believed to have passed long ago (Hinkle & Hinkle, 1954: 21). The value-engaged, ameliorative emphasis in American sociology was soon replaced by a more neutral, scientific approach during the social disorganization period. Although the social pathologists were successful in promoting the idea that the study of social problems and deviance should be a scientific enterprise, they themselves did little to carry out this objective in practice.

The notion of social pathology was found by later sociologists to have limited utility for conceptualizing social problems. The question of what conditions or behaviors are "pathological" depends on the values of the investigator rather than on any objective, empirically identifiable criteria. In the case of these early sociologists, the conditions of urban society at the turn of the century that contrasted or conflicted with their idealized image of rural, Protestant, middle-class life tended to be defined as pathological (Mills, 1942). Put in contemporary, relativistic terms, the concept of social pathology amounted to a *negative label* that was applied to anything or anyone the pathologists viewed as undesirable.

Much of the theoretical writing of the social pathologists was moralistic in its tone even though their works were filled with impressive scientific jargon borrowed from such disciplines as physics, biology, and medicine. Although their use of analogies drawn from more established sciences added prestige to the young discipline of sociology, it also restricted the ability of the social pathologists to formulate distinctly sociological theories of social problems and deviance. Even their main research tool was borrowed—the case study technique developed by social workers.

In short, the end of the social pathology period left sociological theory and research of deviance in an undeveloped state. However, the central issues in the sociology of deviance developed rapidly and became much clearer in the work of sociologists who followed them during the social disorganization period.

The social disorganization period

This next chapter in the history of the sociology of deviance and, indeed, of American sociology in general was written mainly by sociologists who taught and studied at the University of Chicago during the 1920s and 1930s. The Chicago School of sociology, a phrase referring both to these sociologists and to the tradition of theory and research they developed, laid much of the foundation for the contemporary field of deviance. Making a sharp break with the moralistic orientation of the social pathologists, the Chicago School shifted the sociological study of social problems and deviance in a scientific direction (Finestone, 1976; Carey, 1975).

The Chicago School shared with the social pathologists an interest in urban problems and deviance. But there the similarities ended. Whereas earlier sociologists attacked the city as the ultimate symbol of pathology, the Chicago sociologists were fascinated by their urban environment. They viewed the rapidly changing, diverse city of Chicago as an ideal natural laboratory for scientific research on important sociological questions (Faris, 1967). In contrast to the speculative, armchair sociology of the social pathologists, the Chicago sociologists were concerned, above all, with developing a social science that was firmly grounded in empirical research.

Among the major goals of research by the Chicago School was its attempt to describe the nature and consequences of *social disorganization* in urban areas. This concept was introduced by one of the major figures in Chicago sociology, W. I. Thomas, and his collaborator, Florian Znaniecki, in their important early study, *The Polish Peasant in Europe and America*. Thomas and Znaniecki concisely defined social disorganization as a "decrease of the influence of existing social rules of behavior upon individual members of the group" (Traub & Little, 1980: 44). Although Thomas and Znaniecki were careful to distinguish social disorganization from their more individualistic conception of *personal disorganization* ("a decrease of the individual's ability to organize his whole life"), this distinction became blurred in later work by other Chicago sociologists (Winslow, 1970: 46–66). More often than not, community social problems and individual deviance, crime rates and individual criminal careers were all lumped together as *indicators* or manifestations of the general phenomenon of social disorganization.

Although the micro and macro levels of analysis were only loosely and inconsistently distinguished in most conceptual discussions of social disorganization, a clear division between these levels of analysis emerged in the research conducted by the Chicago School. Empirical work on deviance and social problems by these sociologists tended to fall into two general categories: *micro-level case studies* of individual deviants and *macro-level ecological studies* of rates of social problems and deviance in different parts of the city. The case study technique, of course, had been used by the social pathologists; but at the hands of the Chicago sociologists, this methodological approach was developed into a fine art. The method of studying rates of deviance and social problems through an ecological approach, on the other hand, was a unique contribution of the Chicago School.

Two varieties of the case study technique were used by the Chicago sociologists. Some case studies took the form of *life histories*, where the impact of social disorganization upon individuals was documented autobiographically. In their early work, *The Polish Peasant*, Thomas and Znaniecki used life histories (as well as other materials) to trace the declining influence of conventional norms and social controls upon rural Polish immigrants when they moved to urban slums in the United States. Another classic example of a life history case study is Clifford Shaw's *The Jack-Roller* (1930). Based on intensive interviews with a young man who made his living by robbing skid-row drunks (jack-rolling), Shaw vividly depicted the process by which this individual's ties to conventional society became increasingly unstable and disorganized as he drifted into his unconventional way of life on the street in the skid-row district.

The *urban ethnography* was the second form of case study employed by the Chicago sociologists. In contrast to life histories, ethnographic techniques involved *direct observation of individuals in their natural settings*, a method that continues to be used by contemporary sociologists in the labeling tradition. In such ethnographic studies as Anderson's *The Hobo* (1923) or Cressey's *The Taxi-Dance Hall* (1932), sociologists observed and recorded in rich detail the daily existence of persons living in "disorganized" areas or engaged in unconventional occupations.

These two case study techniques were designed to obtain a close-up view of the effects of social disorganization on the lives of individuals in the urban setting. However, particularly in the ethnographic studies, these detailed portraits also revealed a good deal of organization and social patterning in the life worlds of deviant, unconventional individuals (Matza, 1969). Rather than confirming the disorganizing influences of urban life, these case studies tended to reflect the *diversity* of urban life by depicting deviant activity as an *alternative* form of organized behavior. A similar insight was to emerge from the second, macro-level research tradition of the Chicago School—the ecological studies.

The ecological research of the Chicago School was mainly inspired by the teaching and theoretical writings of Robert Park and Ernest Burgess, the most influential sociologists at the University of Chicago during the social disorganization period. Although the organismic model of society and other biological analogies were taken less seriously by the Chicago sociologists than they were by the social pathologists, Park, particularly, made extensive use of ideas adapted from the biological field of plant and animal ecology in his theoretical work on the structure and change of urban communities (1952). Without denying the importance of social and cultural aspects of urban life, Park argued that community organization was additionally based on nonsocial processes, such as the competition for space in urban areas. Patterns of land use and the distribution of populations in the urban community were shaped by an ecological struggle for existence as well as by cultural factors.

Burgess, Park's close colleague, proposed a systematic application of this general ecological theorizing in his *concentric zone model* of urban growth (Burgess, 1925). Burgess used the city of Chicago as a concrete illustration of his graphic model, which is shown in Figure

Figure 2–1
Burgess' concentric zone model of urban land use and growth

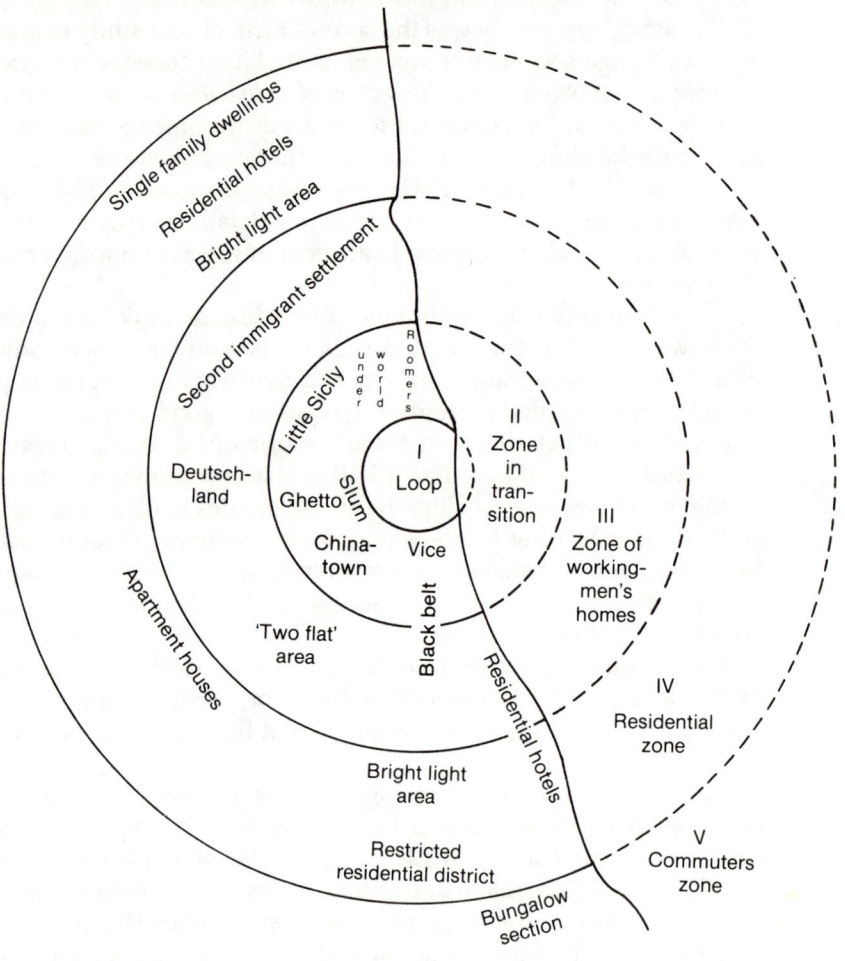

Source: Adapted from Ernest W. Burgess, "The Growth of the City," in Robert E. Park, Ernest W. Burgess, and R. D. McKenzie, eds., *The City* (Chicago: University of Chicago Press, 1925), p. 51.

2–1. This model divides urban areas into five concentric zones based on typical patterns of land use for commercial or residential purposes. Zone I, the central business district or Loop in Chicago, is restricted to commercial uses, whereas Zones III–V are residential areas, ranging from a Zone of Workingmen's Homes to the suburban Commuters' Zone. Zone II, the Zone in Transition, is a mixed area, where low-rent, slum residences are being replaced by businesses and factories.

While Burgess' model was, in part, an attempt to describe the typical patterns of urban land use at a given point in time, he believed that it was most useful for understanding the process of ecological change in the city. As the central business district (Zone I) expands, commercial uses increasingly invade the residential areas in the Zone in Transition (Zone II). Because residential properties in Zone II will eventually be sold for commercial purposes, landlords allow them to deteriorate. This, in turn, leads to an expansion of the transitional, slum area into Zone III and so on. As a result of the ecological competition for space which originates in Zone I, all of the zones in Burgess' model steadily expand outward over time.

Although the ecological change suggested by Burgess' model rippled throughout the entire urban area, the impact of ecological competition and change was most marked in Zone II, the Zone in Transition. In addition to the residential deterioration in Zone II, Burgess and other Chicago sociologists emphasized that this zone was also characterized by rapid social change and severe social disorganization. Because of low rents, this area tended to attract a diverse assortment of immigrants, transients, and impoverished persons who could not afford to live elsewhere. Thus, the population of Zone II was constantly changing and extremely heterogenous in composition. People from radically different backgrounds lived side by side in this impersonal slum environment. With these and other factors at work in Zone II to produce an absence of close interpersonal relationships and a breakdown of informal social controls, the Chicago sociologists viewed it as inevitable that this area would experience a high degree of social disorganization and high rates of social problems and deviance.

The life histories and ethnographic studies of people living in various parts of the Zone in Transition provided some important pieces of evidence in support of these hypotheses. However, the broad, macro-level focus of ecological theorizing demanded a more comprehensive empirical approach that could give an overview of the effects of social disorganization (or lack thereof) across the entire urban area. The ecological research techniques developed by the Chicago School were designed to meet this need. Generally, the ecological studies analyzed how population rates of various indicators of social disorganization, such as crime, divorce, or mental disorder, were distributed geographically throughout an urban area. The official records of law enforcement agencies and other governmental sources were used to obtain information on the residential locations of persons who had been arrested, divorced or committed to an institution. Combining this information with population data from urban census tracts, the ecological researchers were able to plot on maps the different rates at which deviance and social problems occurred in various sections of the city.

Using this statistical approach, faculty and students at the University of Chicago conducted extensive investigations of the ecological distributions of crime, delinquency, suicide, mental disorder, divorce, and other indicators of social disorganization in their city. The results of these studies were impressively consistent. With only a few exceptions, the highest rates of these various forms of deviance and social problems were found in the areas designated as Zone I and, particularly, Zone II of Burgess' model. Furthermore, these studies found that as the distance of a zone from the center of the city *increased*, the rates of deviance and social problems steadily *decreased*, with the lowest rates for the entire city appearing in Zone V. These consistent, repeated findings from the ecological research by the Chicago School provided the sociology of deviance with its first well-supported empirical generalizations about the environmental characteristics of deviants.

During the 1920s and early 1930s, these results were typically interpreted as evidence of variation in the severity of social disorganization throughout the urban area as represented by Burgess' concentric zone model. However, here, as in the case studies by the Chicago sociologists, another interpretation of how persistently high rates of deviance were maintained in slum areas was possible: that deviant behavior is a product of organized, rather than disorganized, social conditions. Some Chicago sociologists recognized this possibility. For instance, in a 1929 ecological study of juvenile delinquency rates, Shaw and his colleagues suggested the following interpretation of how a stable pattern of crime and delinquency becomes established in the slum communities of the Zone in Transition (1929: 205–206):

> when business and industry invade a community, the community thus invaded ceases to function effectively as a means of social control. Traditional norms and standards of the conventional community weaken and disappear. Resistance on the part of the community to delinquent and criminal behavior is low, and such behavior is tolerated and may even become accepted and approved. . . . Delinquent and criminal patterns arise and are transmitted socially just as any other cultural and social pattern is transmitted. In time these delinquent patterns may become dominant and shape the attitudes and behavior of persons living in the area.

In other words, traditional norms and values do not simply break down in slum communities; they are *replaced by an alternative set of norms and values* that may be no less organized than is the culture of the "conventional" community.

This idea heralded the beginning of the end for the social disorganization period and its oversimplified conception of deviant behavior. By 1942, in a more extensive ecological study of delinquency, Shaw and McKay had completely dropped the social disorganization interpretation in favor of the argument that delinquent behavior is *culturally transmitted* in slum areas. The following passage from Shaw and McKay's conclusion (1942: 436) shows how this changing interpretation of the slum environment carried with it a new conception of the deviant actor:

> from the point of view of the delinquent's immediate social world, he is not necessarily disorganized, maladjusted or antisocial. Within the limits of his social world and in terms of its norms and expectations, he may be a highly organized and well-adjusted person.

This image of the deviant as *normal* rather than disorganized reveals that ecological research, in particular, and the sociology of deviance, in general, had moved beyond the social disorganization period by the early 1940s.

During the social disorganization period, the Chicago sociologists did not succeed in overcoming the simplistic formula for the study of deviance that had been introduced by the social pathologists: "Bad things result from bad conditions" (Matza, 1969: 21). In spite of their conscious effort to avoid the moralistic stance of the social pathologists toward the city and its changing environment, the Chicago sociologists still tended to equate the "good life" of an organized society with a stereotyped image of the stable, rural community. Against such an idealized standard of organization, it was natural for the Chicago sociologists to *assume* that the urban slum, with its ecological instability and social diversity, was disorganized. Since they also *assumed* that personal disorganization and deviance were the result of social disorganization, the Chicago sociologists did not seriously entertain alternative explanations of the high rates of deviant behavior they found in slum areas. As a consequence, the Chicago School was locked into a circular argument in their theorizing about social disorganization and deviance. Why does deviant behavior occur in the urban slum? Because the slum area is disorganized. But, how do we know the slum is disorganized? Because it has high rates of deviant behavior. And so it goes with no way of distinguishing the cause from its effects (see Clinard & Meier, 1979: 63–67).

While failing to develop an explicit, systematic theory of deviance, the Chicago sociologists did prepare the way for the emergence of the normative perspective in the late 1930s. For all its weaknesses, the concept of social disorganization was a more strictly sociological notion than was the earlier concept of social pathology with its medical and biological overtones. By viewing deviance as a social phenomenon that has its roots in the normative structure of the community as well as in the nature of the individual, the Chicago sociologists also began to move away from the micro level of analysis which had preoccupied the social pathologists.

However, more significant for the development of the sociology of deviance were the advances in empirical research accomplished by the Chicago School. On the micro level, the Chicago sociologists skillfully used case study techniques to gain detailed insights into the complex and dynamic social worlds of individual deviants. Their concern with the development of deviant careers and with the direct observation of interactional processes in natural settings continues to be apparent in contemporary, micro-relativistic research on labeling processes. Matza (1969), in fact, has called the modern labeling researchers neo-Chicagoans because of their obvious debt to the methods and objectives of case study research during the social disorganization period.

The macro-level, ecological research of the Chicago School had an even more immediate impact on the sociology of deviance. Research on rates of deviant behavior became a dominant theme in the empirical literature of the normative perspective during the 1940s and 1950s. Although the focus of this research on rates shifted from *ecological* variations to *social class* variations in crime and delinquency, macro-normative researchers followed the influential precedent of the Chicago sociologists by relying on data taken from official records.

The dual nature of empirical research by the Chicago School, case study versus ecological techniques, led to the initial appearance of one of the most enduring and controversial issues in the field of deviance. Some Chicago sociologists who favored the "soft," qualitative approach of the case study techniques found themselves at odds with colleagues who advocated research methods such as the ecological techniques that provided "hard," quantitative data on social phenomena (Hinkle & Hinkle, 1954: 25–25). Those who advocated the latter position were motivated by a desire to make sociology a truly objective, scientific discipline—a goal they felt was inconsistent with the subjective, impressionistic approach of case study techniques. Some Chicago sociologists, such as Shaw in his studies of delinquency, felt that they had resolved this hard data versus soft data controversy by drawing upon both kinds of evidence in their research. Yet, this debate has been renewed by neo-Chicagoan labeling theorists who have sharply criticized the quantitative orientation that became dominant in the research on deviant behavior during the normative period.

THE NORMATIVE PERIOD AND DEVIANT BEHAVIOR

The beginning of the normative period was marked by the appearance of several new theoretical developments in the deviance literature rather than by the disappearance of the older notions of social pathology and social disorganization. These earlier conceptions lingered on throughout the 1940s and 1950s as pedagogical frameworks in general textbooks on social problems (Rubington & Weinberg, 1981). In the meantime, a split was occurring between the broad area of social problems and a new area devoted strictly to the study of deviant phenomena. Although it was not until the 1950s that this specialized field was formally recognized as the *Sociology of Deviant Behavior* in an important textbook by Clinard (1957), the conceptual boundaries and core issues of this field had been established in the late 1930s by Merton, Sutherland, and others who introduced the normative perspective on deviance.

The emergence of the normative perspective

Merton and, to a lesser extent, Sutherland were the principal architects of the normative perspective and the developing field of deviant behavior. In addition, some early, but less-enduring contributions were made by sociologists such as Sellin (1938) and Shaw and McKay (1942) who pointed to conflict between cultures or values as a factor in deviant behavior. However, no other work matched the initial impact and continuing influence of Merton's anomie theory (1938; 1957) and Sutherland's differential association theory (1939; 1947) on the central issues of the normative perspective.

In at least three major respects, Merton and Sutherland advanced well beyond the theoretical efforts of earlier sociologists. First, anomie theory and differential association theory were *specialized in scope*. Whereas the Chicago sociologists had lumped deviance and social problems together as indicators of social disorganization, Merton and Sutherland focused on the more specific theoretical goal of explaining various forms of deviant behavior. In so doing, they provided a theoretical foundation for the field of deviant behavior as an independent, specialized area of study. Second, these two theories were *systematic in structure*. In contrast to the vague and loosely connected nature of theoretical work during the social disorganization period, Merton and Sutherland attempted to present explicit, coherent theoretical frameworks for the analysis of deviant behavior. Finally, Merton and Sutherland treated deviant behavior as a _sociologically "normal" phenomenon_. With the normative definition of deviance, these theorists were able to conceptualize deviant behavior as a predictable choice made by normal social actors in response to certain kinds of environmental pressures. It was no longer necessary to link deviant behavior to the maladjustment or disorganization of individuals who had lost their ties to organized society. In this new conception, deviants could be just as social, just as well adjusted to their particular social environment as nondeviants.

A concern with these theoretical aims and the outlines of the emerging normative perspective are clearly apparent in Merton's introduction to his classic article, "Social Structure and Anomie" (1938: 672, emphasis in original):

> it will be suggested that certain phases of social structure generate the circumstances in which infringement of social codes constitutes a "normal" response. The conceptual scheme to be outlined is designed to provide a coherent, systematic approach to the study of sociocultural sources of deviate behavior. Our primary aim lies in discovering how some social structures *exert a definite pressure* upon certain persons in the society to engage in nonconformist rather than conformist conduct.

Here, the central concept of the normative perspective is introduced in Merton's definition of deviate behavior as the infringement of social codes. Equally important is Merton's argument that the choice of nonconformist rather than conformist conduct represents a normal response to structural pressures. In other words, the causes of deviant behavior are not to be found in the *kinds of people* who choose to violate social norms. Rather, the crucial theoretical issue is what *kinds of social environments* force normal people to make a deviant choice. With his broad-scale environmental focus on the "sociocultural sources" of rates of deviant behavior, Merton made a bold attempt to move away from the individualistic orientation that had characterized American conceptions of deviance since the social pathology period.

Sutherland's break with previous developments in the American deviance tradition was less dramatic than Merton's. Unlike Merton, Sutherland received his doctorate at the University of Chicago (in 1913) and continued to be strongly influenced by the work of the Chicago School during his later career at the University of Illinois. Sutherland's initial statement of differential association theory (1939), in fact, referred to social disorganization as a basic cause of criminal behavior. However, this reference was dropped from the final version of Sutherland's theory in 1947, where he gave central emphasis to his argument that "the process of learning criminal behavior . . .

involves all of the mechanisms that are involved in any other learning" (Sutherland & Cressey, 1974: 76). Thus, Sutherland made his micro-level contribution to the emerging normative perspective by placing criminal behavior on an equal basis with noncriminal behavior as "normal," socially learned phenomena.

Even more closely linked to the Chicago School was a third line of development in the normative perspective that was eventually overshadowed by the more systematic theoretical formulations of Merton and Sutherland. Shaw and McKay (1942), Sellin (1938), and Sutherland himself (1939) introduced the relatively short-lived notion that conflict between cultures and value systems accounted for a significant amount of criminality and deviance, particularly in urban areas. As we saw earlier, Shaw and McKay interpreted their later ecological research on delinquency as evidence for the cultural transmission of a system of delinquent values that conflicts with the dominant, conventional system of values in slum areas. Sellin analyzed how immigrants may engage in criminal behavior because the conduct norms of their native culture conflict with the cultural norms of American society. The concept of culture conflict played a major part in Sutherland's early theoretical work and appeared in the initial version of differential association theory (see Cohen et al., 1956: 13–29). Sutherland also developed the concept of differential social organization as a macro-level counterpart to his micro-level analysis of differential association. Similar to Shaw and McKay's analysis of conflicting value systems, Sutherland argued that communities can contain groups organized for crime and groups organized against crime.

What is most interesting about these conceptions of culture and value conflict, however, is their failure to influence significantly the development of the normative perspective. Their mutual emphasis on the fundamental *diversity* of social life and on the importance of *conflict processes* as a source of deviant behavior ran counter to the *consensual* model of society that formed the groundwork for Merton's anomie theory. Whereas Merton saw deviant behavior as a product of the pursuit of *common* cultural goals by *all* members of society, the pursuit of *conflicting* goals and values by various *subgroups* in American society was the major theme of the culture conflict theorists. But in the 1940s and 1950s, it was Merton's approach that prevailed as the dominant macro-level theory of deviance. Conflict ideas were shunted aside as the consensual model of society became increasingly popular in the study of deviant behavior and in sociology in general. Sutherland's theoretical influence on the normative perspective was mainly seen in micro-level work, and his conception of differential social organization and other macro-level conflict approaches fell into disuse until the late 1950s.

Cumulative development of the sociology of deviant behavior

The term *consensus* does not just describe the prevailing model of society during the normative period. Sociologists engaged in the study of deviant behavior also appeared to have reached a general consensus on the central issues in their field. The normative definition seemed to have resolved the problem of finding a truly sociological conception of deviant phenomena that could be objectively measured and usefully applied in scientific research. Sociologists also agreed on the central theoretical issue for the normative perspective: explaining the environmental causes of deviant behavior. While different theorists emphasized different kinds of environmental factors in their explanations of deviant behavior, Merton's focus on the class structure of American society had the greatest impact on research during the normative period. Thus, class variations in deviant behavior replaced ecological variations in social disorganization as the central descriptive issue for empirical studies of deviant phenomena. Finally, the vast majority of sociologists within the normative perspective agreed that the study of deviant behavior should be a value-free, scientific endeavor. Sociologists during the normative period were even more insistent than the Chicago School on the need to eliminate personal biases and value judgments from the scientific study of deviant phenomena.

Since most sociologists agreed on the general perspective, problems, and goals of the study of deviant behavior, they devoted most of their effort to the *cumulative* development of theory and research along the lines laid out by these central issues. This is not to say that scholarly criticism and debate were absent from the deviance tradition during the normative period. However, criticisms were aimed at advancing the theoretical and empirical issues raised by the normative perspective rather than challenging its basic viewpoint on deviant phenomena.

A good example of the cumulative nature of sociological inquiry and criticism during the normative period can be found in the progressive development of subcultural theories of lower-class juvenile delinquency during the 1950s (Cohen, 1955; Sykes & Matza, 1957; Miller, 1958; Cloward & Ohlin, 1960). Many of the subcultural theorists were quite critical of Merton's macro-level explanation of lower-class crime and delinquency. But rather than attempting to discredit Merton's approach, theorists such as Cohen (1955) and Cloward and Ohlin (1960) used their criticisms to point out the need for more extended and refined analyses of the issues raised by anomie theory. Building upon Merton's idea that the lower-class environment is characterized by restricted opportunities for achieving success through legitimate channels, these theorists argued further that lower-class youths *collectively* attempt to adjust to such frustrating circumstances by forming delinquent subcultures. In place of the conventional activities such as academic achievement that are valued and required by the dominant, middle-class culture, the norms and values of delinquent subcultures reward and encourage deviant activities such as vandalism, organized crime, and gang violence. Although they might be failures by middle-class standards, lower-class youths can gain self-esteem and respect in the eyes of their peers by excelling at the deviant activities defined as appropriate in the social environment of the delinquent subculture.

The cumulative nature of subcultural theory is not only exemplified by positive criticism and extension of Merton's macro-level focus on the lower-class environment. In addition, subcultural theorists attempted to integrate Merton's approach with the micro-level approach of Sutherland's differential association theory. Sutherland's focus on interpersonal relationships was used to account for how particular individuals become socialized into an ongoing delinquent subculture and for how certain deviant acts are rationalized and defined as appropriate in delinquent groups (Cohen, 1955; Sykes & Matza, 1957; Cloward & Ohlin, 1960).

However, one particular "subcultural" theory of delinquency is noteworthy for its departure from the work of Merton and the other subcultural theorists. In his lower-class culture theory of gang delinquency, Walter B. Miller (1958) emphasized a theme that had been played down since the early part of the normative period: societal diversity and culture conflict. Miller, in contrast to Merton and the other subcultural theorists, argued that American society is *not* characterized by a general, uniform consensus regarding cultural goals and values. Lower-class behavior, including the deviant behavior of delinquent gangs, is motivated by the standards and concerns of a *separate* lower-class cultural system. Rather than representing a subcultural adjustment to the frustrations of striving for middle-class goals, the behavior of lower-class youths is strictly oriented toward such lower-class cultural concerns as being tough or seeking excitement. It so happens that behavior that conforms to the demands of lower-class culture sometimes conflicts with the values and legal norms of middle-class culture. In such cases, lower-class youths may be "perceived as deliberately non-conforming or malicious by an observer strongly (attached) to middle class norms" (Miller, 1958: 19). Implicit here is the idea that lower-class behavior is delinquent mainly because it is labeled as such by middle-class audiences.

However, Miller did not make a concerted effort to explore the critical questions for the normative perspective that were implicit in his analysis of cultural diversity in American society. Instead, taking middle-class norms as his standard for defining delinquency, he focused on certain features of lower-class culture that served as important environmental causes of the norm-violating behavior of delinquent gangs. Nonetheless, the renewed interest in societal diversity reflected in Miller's work and in other conflict analyses in the late 1950s (Vold, 1958; see also Coser, 1956; Dahrendorf, 1959) was a sign of growing dissatisfaction with Merton's consensual model of society. With the emergence of the relativistic perspective a few years later, of course, this dissatisfaction materialized as an open challenge of the normative perspective and of its dominant influence on the central issues in the study of deviant phenomena.

Apart from these theoretical developments, difficulties for the normative perspective were also appearing in the findings of research conducted during the normative period. Merton and the subcultural theorists took comfort in the fact that rates of criminal and delinquent behavior compiled from official records of law enforcement agencies were consistently highest within the lower class. High lower-class rates of serious mental disorders, determined from research on the records of mental hospitals and treatment agencies, appeared to provide further evidence for the deviance-producing nature of the lower-class environment (Hollingshead & Redlich, 1953; 1958).

However, beginning in the 1940s, survey research techniques came into widespread use, particularly in micro-level studies of the characteristics of individual deviants. Evidence for Sutherland's differential association theory accumulated from surveys focusing on attitudinal and peer group influences on delinquent behavior (Ball, 1957; Short, 1957; 1958). Other survey investigations attempted to provide *micro-level* evidence for Merton's anomie theory. The results of interview surveys in the general public found that lower-class individuals tended to score highest on a measure of *anomia*, a personal, subjective feeling of normlessness or meaninglessness to life (Srole, 1956; Bell, 1957).

While such findings were generally consistent with the major normative theories of deviant behavior, the results from another application of survey techniques were less supportive. A number of studies attempted to measure hidden deviance—deviant behavior that had not come to the attention of social control agencies (Porterfield, 1943; Murphy et al., 1946; Short & Nye, 1957–58; Nye et al., 1958). During interviews or on questionnaires, respondents were asked to report the various kinds of deviant acts they had committed, including those acts where they *had not been caught or arrested*. A major conclusion of these *self-report* surveys was that a great many more criminal and delinquent acts are committed by the general public than are reflected in official statistics. However, another finding from these studies was more surprising. When the numbers of self-reported deviant acts were related to measures of the respondents' social class, a number of these studies found *very little difference* between lower- and middle-class respondents in the incidence of hidden deviance (Short & Nye, 1957–58; Nye et al., 1958; Dentler & Monroe, 1961).

The results of these studies, which were primarily concerned with self-reported delinquency, raised serious questions for anomie theory and the subcultural theories. Although official statistics on arrests and appearances in juvenile court supported their predictions of high rates of lower-class delinquency, the self-report studies did not. While sociologists in the normative perspective began to doubt the reliability of official statistics as measures of the "true" extent of deviant behavior, they, like the Chicago sociologists before them, did not grasp the full significance of this evidence. Only later did relativistic critics seriously argue that official statistics reflected a high rate of *social control* in the lower class rather than a high rate of norm-violating behavior (Kitsuse & Cicourel, 1963), In other words, lower-class persons were not more likely to commit deviant acts than middle-class persons; they were only more likely to be arrested and to show up in official statistics.

The controversy regarding descriptive evidence from official statistics versus self-report studies is still unresolved. However, the self-report research cast serious doubts on normative theories of delinquency and directed attention to new issues in the description of deviant phenomena.

THE RELATIVISTIC PERIOD AND DEVIANCE

As we noted in Chapter 1, the relativistic perspective on deviance was forcefully brought to the attention of sociologists by three different theoretical analyses published in the early 1960s (Kitsuse, 1962; Erikson, 1962; Becker, 1963). The general viewpoint presented in these works was quickly recognized as an important step forward in the study of deviant phenomena. The immediate success of labeling theory is not surprising. Kitsuse, Erikson, Becker, and other recent relativistic theorists offered some novel insights into the central issues in the deviance tradition. More puzzling is why relativistic theorizing did not have a major impact on the deviance tradition until the 1960s.

As early as 1938, Tannenbaum suggested that the experience of being tagged as a delinquent is a major turning point toward a deviant career for young boys. Many, if not most, of the major themes of labeling theory were first presented in 1951 in a textbook by Lemert that carried the misleading title *Social Pathology*. Although this book is now acknowledged to be an important contribution to micro-relativistic theorizing, it received relatively little notice when it initially appeared during the heyday of the normative period. Relativistic ideas were also apparent in other early writings on social problems and deviant behavior (Waller, 1936; Fuller & Myers, 1941a; Sutherland, 1949). With so many early precedents in the sociological literature, why did it take so long for the relativistic perspective to emerge as a distinct viewpoint on deviant phenomena?

What seems to have set relativistic work in the 1960s apart from earlier writings was the *fundamentally critical posture* which Kitsuse, Erikson, and Becker took toward the normative perspective. Each of these theorists prefaced their relativistic analyses with pointed criticisms of the normative perspective and its definition of deviance as norm-violating behavior. This critical quality had been missing in earlier sociological work containing relativistic ideas. In *Social Pathology* (1951), for instance, Lemert noted a number of problems with the normative definition and with existing theories of deviant behavior such as Merton's, but he stopped short of a full-scale critique of the normative perspective. Instead, his early work can best be seen as a *cumulative* effort to bring relativistic ideas to bear on the normative issue of explaining the causes of various forms of deviant behavior (see Rains, 1975). Lemert's treatment of the normative perspective and its central issues contrasted markedly with that of his student, Kitsuse, who issued the following challenge 10 years later (1962: 248, emphasis added): "I propose to *shift the focus of theory and research from the forms of deviant behavior to the processes by which persons come to be defined as deviant by others.*" In other words, Kitsuse and his contemporaries intended to use relativistic ideas to replace, rather than to develop, the normative position on the central issues in the deviance tradition.

The successful emergence of the relativistic perspective is due as much or more to the trenchant and fundamental criticisms of the normative perspective by relativistic sociologists as it is to the actual progress they made in their own studies of deviant phenomena. While relativistic sociologists have not completely shifted the focus of deviance theory and research away from the issues considered important in the normative perspective, they have at least been able to make those issues highly controversial. During the relativistic period, *critical analysis* of those issues has to some extent rivaled *cumulative development* of theory and research as the primary mode for advancing sociological knowledge in the area of deviance. Particularly in the 1970s, the critical orientation of the relativistic perspective was strengthened by the work of neo-Marxists and other "radical" conflict theorists (Liazos, 1972; Thio, 1973; Taylor, Walton, & Young, 1973;

1975; Quinney, 1977; Davis, 1980; Balkan, Berger, & Schmidt, 1980). These so-called critical sociologists went beyond earlier attacks on the normative perspective to take on new targets such as labeling theory and other relativistic approaches.

Thus, the scene is now set for the next chapter, where we will discuss the debates over several central issues in the contemporary sociological literature on deviance. While Chapter 3 will emphasize the critical side of recent work in this area, later chapters will return to cumulative developments in theory and research that have continued into the relativistic period.

Central issues in the study of deviance: Definitions, descriptions, theories, and values

THE ISSUE OF DEFINING DEVIANCE

As we saw in Chapter 1, if any sociological problem were to be singled out as *the* most crucial issue in the contemporary field of deviance, it would be the question of how to define the concept deviance. Not only does this issue affect virtually all of the major theoretical, conceptual, and empirical problems in the sociology of deviance, but the very identity of the field itself hinges on this definitional question.

During the 1940s and 1950s, of course, the normative definition of deviance provided a conceptual identity for the specialized field of deviant behavior. As compared to the vague notions of social pathology and social disorganization it replaced, the concept of norm violation is simple, precise, and objective. The social norms of a community or society can be measured scientifically. Therefore, empirically based standards, rather than the subjective values of the sociologist, can be used to rule if a given act is deviant or not. Similarly, a person who is observed to engage in norm-violating behavior can be objectively defined as deviant.

What could be controversial about this definition of deviance? For one thing, relativistic critics such as Becker (1963) and Lemert (1972) seriously question the tendency of Merton (1938) and others to speak of the norms of American society as if this society were characterized by uniform consensus regarding rules for behavior. Becker (1963: 8), for example, summarily dismisses Merton's implicit assumption of normative consensus as follows:

> (American) society has many groups, each with its own set of rules, and people belong to many groups simultaneously. A person may break the rules of one group by the very act of abiding by the rules of another group. Is he, then, deviant?

In other words, an absence of *general* agreement on the norms of American society makes it difficult if not impossible to specify exactly what behaviors are *generally* deviant in that society.

Furthermore, Kitsuse (1962) argues that abstract sociological definitions of certain behaviors as norm violations often correspond poorly to how those behaviors are reacted to in actual social situations. He states that there are frequent instances "when the societal reaction to behaviors defined as deviant by the (normative) sociologist is nonexistent, indifferent, or at most mildly disapproving" (1962: 248). Erikson (1962) similarly points out that the fact that an *act* violates a social norm tells us little about how the *person* who committed the act will be treated by social audiences. He illustrates this point with the following example:

> working class boys who steal cars are far more likely to go to prison than upper class boys who commit the same or even more serious crimes, suggesting that from the point of view of the community lower class offenders are somehow more deviant (1962: 308).

In general, these and other critical points raised by relativistic theorists during the 1960s represented a concerted effort to challenge the *utility* of the normative definition for theoretical and empirical work on deviance. While the labeling theorists did not deny that groups share norms or rules for behavior, they did argue that a definition based strictly on the notion of norm violation fails to focus attention on the most crucial aspects of the social phenomena studied by the field of deviance. From the relativistic point of view, the nature of an actor's behavior and the question of whether it "objectively" violates social norms are relatively unimportant considerations in understanding the phenomena "which sociologically differentiate deviants from non-deviants" (Kitsuse, 1962: 248). Rather, it is the *reactions* or interactional "responses of the conventional and conforming members of the society who identify and interpret behavior as deviant which sociologically transform persons into deviants" (Kitsuse, 1962: 253). In other words, a relativistic definition of deviance is more useful than a normative definition because it focuses on the phenomena which distinguish deviants from nondeviants in the real world. In its purest form, the relativistic conception would ignore the nature of an actor's behavior and take the nature of an audience's reaction as the sole criterion for defining deviance.

In the ensuing controversy over the issue of defining deviance during the relativistic period, the arguments of the labeling theorists have not gone unanswered. Perhaps the most articulate defender of the normative position on this issue has been Jack Gibbs (1966; 1972). Gibbs has criticized the relativistic definition of deviance for being vague and difficult to apply in empirical research. The definition used by normative sociologists provides an explicit standard (i.e., social norms) for classifying behavior as deviant, but "Becker, Erikson, and Kitsuse have never specified exactly what kind of reaction identifies deviant acts" (Gibbs, 1966: 13). How severe must a reaction be before an actor can be considered to be defined as deviant by a social audience? Must the reaction be an overt, public response? Who must react to identify an act as deviant? Can people be their own social audiences and define themselves as deviant? The labeling theorists, according to Gibbs, are unclear or inconsistent in their answers to these questions. Because of such ambiguities in the relativistic definition of deviance as it was presented in the early 1960s, Gibbs concludes that it has limited utility for empirical research on deviant phenomena.

However, Gibbs (1972) more recently granted that the notions of societal reaction or labeling are potentially useful for determining whether certain *persons* can be classified as deviant. While he maintains that sociological questions relating to the identification of deviant *acts* are better answered by the normative definition, the *separate* question of whether the norm-violating person is actually labeled as deviant depends on the relativistic standard of audience reaction. Although "the labeling of someone as an alcoholic, common drunk, psychotic, nut, homosexual, fag, communist, or red is not unrelated to the fact or suspicion of previous acts by that individual," the particular label applied to a person is ultimately a matter of audience definition (Gibbs, 1972: 49).

The critical stance of the normative theorist Gibbs bears many similarities to another attack on the work of Becker and Erikson by Lemert (1972), whose book *Social Pathology* (1951) was mentioned above as an early effort at relativistic theorizing. In objecting to Becker and Erikson's focus on the subjective definition of deviance by social audiences, Lemert contends that the "extreme relativism in some statements of labeling theory leaves the unfortunate impression that almost any meaning can be assigned to human attributes and actions" (1972: 22). In Lemert's view, labeling theorists overreacted to the normative definition by completely deemphasizing the nature of an actor's behavior and the social norms that it might violate. Like Gibbs, Lemert believes that relativistic conceptions of deviance should remain sensitive to the "way in which the societal reaction varies with objective differences in behavior . . . and its consequences" (1972: 21). Both of these critics appear to be calling for definitions that combine the normative focus on the objective features of deviant behavior with the relativistic focus on subjective definitions of persons as deviants.

Finally, during the past decade, radical conflict theorists sharply criticized both the normative definition and the relativistic definition as it has been used in micro-level work by labeling theorists. These critics have gone beyond the scientific concern with theoretical and empirical utility to object to the values and ideological positions implied by various definitions of deviance. For instance, in an article subtitled "Nuts, Sluts, and Preverts," Alexander Liazos (1972) objects to the moral implications of the term *deviance* itself. He argues that this term tends to focus attention on powerless underdogs in society rather than on violence and oppression by powerful groups. Although the labeling theorists have stressed the need to understand

and tolerate powerless deviants such as mental patients, prostitutes, and homosexuals, "one *tolerates* only those one considers less than equal, morally inferior, and weak; those equal to oneself, one accepts and respects" (1972: 105, emphasis added). Instead, Liazos feels sociologists should be concerned with covert institutional violence by the powerful, such as war, economic exploitation and political oppression. Deviants, like most of the rest of us, should be redefined as victims of an institutional structure controlled by powerful elites.

Similar objections to conventional definitions of deviance have been voiced by other critics who take a conflict approach (Thio, 1973; Schervish, 1973; Taylor, Walton, & Young, 1973; Davis, 1980). Whether deviance is defined as norm violation or as audience definition, sociological attention is drawn away from those who make the rules and have the power to enforce their definitions of deviance on the powerless. Despite these objections, however, conflict theorists continue to rely on relativistic definitions in their macro-level analyses of the formation of laws and application of social control in capitalist society.

This section has only touched on some of the heated controversies that surround the central issue of defining deviance. As we have seen here and in Chapter 1, much of this debate consists of critical exchanges between sociologists who favor a relativistic definition and those who favor a normative definition. However, the distinction between macro and micro levels of analysis also enters into this issue. Criticisms of Merton by the labeling theorists were not only directed at his use of the concept "norm" to define deviant behavior but also at his broad, macro-level attempt to characterize the norms of American society in general. Similarly, conflict theorists criticize the tendency of labeling theorists to apply the relativistic definition to micro-level problems rather than to macro-level analyses of social control in capitalist society. The extent of controversy over this issue should make it clear to you that sociologists are very concerned with the question "what is deviance?" This concern is well justified. The concepts used to "see" deviant phenomena determine to a great degree the way sociologists deal with all of the other major issues in the contemporary field of deviance.

THE ISSUE OF DESCRIBING DEVIANCE

The far-reaching implications of the definitional issue for other issues are most apparent in the sociological problem of describing deviance. This problem can be generally stated as a concern with how deviant phenomena are empirically distinguishable from nondeviant phenomena. From the perspective of the *normative* definition, description is focused on empirical characteristics that differentiate persons who violate norms from those who do not. As we noted in Chapter 1, descriptive research by sociologists who use this definition attempts to find distinctive features of the social environments of deviants. The *relativistic* definition, on the other hand, provides quite a different view of the problem of description. As the quotation in the previous section from Kitsuse (1962) pointed out, audience definitions and reactions rather than inherent characteristics are what differentiate deviants from nondeviants. Therefore, descriptive research from a relativistic perspective focuses on the interpersonal and conflict processes that create deviants by socially distinguishing them from nonlabeled members of conventional society.

These contrasting views of the problem of description translate into an important difference in the investigative strategies used by sociological researchers in the two perspectives. Normative researchers devote a great deal of effort to the conceptualization, measurement, and analysis of social variables that they hope will effectively distinguish various types of deviants from nondeviants. One of the worst outcomes of descriptive research, at least from the normative point of view, is to find no significant differences between the characteristics of deviants and other people. At most, such negative findings are a signal to look elsewhere or to use different research techniques in the search for variables that yield empirical differences between deviants and nondeviants.

Relativistic researchers are neither surprised nor dismayed by descriptive findings that fail to distinguish the characteristics of deviants from those of other people, particularly in cases where norm violators have not been labeled and processed by official agencies of social control. In fact, one of the principal aims of descriptive studies by labeling researchers has been to humanize persons who are labeled as deviant by showing that they differ from conventional members of society mainly with respect to the label that has been imposed upon them. Relativistic interpretations and criticisms of significant findings from descriptive research by normative investigators also attempt to minimize the *inherent* distinctiveness of norm violators. Some findings, such as high arrest rates among blacks, are interpreted as reflecting biased or prejudicial reactions of law enforcement agents to minorities rather than any special tendency of blacks to engage in deviant behavior. The findings of other normative research, such as studies of the values or personalities of convicts or mental patients, are criticized for failing to recognize how the distinctive features of such persons are a product of labeling and incarceration processes. In their own investigations, relativistic researchers attempt to provide vivid observational and historical descriptions of the interactional and conflict processes involved in reactions to deviance. While minimizing the distinctive character of deviants, they attempt to find evidence for maximal variation in the social definition of similar acts and in the application of social controls to certain members of society who in most ways are similar to the rest of us.

To illustrate the controversies generated in the field of deviance by the issue of strategy in descriptive research, we can pull together some of our earlier comments on the relationship between social class and criminal deviance. During the social disorganization period and the normative period, a key descriptive generalization from research using official records was the strong association between the lower-class, slum environment and criminal behavior (as measured by arrest rates). This finding assumed great importance in the theoretical work of Merton and others in the normative perspective as evidence for the distinctively lower-class character of criminals. In contrast, the initial self-report studies during the 1940s and 1950s were extremely problematic for the normative perspective. They failed to find a significant difference in the number of deviant acts admitted by lower-class and middle-class persons. Although later, more sophisticated self-report studies found some evidence that lower-class persons are more likely than middle-class persons to commit *serious* deviant acts (Reiss & Rhodes, 1961; Clark & Wenninger, 1962), there was still good reason to doubt whether the variable of social class was as useful for empirical description of criminals and delinquents as it was once thought to be.

While the discrepancy between official records and self-report studies posed a perplexing descriptive problem for the normative perspective, this evidence was entirely consistent with the descriptive aims of relativistic sociologists. As we saw earlier, Kitsuse and Cicourel (1963) interpreted class differences in arrest rates as evidence for variations in social control rather than for variations in law-violating behavior. Relativistic researchers attempted to describe how social class entered into legal reaction processes by directly observing interactional encounters between law enforcement agents and lower- and middle-class persons (Piliavin & Briar, 1964; Black & Reiss, 1970; Black, 1970). However, in this case the evidence has been disappointing for the descriptive strategy of the relativistic perspective. Studies of class discrimination in the reaction process have failed to yield strong or consistent evidence that lower-class persons are more likely to be arrested than middle-class persons for similar offenses (Black, 1973; Williams, 1976; Carter & Clelland, 1979).

Thus, at least in the specific case of social class, neither the research strategy of the normative perspective nor that of the relativistic perspective has been able to obtain convincing evidence for the usefulness of this social factor in the description of deviant phenomena. However, the main point to be gained from this illustration is how the strategies of descriptive research in the two perspectives are directed at quite different sources of variation in the empirical world. Where normative researchers look for variation in the distinctive characteristics of deviants and nondeviants, relativistic researchers look for variations in reaction processes that impose the social distinction of deviant on some people but not others. The conflicting aims and research methods of the two perspectives have made the issue of describing deviance an arena for considerable criticism and debate over the evidence from studies of deviant phenomena. Conflicts over empirical descriptions of deviance are not only related to the issue of defining deviance but also to controversial theoretical questions in this area. Most deviance research is not purely descriptive, being guided by and addressed to various theoretical approaches. The relevance of empirical work to theoretical problems will become clearer as we examine the issue of theorizing about deviance.

THE ISSUE OF THEORIZING ABOUT DEVIANCE

In our brief discussion of theoretical work in the contemporary field of deviance in Chapter 1, somewhat different terms were used to describe the theoretical goals of the normative and relativistic perspectives. The main concern of normative theories was presented as *explaining* the causes of deviant behavior. The goal of relativistic theories, however, was described as *understanding* the sources and implications of reactions to deviance. The terms *explaining* and *understanding* were chosen carefully, for they refer to important but often subtle differences in the styles, assumptions, and goals of theoretical work in the two perspectives. These differences have also generated a good deal of controversy over the issue of theorizing about deviance.

Theories that are primarily aimed at *explaining* deviant behavior or other phenomena are usually *deterministic* in nature. When used in the field of deviance or in other areas of sociology, deterministic theories are based on the assumption that social phenomena, like physical or biological phenomena, can be explained by general theoretical statements about *cause-and-effect relationships* between variables. Although the specific words *determinant* or *cause* may not be used in a particular theory of deviant behavior, such phrases as "*pressure* upon certain persons" (Merton, 1938: 672) or "*counteracting forces*" (Sutherland & Cressey, 1974: 76, emphasis added) are usually a good indication that the theory is attempting a deterministic explanation of deviant phenomena.

Theories addressed to the goal of *understanding* deviance or other areas of social life typically take the form of *interpretive analysis*. Sociologists who engage in interpretive theorizing usually reject or, at least, consider problematic the assumption that the deterministic form of theoretical explanation used in the natural sciences can be applied to social phenomena (see Blumer, 1969; Wilson, 1970). Above all, interpretive theorists emphasize that social action, as opposed to the actions of physical objects, is *meaningful* to those who engage in it. Social actors do not merely respond passively to forces or pressures in their environment but actively interpret and construct their social environment through meaningful interaction with others. This theoretical position implies that social behavior is complex and dynamic, but it does not imply that it lacks order and predictability. However, to understand the orderly nature of social action, the sociologist must adopt the viewpoint of social actors and attempt to interpret the meanings they attach to themselves, to others, and to their behavior. The goal of interpretive theories of deviance, then, is to arrive at a general understanding of the dynamic social processes through which deviant identities and meanings become attached to certain persons and their behavior.

It would be a gross and misleading oversimplification to state that all normative theories are deterministic and that all relativistic theories are interpretive in form. Some important efforts have been made to formulate interpretive or nondeterministic theories of norm-violating behavior (Becker, 1953; Matza, 1964). Conversely, some relativistic theories of deviance have a distinctly deterministic flavor, particularly the work of some conflict theorists who have been heavily influenced by the ideas of Karl Marx (Chambliss, 1973; Spitzer, 1975; see also Taylor, Walton, & Young, 1973). Nonetheless, with regard to the issue of how sociologists should go about their theoretical work on deviance, normative theorists are clearly more likely to advocate deterministic explanations than are relativistic theorists.

The distinction between deterministic and interpretative theorizing has been clearest and most controversial at the micro level of analysis in social psychological theories of deviance. Although there is some dispute regarding the extent to which Sutherland's differential association theory is deterministic in nature, this micro-normative theory at least presents the appearance of a rigorous attempt at a cause-and-effect explanation of law-violating behavior (Taylor, Walton, & Young, 1973; Davis, 1980; Glaser, 1956). However, there is no question about the deterministic quality of more recent attempts to translate Sutherland's theory into the terminology of psychological reinforcement or learning theory (Jeffrey, 1965; Burgess & Akers, 1966). Burgess and Akers, for instance, apply to Sutherland's theory the general psychological principle that behavior is a conditioned response to reinforcing environmental stimuli and propose that criminal behavior is "emitted" by humans when it is more highly reinforced than noncriminal behavior. Akers (1977; Akers et al., 1979) has continued to develop this differential association–reinforcement theory and has attempted to show how it can be used to explain the environmental causes of a variety of forms of deviant behavior other than criminality.

Burgess and Akers' work is an especially clear example of the deterministic style that tends to characterize most normative theories of deviant behavior. We should note that this theory has also provoked extreme reactions from relativistic critics. Taylor, Walton, and Young (1973: 131–133) rail against this reformulation as a "travesty of Sutherland's position" that "is based on a fundamental theoretical illiteracy." This illiteracy, they argue, stems from the failure of Burgess and Akers to recognize the "element of human choice and purpose" as an essential ingredient of deviant acts.

In contrast to the strong deterministic quality of some micro-normative theorizing, the micro-relativistic work of labeling theorists provides some of the best examples of interpretive analyses of deviance as a meaningful, processual phenomenon. The general analytical style of labeling theory is succinctly characterized by Schur (1969: 311):

> To understand the social psychology of deviance, we must examine the ongoing processes of action and reaction, of response and counterresponse, through which individual behavior and outlooks always develop. The self-conceptions of the deviating individual should be considered . . . crucial, for personal identity is viewed not as a fixed object, but rather as a constantly changing, multifaceted emergent quality.

Taylor, Walton, and Young's comment about the lack of concern with the element of human choice and purpose in deterministic theorizing would not seem to apply to the labeling theorists. For instance, Becker (1963: 37) writes the following about the choices open to an individual who has been initially apprehended for a rule-breaking act:

> Apprehension may not lead to increasing deviance if the situation in which the individual is apprehended for the first time occurs at a point where he can still choose between alternate lines of action. Faced, for the first time, with the possible ultimate and drastic consequences of what he is doing, he may decide that he does not want to take the deviant road, and turn back.

Whatever the merits of the attempts of labeling theorists and others to achieve an interpretive understanding of the interactional processes involved in deviant phenomena, theirs is clearly a minority position on the issue of theorizing about deviance. Deterministic explanation continues to be the dominant mode for theoretical work in the field of deviance. Critics more accustomed to deterministic forms of theory have wondered whether labeling theory is really theory at all (Gibbs, 1966; Schur, 1969). A more serious problem which the labeling theorists face, however, is the tendency of other sociologists to "vulgarize" their work by interpreting it from a strictly *deterministic* point of view (Lemert, 1972). Such an interpretation is presented by Akers (1968: 463) in his critique of the labeling literature:

> One sometimes gets the impression from reading this literature that people go about minding their own business, and then—"wham"— bad society comes along and slaps them with a stigmatized label. Forced into the role of deviant the individual has little choice but to be deviant.

While labeling theorists have objected to this "impression of crude sociologistic determinism" sometimes gained from their work (Lemert, 1972; Kitsuse, 1975), the loose and rather unsystematic nature of their theorizing does leave it open to such impressions.

Some conflict theorists have sympathized with the efforts of labeling theorists to avoid deterministic forms of theorizing and have extended the goal of interpretative understanding to macro-level theory (Quinney, 1972; Taylor, Walton, & Young, 1973). However, there is little reason to doubt that most sociologists in the field of deviance will continue to see some form of deterministic explanation as the preferable mode for theoretical work. Even so, the interpretative theorizing of the labeling theorists and conflict theorists has at least made sociologists aware of some of the problems and limitations of the traditional deterministic orientation of deviance theory. In particular, by advocating a position based on empathy and understanding of social actors who are defined as deviant, interpretive theorists have called into question the conventional role of the sociologist as a neutral, detached analyst of deviant behavior. In attempting to *empathize* with the underdogs they study, labeling theorists such as Becker (1967) have been prone to *sympathize* with their plight as victims of social control. As a result, the issue of values in the study of deviance has become a major concern for labeling theorists and other relativistic sociologists.

THE ISSUE OF VALUES IN THE STUDY OF DEVIANCE

The issues of definition, description, and explanation of deviance are primarily related to scientific problems in the study of deviant phenomena. The issue of values, on the other hand, involves more than just scientific questions. Science, ideally, is concerned with questions about the existing nature of empirical reality; that is, questions about *what is*. Values, however, are concerned with preferences about the desirability or undesirability, the goodness or badness of certain aspects of the empirical world. In other words, values represent conceptions of *what should be*.

Scientific inquiry is traditionally viewed as an activity that should be value free. No matter what a scientist's personal values might be regarding the phenomena he or she investigates, these value judgments must not be allowed to influence, distort, or bias the scientific tasks of theorizing about or conducting research on those phenomena. Until recently, this value-free conception of science, which itself is a value, was held by virtually all sociologists engaged in the study of deviance. Ever since the early social pathology period, sociologists made a conscious effort to avoid moralistic statements about deviant phenomena. No matter what opinions or values sociologists might hold toward deviant behavior as a *private citizen*, these personal views could not be allowed to influence the work of sociologists in their role as *social scientist*. The normative sociologists, in particular, were concerned with the development of *basic*, value-free knowledge about deviant phenomena. They left to others the responsibility of *applying* that knowledge in programs and policies designed to change, control, or otherwise cope with deviance as a threat to societal values. This value-free position, like most other features of the normative perspective, has now become controversial.

Becker, as usual, is right in the center of this controversy. In his presidential address before The Society for the Study of Social Problems, Becker (1967: 239) stated bluntly that it is *impossible* to conduct research on deviance "that is uncontaminated by personal and political sympathies." The question for Becker is not *whether* sociologists should hold values in their work on deviance. The only question is *what* values will sociologists adopt? *Whose* side will they be on?

Becker implies that the "value-free" position of the normative perspective was not free of values at all. By focusing the attention of the field of deviance on behavior and persons who violate the dominant legal and moral norms of society, the normative sociologists were actually *siding with* the values of groups that have the power to make and enforce rules in society. How could normative sociologists maintain that their viewpoint was value free? Nobody *in authority* questioned their perspective, since it corresponded with the dominant moral values of those in power. Dissenting points of view on the *other side of deviance*—the values and moral positions of the underdogs who were labeled as deviant—were ignored or discounted by normative sociologists just as they were by official agents of social control.

Because their own research and theory required close contact and identification with the underdog's point of view, Becker and other labeling theorists became especially sensitive to alternative moral positions in the study of deviance. In fact, in their focus on the sources and implications of societal reactions to deviance, relativistic sociologists made official values and policies of social control a major topic of investigation. Thus, relativistic analyses of deviance typically tend to side with the underdog by depicting the stigmatizing effects of moral labels and the often arbitrary nature of social control in American society. The value position conveyed by such work, in its open criticism of conventional values and systems of social control, is clear and explicit. Yet, Becker (1967) argues that normative analyses of deviant behavior are no less committed to conventional values than labeling analyses are to unconventional values. It is only that the latter position is more objectionable to powerful interests in society and is more likely to be attacked as biased and politically motivated.

Becker is correct, at least, in recognizing that labeling theory would be criticized for its explicit value-engaged approach to the study of deviance. Bordua (1967: 153) argues that labeling theory has "become an ideology of the underdog" by placing all of the blame for deviance on social control agents in positions of power. Lemert (1972: 24), himself a relativistic theorist, has objected that the work of Becker and other recent labeling theorists "is more social criticism than science."

Other critics, however, have argued that Becker does not go far enough in his advocacy of value-engaged sympathy with underdogs who are labeled as deviant. Some conflict theorists believe that the sociology of deviance should not merely attempt to appreciate the underdog's plight as a victim of social control but should actively attempt to *change* the power structure which oppresses deviants and other underdogs (Taylor, Walton, & Young, 1973; 1975; Gouldner, 1968). In a recent statement of this more radical value-engaged position, three British sociologists advocate a form of deviance theory that does not "rest content with the *description* of existing social arrangements. . . . Radical theory and practice can become a full-blown form of political practice . . . if it can find ways of changing the social world whilst investigating it" (Taylor, Walton, & Young, 1975: 24). These sociologists feel that the results of research on the exploitation of lower-class persons by agents of social control and other powerful interests *could* and *should* be used to mobilize the lower classes toward radical change of the current social arrangements of capitalist society.

Relatively few sociologists in the field of deviance go this far in advocating an activistic value-engaged approach to theory and research. However, sociologists no longer take it for granted that their work is value free. Becker and the labeling theorists have made it clear to all that personal and political preferences enter into many phases of research and theorizing on deviant phenomena. This does not mean that studies of deviant phenomena are completely determined by one's values and personal biases. Rather, Becker's position is that sociologists should make explicit their moral commitments so as to better recognize and guard against whatever biasing effects those values might have upon their studies of deviant phenomena. As Becker puts it (1967: 247): "We take sides as our personal and political commitments dictate . . . [and] . . . use our theoretical and technical resources to avoid the distortions that might introduce into our work."

In general, the controversy over the issue of values in the study of deviance represents a logical extension of the relativistic perspective. In this case, sociological conceptions of deviance rather than audience conceptions of deviance have become the object of critical analyses. Many sociologists disagree with Becker's assessment of the extent to which values influence their studies of deviance, but all would agree that these influences will no longer go unexamined.

CONCLUSION

The four broad issues considered in this chapter do not exhaust the dilemmas confronting sociologists in the field of deviance, of course. In later chapters we will encounter a variety of debates between advocates of opposing theories or between researchers who favor different methods of research on particular forms of deviance. Implicit in most of these more limited controversies, however, will be one or two of the core issues reviewed above. Therefore, this chapter has aimed at providing you with some basic tools for critical analysis that will help you evaluate and appreciate specific theoretical arguments and empirical conclusions discussed throughout the rest of this book. Use these tools. *Think critically* about the problems of definition, description, theorizing, and values as they become apparent in this or other works you will be reading in the sociology of deviance.

The macro-normative approach: Anomie and subculture theory

4

What causes people to engage in norm-violating behavior? You are now familiar with this central theoretical question of the normative perspective on deviance. Even with the emergence of the relativistic perspective and the new questions it raises for the field of deviance, explanation of the social causes of deviant behavior continues to be the primary objective of many contemporary sociologists. It is not difficult to understand why this theoretical goal has survived the barrage of criticism that has been directed against it in recent years. One does not have to be a sociologist to recognize that deviant behavior is a topic that fascinates and concerns most members of society. The desire to know more about the causes of alcoholism, interpersonal violence, or mental disorder seems natural and proper to nearly everyone. The long-standing interest of social scientists in the etiology of deviant behavior has itself become a topic for analysis by relativistic theorists (e.g., Taylor, Walton, & Young, 1973), but this interest continues to inspire a substantial amount of scholarly activity within the normative perspective.

This is the first of four chapters that will examine normative theory and research. It will be helpful if we begin this examination by mapping out the major traditions or theory groups within this broad perspective on deviance.

THEORETICAL TRADITIONS IN THE NORMATIVE PERSPECTIVE

The historical development of the field of deviance was described generally in Chapter 2 as a cumulative tradition of sociological inquiry. In this and subsequent chapters, the notion of tradition will be used in a more limited sense to refer to several coherent lines of cumulative theoretical work within the normative perspective. We will consider four more or less distinct traditions of normative theory. Each has its roots in early work that predates the emergence of the normative period in the 1930s; but the major contributions to most of these traditions occurred during the 1940s and 1950s. Most important, each tradition has continued to generate new theoretical and empirical insights into deviant phenomena during the most recent relativistic period.

The current chapter will deal with two normative traditions that are primarily concerned with *macro*-level explanations of deviant behavior: the *anomie tradition* and the *subcultural tradition*. The anomie tradition, of course, is closely identified with Merton's (1938; 1957) macro-normative analysis of the cultural and structural sources of variations in rates of deviant behavior in American society. However, we must also look to the earlier work of an important 19th-century French sociologist, Emile Durkheim (1933; 1951), for the initial use of the concept of anomie and for the classic analytical approach that characterizes the anomie tradition. Several more recent theoretical contributions have carried the anomie tradition well into the relativistic period. The subcultural tradition has also tended to emphasize macro-level questions, although some subculture theories have important social psychological implications as well. The major contributions to this tradition appeared during the 1950s and early 1960s in a series of theoretical analyses of the nature and formation of lower-class, delinquent subcultures (Cohen, 1955; Sykes & Matza, 1957; Miller, 1958; Cloward, 1959; Cloward & Ohlin, 1960). This tradition extends back to the works of Merton, Sutherland, and the Chicago School, and forward to Wolfgang and Ferracuti's (1967) analysis of the "subculture of violence."

In Chapter 6, we will examine two *micro*-normative traditions, the *social learning tradition* and the *control tradition*. Sutherland's (1939; 1947) differential association theory of individual criminal behavior is the anchorpoint of the social learning tradition, of course. As we have already noted in Chapter 3, several efforts have been made to extend the social learning tradition by translating Sutherland's formulation into the rigorous conceptual language of reinforcement theory (Jeffrey, 1965; Burgess & Akers, 1966; Akers, 1977). Finally, the control tradition has its origins in Durkheim's early macro-level theorizing, but it has moved steadily toward the micro-level of analysis in later work by control theorists (Reiss, 1951; Nye, 1958; Matza, 1964; Hirschi, 1969). Unlike the other three normative traditions, control theories have become most influential during the relativistic period rather than earlier. The control tradition also differs from the others by taking as its original analytical question "why do people conform?" rather than "why do people deviate?" Nonetheless, control theorists are ultimately aiming at the same goal that has captured the attention of normative theorists since Durkheim: explanation of the social causes of deviant behavior.

THE ANOMIE TRADITION

Durkheim's classic contribution

Emile Durkheim is just considered to be one of the founders of modern sociology. This French sociologist began his academic career in the late 1800s, a time when sociology was not widely accepted in Europe or elsewhere as an independent scientific discipline. Durkheim devoted his life's work to the advancement of this new field of study. In his first two major books originally published in the early 1890s, *The Division of Labor in Society* (1933) and *The Rules of Sociological Method* (1938), Durkheim outlined what he saw to be the distinctive theoretical problems and methodological strategies of sociological inquiry. In the latter book, he identified the analysis of "social facts" as the unique subject matter for the science of sociology. Social facts, according to Durkheim, are phenomena that are properties of societies rather than of individual members of societies. The rate of divorce or suicide in a society or the nature of a society's legal or religious systems are examples of social facts that Durkheim considered to be external to individuals. Most important, Durkheim argued that social facts could only be explained *sociologically*; that is, by reference to other social facts: "The determining cause of a social fact should be sought among the social facts preceding it and not among the states of the individual consciousness" (1938: 110).

Durkheim applied these general principles to a particular research problem in his third major book, originally published in 1897, *Suicide* (1951). He deliberately focused on the seemingly individualistic phenomenon of suicide in order to demonstrate the power and distinctiveness of sociological inquiry. What better or more dramatic way is there to build a strong case for sociology than to look *beyond the individual*—to society—for the causes of suicidal behavior? Using a vast body of data from official records on suicides in different parts of Europe, Durkheim documented marked variations between countries in suicide rates. This evidence, Durkheim argued, shows that "each society has a definite aptitude for suicide" (1951: 48)—a social fact that is external to the individual members of a given society. Additional analyses of these data convinced Durkheim that the suicide rate of a given society could not be explained by racial characteristics, psychological abnormalities, or other extrasocial causes, and that "by elimination, it must necessarily depend upon social causes" (1951: 145). Throughout the remainder of *Suicide*, Durkheim attempted to prove that "certain states of (the) social environment" (1951: 299) are the determining causes of different patterns of suicide rates.

Durkheim identified four distinct environmental conditions that he believed to be responsible for various patterns of high suicide rates: egoism, altruism, anomie, and fatalism. At this point, we shall focus only on the best known of these four causes of suicide, anomie.

Anomie refers to an environmental state where society fails to exercise adequate regulation or constraint over the goals and desires of its individual members (Durkheim, 1951: 241–276). It is important to note that Durkheim's conceptualization of anomie is based on a general assumption about the psychological or biological nature of individual human beings. He wrote that the human "capacity for feeling is in itself an insatiable and bottomless abyss" (1951: 247). From Durkheim's viewpoint, individual happiness and well-being depend on the ability of society to impose *external limits* on the potentially limitless passions and appetites that characterize human nature in general. Under the condition of anomie, however, society is unable to exert its regulatory and disciplining influences. Human desires are left unchecked and unbounded—the individual "aspires to everything and is satisfied with nothing" (1951: 271). Out of disillusionment and despair with the pursuit of limitless goals, many individuals in the anomic society take their own lives. Therefore, high rates of anomic suicide are the product of the environmental condition of anomie.

Durkheim argued that the condition of anomie could explain at least three kinds of suicidal phenomena. First, in historical data on suicide rates in Europe, Durkheim found that sharp *increases or decreases* in the economic prosperity of a society were associated with increasing rates of suicide. Suicide rates were lowest during times of economic stability. Durkheim reasoned that economic crises disrupted society's regulatory influence on the material desires of its members. Economic booms or depressions undercut the predictable material goals from which individuals would ordinarily derive satisfaction. Second, in addition to cases where anomie resulted from rapid economic change, Durkheim also presented evidence that "one sphere of social life—the sphere of trade and industry—is actually in a *chronic* state" of anomie (1951: 254, emphasis added). In commercial segments of society where far-reaching economic goals are continually sought and "greed is aroused without knowing where to find ultimate foothold" (1951: 256), a lack of regulation over material desires becomes a constant state of the social environment. Durkheim explained high rates of suicide among business people as a result of this chronic state of anomie. Finally, Durkheim analyzed how inadequate regulation of sexual desires could also produce high rates of anomic suicide among certain social groups. Single males, in particular, are in social circumstances where their unrestrained pursuit of physical pleasure is likely to lead to disillusionment and suicide. Marriage functions to regulate sexual desire, and husbands typically have lower rates of suicide than unmarried males. Thus, the concept of anomie is used by Durkheim to explain a variety of social facts. Variations in suicide rates across time, by occupation and by marital status, are all linked theoretically to this general environmental condition.

Durkheim's work has been the subject of extensive discussion and criticism (see, for example, Parsons, 1937; Johnson, 1965; Nisbet, 1965; Douglas, 1967; Pope, 1973; 1976; Marks, 1974; Hawkins, 1979). Nonetheless, his work on suicide has endured as a classic example of the macro-normative approach to theory and research on deviance. We should note that Inkeles (1959) has questioned the sociological purity of Durkheim's analysis by pointing out that psychological assumptions about the limitless nature of human desires can be found in *Suicide*. However, Durkheim generally treats psycho-biological qualities or potentials as *constants* rather than as *variables* in his analytical scheme: "human nature is substantially the same among all men, in its essential qualities" (1951: 247). Variations in suicide rates cannot be explained by psychological constants but only by variations in the social environment that "lies outside individuals" and exerts external influences upon them (1951: 324). Following the clear directions laid down by Durkheim, the anomie tradition has continued to focus its search for the causes of deviant behavior on large-scale variations in the environmental features of society.

Merton's theory of social structure and anomie

We have already devoted some attention to the other major contribution to the anomie tradition, Merton's theory of "Social Structure and Anomie" (1938; 1957). It should now be evident that Durkheim's work provided the intellectual foundation for Merton's attempt to develop a macro-level explanation of rates of norm-violating behavior in American society. But, in Merton's hands, the anomie tradition advanced well beyond Durkheim's singular concern with suicide to become a truly general sociological approach to deviance.

In contrast to Durkheim, Merton bases his theory on sociological assumptions about human nature. Merton replaces Durkheim's conception of insatiable passions and appetites with the assumption that human needs and desires are primarily the product of a *social* process; i.e., cultural socialization. People reared in a society where cultural values emphasize material goals will *learn* to strive for economic success.

As we saw in Chapter 1, Merton does indeed attribute an extreme emphasis on material goals to the cultural environment of American society. In this respect, Merton's description of American society is quite similar to Durkheim's observations regarding the unrelenting pursuit of economic gain in "the sphere of trade and industry." However, Merton extends this materialistic portrait to include all of American society. Merton not only argues that all Americans, regardless of their position in society, are exposed to the dominant materialistic values, but that cultural beliefs sustain the myth that *anyone* can succeed in the pursuit of economic goals.

Anomie, for Durkheim, referred to the failure of society to regulate or constrain the ends or *goals* of human desire. Merton, on the other hand, is more concerned with social regulation of the *means* people use to obtain material goals. First, Merton perceives a "strain toward anomie" in the relative lack of cultural emphasis on institutional norms—the established rules of the game—that regulate the legitimate means for obtaining success in American society. Second, structural blockages that limit access to legitimate means for many members of American society also contribute to its anomic tendencies. Under such conditions, behavior tends to be governed solely by considerations of expediency or effectiveness in obtaining the goal rather than by a concern with whether or not the behavior conforms to institutional norms.

Together, the various elements in Merton's theoretical model of American society add up to a social environment that generates strong pressures toward deviant behavior (1957: 146, emphasis in original):

> when a system of cultural values extols, virtually above all else, certain *common* success-goals *for the population at large* while the social structure rigorously restricts or completely closes access to approved modes of reaching these goals *for a considerable part of the same population* . . . deviant behavior ensues on a large scale.

This chronic discrepancy between cultural promises and structural realities not only undermines social support for institutional norms but also promotes violations of those norms. Blocked in their pursuit of economic success, many members of society are forced to adapt in deviant ways to this frustrating environmental condition.

Just how do people adapt to these environmental pressures? Merton's answer to this question is perhaps his single most important contribution to the anomie tradition. Merton presents an analytical typology, shown in Table 4–1, of individual adaptations to the discrepancy between culture and social structure in American society. These adaptations describe the kinds of social roles people adopt in response to cultural and structural pressures. *Conformity*, for instance, is a nondeviant adaptation where people continue to engage in legitimate occupational or educational roles despite environmental pressures toward deviant behavior. That is, the conformist accepts and strives for the cultural goal of material success (+) by following institutionalized means (+). *Innovation*, on the other hand, involves acceptance of the cultural goal (+) but rejection of legitimate, institutionalized means (−). Instead, the innovator moves into criminal or

Table 4-1
Merton's typology of individual adaptations to environmental pressures

Type of adaptation	Cultural goal	Institutionalized means
I. Conformity	+	+
II. Innovation	+	−
III. Ritualism	−	+
IV. Retreatism	−	−
V. Rebellion	±	±

Note: + signifies acceptance, − signifies rejection, and ± signifies rejection of prevailing goal or means *and* substitution of new goal or means.
Source: Adapted from Robert K. Merton, *Social Theory and Social Structure*, rev. ed. (New York: Free Press, 1957), p. 150.

delinquent roles that employ illegitimate means to obtain economic success. As our discussion of this deviant adaptation in Chapter 1 pointed out, Merton proposes that innovation is particularly characteristic of the lower class—the location in the class structure of American society where access to legitimate means is especially limited and the "strain toward anomie" is most severe. Driven by the dominant cultural emphasis on material goals, lower-class persons use illegitimate but expedient means to overcome these structural blockages. Thus, Merton's analysis of innovation, like Durkheim's analysis of anomic suicide, arrives at an environmental explanation of an important set of social facts; i.e., the high rates of lower-class crime and delinquency found in official records.

However, Merton goes on to explain a much broader range of deviant phenomena than just lower-class crime and delinquency. His third adaptation, *ritualism*, represents quite a different sort of departure from cultural standards than does innovation. The ritualist is an *over*conformist. Here, the pursuit of the dominant cultural goal of economic success is rejected or abandoned (−) and compulsive conformity to institutional norms (+) becomes an end in itself. Merton argues that this adaptation is most likely to occur within the lower middle class of American society where socialization practices emphasize strict discipline and rigid conformity to rules. This adaptation is exemplified by the role behavior of the bureaucratic clerk who, denying any aspirations for advancement, becomes preoccupied with the ritual of doing it "by the book." Since the ritualist outwardly conforms to institutional norms, there is good reason to question, as does Merton, "whether this (adaptation) represents genuinely deviant behavior" (1957: 150).

Merton has no doubts about the deviant nature of his fourth adaptation, *retreatism*, the rejection of both cultural goals (−) and institutionalized means (−). Therefore, retreatism involves complete escape from the pressures and demands of organized society. Merton applies this adaptation to the deviant role "activities of psychotics, autists, pariahs, outcasts, vagrants, vagabonds, tramps, chronic drunkards, and drug addicts" (1957: 153). Despite the obvious importance of ritualism to the study of deviant behavior, Merton provides few clues as to where, in the class structure of society, this adaptation is most likely to occur. Instead, Merton's analysis of retreatism has a more individualistic flavor than does his discussion of other types of adaptation. Retreatism is presented as an escape mechanism whereby the individual resolves *internal conflict* between moral constraints against the use of illegitimate means and repeated failure to attain success through legitimate means. As we shall see later, Merton's conception of retreatism as a private way of dropping out has been given a more sociological interpretation by theorists in the subcultural tradition (Cloward, 1959; Cloward & Ohlin, 1960).

The final adaptation in Merton's typology, *rebellion*, is indicated by different notation than the other adaptations. The two ± signs show that the rebel not only rejects the goals and means of the established society but actively attempts to substitute *new* goals and means in their place. This adaptation refers, then, to the role behavior of political deviants, who attempt to modify greatly the existing structure of society. In later work (1966), Merton uses the term *nonconformity* to contrast rebellion to other forms of deviant behavior that are "aberrant." The nonconforming rebel is not secretive as are other, aberrant deviants and is not merely engaging in behavior that violates the institutional norms of society. The rebel publicly acknowledges his or her intention to change those norms and the social structure that they support in the interests of building a better, more just society. Merton implies that rebellion is most characteristic of "members of a rising class" (1957: 157) who become inspired by political ideologies that "locate the source of large-scale frustrations in the social structure . . . and portray an alternative structure which would not, presumably, give rise to frustration of the deserving" (1957: 156).

The appeal of Merton's theory and a major reason for its far-reaching impact upon the field of deviance lies in his ability to derive explanations of a diverse assortment of deviant phenomena from a relatively simple analytical framework. This is precisely what a *general* theory of deviance must do. The utility or adequacy of Merton's explanations of these forms of deviant behavior is a separate question, of course, a question that has led to a large body of additional theoretical and empirical work in the anomie tradition. Merton has continued to play an active part in the cumulative development of this macro-normative tradition through his published responses to various criticisms, modifications, and empirical tests of his theory of social structure and anomie (1957: 161–194; 1959; 1964; 1966; 1976).

Later developments in the anomie tradition

Throughout the normative period in the sociology of deviance, a number of theorists suggested ways of improving or extending Merton's analytical framework. The most successful modifications of Merton's theory became the basis for a separate theoretical tradition within the normative perspective, subcultural theory. In a later section, we will discuss how some of the major subculture theories represent, in part, attempts to strengthen weaknesses in Merton's analysis of crime and delinquency as innovative deviant behavior (Cohen, 1955; Cloward & Ohlin, 1960). Less successful were several attempts to elaborate on Merton's typology of adaptations to the discrepancy between culture and social structure (Parsons, 1951: 249–325; Dubin, 1959; Harary, 1966). Dubin, for instance, pointed out how Merton's combinations of pluses and minuses could be logically expanded to produce a typology of 14 deviant adaptations. While granting that these complex typologies might be more logical or more general than Merton's, most sociologists found his five types to be far easier to comprehend and quite adequate for their purposes.

The problems of conducting research on Merton's macro-level theory have led to some efforts to extend the anomie tradition to a micro level of analysis. Although several important attempts have been made (Lander, 1954; Bordua, 1959; Chilton, 1964), empirical measurement of anomie and other macro-level variables in Merton's abstract model of American society has proven difficult. As an alternative, Srole (1956) developed a measure of *anomia,* subjective feelings of anomie experienced by *individuals.* Srole's anomia scale consists of five survey questions that indicate the extent to which individuals sense a lack of predictability or meaning in their environment. A number of studies in the 1950s and 1960s relating Srole's scale to the social class and deviant behavior of individuals appeared to provide some support for Merton's theory (see Cole & Zuckerman, 1964). However, Merton (1964) expressed some reservations about this shift of the anomie tradition toward the micro level of analysis. In particular, he objected that the popularity of research on *"anomia*—a condition of the individual—seems to have had an adverse effect on systematic studies of *anomie*—a condition of the social system" (1964: 228, emphasis in original). Analyses of anomia and individual deviant behavior can usefully *complement* analyses of anomie and rates of deviant behavior, but the former approach should not be taken as a *substitute* for the distinctively macro-level focus of the anomie tradition.

Recent theoretical work by Simon and Gagnon (1976) indicates that the anomie tradition is still on its original course as a macro-normative approach to deviance. These theorists, in fact, go all the way back to Durkheim for insights into the contemporary condition of society that they term "the anomie of affluence." Simon and Gagnon are especially critical of Merton's focus on restricted access to legitimate means as a structural source of anomie in American society. Merton's emphasis on "the anomie of scarcity," they argue, is historically dated. In contrast to the Depression years when Merton formulated his theoretical scheme, the central economic fact of life today is that *so many* rather than *so few* members of society obtain a high level of economic success. As Durkheim pointed out, social constraints and limitations on human desires become weakened when sudden economic prosperity places in the hands of many members of society the material goals that once seemed so distant. Applying Durkheim's observation to the contemporary affluent society, Simon and Gagnon propose that the greatest problems of anomie and deviant behavior now involve (1) the degree to which members of society remain committed to the pursuit of cultural goals and (2) the degree to which the achievement of those goals is experienced as gratifying or satisfying to individuals. Forms of deviant behavior during the 1960s and 1970s, such as political radicalism or drug use among middle- and upper-class youths, reflect a lack of commitment to and satisfaction with conventional goals of material success. These deviant adaptations to the anomie of affluence involve a search for alternative goals and gratifications under environmental conditions where conventional goals have lost their luster.

Simon and Gagnon recognize that restricted economic opportunities still confront many members of society, implying that Merton's analysis of the anomie of scarcity may still be applicable to such people (1976: 360). Furthermore, in a postscript to their article (1976: 376–377), they admit that the unexpected economic recession that began in the mid-1970s raises the same question for their theory that they asked of Merton's theory: "to what degree is its applicability (if any) limited to a fixed period of sociocultural time?" No matter which direction further economic trends take us, however, American society will continue to be divided between the haves and the have nots. Although the lasting contribution of Simon and Gagnon's analysis to the anomie tradition cannot be adequately assessed at the present time, they appear to have provided some theoretical balance to the predominantly lower-class emphasis of Merton's work. As self-report studies and other recent research have pointed out, deviant behavior is hardly a phenomenon that is restricted to any particular class. The anomie tradition might regain some of the strength it has lost during the relativistic period if further efforts are made to identify the cultural and structural conditions that cause both the haves and the have nots to engage in various forms of norm-violating behavior.

If anything, an emphasis on lower-class deviance is even more pronounced in a second theoretical tradition within the normative perspective, subcultural theory. Despite this limitation it shares with the anomie tradition, the subcultural tradition did make some important advances beyond Merton's work and provides us with some of the most sophisticated examples of sociological theorizing in the deviance literature.

THE SUBCULTURAL TRADITION

Cohen and the culture of the delinquent gang

The subcultural tradition emerged in the 1950s as an intensive effort by sociological theorists to explain the environmental causes of a relatively specific type of norm-violating behavior: juvenile delinquency committed by gangs of urban, lower-class males. The analytical sophistication and complexity of this theoretical work tended to compensate for limitations in the range of deviant phenomena to which it applied. Although Merton attempted to explain many different forms of deviant behavior, he made little effort to distinguish juvenile delinquency from adult crime, lumping both together under the global category of innovation. The subcultural theorists found that Merton's framework, at best, provided only very general insights into the social determinants of delinquency and, at worst, simply could not account for important kinds of norm-violating behavior performed by delinquent gangs.

In a book that introduced the first subcultural theory of delinquency, *Delinquent Boys: The Culture of the Gang,* Albert K. Cohen (1955) pointed out that the destructive and malicious quality of much delinquent behavior seems far removed from Merton's description of innovation. Rather than pursuing the dominant cultural goal of economic success through illegitimate means, lower-class gangs appear to be more intent on vandalizing and destroying the material objects—such as schools, automobiles, and other property—that symbolize middle-class values. However, despite its weaknesses, Cohen finds Merton's framework useful as a starting point for the development of a more adequate, subcultural explanation of the behavior of delinquent gangs.

Cohen begins his analysis with the assumption that working-class boys are initially influenced by the norms, values, and success goals of the dominant middle-class culture—the consensus model of American society that also underlies Merton's theory. That is, working-class boys enter adolescence with a desire to achieve social status and respect by middle-class standards. However, Cohen, like Merton, argues that environmental blockages stand in the way for these working-class youths. Specifically, Cohen states that socialization practices in working-class families produce young boys who are ill equipped for living up to the standards of the middle-class measuring rod—the norms and values for performance used in schools and other middle-class institutions. Middle-class teachers demand and reward social and intellectual skills that receive relatively little emphasis in working-class homes. The working-class boy soon finds that his desire for social recognition from his teachers and other representatives of the middle class will be unfulfilled. His inability to measure up to middle-class expectations becomes a source of frustration and a constant reminder of his personal inadequacy. At this point, the working-class boy "faces a problem of adjustment and is in the market for a 'solution' " (Cohen, 1955: 119).

Here, where Merton might focus on individual adaptations to environmental blockages, Cohen introduces a more sociological conception of the adjustment process. He proposes that working-class boys accomplish a *collective* rather than an *individual* solution to their mutual problem of adjustment by forming a delinquent subculture. *Interpersonal relationships* between working-class boys who hang around with one another represent the crucial condition for the emergence of a subcultural solution; i.e., "the existence, *in effective interaction with one another, of a number of actors with similar problems of adjustment*" (1955: 59, emphasis in original). Through interaction in the groups or gangs of which they are a part, working-class boys discover that the frustration imposed upon them by the middle-class measuring rod is a *shared* problem. Together, they eventually "establish new norms, new criteria of status which define as meritorious the characteristics they *do* possess, the kinds of conduct of which they *are* capable" (1955: 66, emphasis in original). Cohen argues that the norms and values of this new subculture define as appropriate various behaviors that are in direct opposition to the expectations and standards of middle-class culture. Truancy is encouraged *because* it runs counter to the demands of middle-class schools. Aggressiveness is rewarded *because* it flaunts middle-class standards of politeness and self-control. Vandalism is supported *because* property symbolizes the materialistic values of middle-class culture. In short, the delinquent subculture is the direct antithesis of middle-class culture. It not only provides a new set of standards against which working-class boys can measure up and, by committing delinquent acts, attain status in the eyes of fellow gang members, but also resolves the lingering and frustrating desire for status by middle-class standards through a collective rejection and repudiation of those standards.

The concept of subculture fills in a major theoretical gap left open by the anomie tradition. As Cohen later observed, Merton conceptualized the movement into deviant adaptations "as though each individual . . . were in a box by himself" (1965: 6). Both Merton and Durkheim leave one with the impression that broad structural and cultural pressures act *directly* upon isolated individuals, causing them to engage in deviant behavior. In Cohen's formulation, however, group interaction and subcultural influences *mediate* between strains in the class structure of society and individual responses. The notion of individual adaptation is replaced by a conception of deviant behavior as a group activity which is motivated and given direction by the shared values and norms of a delinquent subculture.

Anomie theory provided a starting point for Cohen's theory, but the ideas of Sutherland and the Chicago sociologists suggested the finishing touches for his analysis of the formation and transmission of delinquent subcultures within working-class gangs. Sutherland's differential association theory (1947) and Shaw and McKay's conception of "cultural transmission" (1942) were instrumental in Cohen's focus on interpersonal relationships between working-class boys as a crucial condition for a subcultural solution to their status problems. Other subcultural theorists followed Cohen's lead by attempting to integrate Merton's macro-level focus on the cultural and structural characteristics of American society with a micro-level focus on interpersonal influences in the group environment of the lower-class delinquent. Still, Cohen's theory and most of the other contributions to the subcultural tradition primarily represent a *macro-normative* approach to the causes of deviant behavior. For Cohen (1955: 148), subcultural theory does not try to explain "why . . . particular individuals engage in delinquency." Rather, the central question is this: "why does a particular subculture, with a certain distinctive content, have its principal locus in a certain . . . sector in our society?"

Cloward and Ohlin: Illegitimate opportunities

The most elaborate attempt to answer Cohen's question was presented by Cloward and Ohlin in their book, *Delinquency and Opportunity: A Theory of Delinquent Gangs* (1960). These theorists also base their work on criticism and cumulative development of Merton's anomie theory. And, like Cohen, by integrating Merton's macro-level approach with Sutherland's micro-level theorizing, Cloward and Ohlin attempt to arrive at a more complete explanation of the formation and content of delinquent subcultures.

Cloward and Ohlin basically agree with Merton's view that an extreme cultural emphasis on the goal of economic success touches all social classes in American society, producing a strain toward anomie. Their main criticism of Merton appears, at first glance, to call for only a minor modification of his theory. Although anomie theory spells out how special pressures are brought to bear on the lower class because of restricted access to legitimate economic opportunities, Merton failed to consider how variations in access to *illegitimate* opportunities might affect deviant adaptations (see Cloward, 1959). Merton's analysis of innovation implicitly assumes that criminal or delinquent means to obtain materialistic goals are readily available in the lower-class environment. Cloward and Ohlin question this general assumption and argue that the availability of illegitimate opportunities, like the availability of legitimate opportunities, is socially structured and varies markedly in different lower-class communities. In some lower-class areas where organized criminal activity flourishes as an integral part of community life, illegitimate opportunity structures will be relatively open. That is, opportunities to learn criminal skills or to participate in criminal organizations, such as the rackets, are open and accessible to many members of the community. In other lower-class communities, where criminal organizations are not integrated into the fabric of community life, the illegitimate (as well as the legitimate) opportunity structure will tend to be closed. Here, community members have relatively few opportunities to follow a systematic career of crime as an alternative means of obtaining economic success.

Cloward and Ohlin's use of this deceptively simple concept of illegitimate opportunity as the foundation for a complex subcultural theory of lower-class delinquency is an excellent example of sociological analysis. Extending Merton and drawing upon Sutherland, Cloward and Ohlin attempt to specify the social conditions under which three different types of delinquent subcultures might develop as lower-class adolescents collectively adapt to their restricted opportunities for legitimate social status and economic success.

A *criminal subculture* tends to form among lower-class adolescents living in communities where illegitimate opportunity structures are *open*. Successful professional criminals are visible role models for youths in the community. Young males may participate in or aspire to low-level jobs in criminal organizations that permeate such communities. As Sutherland's differential association theory would suggest, exposure to these organized patterns of adult criminality encourages the development of a criminal type of delinquent subculture, where adolescents gain recognition and status by demonstrating their skills at theft and other systematic forms of property crime.

A *conflict subculture* emerges in lower-class communities where adult crime is not highly organized and illegitimate opportunity structures are *closed* to adolescents. Cloward and Ohlin characterize such areas as follows (1960: 173–174):

> The disorganized slum . . . contains the outcasts of the criminal world. This is not to say that crime is nonexistent in such areas, but what crime there is tends to be individualistic, unorganized, petty, poorly paid, and unprotected. . . . Because such areas fail to develop criminal learning environments and opportunity structures, stable criminal subcultures cannot emerge.

With both legitimate and illegitimate opportunities for economic success blocked, adolescents in these disorganized areas resort to violence and gang warfare to demonstrate their personal worth and to attain respect. The values of the conflict subculture award high status to those who demonstrate both physical skill and "guts" in gang warfare.

Finally, a *retreatist subculture* that is organized around drug use arises among some lower-class adolescents. Whereas Merton viewed retreatist behavior as a more or less individualistic adaptation to internal conflict, Cloward and Ohlin point out that social conditions are important both in the formation and in the maintenance of the retreatist subculture. They characterize adolescents who form drug-using groups as double failures because they are confronted with complete closure of illegitimate opportunities as well as legitimate opportunities. For either personal or structural reasons, such youths "have failed to find a place for themselves in criminal or conflict subcultures" (1960: 183). A subculture based on shared values and knowledge about drugs is sustained by users who must at least become loosely involved in group activity to maintain a regular supply of their drugs. According to Cloward and Ohlin, the retreat of double failures into drug use depends as much on conditions in the social environment as it does on a personal need to drop out.

The theories of Cloward and Ohlin and of Cohen form the backbone of the subcultural tradition in the sociology of deviance. No other major attempts have been made to tackle the central theoretical problem of these two works, explanation of the *formation* of deviant subcultures. The work of these theorists is also noteworthy for its attempt to weave a variety of theoretical approaches to deviant behavior into an integrated explanation of subcultural delinquency. But, while relying heavily on Merton's work to account for structural pressures conducive to subcultural formation and on Sutherland's work for insight into the interpersonal processes which serve as the mechanism for subcultural adaptations, Cloward and Ohlin and Cohen have synthesized these earlier ideas into a separate and distinctive theoretical tradition.

Other contributions to the subcultural tradition

Much of the other theoretical work in the subcultural tradition can be characterized as efforts to analyze the *content* rather than the formation of deviant subcultures. These theories typically explain high rates of deviant behavior in certain groups or segments of society as a product of conformity to subcultural values and expectations which differ significantly in content from the standards and norms of the dominant culture. A good example of this kind of subcultural explanation is Miller's (1958) lower-class culture theory of gang delinquency that we discussed in Chapter 2. As we noted, Miller takes exception to the idea that a frustrated pursuit of middle-class goals is an underlying cause of lower-class delinquency. Instead, merely by conforming to the ordinary requirements of a distinct and autonomous lower-class cultural system, lower-class adolescents tend to engage in behavior that conflicts with the moral and legal norms of middle-class society.

More recently, during the relativistic period, Wolfgang and Ferracuti (1967) have shifted the subcultural tradition away from a limited focus on juvenile delinquency. Using official records and other data on rates of homicide and other violent acts, these theorists observed that high rates of violent behavior tend to be concentrated in certain population groups, particularly lower-class and minority males ranging in age from late adolescence to the middle adult years. Wolfgang and Ferracuti theorize that a great deal of this violent deviant behavior can be explained as conformity to the values and expectations of a subculture of violence shared in these segments of society. In those groups that share this violent subculture, a variety of social encounters are potentially defined as insulting or threatening to one's honor, such as when one male questions another's masculinity. Furthermore, the norms of this subculture demand a violent response in these situations. Within the subculture of violence, a nonviolent response to a personal insult represents nonconformity and may result in group rejection. Finally, serious consequences often result from violent encounters because of the availability of lethal weapons among those who share the subculture of violence. As Wolfgang and Ferracuti point out, "the carrying of knives or other protective devices becomes a common symbol of willingness to participate in violence, to expect violence, and to be ready for its retaliation" (1967: 159). In many ways, then, the content of the subculture of violence contributes to high rates of serious deviant behavior among those groups that share it and conform to its demands.

Criticism of the major subcultural explanations of delinquency, particularly Cohen's, has also played an important part in the development of the subcultural tradition. Yinger (1960) and Cavan (1961) have pointed out that the negativistic content of the norms and values shared by Cohen's delinquent gangs can be more accurately described as a contraculture (i.e., directly in conflict with or opposed to the dominant culture) than as a subculture (i.e., merely different from or marginal to the dominant culture). Sykes and Matza (1957) seriously question the utility of Cohen's contracultural portrait of the lower-class delinquent gang. If delinquency represented absolute conformity to a set of norms and values that are in direct opposition to middle-class culture, then delinquents would not feel that their behavior was wrong nor would they experience a sense of guilt or shame when apprehended by the police. However, Sykes and Matza observe that delinquents do recognize the overall legitimacy of middle-class standards and laws, frequently exhibiting shame and guilt for delinquent acts that they admit to be wrong.

As an alternative to Cohen's theory, Sykes and Matza suggest that delinquent acts are facilitated by various "techniques of neutralization" learned through social interaction in delinquent gangs. These techniques are shared rationalizations or excuses that allow delinquents to justify their violations of social norms in a given situation. For instance, using the denial of injury as a neutralization technique, delinquents justify auto theft as "borrowing" a car, an act that doesn't really hurt anyone. By the denial of the victim, delinquents might rationalize an attack on a school teacher who is "unfair" and who "had it coming." Instead of conforming to the norms of a negativistic delinquent subculture, then, delinquents temporarily loosen their commitment to the dominant cultural system through the use of these and other techniques of neutralization.

The major macro-level theories of subcultural formation, Cohen (1955) and Cloward and Ohlin (1960), have also been criticized for being overly deterministic (Matza, 1964), difficult to test empirically (Kitsuse & Dietrick, 1959), and insensitive to important group and psychological processes at a micro level of analysis (Short & Strodtbeck, 1965; Bordua, 1961; 1962). Many of these same criticisms can be leveled at any macro-level theory of deviant behavior, such as Merton's anomie theory. Focusing primarily on large-scale units of analysis and broad patterns of variation in rates of deviant behavior, macro-normative theories tend to blur the details of complex interactional processes involved in the actions of deviant individuals. Nonetheless, the contributions of the anomie tradition and the subcultural tradition give substance to Durkheim's (1951: 299) early contention that important and uniquely sociological insights into deviant phenomena can be gained by "forgetting the individual" and seeking the causes of deviant behavior "in the nature of societies . . . themselves."

CONCLUSION

The theories reviewed in this chapter are distinctively sociological in heritage and approach, firmly rooted in the classic Durkheimian and Chicago traditions, and dedicated to the explanation of macro-level social facts. The discipline of sociology owes much to the strategic insights into the organization of modern society provided by Durkheim and Merton's analyses of anomie and rates of deviant behavior. The more concentrated efforts of subcultural theorists to unravel the causes of juvenile delinquency stands as one of the best examples of how general sociological principles can be applied to a particular social problem. Yet, these grand theoretical frameworks, like any scientific theory, must at some point be "brought down to reality" and subjected to empirical evaluation. After all is said and done, do these theories work? The next chapter turns to the methods that macro-normative researchers have employed to gather the social facts necessary for answering this most crucial question.

Research on rates of deviant behavior

5

Suppose that one of your professors asked you to help with some research he or she was doing for a book on suicide. The professor's request sounds simple enough; you must obtain information on the age, sex, and marital status of people who took their own lives over a three-year period. This information will be used mainly to construct two statistical tables for a book. As a reward for your efforts, the professor offers to acknowledge your assistance in the preface to the book. Unfortunately, you discover that the necessary data are not available in any government publications nor are they stored on a computer. In fact, the only way you can obtain this information is to copy it, case by case, from the official records on 26,000 individual suicides! Would you be willing to take on this job?

This incredible task was actually carried out in the early 1890s by one of Durkheim's students, Marcel Mauss. His contribution to Durkheim's *Suicide* (1951: 39) not only stands as a monument to the countless hours of labor that student assistants have performed for their professors over the years but also serves as a fitting introduction to the realities and problems of sociological research on rates of deviant behavior. Mauss's work was undertaken because of Durkheim's concern with the limitations of existing official statistics on suicide. This same concern lies at the core of much contemporary research within the macro-normative approach to deviance. Like many sociologists today, Durkheim questioned both the accuracy and the scientific utility of statistical data compiled for administrative purposes by governmental agencies. Specifically, when Durkheim attempted to examine the effects of marital status on the suicide rates for males and females at different ages, he found that "official publications do not contain the necessary data for this comparison" (1951: 175). Thus, Durkheim's need for sociologically relevant data that went beyond the "valueless information" in official reports resulted in Marcel Mauss's painstaking classification of individual suicides recorded in the files of the French Ministry of Justice.

While the quality and utility of official reports on various forms of deviance have improved considerably since Durkheim's time, sociologists are now much more likely to rely on alternative ways of documenting the social facts about rates of deviant behavior. As we noted in Chapter 1, some researchers continue to follow the example of Mauss and Durkheim by gaining access to the original, raw records of agencies of social control and by conducting specialized reanalyses of these secondary data. However, in many areas of deviance research, sociologists have attempted to escape the constraints of official record-keeping altogether by gathering their own primary data on social variations in deviant behavior. Modern techniques of survey research make it possible for investigators to obtain reliable estimates of rates of norm-violating behavior in various populations through interviews with relatively small samples of people within those populations. We have already seen in Chapter 2 that the results of survey research have occasionally raised serious doubts about certain "social facts" that seemed to be well established by official statistics on deviant behavior.

In this chapter, we will concentrate on two areas of research where both official records and survey techniques have provided important insights into the social patterning of deviant behavior: the study of rates of mental disorder and the study of crime rates. As in later chapters, we will examine three empirical articles written by social scientists that illustrate the research strategies and problems characteristic of the analytical approach to deviance being considered. First, we will look at a classic contribution to macro-normative research on mental disorder that makes use of psychiatric records in conjunction with survey data—Hollingshead and Redlich's "Social Stratification and Psychiatric Disorders" (1953). Then, we will turn to two more recent articles by Hindelang (1978) and Erlanger (1976) that focus on the implications of official data and survey data on crime rates for several of the macro-normative theories of deviance reviewed in Chapter 4.

INTRODUCTORY COMMENTS ON HOLLINGSHEAD AND REDLICH'S RESEARCH

In what social locations or segments of society do people stand the greatest risk of developing mental disorders? This, in a nutshell, is the central question of a specialized area of research known as the *social epidemiology of mental illness*. By studying and describing social variations in the distribution of mental disorders, social epidemiologists attempt to gather evidence that points to significant environmental causes of psychiatric problems. One of the major landmarks in epidemiological research is an investigation of the relationship between social class and the prevalence of mental disorders conducted in 1950 by a large team of researchers headed by August Hollingshead, a sociologist, and Frederick Redlich, a psychiatrist. Although Hollingshead and Redlich did not publish their final, detailed report on this project until 1958, the initial findings presented in the 1953 article reprinted below make clear the main conclusion of their research: *serious mental disorders are heavily concentrated at the bottom of the class structure.*

Some social epidemiological investigators limit their attention to the *incidence* of mental disorders; that is, they study the rate at which *new cases* of mental illness occur in a population over a given period of time. Hollingshead and Redlich, however, attempted to study social variations in the *treated prevalence* of mental disorders—that is, rates of *existing cases* (both new and continuing) under treatment—in a large urban community, New Haven, Connecticut. In order to accomplish this objective, Hollingshead, Redlich, and their research team gathered a massive body of data that allowed them to compare the psychiatric population of this community to the normal population on a number of social characteristics including, especially, social class. As you will see, Hollingshead and Redlich's measure of social class, the *Index of Social Position*, is actually based on a combination of three social characteristics that reflect a person's relative prestige or status within the community: area of residence, occupation, and education. Preliminary research by Hollingshead and another sociologist, Jerome Myers, had shown that this combined index was more effective than any single characteristic in assigning a person to an appropriate class level or stratum in the class structure of New Haven (Hollingshead & Redlich, 1958: 387–397). Community studies had revealed that New Haven itself was stratified into five social classes, ranging from Class I, the highest or most prestigious stratum, to Class V, the bottom stratum in the stratification system. The basic research problem, then, was to determine how the distribution of the psychiatric population differed from the distribution of the normal population across these five classes as measured by the Index of Social Position.

Hollingshead and Redlich's procedures for obtaining necessary data on the social characteristics, diagnoses, and treatment of the psychiatric population extended well beyond the use of official records on patients in state mental hospitals, a point at which many earlier epidemiological studies had stopped. The Psychiatric Census described briefly in the article below was a far-reaching effort to identify *every* resident of New Haven who was under psychiatric treatment as of December 1, 1950. Initial contacts were made with 1,287 public and private mental hospitals, psychiatric clinics, and psychiatrists in private practice, some as far away as Kansas and Florida. Eventually, the researchers were able to narrow this list down to 29 public and private mental institutions, and 66 private practitioners actually treating patients from New Haven. All of the mental institutions and 70 percent of the private practitioners agreed to give the researchers access to relevant information in patients' records (Hollingshead & Redlich, 1958: 18–24). Since a large majority (68 percent) of the 1,963 New Haven residents finally included in the psychiatric population were patients in state mental hospitals, you might ask yourself why Hollingshead and Redlich went to the additional trouble of identifying the relatively small proportion of patients in private treatment? Or, you might consider the fact that information was lost on 30 New Haven residents whose private psychiatrists in New York City refused to cooperate with the study. From what segment of the class structure would these patients be likely to come? How would their exclusion from the psychiatric population affect or bias Hollingshead and Redlich's findings on the class distribution of mental disorder? By asking critical questions about the strengths and limitations of Hollingshead and Redlich's procedures for gathering data on this form of deviance, you can gain a greater understanding of the overall purpose and implications of their research.

Some of the results reported below in Hollingshead and Redlich's article are based strictly on data from the psychiatric population. For instance, Table II in the article shows how the patients at each class level are distributed according to two broad diagnostic categories—neuroses and psychoses (the more serious diagnosis). Similarly, Table IV in the article reveals some striking variations in the types of psychiatric treatment patients at different class levels receive. It is important to note here that these data were gathered before tranquilizing and antipsychotic drugs came into widespread use in the treatment of mental disorders. Therefore, the category of organic therapy in Table IV does not refer to this contemporary type of treatment but to more drastic "neurosurgical procedures such as lobotomies . . . and various shock treatments such as electro-convulsive therapy and insulin coma therapy" (Hollingshead & Redlich, 1958: 256).

However, Hollingshead and Redlich's crucial epidemiological findings on the treated prevalence of mental disorders in New Haven also involve additional baseline data on the normal population of the community. The distributions of the normal population in Tables I and III in the article are based on survey data gathered by interviews in 5 percent of the households in New Haven. This survey, which included 3,559 interviews and took four months to complete, was designed so that its results could be generalized to the entire residential population of New Haven (Hollingshead & Redlich, 1958: 30–37). The households where interviews were conducted were selected or sampled *randomly* from a complete list of residential addresses in the community. This random selection process insured, within a very small margin of error, that the characteristics of households in the 5 percent sample would be representative of the characteristics of all households in the general population. More specifically, Hollingshead and Redlich could confidently treat their interview data on the Index of Social Position for members of sample households as if these data had been gathered on all members of the normal population of New Haven. Therefore, Tables I and III in the article provide an accurate estimate of the actual proportions of the general population that would be assigned to the five strata in the class structure of this community. By comparing these percentages to the proportions of the total psychiatric population (Table I) and the proportions of schizophrenic patients (Table III) falling into the five social classes, you will clearly see why Hollingshead and Redlich were able to conclude that serious mental disorders are disproportionately located at the bottom of the class structure.

RESEARCH ILLUSTRATION 5–A

Social stratification and psychiatric disorders*

August B. Hollingshead and Frederick C. Redlich

The research reported here grew out of the work of a number of men, who, during the last half century, have demonstrated that the social environment in which individuals live is connected in some way, as yet not fully explained, to the development of mental illness.[1] Medical men have approached this problem largely from the viewpoint of epidemiology.[2] Sociologists, on the other hand, have analyzed the

---

Source: Article reprinted from *American Sociological Review* 18 (April 1953), pp. 163–169.

* Paper read at the annual meeting of the American Sociological Society, September 3–5, 1952. The research reported here is supported by a grant from the National Institute of Mental Health of the United States Public Health Service to Yale University under the direction of Dr. F. C. Redlich, Chairman, Department of Psychiatry, and Professor August B. Hollingshead, Department of Sociology.

[1] For example, see, A. J. Rosanoff, *Report of a Survey of Mental Disorders in Nassau County, New York,* New York: National Committee for Mental Hygiene, 1916; Ludwig Stern, *Kulturkreis und Form der Geistigen Erkrankung* (Sammlung Zwanglosen Abshandlungen aus dem Gebiete der Nerven-und-Geiteskrankheiten), X, No. 2, Halle a. S:C. Marhold, 1913, pp. 1–62; J. F. Sutherland, "Geographical Distribution of Lunacy in Scotland," *British Association for Advancement of Science,* Glasgow, Sept. 1901; William A. White, "Geographical Distribution of Insanity in the United States," *Journal of Nervous and Mental Disease,* XXX (1903), pp. 257–279.

[2] For example, see: Trygve Braatoy, "Is it Probable that the Sociological Situation is a Factor in Schizophrenia?" *Psychiatrica et Neurologica,* XII (1937), pp. 109–138; Donald L. Gerard and Joseph Siegel, "The Family Background of Schizophrenia," *The Psychiatric Quarterly,* 24 (January, 1950), pp. 47–73; Robert W. Hyde and Lowell V. Kingsley, "Studies in Medical Sociology, I: The Relation of Mental Disorders to the Community Socio-economic Level," *The New England Journal of Medicine,* 231, No. 16 (October 19, 1944), pp. 543–548; Robert W. Hyde and Lowell V. Kingsley, "Studies in Medical Sociology, II: The Relation of Mental Disorders to Population Density," *The New En-*

question in terms of ecology,[3] and of social disorganization.[4] Neither psychiatrists nor sociologists have carried on extensive research into the specific question we are concerned with, namely, interrelations between the class structure and the development of mental illness. However, a few sociologists and psychiatrists have written speculative and research papers in this area.[5]

The present research, therefore, was designed to discover whether a relationship does or does not exist between the class system of our society and mental illnesses. Five general hypotheses were formulated in our research plan to test some dimension of an assumed

---

gland *Journal of Medicine*, 231, No. 17 (October 16, 1944), pp. 571–577; Robert M. Hyde and Roderick M. Chisholm, "Studies in Medical Sociology, III: The Relation of Mental Disorders to Race and Nationality," *The New England Journal of Medicine*, 231, No. 18 (November 2, 1944), pp. 612–618; William Malamud and Irene Malamud, "A Socio-Psychiatric Investigation of Schizophrenia Occurring in the Armed Forces," *Psychosomatic Medicine*, 5 (October, 1943) pp. 364–375; B. Malzberg, *Social and Biological Aspects of Mental Disease*, Utica, N.Y.: State Hospital Press, 1940; William F. Roth and Frank H. Luton, "The Mental Health Program in Tennessee: Statistical Report of a Psychiatric Survey in a Rural County," *American Journal of Psychiatry*, 99 (March, 1943), pp. 662–675; J. Ruesch and Others, *Chronic Disease and Psychological Invalidism*, New York: American Society for Research in Psychosomatic Problems, 1946; J. Ruesch and others, *Duodenal Ulcer: A Socio-psychological Study of Naval Enlisted Personnel and Civilians*, Berkeley and Los Angeles: University of California Press, 1948; Jurgen Ruesch, Annemarie Jacobson, and Martin B. Loeb, "Acculturation and Illness," *Psychological Monographs: General and Applied*, Vol. 62, No. 5, Whole No. 292, 1948 (American Psychological Association, 1515 Massachusetts Ave., N.W., Washington 5, D.C.); C. Tietze, Paul Lemkau and M. Cooper, "A Survey of Statistical Studies on the Prevalence and Incidence of Mental Disorders in Sample Populations," *Public Health Reports*, 1909–27, 58 (December 31, 1943); C. Tietze, P. Lemkau and Marcia Cooper, "Schizophrenia, Manic Depressive Psychosis and Social-Economic Status," *American Journal of Sociology*, XLVII (September, 1941), pp. 167–175.

[3] Robert E. L. Faris, and H. Warren Dunham, *Mental Disorders in Urban Areas*, Chicago: University of Chicago Press, 1939; H. Warren Dunham, "Current Status of Ecological Research in Mental Disorder," *Social Forces*, 25 (March, 1947), pp. 321–326; R. H. Felix and R. V. Bowers, "Mental Hygiene and Socio-Environmental Factors," *The Milbank Memorial Fund Quarterly*, XXVI (April, 1948), pp. 125–147; H. W. Green, *Persons Admitted to the Cleveland State Hospital, 1928–1937*, Cleveland Health Council, 1939.

[4] R. E. L. Faris, "Cultural Isolation and the Schizophrenic Personality," *American Journal of Sociology*, XXXIX (September, 1934), pp. 155–169; R. E. L. Faris, "Reflections of Social Disorganization in the Behavior of a Schizophrenic Patient," *American Journal of Sociology*, L (September, 1944), pp. 134–141.

[5] For example, see: Robert E. Clark, "Psychoses, Income, and Occupational Prestige," *American Journal of Sociology*, 44 (March, 1949), pp. 433–440; Robert E. Clark, "The Relationship of Schizophrenia to Occupational Income and Occupational Prestige," *American Sociological Review*, 13 (June, 1948), pp. 325–330; Kingsley Davis, "Mental Hygiene and the Class Structure," *Psychiatry*, I (February, 1938), pp. 55–56; Talcott Parsons, "Psychoanalysis and the Social Structure," *The Psychoanalytical Quarterly*, XIX, No. 3 (1950), pp. 371–384; John Dollard and Neal Miller, *Personality and Psychotherapy*, New York: McGraw-Hill, 1950; Jurgen Ruesch, "Social Technique, Social Status, and Social Change in Illness," Clyde Kluckhohn and Henry A. Murray (editors), in *Personality in Nature, Society, and Culture*, New York: Alfred A. Knopf, 1949, pp. 117–130; W. L. Warner, "The Society, the Individual and his Mental Disorders," *American Journal of Psychiatry*, 94, No. 2 (September, 1937), pp. 275–284.

relationship between the two. These hypotheses were stated positively; they could just as easily have been expressed either negatively or conditionally. They were phrased as follows:

I. The *expectancy* of a psychiatric disorder is related significantly to an individual's position in the class structure of his society.
II. The *types* of psychiatric disorders are connected significantly to the class structure.
III. The type of *psychiatric treatment* administered is associated with patient's positions in the class structure.
IV. The *psycho-dynamics* of psychiatric disorders are correlative to an individual's position in the class structure.
V. *Mobility* in the class structure is neurotogenic.

Each hypothesis is linked to the others, and all are subsumed under the theoretical assumption of a functional relationship between stratification in society and the prevalence of particular types of mental disorders among given social classes or strata in a specified population. Although our research was planned around these hypotheses, we have been forced by the nature of the problem of mental illness to study *diagnosed* prevalence of psychiatric disorders, rather than *true* or *total* prevalence.

METHODOLOGICAL PROCEDURE

The research is being done by a team of four psychiatrists,[6] two sociologists,[7] and a clinical psychologist.[8] The data are being assembled in the New Haven urban community, which consists of the city of New Haven and surrounding towns of East Haven, North Haven, West Haven, and Hamden. This community had a population of some 250,000 persons in 1950.[9] The New Haven community was selected because the community's structure has been studied intensively by sociologists over a long period. In addition, it is served by a private psychiatric hospital, three psychiatric clinics, and 27 practicing psychiatrists, as well as the state and Veterans Administration facilities.

Four basic technical operations had to be completed before the hypotheses could be tested. These were: the delineation of the class

---

[6] F. C. Redlich, B. H. Roberts, L. Z. Freedman, and Leslie Schaffer.
[7] August B. Hollingshead and J. K. Myers.
[8] Harvey A. Robinson.
[9] The population of each component was as follows: New Haven, 164,443; East Haven, 12,212; North Haven, 9,444; West Haven, 32,010; Hamden, 29,715; and Woodbridge, 2,822.

structure of the community, selection of a cross-sectional control of the community's population, the determination of who was receiving psychiatric care, and the stratification of both the control sample and the psychiatric patients.

August B. Hollingshead and Jerome K. Myers took over the task of delineating the class system. Fortunately, Maurice R. Davie and his students had studied the social structure of the New Haven community in great detail over a long time span.[10] Thus, we had a large body of data we could draw upon to aid us in blocking out the community's social structure.

The community's social structure is differentiated *vertically* along racial, ethnic, and religious lines; each of these vertical cleavages, in turn, is differentiated *horizontally* by a series of strata or classes. Around the socio-biological axis of race two social worlds have evolved: A Negro world and a white world. The white world is divided by ethnic origin and religion into Catholic, Protestant, and Jewish contingents. Within these divisions there are numerous ethnic groups. The Irish hold aloof from the Italians, and the Italians move in different circles from the Poles. The Jews maintain a religious and social life separate from the gentiles. The *horizontal* strata that transect each of these vertical divisions are based upon the social values that are attached to occupation, education, place of residence in the community, and associations.

The vertically differentiating factors of race, religion and ethnic origin, when combined with the horizontally differentiating ones of occupation, education, place of residence and so on, produce a social structure that is highly compartmentalized. The integrating factors in this complex are twofold. First, each stratum of each vertical division is similar in its cultural characteristics to the corresponding stratum in the other divisions. Second, the cultural pattern for each stratum or class was set by the "Old Yankee" core group. This core group provided the master cultural mold that has shaped the status system of each sub-group in the community. In short, the social structure of the New Haven community is a parallel class structure within the limits of race, ethnic origin, and religion.

---

[10] Maurice R. Davie, "The Pattern of Urban Growth," G. P. Murdock (editor), in *Studies in the Science of Society*, New Haven: 1937, pp. 133–162; Ruby J. R. Kennedy, "Single or Triple Melting-Pot: Intermarriage Trends in New Haven, 1870–1940," *American Journal of Sociology*, 39 (January, 1944), pp. 331–339; John W. McConnell, *The Influence of Occupation Upon Social Stratification*, Unpublished Ph.D. thesis, Sterling Memorial Library, Yale University, 1937; Jerome K. Myers, "Assimilation to the Ecological and Social Systems of a Community," *American Sociological Reviews*, 15 (June, 1950), pp. 367–372; Mhyra Minnis, "The Relationship of Women's Organizations to the Social Structure of a City," Unpublished Ph.D. Thesis, Sterling Memorial Library, Yale University, 1951.

This fact enabled us to stratify the community, for our purposes, with an *Index of Social Position*.[11] This *Index* utilizes three scaled factors to determine an individual's class position within the community's stratificational system: ecological area of residence, occupation, and education. Ecological area of residence is measured by a six point scale; occupation and education are each measured by a seven point scale. To obtain a social class score on an individual we must therefore know his address, his occupation, and the number of years of school he has completed. Each of these factors is given a scale score, and the scale score is multiplied by a factor weight determined by a standard regression equation. The factor weights are as follows: Ecological area of residence, 5; occupation, 8; and education, 6. The three factor scores are summed, and the resultant score is taken as an index of this individual's position in the community's social class system.

This *Index* enabled us to delineate five main social class strata within the horizontal dimension of the social structure. These principal strata or classes may be characterized as follows:

Class I. This stratum is composed of wealthy families whose wealth is often inherited and whose heads are leaders in the community's business and professional pursuits. Its members live in those areas of the community generally regarded as "the best;" the adults are college graduates, usually from famous private institutions, and almost all gentile families are listed in the New Haven *Social Directory*, but few Jewish families are listed. In brief, these people occupy positions of high social prestige.

Class II. Adults in this stratum are almost all college graduates; the males occupy high managerial positions, many are engaged in the lesser ranking professions. These families are well-to-do, but there is no substantial inherited or acquired wealth. Its members live in the "better" residential areas, about one half of these families belong to lesser ranking private clubs, but only 5 per cent of Class II families are listed in the New Haven *Social Directory*.

Class III. This stratum includes the vast majority of small proprietors, white-collar office and sales workers, and a considerable number of skilled manual workers. Adults are predominantly high school graduates, but a considerable percentage have attended business schools and small colleges for a year or two. They live in "good" residential areas, less than 5 percent belong to private clubs, but they are not included in the *Social Directory*. Their social life

---

[11] A detailed statement of the procedures used to develop and validate this *Index* will be described in a forthcoming monograph on this research tentatively titled *Psychiatry and Social Class* by August B. Hollingshead and Fredrick C. Redlich.

tends to be concentrated in the family, the church, and the lodge.

Class IV. This stratum consists predominately of semi-skilled factory workers. Its adult members have finished the elementary grades, but the older people have not completed high school. However, adults under 35 have generally graduated from high school. Its members comprise almost one half of the community; and their residences are scattered over wide areas. Social life is centered in the family, the neighborhood, the labor union, and public places.

Class V. Occupationally, class V adults are overwhelmingly semi-skilled factory hands and unskilled laborers. Educationally most adults have not completed the elementary grades. The families are concentrated in the "tenement" and "cold-water flat" areas of New Haven. Only a small minority belong to organized community institutions. Their social life takes place in the family flat on the street, or in neighborhood social agencies.

The second major technical operation in this research was the enumeration of psychiatric patients. A Psychiatric Census was taken to discover the number and kinds of psychiatric patients in the community. Enumeration was limited to residents of the community who were patients of a psychiatrist or a psychiatric clinic, or were in a psychiatric institution on December 1, 1950. To make reasonably certain that all patients were included in the enumeration, the research team gathered data from all public and private psychiatric institutions and clinics in Connecticut and nearby states, and all private practitioners in Connecticut and the metropolitan New York area. It received the cooperation of all clinics and institutions, and of all practitioners except a small number in New York City. It can be reasonably assumed that we have data comprising at least 98 percent of all individuals who were receiving psychiatric care on December 1, 1950.

Forty-four pertinent items of information were gathered on each patient and placed on a schedule. The psychiatrists gathered material regarding symptomatology and diagnosis, onset of illness and duration, referral to the practitioner and the institution, and the nature and intensity of treatment. The sociologists obtained information on age, sex, occupation, education, religion, race and ethnicity, family history, marital experiences, and so on.

The third technical research operation was the selection of a control sample from the normal population of the community. The sociologists drew a 5 percent random sample of households in the community from the 1951, New Haven *City Directory*. This directory covers the entire communal area. The names and addresses in it were compiled in October and November, 1950—a period very close to the date of the Psychiatric Census. Therefore there was comparability of residence and date of registry between the two population groups. Each household drawn in the sample was interviewed, and data on the age, sex, occupation, education, religion, and income of family members, as well as other items necessary for our purposes were placed on a schedule. This sample is our Control Population.

Our fourth basic operation was the stratification of the psychiatric patients and of the control population with the *Index of Social Position*. As soon as these tasks were completed, the schedules from the Psychiatric Census and the 5 percent Control Sample were edited and coded, and their data were placed on Hollerith cards. The analysis of these data is in process.

SELECTED FINDINGS

Before we discuss our findings relative to Hypothesis I, we want to reemphasize that our study is concerned with *diagnosed or treated* prevalence rather than *true* or *total* prevalence. Our Psychiatric Census included only psychiatric cases under treatment, diagnostic study, or care. It did not include individuals with psychiatric disorders who were not being treated on December 1, 1950, by a psychiatrist. There are undoubtedly many individuals in the community with psychiatric problems who escaped our net. If we had *true* prevalence figures, many findings from our present study would be more meaningful, perhaps some of our interpretations would be changed, but at present we must limit ourselves to the data we have.

Hypothesis I, as revised by the nature of the problem, stated: *The diagnosed prevalence of psychiatric disorders is related significantly to an individual's position* in the class structure. A test of this hypothesis involves a comparison of the normal population with the psychiatric population. If no significant difference between the distribution of the normal population and the psychiatric patient population by social class is found, Hypothesis I may be abandoned as unproved. However, if a significant difference is found between the two populations by class, Hypothesis I should be entertained until more conclusive data are assembled. Pertinent data for a limited test of Hypothesis I are presented in Table I. The data included show the number of individuals in the normal population and the psychiatric population, by class level. What we are concerned with in this test is how these two populations are distributed by class.

When we tested the reliability of these population distributions by the use of the chi square method, we found a *very significant* relation between social class and treated prevalence of psychiatric disorders in the New Haven community. A comparison of the percentage distri-

Table I
Distribution of normal and psychiatric population by social class

Social class	Normal population*		Psychiatric population	
	Number	Percent	Number	Percent
I	358	3.1	19	1.0
II	926	8.1	131	6.7
III	2500	22.0	260	13.2
IV	5256	46.0	758	38.6
V	2037	17.8	723	36.8
Unknown†	345	3.0	72	3.7
Total	11,422	100.0	1,963	100.0

Chi square = 408.16, P less than .001.
* These figures are preliminary. They do not include Yale students, transients, institutionalized persons, and refusals.
† The unknown cases were not used in the calculation of chi square. They are individuals drawn in the sample, and psychiatric cases whose class level could not be determined because of paucity of data.

bution of each population by class readily indicates the direction of the class concentration of psychiatric cases. For example, Class I contains 3.1 percent of the community's population but only 1.0 percent of the psychiatric cases. Class V, on the other hand, includes 17.8 percent of the community's population, but contributed 36.8 percent of the psychiatric patients. On the basis of our data Hypothesis I clearly should be accepted as tenable.

Hypothesis II postulated a significant connection between the *type* of psychiatric disorder and social class. This hypothesis involves a test of the idea that there may be a functional relationship between an individual's position in the class system and the type of psychiatric disorder that he may present. This hypothesis depends, in part, on the question of diagnosis. Our psychiatrists based their diagnoses on the classificatory system developed by the Veterans Administration.[12] For the purposes of this paper, all cases are grouped into two categories: the neuroses and the psychoses. The results of this grouping by social class are given in Table II.

A study of Table II will show that the neuroses are concentrated at the higher levels and the psychoses at the lower end of the class structure. Our team advanced a number of theories to explain the

---
[12] *Psychiatric Disorders and Reactions*, Washington: Veterans Administration, Technical Bulletin 10A-78, October, 1947.

Table II
Distribution of neuroses and psychoses by social class

Social class	Neuroses		Psychoses	
	Number	Percent	Number	Percent
I	10	52.6	9	47.4
II	88	67.2	43	32.8
III	115	44.2	145	55.8
IV	175	23.1	583	76.9
V	61	8.4	662	91.6
Total	449		1,442	

Chi square = 296.45, P less than .001.

sharp differences between the neuroses and psychoses by social class. One suggestion was that the low percentage of neurotics in the lower classes was a direct reaction to the cost of psychiatric treatment. But as we accumulated a series of case studies, for tests of Hypotheses IV and V, we became skeptical of this simple interpretation. Our detailed case records indicate that the social distance between psychiatrist and patient may be more potent than economic considerations in determining the character of psychiatric intervention. This question therefore requires further research.

The high concentration of psychotics in the lower strata is probably the product of a very unequal distribution of psychotics in the total population. To test this idea, Hollingshead selected schizophrenics for special study. Because of the severity of this disease it is probable that very few schizophrenics fail to receive some kind of psychiatric care. This diagnostic group comprises 44.2 percent of all patients, and 58.7 percent of the psychotics, in our study. Ninety-seven and six tenths percent of these schizophrenic patients had been hospitalized at one time or another, and 94 percent were hospitalized at the time of our census. When we classify these patients by social class we find that there is a very significant inverse relationship between social class and schizophrenia.

Hollingshead decided to determine, on the basis of these data, what the probability of the prevalence of schizophrenia by social class might be in the general population. To do this he used a proportional index to learn whether or not there were differentials in the distribution of the general population, as represented in our control sample, and the distribution of schizophrenics by social class. If a social class exhibits the same proportion of schizophrenia as it comprises of the general population, the index for that class is 100. If schizophrenia is disproportionately prevalent in a social class the index is above 100; if schizophrenia is disproportionately low in a social class the index is below 100. The index for each social class appears in the last column of Table III.

Table III
Comparison of the distribution of the normal population with schizophrenics in class, with index of probable prevalence

Social class	Normal population		Schizophrenics		Index of prevalence
	Number	Percent	Number	Percent	
I	358	3.2	6	.7	22
II	926	8.4	23	2.7	33
III	2,500	22.6	83	9.8	43
IV	5,256	47.4	352	41.6	88
V	2,037	18.4	383	45.2	246
Total	11,077	100.0	847	100.0	

The fact that the Index of Prevalence in class I is only one-fifth as great as it would be if schizophrenia were proportionately distributed in this class, and that it is two and one-half times as high in class V as we might expect on the basis of proportional distribution, gives further support to Hypothesis II. The fact that the Index of Prevalence is 11.2 times as great in class V as in class I is particularly impressive.

Hypothesis III stipulated that the type of psychiatric treatment a patient receives is associated with his position in the class structure. A test of this hypothesis involves a comparison of the different types of therapy being used by psychiatrists on patients in the different social classes. We encountered many forms of therapy but they may be grouped under three main types; psychotherapy, organic therapy, and custodial care. The patient population, from the viewpoint of the principal type of therapy received, was divided roughly into three categories: 32.0 percent received some type of psychotherapy; 31.7 percent received organic treatments of one kind or another; and 36.3 percent received custodial care without treatment. The percentage of persons who received no treatment care was greatest in the lower classes. The same finding applies to organic treatment. Psychotherapy, on the other hand, was concentrated in the higher classes. Within the psychotherapy category there were sharp differences between the types of psychotherapy administered to the several classes. For example, psychoanalysis was limited to classes I and II. Patients in class V who received any psychotherapy were treated by group methods in the state hospitals. The number and percentage of pa-

Table IV
Distribution of the principal types of therapy by social class

Social class	Psychotherapy		Organic therapy		No treatment	
	Number	Percent	Number	Percent	Number	Percent
I	14	73.7	2	10.5	3	15.8
II	107	81.7	15	11.4	9	6.9
III	136	52.7	74	28.7	48	18.6
IV	237	31.1	288	37.1	242	31.8
V	115	16.1	234	32.7	367	51.2

Chi square = 336.58, P less than .001.

tients who received each type of therapy is given in Table IV. The data clearly support Hypothesis III.

At the moment we do not have data available for a test of Hypotheses IV and V. These will be put to a test as soon as we complete work on a series of cases now under close study. Preliminary materials give us the impression that they too will be confirmed.

CONCLUSIONS AND INTERPRETATIONS

This study was designed to throw new light upon the question of how mental illness is related to social environment. It approached this problem from the perspective of social class to determine if an individual's position in the social system was associated significantly with the development of psychiatric disorders. It proceeded on the theoretical assumption that if mental illnesses were distributed randomly in the population, the hypotheses designed to test the idea that psychiatric disorders are connected in some functional way to the class system would not be found to be statistically significant.

The data we have assembled demonstrate conclusively that mental illness, as measured by diagnosed prevalence, is not distributed randomly in the population of the New Haven community. On the contrary, psychiatric difficulties of so serious a nature that they reach the attention of a psychiatrist are unequally distributed among the five social classes. In addition, types of psychiatric disorders, and the ways patients are treated, are strongly associated with social class position.

The statistical tests of our hypotheses indicate that there are definite connections between particular types of social environments in which people live, as measured by the social class concept, and the emergence of particular kinds of psychiatric disorders, as measured by psychiatric diagnosis. They do not tell us what these connections are, nor how they are functionally related to a particular type of mental illness in a given individual. The next step, we believe, is to turn from the strictly statistical approach to an intensive study of the social environments associated with particular social classes, on the one hand, and of individuals in these environments who do or do not develop mental illnesses, on the other hand. Currently the research team is engaged in this next step but is not yet ready to make a formal report of its findings.

INTRODUCTORY COMMENTS ON HINDELANG'S RESEARCH

Viewed generally, Hollingshead and Redlich's study is a prime example of the analytical concern with relationships between *social inequality* and rates of deviant behavior that runs through much of the research within the macro-normative approach. This concern is also evident in the next research illustration by Hindelang (1978) that explores several theoretical interpretations of the impact of racial inequality on rates of criminal arrest in the United States. At issue in Hindelang's research is the question of why official statistics on a variety of criminal offenses show disproportionately high rates of arrest for blacks. As Hindelang points out, virtually all sociological theories of deviance can provide plausible interpretations of the nature and underlying causes of this statistical relationship. On the one hand, the macro-normative theories discussed in Chapter 4 treat high arrest rates as evidence of *deviant adaptations* or *subcultural responses* by blacks and other minority groups that have been denied equal opportunities for economic success and social advancement in American society. On the other hand, relativistic theorists—such as those in the labeling or conflict traditions—argue that racial variations in arrest statistics are primarily due to differences in the *social controls* applied to minorities rather than to differences in the actual behavior of disadvantaged groups. In this latter view, high arrest rates among blacks are seen as the product of unequal, discriminatory treatment of minorities in a criminal justice system dominated by the white minority. Which of these views is more accurate? Do arrest statistics reflect actual racial differences in law-violating behavior or are blacks simply more likely to be arrested for engaging in the same patterns of behavior as whites?

Since neither of these alternative interpretations of the effects of racial inequality on crime rates can be ruled out solely on the basis of official arrest statistics, Hindelang turns to another source of data that can shed additional light on patterns of law-violating behavior in

American society: *victimization surveys*. The victimization survey is a fairly recent development in criminological research that, as the term implies, gathers data on criminal incidents through interviews conducted with the victims of such incidents. In the typical victimization survey, interviewers contact a representative sample of people living in a given geographical area and ask these respondents whether they have been the victims of specific crimes during the past six months (or some other time interval). Those respondents who report having been the victim of one or more crimes are then asked to provide details about each incident of victimization, including such information as the perceived race of the offender and whether the incident was reported to the police. Since a large proportion of criminal incidents are not, in fact, reported to the police, the victimization survey presumably can provide a more complete picture of the true rates of crime in an area and of the kinds of offenders involved in these incidents than can official statistics on crimes known to the police or on arrest. Furthermore, victimization data can be compared to police statistics in order to determine whether any particular kinds of incidents or offenders are more likely than others to be singled out and subjected to official action or arrest.

Hindelang's analysis of competing interpretations of high arrest rates among blacks is based on this comparative strategy. Using data from a national victimization survey, he compares the proportions of black and white offenders involved in victimization incidents against the racial distributions of arrests in the United States for four major crimes. Hindelang's victimization data are taken from the 1974 National Crime Panel (NCP), a survey conducted annually by the U.S. Bureau of the Census on representative samples of American households and businesses. His statistics on arrests by race are drawn from the 1974 annual edition of the *Uniform Crime Reports* (UCR) published by the Federal Bureau of Investigation. The UCR is by far the most comprehensive and influential source of official statistics on crime in the United States. National arrest data, rates of crimes known to the police and other statistical information presented in the UCR are compiled from standardized (i.e., uniform) reports submitted monthly to the FBI by local law-enforcement agencies. Although the UCR presents racial classifications of arrests for a variety of crimes, Hindelang limits his attention to four crimes for which victims interviewed in the NCP could report their perceptions of the race of the offender: rape, robbery, aggravated assault, and simple assault.

Table 1 in Hindelang's article compares the percentage distributions by race for NCP offenders and UCR arrestees for each crime. As you read this important table, pay particular attention to whether the percentage of blacks in UCR arrests for a given crime is *higher* than the percentage of blacks involved in victimization incidents of that kind. In other words, is there evidence of racial inequality or selection bias in law enforcement where blacks are more likely to be arrested than they are to be offenders? At the bottom of Table 1, Hindelang also shows the proportions of blacks and whites in the general population of the United States. Compared to the percentage of blacks in the American population (11 percent), is this racial group disproportionately involved in criminal incidents reported by NCP victims? In general, do you agree with Hindelang that the comparisons presented in Table 1 add up to much stronger support for the criminal involvement interpretation than for the selection bias interpretation of high arrest rates among blacks?

By making sure that you grasp the basic logic behind Hindelang's comparisons of victimization and arrest distributions in Table 1, you will be in a better position to understand his discussion of additional findings from the NCP victimization data that further strengthen his main conclusion. For instance, he presents data in Table 2 indicating that the overrepresentation of blacks in arrests for at least one crime, rape, is not due to police selection bias but to the relatively high proportion of blacks involved in rape incidents actually reported to the police by *victims*. Here, as elsewhere in his article, Hindelang finds little solid evidence to support the view that high arrest rates among blacks are a product of discriminatory treatment by the criminal justice system. Instead, Hindelang argues that victimization data and official statistics are, on the whole, mutually consistent with anomie and subcultural theories that predict high rates of law-violating behavior among socially and economically disadvantaged minorities in American society.

RESEARCH ILLUSTRATION 5-B

Race and involvement in common law personal crimes*

Michael J. Hindelang

Most contemporary sociological theories of crime predict that blacks will be overrepresented among arrestees in common law personal crimes. These theories differ, however, in the extent to which this over-

---

Source: Article reprinted from *American Sociological Review* 43 (February 1978), pp. 93–109.

* Special gratitude is due to Michael R. Gottfredson who offered critical comments on several drafts of this paper.

representation is attributed to disproportionate involvement in criminal offenses vs. criminal justice system selection biases. Studies that have relied upon official data have generally supported the differential involvement hypothesis, whereas studies relying on self-report techniques generally have supported the differential selection hypothesis. National victimization survey data on victims' reports of racial characteristics of offenders are introduced as a third measurement technique in order to shed additional light on this controversy. These data for rape, robbery, and assault are generally consistent with official data on arrestees and support the differential involvement hypothesis. Some evidence of differential selection for criminal justice processing is found; however, most of the racial disproportionality in arrest data is shown by victimization survey data to be attributable to the substantially greater involvement of blacks in the common law personal crimes of rape, robbery, and assault. These results suggest that traditional admonitions against using arrest data as an index of involvement in these crimes may be overly cautious. In fact, the results imply that more caution should attend the use of self-report data in this vein and that more attention should be given to sampling and instrument concerns in self-report techniques. *As currently used*, the method may not be adequate for assessing the correlates of serious illegal conduct. The results also suggest that research emphasis be placed on those theories, such as the subcultural and differential opportunity perspectives, which attempt to explain differential racial involvement in these common law personal crimes.

INTRODUCTION

One of the most important theoretical questions facing criminology is whether, and to what extent, race is related to involvement in common law personal crimes.[1] Perhaps because of the sensitivity of this question, assertions and speculations about this relationship have outdistanced the research attention focused on it. Despite the limited research on the relationship between race and common law personal crime, this relationship is central to many contemporary criminological theories, and therefore it deserves the empirical attention that must be given to any important theoretical question.

Most sociological theories of crime agree that blacks are disproportionately arrested for common law personal crimes but disagree about the extent to which *arrest* data are indicative of disproportionate offending behavior vs. criminal justice system selection biases. Although most sociological theories of crime can accommodate a race-

---

[1] Included among the common law crimes are murder, rape, robbery, assault, burglary, larceny, and arson; the first four of these are designated personal common law crimes in this discussion. See Blackstone (1778) and Clark and Marshall (1967).

crime relation in arrest data, it is possible to conceive of these theories as falling along a continuum in terms of the proportion of variation in racial differences in rates of arrest that is attributed to differential *involvement* in common law crimes vs. differential *processing* by the agents of the criminal justice system. For purposes of discussion, "low" on the continuum will refer to theories which attribute very little of the variation in racial differences in rates of arrest to differences in the involvement of blacks and whites in common law crimes. "High" on the continuum will refer to theories which attribute much of the variation to actual behavioral differences between blacks and whites.[2]

Theories which fall at the higher end of the continuum suggest that concomitants of race, such as cultural or economic factors, are etiologically related to involvement in criminal activity. Characteristic of theories in this range on the continuum is Wolfgang and Ferracuti's (1967) subculture-of-violence thesis. In the *Subculture of Violence*, the authors observe:

> Statistics on homicide and other assaultive crimes in the United States consistently show that Negroes have rates between four and ten times higher than whites. Aside from a critique of official statistics that raises serious questions about the amount of Negro crime, there is no real evidence to deny the greater involvement that Negroes have in assaultive crimes. . . . There is reason to agree . . . that whatever may be the learned responses and social conditions contributing to criminality, persons visibly identified and socially labeled as Negroes in the United States appear to possess them in considerably higher proportions than do persons labeled white. Our subculture-of-violence thesis would, therefore, expect to find . . . [widespread] learning of, resort to, and criminal display of the violence value among minority groups such as Negroes. (264)

Thus, although Wolfgang and Ferracuti (1967) acknowledge the difficulties in using official police statistics to investigate the relationship between race and crime, they nonetheless conclude that blacks are disproportionately *involved* in assaultive crimes. More generally, the theories of Merton (1938) and Cloward and Ohlin (1960), because of their emphasis on structural impediments to the achievement of success goals via legitimate avenues, are also consistent with the hypothesis that blacks will have rates of involvement in common law criminal activity which exceed those of whites.

Theories which fall toward the middle of the continuum include those commonly referred to as conflict theories. These theories sug-

---

[2] In a paper on minorities as victims of police shootings, Goldkamp (1977) has presented a dichotomous characterization of labeling theories vs. theories that predict greater involvement of blacks in violent crimes.

gest that laws are enacted to protect the interests of the more powerful segments of society, and hence many of the activities that are criminalized are activities in which less powerful persons (blacks, the poor, the young, etc.) are disproportionately involved. Although such theories generally imply or state that blacks and other less powerful members of society will be disproportionately *involved* in common law criminal activity, these theories strongly emphasize that the overrepresentation of blacks in arrest statistics is considerably influenced by enforcement practices that discriminate against the less powerful.

Within the conflict group, it is perhaps Bonger (1916; 1943) who places highest on this continuum. In *Criminality and Economic Conditions*, Bonger (1916: 379) suggested that in "every society which is divided into a ruling class and a class ruled, penal law has been principally constituted according to the will of the former." Under capitalism, individuals are encouraged to use any means available, including criminal activity, to obtain material goods. Furthermore, the widespread poverty that abounds under capitalism "kills the social sentiment in man, destroys in fact all relations among men" and fosters criminality (1916: 436). After having studied prison statistics in the United States, he concluded that:

> Crime among Negroes is significantly higher than among whites. It is three or four times higher among the men, and four or five times higher among the women. To me this appears to eliminate the idea that actual criminality among Negroes is no greater than among whites. (1943: 43)

It was Bonger's (1943) view that the higher rate of crime among blacks was attributable to the unfavorable economic circumstances in which blacks were disproportionately found.

Because of a greater emphasis on differential enforcement, other conflict theorists place lower on the continuum than does Bonger. Quinney (1970: 129–30), for example, notes that "the differences in arrest rates are not, however, due entirely to the fact that Negroes may be involved more than whites in law-violating behavior, but that in similar situations Negroes are more likely than whites to be apprehended." Chambliss (1969: 856) and Chambliss and Seidman (1971) emphasize that the "administration of the criminal law is a highly selective process and involves the use of a wide range of discretion" that results in "systematic bias in law enforcement." Although most of their discussion of such biases is couched in terms of lower-class persons, many of their examples are of discrimination against blacks. They observe that such persons are "more likely to be scrutinized and therefore to be observed in any violation of the law and more likely to be arrested if discovered under suspicious circumstances" (Chambliss, 1969: 86; see also Chambliss and Seidman, 1971: 322–46). In general, the conflict theorists are careful not to deny that personal characteristics such as race are related to involvement in criminal behavior but tend instead to focus on power-related differentials in enforcement which introduce an unspecified proportion of contamination into arrest statistics.

At the lowest point on the continuum, those who subscribe to the labeling perspective in its most extreme form are found. Those at this pole argue that there are no demographic, sociological, or psychological correlates of involvement in criminal behavior but rather that any differences in arrest rates along social, demographic, or other dimensions are attributable to biases in official processing. Characteristic of this position is the thesis presented by Chapman (1968: 4) in *Sociology and the Stereotype of the Criminal:*

> . . . 3. That apart from the factor of conviction there are no differences between criminals and non-criminals.
> 4. That criminal behavior is general, but the incidence of conviction is controlled in part by chance and in part by social processes which divide society into the criminal and non-criminal classes, the former corresponding to, roughly, the poor and underprivileged.

Lemert (1967: 24), in his discussion of "the new deviance sociology"—Lemert (1951), Tannenbaum (1938), Kitsuse (1964), Goffman (1961), Erikson (1962), Becker (1963)—notes,

> In extreme statements deviance is portrayed as little more than the result of arbitrary, fortuitous, or biased decision-making, to be understood as a sociopsychological process by which groups seek to create conditions for perpetuating established values and ways of behaving or enhancing the power of special groups.

Lemert's exception to this extreme position places him more toward the middle of our continuum, in light of his observation that "striving to validate a conception of deviance as primarily a definitional phenomenon overlooks the way in which the societal reaction varies with *objective differences in behavior, its context, and its consequences*" (1967: 21, emphasis added).

This brief review of contemporary sociological theories relevant to the question of the relationship between race and crime demonstrate that although all of these theories can accommodate higher arrest rates for blacks than whites, they differ substantially in the extent to which such racial differences are attributable to objective differences in behavior. Because each of these positions claims support from research findings, it is necessary to turn our attention to that body of research.

PRIOR RESEARCH

Official data

Among the sources of official data on race and crime, the Federal Bureau of Investigation's *Uniform Crime Reports* (UCR) is the most extensive. In the UCR, characteristics of arrestees, including race, are published for the United States in the aggregate. These data for 1975 show that in relation to their representation in the general population (about 11 percent), blacks were substantially overrepresented among arrestees for murder and nonnegligent homicide (54 percent), forcible rape (45 percent), robbery (59 percent), aggravated assault (40 percent), burglary (28 percent), larceny and theft (31 percent), and motor vehicle theft (26 percent). For all of the remaining (Part II) offenses, blacks constituted 22 percent of the arrests (Kelley, 1976).

Police data were used by Mulvihill et al. (1969) to investigate the relationship between race and crime in a study published under the auspices of the President's Commission on the Causes and Prevention of Violence. Data were gathered on a probability basis from offense and arrest reports in police files in 17 large cities covering all regions of the United States. The authors report that the race of the offender was black in 72 percent of the criminal homicides, in 74 percent of the aggravated assaults, in 70 percent of the forcible rapes, in 85 percent of the armed robberies, and in 81 percent of the unarmed robberies (Mulvihill et al., 1969: 271–83).

Wolfgang et al. (1972: Table 5.3) in their *Delinquency in a Birth Cohort* use as their criterion recorded police contacts of their cohort when the subjects were 7 through 17 years old. For the offenses of homicide, rape, robbery, and aggravated assault, the number of contacts per 1,000 cohort subjects was 139.9 for nonwhites and 9.2 for whites. For the remaining offenses (burglary, larceny, and auto theft), the number of contacts per 1,000 cohort subjects was 476.6 for the nonwhites and 124.0 for the whites.

These official data from the UCR, the Violence Commission study, and the Wolfgang et al. (1972) cohort study are typical of comparisons of the offending of whites and blacks as measured by a variety of official data (arrest data, victim reports to the police, and police contacts). Theorists at the higher end of the continuum use such data as evidence of disproportionate involvement by blacks in the common law crimes. Theorists at the lower end of the continuum, by definition, argue that such official data are reflective of differential selection patterns, and hence they rely heavily on research data that are generated independently of the criminal justice system to support their arguments—typically data on self-reported involvement in illegal activities. To date, such studies have focused almost exclusively on juveniles.

Self-report measures

Relatively few self-report studies have compared the extent and nature of delinquency among whites and blacks. Three of the earliest research efforts to do so were those of Chambliss and Nagasawa (1969), Gould (1969), and Hirschi (1969). In the Chambliss and Nagasawa (1969: 73) study, lower-class white, black, and Japanese high school boys responded to self-reported delinquency questionnaires; in addition, juvenile court records were canvassed to ascertain the official delinquency status of the respondents. Despite the finding that blacks had an official delinquency rate that was substantially higher than that of whites, when self-reported delinquency was used as the criterion, whites were found to have a slightly higher rate than blacks. Similarly, Gould (1969: 330) studied junior high school boys in Seattle and found that although race (white vs. nonwhite) was moderately related to official delinquency in the usual direction (theta = .46), race was virtually unrelated (theta = .07) to self-reported delinquency on equivalent offenses.

In his study of more than 800 black and 1,300 white boys in California high schools, Hirschi (1969: Table 14) found that the former were more likely than the latter (42 percent vs. 18 percent) to have police records. When self-reported delinquency was used as the criterion, however, 49 percent of the blacks and 44 percent of the whites reported one or more delinquent acts. Once again, the racial differences for official delinquency were found to be much greater than for self-reported delinquency.

In two national studies, Gold and his colleagues (Williams and Gold, 1972; Gold and Reimer, 1975) made sex-specific comparisons of the self-reported delinquent behavior of black and white respondents. In the first study, a national probability sample of 736 white and 101 black respondents, 13 to 16 years old, was interviewed in 1967; in the second study, a national probability sample of 481 white and 67 black respondents, 13 to 16 years old, was interviewed in 1972. For both years and sex groups, whites and blacks reported involvement in 17 delinquent behaviors with similar *frequencies*. When the *seriousness* of eight items amenable to the Sellin-Wolfgang (1964) seriousness scoring procedure were tallied, the seriousness-weighted rate of self-reported delinquency was slightly greater for black males than for white males for both years.[3]

---

[3] For the 1967 results, Williams and Gold (1972: 215) report Mann-Whitney U-test p-levels for racial comparisons on seriousness of .49 and .06 for females and males,

The research findings on racial differences in offending behavior can be summarized succinctly: studies using official measures of criminal and delinquent behavior (e.g., arrests) have repeatedly found that blacks have markedly higher rates of arrest than do whites. However, studies using self-report measures of illegal behavior (almost exclusively illegal behavior of juveniles) have found that blacks and whites report only minimal differences on self-report inventories. This discrepancy between the self-report results and the official results requires some explanation and ultimate resolution, especially in light of the theoretical controversy. Thus, it is essential that a third source of data be brought to bear on this question.

THE PRESENT STUDY

Victimization surveys

Victimization surveys, in which representative samples from the general population are asked to report on victimizations they may have suffered during a specific reference period, provide data on the relationship between race and common law crime that are independent of criminal justice system selection biases. In these surveys respondents are asked to tell interviewers about victimizations, regardless of whether or not they reported them to the police.

The data used here derive from a national survey of victims of crimes, undertaken by the U.S. Bureau of the Census under the sponsorship of the U.S. Department of Justice, commonly referred to as the National Crime Panel (NCP).[4]

There are two parts of the NCP—a national probability sample of households (and individuals) and a national probability sample of businesses. In a period of six months, six independent probability samples of households and businesses are interviewed (see LEAA,

---

respectively. For the 1972 results (Gold and Reimer, 1975: Tables 3 and 4) comparable U-tests are not reported. However, because the mean racial difference in seriousness rates for females is smaller in 1972 than in 1967 and the mean racial difference in seriousness rates for males is larger in 1972 than in 1967, we infer (in light of the 1967 U-test results) that in 1972 the racial difference for males is probably significant beyond the .06 level and the racial difference for females probably has a p-level of greater than .49. This inference depends, of course, on the assumption that the standard errors in seriousness rates are comparable across years. See Gold (1970: 79) in which black-white differences in the seriousness and frequency of self-reported delinquency are not significant when SES is controlled.

[4] A good deal of developmental work in the area of surveying victims of crime was undertaken by the U.S. Bureau of the Census and others prior to the implementation of the National Crime Panel. For the sake of brevity, this research will not be reviewed here, but the interested reader is referred to Hindelang (1976: Chaps. 2 and 3) for a summary of this research.

1976 for a fuller description of sampling techniques). For purposes of estimating victimizations occurring during 1974 (the data to be used here), a total of approximately 80,000 housing units and other living quarters as well as approximately 17,000 businesses were selected for the sample (Law Enforcement Assistance Administration [LEAA], 1976: 45).

From the 80,000 housing units selected to make victimization estimates for 1974, interviews were completed in about 65,000. The majority of the 15,000 housing units in which interviews were not obtained were found to be vacant, demolished, converted to nonresidential use, or otherwise ineligible to be sampled (LEAA, 1976: 46). Overall, "interviews were obtained in about 96 percent of all eligible housing units, and about 99 percent of the occupants of these households participated in the survey" (LEAA, 1976: 46).

In the survey of households there are three types of respondents: household respondents, self-respondents, and proxy respondents. The household respondent, usually the head of household, answers such questions as whether the residence is owned or rented and what is the family income. In addition, the household respondent answers questions about victimizations affecting the entire household, such as burglary and vehicle theft.

Self-respondents are all household respondents 14 years of age or older. In addition to background information (e.g., age, sex, and education), each of these household members is asked a series of "screen" questions designed to elicit whether or not the person has been the victim of a crime of rape, robbery, assault, or personal larceny during the preceding six months. After all screen questions have been asked, a series of detailed incident questions is asked about each victimization uncovered in the screen questions. Proxy respondents are used to elicit the same information about household members 12 and 13 years old and for individuals who are physically or mentally unable to answer for themselves. Thus, the estimates derived in the household portion of the survey are national estimates for those 12 years of age or older.[5]

---

[5] Some personal victimizations are classified as series victimizations and an incident report is completed only for the last crime in a series of crimes. To be counted as a series victimization *all* of the following criteria must be met:

(a) the respondent must be unable to recall the details of the victimizations in the series well enough to report on the circumstances of each victimization separately;
(b) the victimizations must be of a similar type; and
(c) there must be at least three victimizations to constitute a series.

Series victimizations are tabulated separately from nonseries victimizations and tend disproportionately to be either assaults, more likely simple than aggravated, or household larcenies under $50 (LEAA, 1976: 51). I have excluded series victimizations from the analyses for two reasons: (1) because detailed information, such as the per-

In the commercial portion of the survey, the owner, manager, or someone knowledgeable about the affairs of the business is interviewed about robbery and burglary victimizations occurring during the reference period. As in the household portion of the survey, the screen method is used to elicit victimizations and is followed by a detailed incident report. Businesses eligible for interviews, but in which interviews were not completed, amounted to fewer than 1 percent of those eligible (LEAA, 1976: 60).

The data derived from the interviews are then weighted to give estimates for the nation (see LEAA, 1976; App. 1 and 2 for a detailed discussion of the weighting procedures and standard errors). The estimates used here are for incidents rather than victimizations. In the former, one incident is counted for each event uncovered during the survey regardless of the number of victims involved in the crime, whereas in the latter, one victimization is counted for each person victimized during an event. The incident weight assigned to each sample case is adjusted in those cases in which an event involved more than one victim because such cases would have more than a single chance of being included in the sample (LEAA, 1976: 49–50). The mean incident weight for the crimes studied here (rape, robbery, aggravated assault, and simple assault) in the household portion of the survey is about 1,023.

Because the UCR arrest data include business robbery arrestees in tables on the race of offenders, it was necessary also to include business robberies in the NCP data. This was accomplished by combining the results on the race of offender in business incidents from the 1974 NCP with those for personal robberies.

Results

In the course of the interview, respondents who had been confronted by offenders were asked a series of questions about the offender(s), including the number of offenders involved and the sex, race, and estimated age of the offender. The data presented here have been tabulated according to the responses to these questions. Before proceeding to the findings, it is necessary to discuss briefly how they were generated.

Each incident reported to survey interviewers was weighted by the

---

ceived race of the offender is collected only for the last crime in a series, details of series crimes are not known; and (2) because the respondent may not have reported accurately on the time of occurrence, it is less certain that these events fall within the reference period. In 1973, about 5 percent of the personal victimizations reported to interviewers were classified as series victimizations. See Hindelang (1976: App. F) for a discussion of some of the problems inherent in the use of series data.

number of offenders that the victim reported was involved in the incident.[6] Incidents in which the number of offenders was unknown or not ascertained or in which there was a group of offenders of mixed races (i.e., in which some were white and some were black or of other races) were excluded from analysis. It was necessary to exclude incidents in which the number of offenders was unknown because in such cases the victim was not asked the race of the offender(s). It was necessary to exclude incidents involving multiple offenders of mixed races because victims were not asked how many offenders were from each racial group. Of the total estimated number (8,130,059) of incidents of robbery, rape, and assault elicited by the survey for the 1974 calendar year, 3 percent or 210,824 were excluded from the analysis because they met at least one of the exclusionary conditions noted above.

The analyses presented here are limited to robbery, rape, and assault because it is in victimizations of these types that the victim is confronted by the offender and hence is able to report on the offender's characteristics. In the crimes of burglary, household larceny, and vehicle theft, the victim usually does not see the offender during the commission of the crime and therefore cannot report on the offender's personal characteristics.

The UCR annually publishes data on the racial characteristics of arrestees. It is possible to compare the racial characteristics of offenders as reported by victims in the 1974 national sample of the National Crime Panel to the racial characteristics of arrestees as reported in the 1974 UCR. If there are substantial biases in the UCR data for *any* reason, we would expect, to the extent that victimization survey reports are unbiased, to find large discrepancies between the UCR arrest data and victimization survey reports on racial characteristics of offenders. Specifically, the theories at the lowest point of the continuum predict a very substantial overrepresentation of blacks in the population of UCR arrestees, whereas theories at the highest point of the continuum predict a very small overrepresentation of blacks in arrest statistics *when compared with victimization survey reports*.[7] Furthermore, the former theories (low on continuum) would predict a small overrepresentation of black offenders in victimization survey reports relative to the representation of blacks in the general popula-

---

[6] As noted above, each incident had a weight that was inversely proportional to the probability of appearing in the sample. It was actually this incident weight that was weighted by the number of offenders that the victim reported having been involved in the incident.

[7] It should be noted here that this comparison will be sensitive not only to biases on the part of police but also to such potential biases as would be introduced if white victims were more likely to notify the police when victimized by black offenders.

Table 1
National comparisons between Uniform Crime Reports (UCR) and National Crime Panel (NCP) estimates* for race of arrestees and offenders, 1974

		White	Black	Other	Total
Rape	NCP	60% (125,890)	39% (82,873)	1% (1,847)	210,609
	UCR	49% (7,665)	48% (7,482)	3% (453)	15,600
Robbery	NCP	34% (797,246)	62% (1,465,838)	4% (105,587)	2,368,671
	UCR	35% (31,477)	62% (55,728)	3% (2,210)	89,415
Aggravated assault	NCP	66% (1,473,341)	30% (659,814)	4% (93,044)	2,226,199
	UCR	56% (75,136)	41% (54,870)	2% (3,330)	133,336
Simple assault	NCP	66% (2,204,576)	29% (969,432)	5% (150,572)	3,324,580
	UCR	61% (154,757)	37% (92,417)	2% (6,337)	253,511
Representation in general population		88%	11%	1%	

* Weighted by number of offenders in incident.
Source: UCR data, Kelley (1975: 191). General population data, U.S. Bureau of the Census (1975a).

tion, whereas the latter (high on continuum) would predict a very substantial overrepresentation. The victimization survey reports are thus an independent measure of the involvement of whites and blacks in rape, robbery, and assault—a measure that cannot be affected by the kind of contamination with which theorists falling at the lower end of the continuum contend police data are rife.[8]

The UCR victimization comparisons for 1974 are presented in Table 1. Both sources follow the U.S. Bureau of the Census convention of counting Spanish-Americans as white; "other races" include American Indian, Chinese, and Japanese. As expected, for each of the offenses shown, the ratio of offenders in incidents reported by victims in the survey to the number of UCR arrestees is large. This results primarily from three factors: first, the victimization survey data include many crimes that have not been reported to the police; second, even for reported crimes, the clearance rates for these offenses are

---

[8] Some of the limitations of victim survey data are discussed later.

small;[9] third, the UCR data on race of arrestees in 1974 were based on reports of police agencies covering an estimated population of 124 million persons rather than on the entire population (211 million), whereas the victimization survey results are estimates of victimization experiences of the entire U.S. population 12 years of age or older.

For convenience, the discussion will focus on the results for blacks. Table 1 shows that the UCR and the victimization data are identical for the crimes of robbery: 62 percent of the victimization survey offenders and 62 percent of the UCR arrestees were reported to have been black. For the remaining crime categories (rape and assault), in relation to the victimization reports, blacks are overrepresented by about ten percentage points in the UCR arrest data. Thus, for the crimes of rape and assault, but not for robbery, these results are consistent with the hypothesis that a small proportion of the white/black discrepancy in arrest rates is attributable to selection bias of some sort. The nature of this selection bias and some competing hypotheses will be discussed below.

In 1974 an estimated 88 percent of the U.S. population was white, 11 percent was black, and 1 percent was of other races (U.S. Bureau of the Census, 1975a: 26). Regardless of whether the UCR or the victimization survey data are taken as the indicator, blacks are substantially overrepresented in relation to their representation in the general population. This overrepresentation is by a factor of three or three and one-half times for assault, about four times for rape, and more than five times for robbery. In light of these data, it is difficult to argue that blacks are no more likely than whites to be *involved* in the common law crimes of robbery, forcible rape, and assault. At the same time, in UCR arrest data for assault and rape, blacks are found with a greater relative frequency than victimization survey data would predict, under the assumption that race-linked biases have not been introduced at some point in the arrest selection process.

Both the NCP and the UCR data can be dichotomized into groups of offenders (or, in the case of the UCR, arrestees) under 18 years of age and 18 years of age or older. Although not shown in tabular form, these results closely parallel those reported in Table 1.[10] Thus, both among adults and juveniles, blacks are substantially overrepresented in relation to their representation in the general population regardless of whether the NCP data or the UCR data are used.

---

[9] In 1974, 51 percent of the forcible rapes, 63 percent of the aggravated assaults, and 27 percent of the robberies were cleared by arrest (Kelley, 1975: 43).

[10] For the UCR data, see Kelley (1975: 192–3). Forcible rapes committed by offenders under 18 years of age are relatively rare; the number of NCP sample (unweighted) cases is very small (23 cases).

One major source of potential bias in the UCR data, one that is independent of the actions of criminal justice functionaries, is differential reporting of crimes by victims to the police. It is possible that the UCR/NCP differences, as reported in Table 1, are attributable not to discriminatory enforcement patterns but rather are attributable to victims' reporting to the police offenses committed by blacks proportionately more often than offenses committed by whites. Because research has demonstrated that offenses of these types almost exclusively come to the attention of the police through victim reporting (Reiss, 1971; Hindelang and Gottfredson, 1976), the reporting decision obviously affects arrest patterns; offenses not reported to the police almost certainly will not result in an arrest.[11]

The data in Table 2 indicate that when only those NCP victimizations which the victims told interviewers were reported to the police are considered, blacks are found to constitute 47 percent of the NCP rape offenders as compared with 48 percent of the UCR rape arrestees (Table 1). For both aggravated and simple assault, on the other hand, there is a slightly greater discrepancy between the NCP and the UCR percentages when only those NCP crimes which victims said were reported to the police are considered. For instance, 26 percent of the offenders involved in aggravated assaults which victims said were reported to the police were black, whereas 41 percent of the aggravated assault arrestees were black. If we operationally define criminal justice system selection bias as the discrepancy between the proportion of blacks involved in victimizations which victims said were reported to the police and the proportion of blacks among UCR arrestees, then these data suggest that there is virtually no criminal justice system selection bias for either rape or robbery but that there is such bias for assault, especially aggravated assault. Thus, once the victim's reporting (to the police) behavior is taken into account, differences between NCP crimes reported to the police and UCR data on arrestees remain only for assault.

Some NCP measurement problems

It is essential to note at this point that the crime of assault is the NCP crime which has the most measurement difficulties. In reverse record checks (U.S. Bureau of the Census, 1970a; 1970b; LEAA, 1972), checks in which victims are selected from police files and ideally

---

[11] In a small proportion of victimizations (about 3 percent of the victimizations in the NCP data), the police do come across the crime in progress. In addition, it is possible for police to discover incriminating evidence in the possession of an offender (e.g., another person's wallet) even though the victim may not have reported it to the police.

Table 2
Race of offender in National Crime Panel estimates* (1974) by whether the crime was reported to the police

	White	Black	Other	Total
	\multicolumn{4}{c}{Rape}			
Not reported to police	66%	33%	1%	100%
	(78,058)	(39,442)	(1,261)	(118,762)
Reported to police	52%	47%	1%	100%
	(47,832)	(43,431)	(585)	(91,848)
Total	60%	39%	1%	100%
	(125,890)	(82,873)	(1,847)	(210,609)
	Robbery			
Not reported to police	38%	57%	5%	100%
	(370,800)	(550,378)	(44,405)	(965,583)
Reported to police	30%	65%	4%	100%
	(426,445)	(915,454)	(61,182)	(1,403,081)
Total	34%	62%	4%	100%
	(797,245)	(1,465,832)	(105,587)	(2,368,664)
	Aggravated assault			
Not reported to police	62%	33%	5%	100%
	(629,837)	(341,198)	(49,123)	(1,020,158)
Reported to police	70%	26%	4%	100%
	(843,503)	(318,617)	(43,921)	(1,206,041)
Total	66%	30%	4%	100%
	(1,473,341)	(659,814)	(93,044)	(2,226,199)
	Simple assault			
Not reported to police	65%	31%	4%	100%
	(1,401,374)	(669,775)	(95,904)	(2,167,053)
Reported to police	69%	26%	5%	100%
	(803,202)	(299,657)	(54,668)	(1,157,527)
Total	66%	29%	5%	100%
	(2,204,576)	(969,432)	(150,572)	(3,324,580)

* Weighted by number of offenders in incident.

interviewed on a double-blind basis by Bureau of the Census interviewers, assault has been found to be the most poorly measured offense in the sense that: (*a*) assault victims from police files are more difficult, for a variety of reasons, than other victims to locate and interview; (*b*) of those victims who are interviewed, a smaller proportion of assault victims than other victims from police files mention having been victimized when they are interviewed.

In the three reverse record check studies, assault victims selected from police files had the lowest rate of completed interviews, about three out of five. Furthermore, among those victims selected from police files with whom interviews were completed, assault victims consistently had the poorest "recall" rate, that is, the smallest proportion of known victims who reported to survey interviewers that they had been victims of the crime selected from police files. For example, in completed interviews in all three studies combined, 88 percent of the burglary victims, 80 percent of the robbery victims, and 67 percent of the rape victims reported the crime selected from police files to survey interviewers; however, only 47 percent of the assault victims did so. In addition, it was found that when the offender was known to the victim, especially when the offender was *related* to the victim, the rate of "recall" was smaller than when the offender was a stranger (LEAA, 1972). This finding is important for two reasons. First, among the crimes studied here, assault is the most likely to involve non-strangers.[12] Second, victimization data suggest that nonstranger victimizations account for a larger proportion of black than of white victimizations.[13] For example, in the NCP data used here, 32 percent of the white victims and 48 percent of the black victims were reportedly victimized in aggravated assaults by nonstrangers.[14] If we assume that the "recall" problem for assaults in victimization surveys is comparable for nonstranger victimizations suffered by both blacks and whites, it follows that the *total* number of assaults suffered by black victims will be underestimated in victimization data more so than those suffered by whites because blacks apparently are victimized by nonstrangers in a greater proportion of the assaults than are whites. In light of this and because the victims in assaults are likely to be victimized by persons of the same race (Hindelang, 1976: 184–6), we can infer that the victimization data on assault probably underestimate the proportion of black offenders.

SUMMARY AND CONCLUSIONS

These results demonstrate that both the victimization data and the official arrest data show blacks to be substantially overrepresented, in relation to their representation in the general population, as offenders/arrestees for the common law crimes of forcible rape, robbery, and assault. Both data sources show that this disproportionality is greatest for robbery, followed by rape, aggravated assault, and simple assault. Furthermore, both sources of data show virtually the same

---

[12] This holds generally whether victimization survey data or police data on offenses known are used. See Hindelang (1976: Table 7.16).

[13] Of course, the victim-offender relationship affects the data, because, as noted above, the "recall" rate in victimization data is related to the relationship between the victim and the offender.

[14] Nonstrangers include family members and other relatives, persons well-known to the victim, and casual acquaintances of the victim.

percent figure for robbery but for the remaining three crimes the official data show a somewhat greater proportion of black offenders than do the victimization data. The discrepancy for rape is accounted for by the finding that rapes involving black offenders are more likely to be reported to the police than are rapes involving white offenders. When only those rape victimizations that are reported to the police are examined, there is virtually no difference between the two sources. Parenthetically, it should be noted that the UCR/victimization survey similarity for robbery maintains when only victimizations reported to the police are studied. For both aggravated and simple assault, however, the NCP/UCR discrepancy is slightly greater when only victimizations reported to the police are examined. For the reasons noted above, the NCP data on assault must be viewed with less confidence than the NCP data for robbery and rape.

In general, the results on the disproportionate involvement of blacks in rape, robbery, and assault as shown in these nationwide victimization data are much more congruent with studies that have used police data than with studies that have used self-reports of offenders. This is true even when the data for offenders reported by victims to be under 18 years of age, the age group most often studied in self-report research, are examined separately.

There are several reasons why the self-report studies discussed earlier may be incompatible with the NCP and UCR data.[15] First, with the exception of Gould's (1969) study, these self-report studies did not examine official and self-reported offenses of comparable seriousness; the self-report studies are weighted toward the least serious offenses. Second, with the exception of the Gold (1970; Gold and Reimer, 1975; Williams and Gold, 1972) studies, the self-report studies drew samples from in-school populations; the higher dropout rates for blacks than for whites means that this sampling approach results in a race-linked sampling bias. Third, the Gold studies, which increasingly are the studies most often cited by those arguing that black/white differences are minimal, had numbers of blacks that are certainly too small for reliable conclusions in a national survey (1967: 53 black males, 48 black females; 1972: 33 black males, 34 black females), especially in light of the relative rarity of all but the most trivial illegal behaviors.[16]

---

[15] In the course of discussing theoretical perspectives above, some of the shortcomings of official data were suggested by the theorists. For critiques of police data see Doleschal and Wilkins (1972) and Wolfgang (1963).

[16] For example, the mean number of burglaries reported during the three years prior to the interview was .06 for the white males and .09 for the black males in the 1972 study. Also in 1972, more than one quarter of the males had total Sellin-Wolfgang (1964) seriousness scores of zero. See Nettler (1974) and Reiss (1975) for some recent discussions of suggested methodological shortcomings of the self-report method.

These findings may indicate that at its current level of methodological development, the self-report technique is simply inadequate for assessing racial differences in rates of involvement in serious offenses. Even if the self-report technique itself were well developed from a methodological point of view, it would be necessary to use sample sizes much larger than those used in self-report studies to date in order to estimate reliably correlates of involvement in serious offenses.

Earlier, I discussed a continuum along which selected criminological theories fall in terms of the proportion of variation in arrest statistics which they attribute to involvement in criminal activity. It was noted that because all of these theories can accommodate the higher black arrest rate for common law personal crimes, it is necessary empirically to disentangle involvement in these crimes from selection biases in criminal justice processing. To the extent that a small percentage of the racial disproportionality in arrest rates is attributable to racial disproportionality in offending behavior, theories at the lower end of the continuum (e.g., labeling) are supported and theories at the higher end of the continuum (e.g., subculture of violence) are not. If the victimization data as reported in Table 1 are taken as a measure of involvement in rape, robbery, and assault and the UCR arrest data are taken as a measure of involvement in these crimes *plus* selection biases,[17] then the discrepancy between the two data sources can be taken as a measure of selection bias. The ratio of the percentage of black offenders in the NCP data to the percentage of black arrestees in the UCR data is an index of the proportion of the arrest percentage that can be attributed to criminal involvement; the complement can be attributed to selection bias. For robbery this ratio (62 percent ÷ 62 percent) is 1.0, indicating that none of the arrest percentage can be attributed to selection bias. The ratios for the remaining offenses are

---

[17] These biases include those introduced by differential reporting of offenses by victims to the police as well as criminal justice system selection biases. It should be noted here that the UCR data may also reflect statistical biases due to the fact that not all police jurisdictions report arrest data to the FBI. For data on offenses, the UCR received reports from jurisdictions covering 94 percent of the U.S. population in 1974. The published UCR arrest data are broken out only for cities, suburban areas, and rural areas. Because the offense data cover almost all of the U.S. population, we can examine the extent to which the arrest data come disproportionately from city, suburban, and rural areas by examining the ratio of the U.S. population covered by agencies that report arrest data (Kelley, 1975: Tables 44, 49 and 54) to the U.S. population covered by agencies reporting offense data (Kelley, 1975: Table 13). These ratios are .72 for the cities, .72 for the suburban areas, and .51 for the rural areas. Thus, rural areas are underrepresented in the national arrest data. However, the total number of arrests in rural areas for rape, robbery, and assault (26,000) is relatively small in relation to the total number of arrests in all reporting areas for these crimes (490,000), and even if adjustments were made for the underrepresentation of rural areas, the effect on the aggregate figures would not be substantial.

.84 for rape, .78 for simple assault, and .73 for aggravated assault. This indicates that for these crimes some of the arrest percentage can be attributed to selection bias but, by far, most of the arrest percentage appears to be attributable to the substantially greater involvement of blacks than whites in these crimes.

The complements of these ratios can be thought of as an index of selection bias. These selection biases can be decomposed into criminal justice system biases (differential police patrols, closer scrutinizing of blacks by police, greater propensity of police to arrest blacks once contact has been made, etc.) and victim reporting (to the police) biases. By using the data in Tables 1 and 2, the ratios discussed above can be recomputed, using in the numerator only those incidents which victims said were reported to the police. For example, in rapes elicited in the NCP survey which victims said were reported to the police, offenders were black in 47 percent of the cases (Table 2). In the UCR arrest data, blacks constituted 48 percent of the rape arrestees. This ratio for rape is (47 percent ÷ 48 percent) .98. The comparable ratio is 1.05 for robbery, .63 for aggravated assault, and .70 for simple assault. The complements of the ratios reported in the previous paragraph can be taken as a measure of all selection biases, that is, criminal justice system and victim reporting biases. The complements of the ratios reported in this paragraph can be taken as a measure of selection biases exclusive of victim reporting biases. For aggravated assault the first complement is .22 and the second is .37, which suggests that criminal justice system biases are more pronounced than they first appear once victim reporting biases are taken into account. For rape, the first complement is .16 and the second is .02, which suggests that for this crime category almost all (.16 − .02 = .14) of the deviation of the UCR from NCP data is attributable to the reporting biases of victims rather than to criminal justice system selection bias.

These results suggest that criminal justice system selection bias may be greatest for aggravated and simple assault and may be negligible for rape and robbery. At the same time, these data indicate that such biases account for much less of the racial disproportionality for these crimes than does differential involvement. These results do not support the heavy theoretical emphasis on differential selection manifested in the theories at the lower end of the continuum.[18] Rather,

---

[18] It should be stressed that I am not arguing that these results by any means indicate that racial discrimination in the criminal justice system should cease to be a cause for concern. There is evidence within the data of racially discriminatory enforcement and, obviously, any racial discrimination in the mechanisms by which people enter the criminal justice system is objectionable and demands attention. The argument

these data suggest that theories of criminality must give more attention to explaining disproportionate involvement (or noninvolvement) in common law personal crimes among blacks and whites, as do those theories higher on the continuum.

Of course, there are some measurement problems that may affect the victimization survey results. For example, victims' reports of the racial characteristics of offenders may be affected by popular stereotypes of the criminal. Furthermore, persons of Spanish heritage may be reported by some victims to be black. Because Spanish heritage persons in the general population are counted as white by U.S. Bureau of Census convention, this potential definitional difference may artificially inflate the disproportionality of blacks among the NCP offenders. It is also possible that white victims, who in assault and rape are likely to be victimized by white offenders, underreport their victimizations to survey interviewers. On the other hand, as noted in the discussion above, available evidence indicates that race-linked biases in the measurement of assault in victimization surveys may tend to undercount black offenders. Furthermore, there is some evidence that the most undersampled respondent group consists of young black males (U.S. Bureau of the Census, 1975b), who would be expected to be victimized in these crimes by black offenders. In any event, it is unlikely that biases in the victimization surveys linked to the race of the offender would be of such a magnitude that the substantial overrepresentation of blacks in the offender population would disappear.

The results of this study have important theoretical implications. The analysis indicates that theories at the lower end of the continuum are incapable of accounting for these victimization survey results which show a much higher rate of involvement for blacks than for whites in these common law personal crimes; the data from two independent sources (victimization surveys and arrest data) are in close agreement with each other and in sharp disagreement with the predictions of labeling theory, particularly in its extreme form (e.g., Chapman, 1968). As one moves from the lower to the higher end of the continuum, the predictions of the theories become increasingly compatible with the results. Conflict theory, which is nearer to the middle of the continuum than labeling theory, is somewhat compatible with the results in that it predicts racial differential in involvement in common law personal crimes because the more powerful (white) segments of society will have legislated against those activities in

---

being made is that it appears that these data seriously question sociological explanations which attribute most of the racial disproportionality in arrest data to differential selection rather than to differential involvement.

which the less powerful (black) segments of society engage disproportionately. However, many conflict theorists (e.g., Chambliss, 1969; Chambliss and Seidman, 1971; Quinney, 1970) also strongly emphasize that power differentials result in differential processing by agents of the criminal justice system. Although there was evidence of bias in police processing for assault, there was virtually none for robbery and rape.

Theories at the higher end of the continuum are most consistent with the data. These theories, such as Merton's (1938) anomie theory, Cloward and Ohlin's (1960) opportunity theory, or Wolfgang and Ferracuti's (1967) subculture-of-violence theory are quite compatible with large racial differentials in involvement in common law personal crimes and *comparatively* small racial differentials in police processing.

It is much more difficult, in light of the findings, to choose among theories at the higher end of the continuum than it is to reject, as incompatible with the data, theories at the lowest end. For example, these findings could easily be interpreted within the differential opportunity perspective because the NCP and UCR data indicate that the greatest racial differences in involvement are for the economically motivated crime of robbery.[19] Blocked access to legitimate avenues for material achievement (e.g., Merton, 1938; Cloward and Ohlin, 1960) can be readily invoked to account for the higher rate of black involvement in robbery. Although differential opportunity might seem less capable of encompassing the higher rates of black assault and rape, several strain theorists have suggested mechanisms to account for violent crime. Cloward and Ohlin (1960: 171–8) postulate the existence of a subcultural adaptation to blocked opportunities that is organized around violent behavior. In this conflict subculture, ". . . violence is the keynote; its members pursue status ('rep') through the manipulation of force or threat of force" (1960: 20). Under conditions conducive to the development of conflict subculture:

> . . . tendencies toward aberrant behavior become intensified and magnified. These adolescents seize upon the manipulation of violence as a route to status not only because it provides a way of expressing pent-up angers and frustrations but also because they are not cut off from

---

[19] Another NCP property crime, personal larceny, also shows greater racial differences than those found for assault and rape. A small proportion of larcenies involve a confrontation between the victim and the offender and are differentiated from robberies in that they do not involve force or the threat of force—for example, a purse snatch in which force is not threatened or directed at the victim. The UCR arrest tables do not separate larcenies of this type from larcenies in which there is no personal confrontation between the victim and the offender; the NCP data on larcenies that do involve such a confrontation cannot reasonably be compared with the UCR arrest data. However, the 1974 NCP data reveal that 69 percent (estimated N = 230,091) of the offenders in face-to-face larcenies were black.

> access to violence by vicissitudes of birth. In the world of violence, such attributes as race, socioeconomic position, age, and the like are irrelevant. . . . (1960: 175)

Similarly, Cohen (1955) suggests a strain model which links school failure with an increased probability of engaging in negativistic, nonutilitarian, and malicious behavior. One important emphasis of the anomie theorists which cannot be ignored in accounting for differential rates of violent behavior is their emphasis on the frustration that accompanies blocked opportunities and the use of violence as status-conferring.

On the other hand, those subscribing to the subculture-of-violence perspective have argued that blacks are more likely than whites to be members of the violent subculture and hence are more likely than whites to accept and expect violent behavior in social interactions (Wolfgang and Ferracuti, 1967; Curtis, 1975). To the extent that the crimes studied here, that is, rape, robbery, and assault, are construed to be violent crimes, the results are interpretable within this subcultural perspective. It should be noted, however, that despite the fact that robbery has been defined by some as a violent crime (e.g., in the Uniform Crime Reports; Mulvihill et al., 1969), the primary aim of robbery is to deprive a person of property, whereas assault and rape, if completed, necessarily involve bodily harm to the victim. Among the personal crimes studied here, the least violent crime (robbery) shows the greatest racial difference,[20] and the more violent crimes (assault and rape) show a smaller racial difference. Subculture-of-violence theorists argue, however, that much violent crime is intraracial, particularly blacks victimizing blacks. It may be that intraracial crimes of assault and rape are undercounted in both the NCP and UCR data because, according to this subcultural theory, they are more accepted and expected by blacks in social interactions and hence are less often construed as crimes and/or reported to either the police or to survey interviewers as crimes. Of course, the resolution of this speculation is well beyond the scope of the data.

By the definition of the continuum used here, the theories at the higher end all predict racial differences in involvement in common law personal crimes and the data are not sufficient for choosing among these competing explanations. However, the results do strongly indicate that research attention in this area should focus on these competing (higher-end) explanations of the differential involvement of blacks and whites in common law personal crimes. Is the differential attributable to the disparity between the socioeconomic

---

[20] Similarly for personal larceny (see ftn. 19).

status distributions of blacks and whites as Bonger (1943) has suggested or to actual or perceived differences in structural impediments to the achievement of success goals via legitimate avenues (e.g., Merton, 1938; Cloward and Ohlin, 1960)? Are these differences due to cultural factors as Wolfgang and Ferracuti (1967) argue? Or is the explanation to be found in the historical maltreatment of American blacks? Only further research specifically designed to assess these and other hypotheses can shed additional light on these questions.

Throughout this paper, substantial care has been taken to limit the discussion to common law crimes of forcible rape, robbery, and assault. The NCP data now available only address common law crimes. For the crimes of burglary, household larceny, and vehicle theft, which are also included in the NCP surveys, offender characteristics are generally unavailable because these crimes do not typically involve a face-to-face confrontation between the victim and the offender. Clearly, these results cannot be extrapolated beyond the specific crimes to which the analyses were addressed. If the differential involvement in white-collar offenses, organized crime, corporate crime, or consumer fraud had been studied, the results might have been very different. Obviously, these data and analyses shed no light on racial differences in crime generally.

As Nettler (1974: 126) has noted:

> . . . caution is required in the interpretation of differentials in crime rates between whites and nonwhites. In the light of the sad history of racial relations, it is difficult to make comparisons today of the relative importance of the alleged causes of any differences in observed behaviors.

Although research on this question is difficult for a variety of reasons, the results of this study suggest that it is incumbent upon social scientists to give long overdue research attention to such basic questions as these.

REFERENCES

Becker, Howard S.
    1963   The Outsiders: Studies in the Sociology of Deviance. New York: Free Press.
Blackstone, William
    1778   Commentaries on the Laws of England. 8th ed. Oxford: Clarendon Press.
Bonger, Willem
    1916   Criminality and Economic Conditions. Tr. Henry Horton. Boston: Little, Brown.
    1943   Race and Crime. Tr. M. Hordyk. Montclair: Patterson-Smith.
Chambliss, William
    1969   Crime and the Legal Process. New York: McGraw-Hill.
Chambliss, William and Richard Nagasawa
    1969   "On the validity of official statistics: a comparative study of white, black,

and Japanese high school boys." Journal of Research in Crime and Delinquency 6:71–7.

Chambliss, William and Robert Seidman
    1971   Law, Order, and Power, Reading, Pa.: Addison-Wesley.

Chapman, Dennis
    1968   Sociology and the Stereotype of the Criminal. London: Tavistock.

Clark and Marshall
    1967   A Treatise on the Law of Crimes. 7th ed. New York: Holt.

Cloward, Richard and Lloyd Ohlin
    1960   Delinquency and Opportunity: A Theory of Delinquent Gangs. New York: Free Press.

Cohen, Albert
    1955   Delinquent Boys. New York: Free Press.

Curtis, Lynn
    1975   Violence, Race, and Culture. Lexington: Lexington Books.

Doleschal, E. and Leslie Wilkins
    1972   Criminal Statistics. Rockville, Md.: Center for Studies in Crime and Delinquency.

Erikson, Kai
    1962   "Notes on the sociology of deviance." Social Problems 9:307–14.

Goffman, Erving
    1961   Asylums. New York: Anchor.

Gold, Martin
    1970   Delinquent Behavior in an American City. Belmont, Ca.: Brooks/Cole.

Gold, Martin and David Reimer
    1975   "Changing patterns of delinquent behavior among Americans 13 through 16 years old." Crime and Delinquency Literature 7:483–517.

Goldkamp, John
    1977   "Minorities as victims of police shootings: interpretations of racial disproportionality and police use of deadly force." Justice System Journal 2:169–83.

Gould, Leroy
    1969   "Who defines delinquency: a comparison of self-reported and officially-reported indices of delinquency for three racial groups." Social Problems 16:325–36.

Hindelang, Michael
    1976   Criminal Victimization in Eight American Cities: A Descriptive Analysis of Common Theft and Assault. Cambridge, Ma.: Ballinger.

Hindelang, Michael and Michael Gottfredson
    1976   "The victim's decision not to invoke the criminal process." Pp. 57–78 in W. McDonald (ed.), The Victim and the Criminal Justice System. Beverly Hills: Sage.

Hirschi, Travis
    1969   Causes of Delinquency. Berkeley: University of California Press.

Kelley, Clarence
    1975   Crime in the United States. Washington, D.C.: U.S. Government Printing Office.
    1976   Crime in the United States. Washington, D.C.: U.S. Government Printing Office.

Kitsuse, John
    1964   "Societal reaction to deviant behavior: problems of theory and method." Pp. 87–102 in Howard Becker (ed.), The Other Side: Perspectives on Deviance. New York: Free Press.

Law Enforcement Assistance Administration, U.S. Department of Justice, National Institute of Law Enforcement and Criminal Justice, Statistics Division
    1972   San Jose Methods Test of Known Crime Victims. Statistics Technical Report No. 1. Washington, D.C.: U.S. Government Printing Office.
    1976   Criminal Victimization in the United States. Washington, D.C.: U.S. Government Printing Office.

Lemert, Edwin
    1951   Social Pathology. New York: McGraw-Hill.
    1967   Human Deviance, Social Problems and Social Control. Englewood Cliffs: Prentice-Hall.
Merton, Robert
    1938   "Social structure and anomie." American Sociological Review 3:672–82.
Mulvihill, D., M. Tumin and L. Curtis
    1969   A Staff Report Submitted to the National Commission on the Causes and Prevention of Violence. Crimes of Violence, Vol. 11. Washington, D.C.: U.S. Government Printing Office.
Nettler, G.
    1974   Explaining Crime. New York: McGraw-Hill.
Quinney, Richard
    1970   The Social Reality of Crime. Boston: Little, Brown.
Reiss, Albert Jr.
    1971   The Police and the Public. New Haven: Yale University Press.
    1975   "Inappropriate theory and inadequate methods as policy plagues: self-reported delinquency and the law." Pp. 211–22 in N. J. Demerath, Jr., Otto Larson, and Carl F. Schuessler (eds.), Social Policy and Sociology. New York: Academic Press.
Sellin, T. and M. Wolfgang
    1964   The Measurement of Delinquency. New York: Wiley.
Tannenbaum, Frank
    1938   Crime and the Community. New York: McGraw-Hill.
U.S. Bureau of the Census
    1970a   "Victim recall pretest (Washington, D.C.): household survey of victims of crime." Mimeographed. Suitland, Md.
    1970b   "Household survey of victims of crime: second pretest (Baltimore, Md.)." Mimeographed. Suitland, Md.
    1975a   Statistical Abstract of the United States. Washington, D.C.: U.S. Government Printing Office.
    1975b   "Comparison of the second stage ratio factors produced in the National Crime Survey and the Current Population Survey." Mimeographed memorandum. Suitland, Md.
Williams, Jay and Martin Gold
    1972   "From delinquent behavior to official delinquency." Social Problems 20:209–28.
Wolfgang, Marvin
    1963   "Uniform crime reports: a critical appraisal." University of Pennsylvania Law Review 111:708–38.
Wolfgang, Marvin and Franco Ferracuti
    1967   The Subculture of Violence: Toward an Integrated Theory in Criminology. London: Tavistock.
Wolfgang, Marvin, Robert Figlio and Thorsten Sellin
    1972   Delinquency in a Birth Cohort. Chicago: University of Chicago Press.

INTRODUCTORY COMMENTS ON ERLANGER'S RESEARCH

The two previous research illustrations have presented rather clear and consistent descriptions of the social distribution of deviant behavior in American society. Marshalling evidence from official records and victimization surveys, these studies indicate that mental disorder and crime are indeed disproportionately located in the kinds of disadvantaged social environments emphasized by anomie and subcultural theories of deviance. However, in the next article by Erlanger (1976) this coherent picture is muddied by evidence gathered through a third technique for research on macro-level variations in norm-violating behavior: *self-report surveys*. By asking people to report the nature and extent of their *own* involvement in deviant behavior, self-report surveys seemingly represent a more direct source of data on deviant activity than are the observations of official agencies or victims. Most important, self-report interviews or questionnaires designed by sociologists can obtain more detailed and theoretically relevant information on the social and personal characteristics of deviants and nondeviants than is available from other sources. Thus, as Erlanger's article will demonstrate, self-report data cannot only be used to *describe* variations in deviant behavior across different segments of society, but they can also provide measures of factors in the social environment that are theoretically expected to *explain* those variations. In fact, the lack of support for anomie and subcultural explanations in self-report surveys is one of the major reasons why many sociologists have lost confidence in these macro-normative theories. In this respect as well as in others, Erlanger's study serves as a good example of how empirical analyses based on self-report data have contributed to sociological knowledge about rates of deviant behavior.

The main focus of Erlanger's analysis is on *regional* variations in rates of interpersonal violence in the United States. Official statistics have consistently shown that states in the South have the highest homicide rates in the nation. Attempting to account for this and other phenomena pointing to the South as a particularly violence-prone region, several observers have argued that Southerners share a regional subculture that permits and even encourages violence in interpersonal encounters. Erlanger notes that these subcultural explanations of regional violence are similar in many ways to Wolfgang and Ferracuti's theory of the subculture of violence (1967), which was discussed briefly in Chapter 4 and in Hindelang's article. A common implication of these theories of subcultural content is that population groups characterized by high rates of violence in official statistics— minority and low-income white males from the South—share distinctive norms and values that support and reward violent behavior. Erlanger examines three basic questions that bear on this theoretical position. First, do self-report surveys confirm the regional and racial differences in violent behavior described by official statistics? Second, are those groups that are thought to share a subculture of violence more likely than others to value or approve of interpersonal violence?

Finally, Erlanger attempts to assess the theoretically crucial question of whether subcultural rewards are *positively related* to acts of violence; for instance, is it true among Southerners (but not Northerners) that the more often they fight, the more likely they are to feel liked and respected by other people?

Erlanger's analyses of the first two descriptive questions involve relatively simple regional and racial comparisons of data for men aged 21–64 who were interviewed in several self-report surveys. Unfortunately, his measures of violent behavior are scores based on respondents' self-reported frequency of fist fighting, a relatively minor form of interpersonal aggression. Do you agree with Erlanger that involvement in "angry fist fights" is an important indicator of the kind of deviant behavior that would be expected in groups that share a subculture of violence? If so, then you will probably also agree that his regional comparisons of mean or average scores for self-reported fist fighting (Tables I and II in his article) tend to contradict subcultural theorizing about southern violence. Erlanger uses the results of two different self-report studies to show that black and white males in the South confess to *less frequent* involvement in fights, on the average than do their counterparts in other regions.

Erlanger's descriptive analysis of regional and racial differences in self-reported approval of various forms of violence, based on the survey results shown in his Table III, further strengthens the case against a Southern subculture of violence. Can you detect any consistent pattern in the mean approval scores presented in Table III that would suggest that Southerners or blacks share distinctive norms and values encouraging violence in interpersonal relationships? Pay particular attention to how southern blacks—the group that is supposedly most influenced by the subculture of violence—compare to others in their approval of violence.

Erlanger's attempt to answer his final research question involves a more complex analysis of the relationship *between* self-reported acts of violence and social approval. Again, if groups such as Southerners, blacks or low-income whites do indeed value and reward violence, then members of these groups who fight frequently should be happier and more respected than those members who avoid violence. In others words, there should be a *positive relationship* between involvement in violence and social approval in these groups; i.e., as one variable increases, the other also increases. Furthermore, this positive relationship should be *especially strong* in groups such as southern, low-income blacks that are expected to be most heavily influenced by the subculture of violence. On the other hand, what if a population group does *not* share the subculture of violence and rejects members who engage in fighting or other forms of aggression? Erlanger singles out higher-income whites in the North as an instance where a *negative relationship* between self-reported acts of violence and social approval should be observed; i.e., as violence increases, approval decreases.

Empirical relationships such as these are examined in Tables IV and V of Erlanger's article. Erlanger divides respondents from a self-report study into eight subgroups according to region, race, and income. For each subgroup, Erlanger states a hypothesis specifying how self-reported violence and social rewards should be related as predicted by subculture of violence theory. Each hypothesis is tested by correlation and regression analyses, statistical procedures that provide measures of the *strength* and *direction* of the empirical relationship between two or more variables. The statistics shown in Tables IV and V, then, reveal how strongly and in what direction (i.e., positive or negative) self-reported fighting is related to three indicators of social rewards (respondents' feelings of respect, liking by others, and happiness). In general, the further the correlation and regression statistics (r and Beta) *depart from zero in either a positive or negative direction*, the stronger the relationship between fighting and the indicators of social reward.

If you inspect Tables IV and V carefully, you will see that the predictions of subculture of violence theory do not compare well with the results of Erlanger's correlation and regression analyses. For instance, Erlanger hypothesizes a very strong positive relationship between self-reported fighting and the indicators of social rewards for low-income blacks in the South (rural North Carolina), the subgroup in which the subculture of violence is presumed to be most pervasive. However, as you will note, the correlation and regression statistics for this subgroup are not only relatively weak (not significantly different from zero) but also consistently *negative* in direction. Therefore, to the extent that any relationship between fighting and social rewards exists at all in this subgroup, it is *opposite* from that predicted by subculture of violence theory. Overall, Erlanger finds virtually no evidence to suggest that low-income blacks or whites in the South or North actually receive subcultural support and rewards for fighting.

No theory of deviance will stand or fall on the basis of a single investigation such as this. Erlanger is well aware of the limitations of the self-report data he had at his disposal and suggests further research that is needed to assess more adequately subcultural explanations of regional violence. Nonetheless, Erlanger's findings add weight to the evidence from many other self-report studies that have raised doubts about the explanatory power of the major macro-normative theories of deviant behavior.

RESEARCH ILLUSTRATION 5-C

Is there a "subculture of violence" in the South?

*Howard S. Erlanger**

For many decades analysts have commented on the disproportionately high rates of homicide in the Southern states. In 1958, for example, the South had a homicide rate about nine per 100,000 as compared to about three per 100,000 for the rest of the country. In recent years the gap has been narrowing, as the rate of increase in the homicide rate has been higher outside the South. In 1972 the homicide rate was 12.6 per 100,000 for the South, compared to about 7.3 per 100,000 for the rest of the country.[1] Hackney, employing regression analysis on aggregate homicide (and suicide) data from 1940, found that the regional effect remained strong even after the effects of degree of urbanization, average level of education, average income, unemployment rate, wealth of state, and average age of inhabitants of state are controlled.[2] Gastil has supplemented these findings in a study relating the degree of Southern influence on a state to the state's homicide rate.[3]

Discussions of Southern violence generally argue or assume that the tendency to use violence is not limited to murder, but is pervasive in interpersonal affairs. Hackney, for example, says:

> In various guises, the image of the violent South confronts the historian at every turn: dueling gentlemen and masters whipping slaves, flatboatmen indulging in a rough and tumble fight. . . . The image is so pervasive that it compels the attention of anyone interested in understanding the South.[4]

Source: Article reprinted from *The Journal of Criminal Law & Criminology* 66, no. 4 (December 1976), pp. 483–490. Reprinted by special permission of The Journal of Criminal Law & Criminology. Copyright © 1976 by Northwestern University School of Law.

* Department of Sociology, The University of Wisconsin, Madison, Wisconsin.

The research reported here was supported in part by the National Institute of Mental Health. The author wishes to thank Russell Middleton and an anonymous reviewer for helpful comments, and Irene Rodgers for her research assistance. Responsibility for interpretations and conclusions rests with the author.

[1] FBI, Uniform Crime Reports 6 (1973).

[2] Hackney, *Southern Violence,* in History of Violence in America: Report of the Task Force of the President's Commission on Causes and Prevention of Violence 387–404 (H. Graham & T. Gurr eds. 1969).

[3] Gastil, *Homicide and a Regional Culture of Violence,* 36 Am. Sociological Rev. 412–27 (1971). *See also* Pettigrew & Spier, *The Ecological Structure of Negro Homicide,* 67 Am. J. Sociology 621–29 (1962).

[4] Hackney, *supra* note 2, at 387.

Similarly Reed, in a study using data on gun ownership and on attitudes towards corporal punishment and gun control legislation, as well as the historical record of lynchings and bombings, concludes that in general, Southerners "do have a tendency to appeal to force to settle differences."[5] But this judgment is not unanimous. Gastil, for example, says that fist fighting and murder may not be related; he cites the example of the Irish, but has no data for the South on this point.

In explanations of regional differences in violence, a subcultural theme has been predominant. Hackney and Gastil argue, for example, that since "Southerness" is strongly related to homicide (or to a low suicide-homicide ratio) even after structural variables are controlled, cultural forces probably account for the violence.[6] Reed writes more generally of a "subcultural persistence" in the South.

Further analysis of the hypothesis that some form of a "subculture of violence" exists in the South is hampered by variations in the concept of subculture used by different writers. Wolfgang and Ferracuti, who have written extensively on the subculture of violence (although not specifically with reference to the American South), argue that the concept of subculture ultimately refers to values, and to actions people take with respect to these values.[7] Writers in this tradition accept verbal statements of preferences as important indicators of subcultural preferences. It seems that Reed would fit into this general tradition, since he bases much of his argument on attitudinal data. Gastil, however, explicitly rejects Wolfgang and Ferracuti's stress on norms and values, while Hackney does not state a position.

The present paper explores five topics related to the issues of the pervasiveness and the subcultural character of violence in the South: (1) self-reported experiences with violence; (2) the effect of migration from the South on rates of fighting in the North; (3) self-reported approval of violence; (4) the association between fighting and perceived esteem by peers; and (5) the association between fighting and a feeling of well-being. All of the findings must be seen as tentative,

---

[5] J. Reed, The Enduring South: Subcultural Persistence in Mass Society 46 (1972).

[6] A recent article by Loftin and Hill has sharply criticized the methodology of both Gastil and Hackney. Loftin & Hill, *Regional Subculture and Homicide: An Examination of the Gastil-Hackney Thesis*, 39 Am. Sociological Rev. 714 (1974). Using different indicators of the structural variables, they arrive at different findings. The Loftin-Hill paper, like those of Gastil and Hackney, is based on ecological data. The present paper, based on individual data, lends a different perspective to the discussion.

[7] M. Wolfgang & F. Ferracuti, The Subculture of Violence: Toward an Integrated Theory in Criminology (1967). For the United States, Wolfgang and Ferracuti have used the subculture of violence thesis mainly as an explanation of the higher homicide rate of blacks and low income white adult males. For recent critiques of the argument see Ball-Rokeach, *Values and Violence* 38 Am. Sociological Rev. 736 (1973), and Erlanger, *The Empirical Status of the Subculture of Violence Thesis*, 22 Social Problems 280 (1974).

both because of the quality of the data and because of the variety of concepts of subculture. The topics flow from a general consideration of Southern violence, the possible subcultural character of that violence, and from the types of data available; the presentation is not meant as an explicit test of the earlier works. Readers who are interested only in a subculture of lethal violence, who reject the relevance of norms, values, or peer processes to the study of subculture, or who do not agree that some types of attitudinal data are suggestive of value preferences, will not see the material here as a challenge to the hypothesis that a subculture of violence exists in the South. However, they may still find the material of interest as an addition to the relatively small fund of knowledge about Southern violence.

The discussion will rely primarily on secondary analysis of two data sets. The first is a national sample of adults taken in 1968 for the President's Commission on the Causes and Prevention of Violence.[8] To obtain comparability with the second data set, only the responses of the 451 men aged 21 to 64 will be presented. The second data set is comprised of separate samples of black and white men aged 21 to 64 living in Milwaukee, Wisconsin, and in the rural areas of two counties in Eastern North Carolina in 1969.[9] Each of the four groups has an N of about 220. Since there is a perfect correlation of regional and urban-rural differences in the latter data set, the alternative hypothesis that the results would change if urban-rural residence were controlled cannot be ruled out. The main argument for a regional interpretation is that for officially recorded criminal violence, differences are primarily regional rather than urban-rural. Although the rate of violent crime (murder, assault, and rape) is somewhat lower in rural North Carolina than in the rest of that state (239 per 100,000 population, as compared to 309 for the whole state in 1968), it is substantially higher than the average rate of violent crime for urban and rural areas outside the South.[10] For example, in 1968 only about a dozen cities out-

---

[8] The data were collected by Louis Harris Associates, using a sample drawn for 100 clusters in all parts of the United States. The specific individual to be interviewed was specified in advance, but no call-backs were made. The questionnaire and preliminary findings may be found in R. Baker & S. Ball, Mass Media and Violence: Report to the National Commission on Causes and Prevention of Violence 503–91 (1969).

[9] These data are from an ongoing study of correlates of self-esteem directed by Russell Middleton (supported by the National Science Foundation). I am grateful to him for permission to analyze and report the relationships presented here.

The data for Milwaukee are based on a multi-stage disproportionate stratified area probability sample of housing units in the Milwaukee city limits in 1960. The data for rural North Carolina are based on a replicated area probability sample of housing units in Nash and Edgecomb counties, outside of towns or cities with 1,000 or more inhabitants. For both the Milwaukee and North Carolina surveys, a modified Kish sampling procedure was used, interviewers and respondents were matched by race, and several call-backs were made when necessary.

[10] N. C. Div'n of Law and Order of the Dep't of Local Affairs, Improvements in the Criminal Justice System—Commitment to Action, vol. III (1970) (A copy of this study is on file with the author.)

side the South had a rate of violent crime higher than that of rural North Carolina,[11] and there is no evidence that the two counties studied are low in their rate of officially recorded crime. The Milwaukee-North Carolina data are also geographically limited and generalization to North-South differences is tentative.

Reference will also be made to the Criminal Victimization survey taken by the National Opinion Research Center (NORC) for the President's Commission on Law Enforcement and Administration of Justice in 1966.[12] This was a national survey of 10,000 households designed in part to check on the accuracy of the F.B.I. Uniform Crime Reports.[13]

SELF-REPORTED EXPERIENCES WITH VIOLENCE

Criminal violence

Although the higher rate of criminal violence in the South is taken as well established fact, the NORC Victimization Survey did not confirm it. The President's Commission on Law Enforcement reports that the South had the highest homicide rate in 1965 to 1966,[14] but this finding is an artifact of the low incidence of homicide. Only one homicide was reported on the survey, and it happened to be in the South. For aggravated assault and simple assault the N's are more acceptable, and self-reported victimization rates for the South are relatively *low* for these crimes. For aggravated assault, the NORC estimate for the South is 173 per 100,000 population, compared to an estimate of 238 per 100,000 for the rest of the country. For simple assault, the estimate for the South is 375 per 100,000 compared to 403 per 100,000 for the rest of the country.

The findings from the Violence Commission Survey are more ambiguous, and depend on the item which is examined. If the responses of all adults are examined (in order to make the findings more comparable to the NORC and Uniform Crime Reports data), then the South tends to be higher than average, but not the highest region, on such items as "Have you (as an adult) ever been threatened with, or actually cut with, a knife?"[15] However, if only males aged 21 to 65 are

---

[11] FBI, Uniform Crime Reports 82–97 (1970).

[12] P. Ennis, Criminal Victimization in the United States: Report to the President's Commission on Law Enforcement and Administration of Justice (1967).

[13] Methodological problems in the NORC survey are discussed in detail in Biederman, *Survey of Population Samples for Estimating Crime Incidence*, 374 Annals 16–33 (1967). Biederman does not indicate any special problem with the data from the South, but some of the problems he pinpoints may be of a different magnitude in the South.

[14] Ennis, *supra* note 12, at 27.

[15] Stark & McEvoy, *Middle Class Violence*, 4 Psychology Today 30 (1970).

Table I
Fighting by region
"How often do you get in angry fist fights with other men?"
(men aged 21–64 in 1969)

	Milwaukee		Rural North Carolina	
	White	Black	White	Black
Mean score (range 0–3)	.25	.40	.10	.22
(N)	(222)	(235)	(218)	(236)

examined, the rate for the South is somewhat higher than for other regions.

Less serious violence

Self-reports of acts of relatively minor physical aggression are an important indicator of the pervasiveness of violence. Although extensive high quality data of this type do not exist at present, some suggestive data are available.

In the Milwaukee-rural North Carolina study, respondents were asked "How often do you get in angry fist fights or the like with other men—never, almost never, sometimes, often?" The responses, shown in Table I, are a striking contrast to the homicide data. Both black and white men in rural North Carolina are, by their reports, less likely to fight. Controlling for age, occupation, income, and "social desirability bias" does not affect this finding.[16] The Violence Commission national survey shows a similar pattern. Items concerning acts of punching or beating reported by the respondent can be combined into an "index of fist fighting in conflict situations," which estimates the number of times the respondent has been involved in fights during his adult lifetime.[17] Table II shows that men in the census South

---

[16] "Social desirability bias" is indicated by a five item adaptation of Crowne and Marlowe's scale, which includes items that are either socially desirable but probably untrue or probably true but socially undesirable. (*E.g.*, True or False: "I never hesitate to go out of my way to help someone in trouble.") D. Crowne & D. Marlowe, The Approval Motive (1964). Respondents scoring high on this scale are somewhat more likely to report that they do not get in fights.

[17] Because of several ambiguities in the questionnaire, the "index of fist fighting in conflict situations" is only a rough indicator of the use of violence. The core item used for the index is: "Have you ever punched or beaten anyone?" The ambiguities are these:

1) The respondent was asked whether the aggression occurred when he was a "child," or "adult," or both, but this was according to his own definition.

2) Although frequency of occurrence is recorded, it was asked independently of

Table II
Fighting by region
Index of fist fighting in conflict situations during adult lifetime (men aged 21–64 in 1968; national sample)

	Non-South		South	
	White	Black	White	Black
Mean score (range 0–3)	.51	.64	.31	.08
(N)	(282)	(44)	(87)	(38)

are less likely, by their reports, to have been in fights than those outside this region. Again this finding is not changed by controls for age and income.[18]

THE EFFECT OF SOUTHERN MIGRATION ON NORTHERN VIOLENCE

Various papers[19] have dealt with the question of whether or not a sizable amount of Northern homicide can be explained by the migration of Southerners who, so to speak, "brought their violence with them." Previous studies have been based on ecological data, as individual data on homicide are apparently not available.

Data from the Milwaukee sample of blacks allows an assessment of the hypothesis at the individual level, but only for relatively minor violence. (The sample of Milwaukee whites has too few migrants to permit analysis.) Analysis indicates that Milwaukee blacks born in the South[20] (64 percent of those in the sample) are somewhat *less* likely than those born outside the South to engage in fist fighting. Controlling for income, occupation, age, and social desirability bias, the net

---

time, thus, unless a person reported that the event(s) occurred *only* during childhood or adulthood, we cannot determine the frequency as an adult. In addition, frequency was recorded in only four categories: 0 score 0; 1 = 1; 2 or 3 = 2; 4 or more = 3.

3) Type of incident, *e.g.*, conflict, military, sports, and play, is recorded only for the most recent incident.

Given these ambiguities, an adjusted index was constructed by reducing the frequency to zero if the aggression occurred only during childhood or if the last instance was not in a situation of "anger or conflict." The latter adjustment is quite stringent and assumes that the more recent incident is representative of the previous ones. Experimentation with less stringent adjustments had no important effect on the findings reported here.

[18] Occupation and "social desirability bias" were not included in this data set.

[19] *See, e.g.*, Gastil, *supra* note 3; Loftin & Hill, *supra* note 6.

[20] In the study, the "South" was defined as: Alabama, Arkansas, Delaware, Florida, Georgia, Kentucky, Louisiana, Maryland, Mississippi, North Carolina, Oklahoma, South Carolina, Tennessee, Texas, Virginia, West Virginia, and Washington, D.C.

effect (standardized regression coefficient) of Southern origin on fighting is $-.15$ (p = .03). Crain and Weisman report a similar finding in their analysis of a large scale national survey done by the National Opinion Research Center in 1966, concluding that "Northern born men are more likely to report being in a fight than are late migrants from the South with the same amount of education."[21]

SELF-REPORTED APPROVAL OF VIOLENCE

Some studies of Southern attitudes towards the use of physical aggression have shown a higher level of support in the South.[22] However, these studies have not been specifically concerned with the use of physical aggression in peer situations, rather they have dealt with political violence and corporal punishment.

In the Violence Commission Survey, respondents were asked about their general approval of the use of physical aggression in different kinds of peer interactions; those who gave their general approval were then asked about four or five more specific situations. The general approval questions asked whether there were "any situations that you can imagine" in which the respondent would approve of such acts as a husband slapping his wife's face; a husband shooting his wife; a man punching (or choking) an adult male stranger; one teenage boy punching (or knifing) another. These general items and their follow-ups[23] were combined into indices. Table III shows the mean score on these indices for Southern and non-Southern whites

---

[21] R. Crain & C. Weisman, Discrimination, Personality, and Achievement 14 (1972).

[22] *See, e.g.*, M. Blumenthal, R. Kahn, F. Andrews & K. Head, Justifying Violence: Attitudes of American Men (1972); J. Reed, The Enduring South: Subcultural Persistence in Mass Society (1972).

[23] For each index, the lead item and its follow-ups were scored 2 for a "yes" response, 0 for "no," and 1 for "not sure." If a "no" was given for the lead item, the follow-ups were not asked. The items were these:

a. Are there any situations that you can imagine in which you would approve of a husband slapping his wife's face? If "yes" or "not sure," would you approve if the husband and wife were having an argument?; If the wife had insulted her husband in public?; if the wife had been flirting with other men?; if the wife had been unfaithful?

b. Are there any situations you can imagine in which you would approve of a teenage boy punching another teenage boy? If "yes" or "not sure," would you approve if he didn't like the other boy?; if he had been challenged by the other boy to a fist fight?; if he had been hit by the other boy?; if he had been ridiculed and picked on by the other boy?

c. Are there any situations that you can imagine in which you would approve of a man punching an adult male stranger? If "yes" or "not sure," would you approve if the stranger was drunk and bumped into the man and his wife on the street?; if the stranger had hit the man's child after the child accidentally damaged the stranger's car?; if the stranger was beating up a woman and the man saw it?; if the stranger had broken into the man's house?

d. Same as c), but change "punching" to "choking" and add "if the stranger had knocked the man down and was trying to rob him?"

Table III
Approval of Violence by Region (men aged 21–64 in 1968; national sample)

		Non-South		South	
		White	Black	White	Black
A.	Approval of a husband slapping his wife's face				
	Mean (range 0–10)	1.4	3.1	1.0	1.1
B.	Approval of a teenage boy punching another teenage boy				
	Mean (range 0–10)	5.4	4.5	4.4	3.3
C.	Approval of a man punching an adult male stranger				
	Mean (range 0–10)	4.3	3.8	4.1	2.7
D.	Approval of a man choking an adult male stranger				
	Mean (range 0–12)	2.1	3.3	2.2	1.7
E.	Approval of a man shooting his wife				
	Mean (range 0–2)	.10	.14	.11	.05
F.	Approval of a teenage boy knifing another				
	Mean (range 0–2)	.09	.11	.05	.08
Number of cases		(282)	(44)	(87)	(38)

and blacks. For each index, there is either essentially no difference in the scores for the South and non-South, or the South actually has a lower mean score. Extensive exploration of control variables does not change the basic conclusion of no substantial South/non-South difference.[24]

Since only an abstract level of approval is being tapped by these indices, the absolute level of the mean score is important as well as the regional comparison. For example, if mean scores were quite high, it could be that the indices were tapping a somewhat trivial dimension of support for violence and that tighter questions would draw out major regional differences in approval. However, the absolute level of support is too low to lend much support to such an objection. For all the indices but one (approval of one teenage boy punching another), the sample means are below the midpoint on the indices, often markedly so, even though most items seem fairly easy to support. In addition, when the frequency distributions are examined (not shown), support at the high end of the index is low for all groups on all indices, with the South again about the same or lower than the non-South.

---

e. Are there any situations you can imagine in which you would approve of a husband shooting his wife?

f. Are there any situations you can imagine in which you would approve of one teenage boy knifing another?

[24] A separate analysis of women shows a slight tendency for women in the South to score higher than those in the non-South on most of the indices.

A few of the indices warrant some additional comment. The index of approval of a boy punching another is of interest because it begins to tap intergenerational transmission of attitudes and because the follow-up items deal with such aspects of "machismo" as taking up the challenge to fight.[25] Yet on this index the South/non-South contrast is sharpest, with the mean score for Southern whites and blacks being 20 to 25 percent lower than for the corresponding non-Southern samples. The last two items in Table III are important because they deal with approval of a husband shooting his wife or one teenage boy knifing another, *i.e.*, the types of extreme violence that are reflected in the official data on homicide and criminal assault. The mean scores here are low, and those for the South are quite incompatible with the thesis that there is at least a moderately high tolerance for extreme violence among peers in the South. In addition, note that again the mean scores for the South are if anything *lower* than those for the non-South.

Granted, all the items analyzed here are general, and responses do not necessarily indicate a person's likely attitude or action in some actual instance he may become (or have been) involved in. But it is just this generality which makes the items useful indications of the general level of tolerance of violence between peers. Given that the items are so easy to agree with, the relatively low mean scores, and especially the low frequency of high scores on the indices, does seem to indicate the absence of a high level of general tolerance.

FIGHTING AND PERCEIVED ESTEEM BY OTHERS

Some formulations of the subculture of violence thesis imply a clear relationship between violence and the general esteem accorded to a person by others. For example, in their discussion of what they see as a subculture of violence among blacks and low income whites. Wolfgang and Ferracuti hold that violence is positively valued and non-violence negatively sanctioned. This sanctioning is, they argue, carried out through informal mechanisms of social control ranging from the "cold shoulder" to ostracism.[26] Under such circumstances violence is important to the subculture, and we would expect that persons who adhere to the values would be more likely than those who do not to be liked, respected, and accorded high status in the group.

Comparison of the South and non-South on violence and peer esteem is complicated by Wolfgang and Ferracuti's hypothesis that

---

[25] *See* note 23 *supra*.
[26] *See, e.g.*, M. Wolfgang & F. Ferracuti, *supra* note 7, at 160.

Table IV
Fighting and perceived esteem by others (men aged 21–64 in 1969)

	Milwaukee				Rural North Carolina			
	White		Black		White		Black	
Hypothesized relationship	<$5,000 Positive	≥$5,000 Strong Negative	<$5,000 Strong Positive	≥$5,000 Positive	<$5,000 Strong Positive	≥$5,000 Positive	<$5,000 Very strong Positive	≥$5,000 Strong Positive
A. Effect of fighting on feeling "respected and listened to by others."								
Zero order r	-.15	.02	-.25	-.18*	.04	-.09	-.10	.15
Beta, net of age, occupation, and social desirability index	†	.08	.02	-.14	.11	-.08	-.08	.21
B. Effect of fighting on feeling "well liked by other people and having lots of friends."								
Zero order r	.22	-.02	-.13	-.01	-.03	.07	-.26	.17
Beta, net of age, occupation, and social desirability index	†	-.03	.16	-.04	.29	.17*	-.24*	.21
(N)	(15)	(207)	(51)	(184)	(39)	(179)	(196)	(40)

* Indicates significance level at .05 or better.
† N is too low to compute beta.

race and income subcultures exist. Thus, the relationship must be analyzed within income and race groups as well as by locale. Given Wolfgang and Ferracuti's assumption that a relatively strong system of sanctions exists, it should follow that the relationship between fighting and peer esteem will be statistically significant and positive for all race-income groups in the rural North Carolina sample. (In the North, prediction would be that the relationship will be negative for non-poor whites, positive for poor whites and non-poor blacks, and highly positive for poor blacks.) If we in addition assume that the hypothesized race, income, and regional effects are additive, then for each race-income group, the association will be more positive in the South than in the North.

These hypotheses can be examined with the Milwaukee-rural North Carolina data. Physical aggression is indicated by the item used in the earlier discussion; perceived esteem accorded by others is indicated by two items, "How do you compare with most men you know on being respected and listened to by other people?" and "How do you compare with most men you know on being well liked by other people and having lots of friends?" Each item had five possible responses, ranging from "much worse" to "much better." Standardized regression coefficients for the relationship between fighting and perceived esteem, controlled for age, occupation, and "social desirability bias," are shown in Table IV. In general, there is a slight tendency for the relationship to be positive and stronger in the rural North Carolina sample than in the Milwaukee sample, as predicted. However, out of 14 beta coefficients, only 2 are significant at the .05 level, and one of these, for poor blacks in the North Carolina sample, is in the direction *opposite* to that predicted. In general, then, these data suggest that the type of subculture discussed by Wolfgang and Ferracuti does not exist in the South.

FIGHTING AND FEELING OF WELL-BEING

As a corollary to the argument in the immediately preceding section, we may explore the relationship between fighting and feeling of well-being. Following Wolfgang and Ferracuti, it would seem that outside the subculture men who are violent would be less likely to be happy both because they were receiving negative sanctions for their violence and because in this group it would be the more marginal persons who would be violent. By contast, within the subculture, this formulation suggests that happiness would be positively correlated with violence, since non-violent men are hypothesized to be negatively sanctioned.

The standardized regression coefficient for the relationship be-

Table V
Fighting and happiness (men aged 21–64 in 1969)

	Milwaukee				Rural North Carolina			
	White		Black		White		Black	
	<$5,000	≥$5,000	<$5,000	≥$5,000	<$5,000	≥$5,000	<$5,000	≥$5,000
Hypothesized relationship	Positive	Strong Negative	Strong Positive	Positive	Strong Positive	Positive	Very strong Positive	Strong Positive
Zero order r	−.09	−.07	−.36*	−.19*	−.01	.05	−.11	−.30
Beta, net of age, occupation, and social desirability index	†	−.09	−.30*	−.18*	−.07	.10	−.07	−.28
(N)	(15)	(207)	(51)	(184)	(39)	(179)	(196)	(40)

* Indicates significance level at .05 or better.
† N is too low to compute beta.

tween fighting and an index of happiness[27] was computed for each of the eight groups in the Milwaukee-North Carolina survey. Predictions are shown on the first line of Table V. This table shows that, contrary to the predictions, there is no significant relationship between fighting and happiness—except for Milwaukee blacks, where it is *negative*.

The data in the last two sections suggest, then, that if there is a subculture of violence in the South, it is probably not such that violence is *required* as a condition of one's being accepted as a "man" by his peers. For if this were the case, then the rural North Carolina coefficients should have been strongly positive. The data further suggest that it is not simply a matter of norms in the South being less specific, in contrast to a sharp rejection of violence in the non-South. For if that were the case, the rural North Carolina coefficients would not be problematic, but the Milwaukee coefficients, particularly for non-poor whites, should have been sharply negative. Together, these findings suggest that a man's fighting is not basic to the evaluations communicated to him by his peers. Violence itself is, then, probably not a prominent part of the normative system in the South.

DISCUSSION

The data presented here from the Violence Commission and Milwaukee-North Carolina surveys contain much that is surprising in the light of previous writing and analysis, but the findings are not necessarily contradictory to those of the earlier work. The Violence Commission survey contains items comparable to those used in earlier research, and on these items the pattern of response is similar to that reported in the literature. For example, the South is higher than the non-South in approval of spanking, in approval of corporal punishment in the schools, and in gun ownership, although the differences tend to be somewhat less than those found by Reed in his analysis of Gallup surveys. The divergence between this and earlier studies lies in the indicators used: individual rather than ecological data on the influence of migration from the South, approval of interpersonal violence among adults rather than in adult-child relationships or in political affairs, and analysis of more commonplace fight-

---

[27] The items in the index of happiness are these: On the whole, how happy would you say you are now? On the whole, how happy would you say you are now compared with other men you know? How often do you feel very discouraged and depressed? How often do you get the feeling that life is not worth living? Each item had four possible responses. Because of the uncertain direction of causality, the partial correlation coefficient may be preferable to the standardized regression coefficient here. However, analysis of partial r's did not change the finding.

ing rather than officially recorded homicide or assault. Like the earlier studies, the present one can only be suggestive. Larger samples of Southern residents and of migrants are needed, and questions need to be more specifically directed to examining hypotheses about a subculture of violence.

Prior to the instigation of such studies, more work is needed in the specification of the content of the hypothesized cultural differences.[28] Gastil, for example, differentiates his notion of a subculture of violence from Wolfgang and Ferracuti's by holding that his is only a subculture of lethal violence. Yet some of the processes suggested as leading to murder (for example, defense of honor, remnants of the frontier ethic, or legitimization of actions that lead to hostile relations within families or between classes), seem just as likely to lead to nonlethal violence. Other factors (such as the high rate of gun ownership relative to other regions or a lesser degree of opprobrium attached to the act of murder), could be unique to a subculture of lethal violence.[29] Moreover, it is not clear whether the hypothesized subculture is defined by its approach to violence itself, or whether violence is hypothesized as a by-product of a subculture centered on something other than violence. Thus, Gastil emphasizes that "a violent tradition may be one that in a wide range of situations condones lethal violence, *or* it may be a tradition that more indirectly raises the murder rate."[30] He seems to prefer the latter notion, and at times refers to the values of "Southern culture," although the title of his paper stresses the idea of a subculture of *violence*. A strong case can certainly be made that the South has had a different history in terms of ideals as well as in experience, and of the writers discussed, Reed is perhaps the clearest in seeing attitudes towards violence as a subset of a broader Southern culture. His discussion of violence is only a part of a broader argument that a distinctive Southern orientation emphasizing traditional values persists today. However, Reed does not attempt to show which parts of that Southern orientation are more central than others.

Future research should thus be directed towards clarifying the origins and precise content of such a "Southern Culture" and its rela-

---

[28] Another aspect of the inquiry which needs refinement is the specification of the area to be compared to "the South." Following Reed, the analysis in this paper has not differentiated among non-southern regions. This method is justifiable in that there is a clearer regional tradition in the South, but it also obscures important variation outside the South. On most items relating to violence, the Northeast is markedly lower than other regions in its approval and reported use of violence; it is also true, however, that this region has had less migration from the South than others.

[29] Recall, however, that the analysis above indicates that men in the South are if anything *lower* in approval of lethal violence.

[30] Gastil, *supra* note 3, at 416.

tionship, if any, to the high rate of recorded homicide in the South. It is possible, for example, that there is a subcultural norm in the South supporting the possession of weapons—perhaps even loaded weapons—in the home, but that use of the weapons for other than "show" or defense against intruders is negatively sanctioned. Shootings during arguments could be opprobrious and yet still be rare enough to be insufficient to lessen the desire to have a gun. Similarly, differences in political violence and in attitudes towards physical punishment in childrearing may be best understood as by-products of other Southern values, such as traditionalism in race relations and in parent-child-relationships.[31] Such indirect influences of a broader Southern culture may prove to be important in the explanation of violence, but current evidence suggests that a subculture directly based on normative support for violence in interpersonal situations does not exist.

The findings here, along with the critique of Gastil and Hackney's methodology,[32] also suggest that more attention should be given to non-cultural explanations of Southern violence. Structural and demographic variables, for example, should be explored in greater depth than has been the case in previous research.

CONCLUSION

A massive body of evidence about the relationship between social inequality and rates of deviant behavior has accumulated since Merton (1938) first emphasized the variable of social class in his original formulation of anomie theory. The three research illustrations presented in this chapter are a reasonably representative sample of the methodological approaches sociologists have taken in examining this

---

[31] If the South does in fact have a higher homicide rate than the non-South, but a lower rate of less extreme violence, it is also possible that psychological differences are important. Megargee's research suggests that there are two types of persons prone to extreme violence: the "under-controlled" type, who frequently engages in the whole range of aggressive acts, and the "overcontrolled" type, who has very rigid inhibitions against aggression, but who, if pushed over the brink" is likely to commit an extreme act. The "overcontrolled" personality could in turn, be an indirect product of a "Southern culture." Megargee, *Undercontrolled and Overcontrolled Personality Types in Extreme Antisocial Aggression*, 80 Psychological Monographs no. 3, at 1 (1966).

The work of H. Haven suggests that the "overcontrolled" person is more likely to have grown up in a conservative, religious family with strong pressures towards conformity. H. Haven, Descriptive and Developmental Characteristics of Chronically Overcontrolled Hostile Prisoners, 1972 (unpublished doctoral dissertation, Florida State University). If, as some studies indicate, these family characteristics are more typical of the South, then a possible explanation of South/non-South patterns of violence is generated. An examination of this model would have to avoid the use of ecological data and instead use individual data, which are not available at this time.

[32] Loftin & Hill, *supra* note 6.

general relationship. These particular studies also provide a fairly accurate reflection of the current state of empirical support for the ideas of Merton and other theorists reviewed in Chapter 4.

The results of Hollingshead and Redlich's (1953; 1958) research seem to bear out the implication of the leading macro-normative theories that the lower class is an especially stressful, frustrating location in the American social structure. A negative or inverse relationship between social class and serious psychiatric problems has also been uncovered in a number of more recent studies that have used survey techniques to measure self-reported symptoms in samples of community populations (Dohrenwend & Dohrenwend, 1969; Dohrenwend et al., 1980; Schwab & Schwab, 1978). Nonetheless, the question of whether mental disorder is actually *caused* by social conditions in the lower class is not much clearer today than it was at the time of Hollingshead and Redlich's investigation. While many researchers would agree with the traditional sociological view of mental disorder as a retreatist adaptation to the environmental pressures of lower-class life (see, for example, Kleiner & Parker, 1963; Langner & Michael, 1963; Liem & Liem, 1978), some investigators support the alternative view that cases of mental disorder become concentrated in the lower class as a result of *social selection* (Dunham et al., 1966; Turner & Wagenfeld, 1967; Turner & Gartrell, 1978; also see Eaton, 1980; Miles, 1981). The latter position postulates that persons selectively become stuck in the lower class or drift downward from other classes as a *consequence* of psychiatric disabilities that were initially caused by genetic factors or other conditions unrelated to social class. In short, the theoretically crucial question of which comes first—membership in the lower class or mental disorder—is still largely unresolved. However, longitudinal surveys that measure environmental variables and psychiatric variables at several points in time are currently being used to unravel causes from effects in epidemiological research (Kessler & Cleary, 1980; Wheaton, 1978; 1980; Thoits & Hannan, 1979; Srole, 1975).

We have seen that the studies by Hindelang (1978) and Erlanger (1976) illustrate opposing sides in a continuing theoretical and methodological debate over the relationship between social inequality and rates of crime and delinquency. The doubts that Erlanger and other self-report researchers have raised about the empirical foundations of anomie and subculture theories reached a zenith in an article by Tittle, Villemez, and Smith (1978) titled "The Myth of Social Class and Criminality." Tittle and his associates attempted an exhaustive review and reanalysis of all previous studies of social class and criminal behavior, including those based on official statistics as well as self-report studies. Not only did a class-crime relationship fail to emerge in the aggregated self-report survey data presented by these authors but, more surprising, the theoretically predicted inverse relationship between class and *officially recorded* crime and delinquency had virtually vanished in studies conducted since the early 1960s. This apparent lack of current empirical support for a central hypothesis of the anomie and subculture theorists led Tittle and his associates to the pessimistic conclusion that it is "now time . . . to shift away from class-based theories" of rates of criminal behavior (1978: 654).

Hindelang, on the other hand, is among a number of sociologists who have vigorously challenged many of the conclusions that Erlanger, Tittle, and others have drawn from self-report data (Hindelang et al., 1979; 1981; Braithwaite, 1979; 1981; Nettler, 1978; 1982). For instance, Hindelang, Hirschi, and Weis (1979) recently argued that self-report researchers, in general, and Tittle et al. (1978), in particular, have focused almost exclusively on relatively minor offenses committed by juveniles (e.g., driving a car without a license, skipping school) that are far removed from the serious forms of criminal behavior that are of primary interest to macro-normative theorists. In a later empirical work, these same authors (Hindelang et al., 1981) found that black youths tend to underreport their involvement in serious crimes—a result suggesting that racial differences in criminal behavior may be greater than what Erlanger and other self-report researchers have observed (see Empey, 1982). These methodological points were reinforced by some initial findings from a national self-report survey designed by Elliott and Ageton (1980) to be especially sensitive to serious personal and property offenses (e.g., rape, aggravated assault, breaking and entering). Among other race and class relationships that emerged in these interview data, Elliott and Ageton (1980: 106) discovered "a relatively high involvement of lower-class black youth in serious offenses against persons." This is in line with Hindelang's (1981) estimate from national victimization data of an extraordinarily high rate of personal crimes committed by black males aged 18–20: approximately 85,000 personal offenses per year for every 100,000 youths in this population subgroup.

At this point, then, the evidence pertaining to the major macro-normative theories is mixed. Class variations—which are central to Merton's (1957) view of deviant behavior—are far more evident in epidemiological research on mental disorder than in corresponding studies of crime and delinquency rates. Recent findings in the latter area, however, point directly to the groups of disadvantaged minority youths that have been emphasized in subcultural theories of delinquency. We will follow this lead in the next two chapters, where we will examine micro-normative theories and research that have attempted to shed light on the inner workings of these and other deviant groups.

The micro-normative approach: Social learning and control theory

6

The theorists whose work will be discussed in this chapter have occasionally had difficulty convincing their colleagues that they are, indeed, sociologists. In contrast to the macro-level theories and research discussed in the last two chapters, work conducted within the social learning tradition and the control tradition characteristically focuses on the deviant behavior of individuals. Furthermore, social learning theorists and control theorists sometimes weave individualistic concepts like attitude, belief, or self-concept into their explanatory frameworks. Such features of the micro-normative approach have led many sociologists to conclude with Cohen (1959: 462) that it falls outside the boundaries of their discipline:

> Much that travels under the name of sociology of deviant behavior . . . is psychology—some of it very good psychology, but psychology. For example, Sutherland's theory of differential association, which is widely regarded as preeminently sociological, is not the less psychological because it makes much of the cultural milieu. It is psychological because it addresses itself to the question: How do people become the kind of individuals who commit criminal acts? A sociological question would be: What is it about the structure of social systems that determines the kinds of criminal acts that occur in these systems and the way in which such acts are distributed within the systems?

In other words, Cohen contends that the only truly sociological explanations of deviant behavior are those theories that deal with the macro-level problem of rates.

Contrary to Cohen, the position of this chapter will be that Sutherland's differential association theory and most of the other micro-normative theories considered here are primarily sociological in nature. This means that the phenomena to be explained (i.e., rates versus individual deviant behavior) will not be taken as the sole distinguishing criterion of sociological theorizing. Rather, a theory will be defined as a sociological explanation to the extent that it focuses attention on *patterned social relationships* or on *cultural meanings associated with those relationships* as the main environmental determinants of deviant behavior. Psychological explanations, while they typically give at least some recognition to environmental influences on learning or personality formation, tend to focus their greatest attention on factors *within* the individual as the primary causes of deviant behavior. Therefore, sociological explanations can be characterized as *interpersonal* in nature (i.e., based on what goes on *between* people) whereas psychological explanations are *intra*personal in nature (i.e., based on what goes on *within* people).

This distinction does not necessarily conflict with Inkeles' (1959) observation that most sociological analyses of deviant behavior or other social phenomena contain, either explicitly or implicitly, some elements of psychological theorizing. There is no denying that assumptions about psychological processes or states of the individual are incorporated to varying degrees in virtually all theories within the normative perspective. However, instead of emphasizing psychological abnormalities or individual differences, these assumptions typically deal with general, normal psychological conditions that make *all* people responsive to variations in the social environment. For example, by assuming that people are normally rewarded by close relationships with others, the sociological analyst can go on to focus on the various kinds of social relationships that are important environmental causes of deviant behavior. Thus, as we saw with Durkheim's work in Chapter 4, psychological assumptions are not incompatible with explanations that are mainly focused on social and cultural variables.

The main problem confronting sociological theorizing about deviant behavior is not the use of *some* psychological or even biological assumptions but the common tendency to resort to explanations that are *dominated* by a focus on the individual. From a commonsense point of view, it is easier to see individuals and their behavior than it is to see social relationships, class structures, or cultures. Even when using macro-level concepts such as culture conflict or the strain toward anomie, it is tempting to think of these conditions as properties of individuals rather than as properties of groups or societies. This temptation to fall back on psychologistic interpretations of social phenomena is even more appealing in micro-level analyses of individual deviant behavior. As Arthur Brittan (1973: 6) has commented, "there is nothing more difficult to sustain than the sociological vision"—the ability to look beyond individuals to the social phenomena of which they are only a part. Unlike anomie or subcultural theorists who stand back and view social phenomena from a safe analytical distance, the micro-level viewpoint of social learning and control theorists necessarily brings them closer to individuals and psychological processes. Nonetheless, this chapter will cover the work of some theorists who have made excellent use of the sociological vision to highlight interpersonal interaction, group bonds, and other distinctively social factors surrounding the norm-violating behavior of individuals.

THE SOCIAL LEARNING TRADITION

Sutherland's differential association theory

At the same time that Merton, Cohen, and Cloward and Ohlin were attempting to develop various aspects of the macro-normative approach to rates of deviant behavior, Sutherland's differential association theory (1974) held a virtual monopoly over the micro-normative approach in the sociology of deviance. Sutherland, of course, had no intention of "forgetting the individual" as Durkheim would have it. Sutherland steadfastly maintained that deviant phenomena at both the individual level and the societal level were appropriate topics for sociological analysis. In fact, as we noted in Chapter 2, Sutherland attempted to complement the micro-level focus of differential association theory with a macro-level analysis of how differential social organization contributes to variations in crime rates across different communities (see Sutherland & Cressey, 1974: 93–112). However, Sutherland's most systematic and influential contribution was his theoretical analysis of individual deviance as a product of social learning in a group environment. Although Sutherland died in 1950, his work has been carried on by his colleague, Donald R. Cressey. The 1947 version of differential association theory has continued to appear unchanged in Cressey's revisions of Sutherland's text, *Criminology* (1974: 71–93). Cressey has also actively defended differential association theory against its critics (1960; 1962).

Sutherland's theory consists of nine statements which specify various elements of the interpersonal process through which individuals learn to engage in law-violating behavior. In Chapter 1, we discussed the crucial proposition in this theory (statement 6) that a person becomes criminal when he or she associates with more "definitions" which are favorable to violation of the law than are unfavorable to violation of the law. However, it is clear from other statements in Sutherland's theory and from his comments on those statements that the content of the criminal learning process includes much more than just definitions that oppose or support legal norms. More broadly, people learn various criminal or anticriminal patterns that are differentially present in their social environment (1974: 76).

A criminal pattern refers to a complex but organized set of behaviors and cultural meanings that support violation of the law. The behavioral component of a criminal pattern "includes . . . techniques of committing the crime, which are sometimes very complicated, sometimes very simple" (1974: 75). But, merely learning how to commit a crime is not sufficient to cause a person actually to engage in criminal behavior. Criminal patterns also include a subjective component—cultural meanings attached to criminal behavior that make a person willing or motivated to violate the law. In addition to unfavorable definitions or evaluations of the law, these cultural meanings also include various "motives, drives, rationalizations, and attitudes" that channel a person's behavior in a criminal direction (1974: 75). Although Sutherland does not devote detailed attention to anticriminal patterns, we can reasonably assume that this concept refers to patterns of law-abiding behavior and conventional cultural meanings. Most of us are not criminals, Sutherland would argue, because our associations with anticriminal patterns predominate over our exposure to criminal patterns. However, this ratio of associations is reversed in the social environment of criminals. Reiterating the central principle of differential association theory, Sutherland states that "(w)hen persons become criminal, they do so because of contacts with criminal patterns and also because of isolation from anticriminal patterns" (1974: 76).

What is the nature of the learning process by which criminal patterns are acquired by the individual? Statements 2, 3, and 8 in Sutherland's theory give concise answers to this question (1974: 75–76):

2. Criminal behavior is learned in interaction with other persons in a process of communication.
3. The principal part of the learning of criminal behavior occurs within intimate personal groups.
8. The process of learning criminal behavior by association with criminal and anticriminal patterns involves all of the mechanisms that are involved in any other learning.

In short, criminal behavior is a product of normal social learning through interaction in primary groups, such as friends or family.

Sutherland's argument that law-violating behavior is socially learned from an excess of interpersonal associations with criminal patterns is appealing for its clarity and simplicity. But, as statement 7 in his theory indicates, he was cautious not to oversimplify his analysis of this micro-level process (1974: 76): "Differential associations may vary in frequency, duration, priority, and intensity." Here, he specifies a number of analytical variables that figure into the misleadingly simple conception of an "excess" of associations. This excess may come about through more *frequent* exposure to criminal patterns than to anticriminal patterns, or it may be a function of greater *duration* of contact with criminal patterns over time. With regard to the variable of *priority*, Sutherland suggests that criminal learning early in life may be especially influential on the individual. Finally, Sutherland does not precisely define the meaning of *intensity*, but he indicates that "it has to do with such things as the prestige of the source of a criminal or anticriminal pattern and with emotional reactions related to the associations" (1974: 76). All of these contingencies in the social learning process can affect the relative impact of criminal patterns or anticriminal patterns on the individual's behavior.

Criticisms and revisions of Sutherland's theory

Throughout the normative period, Sutherland's influence on micro-level theorizing in the sociology of deviance was perhaps even more pervasive than was Merton's influence on macro-level approaches. Theoretical work in the social learning tradition has primarily consisted of critical debates over the merits of Sutherland's explanation of individual criminality and of attempts to revise or extend differential association theory (see Cressey, 1960).

The qualities that made Sutherland a leading social scientist show through in the fact that he, himself, was one of the most astute critics of differential association theory. One of his major reservations about the theory was its failure to incorporate criminal opportunities as an essential factor for the occurrence of criminal behavior (1956b). As we have seen, Cloward and Ohlin (1960) later benefitted from Sutherland's critical scrutiny of his own theory by building their subcultural theory of delinquency around the concept of illegitimate opportunity. Sutherland was also concerned about the part played by variations in individual personality in the differential association process (1956a). His sociological explanation of crime focused attention on variations in the social environment in the form of interpersonal contacts with criminal or anticriminal patterns. However, he felt that this theory should be modified in some way to take into account personality traits, such as bashfulness, that might affect a person's susceptibility to these environmental influences.

Picking up on the latter criticism, Daniel Glaser (1956) proposed a revision of differential association theory that attempts to focus greater attention on individual factors that intervene between environmental contacts and criminal behavior. Glaser states his theory of differential identification as follows (1956: 440, emphasis deleted):

> a person pursues criminal behavior to the extent that he identifies himself with real or imaginary persons from whose perspective his criminal behavior seems acceptable.

Glaser argues that this formulation improves upon Sutherland's mechanistic image of individuals being pushed toward criminal or noncriminal behavior by opposing environmental forces. The theory of differential identification views the individual as a more active, voluntary participant in the criminal learning process. The key question in explaining criminal behavior, according to Glaser, is with whom does the individual subjectively choose to identify, criminals or noncriminals? Criminal associations and other environmental factors external to the individual are primarily relevant only "to the extent that they can be shown to affect the choice of the other from whose perspective the individual views his own behavior" (1956: 440).

It is not clear whether Glaser intended to revise differential association theory completely or merely to substitute his brief statement of differential identification for some of the statements in Sutherland's theory. As it stands, differential identification theory is less specific than differential association theory regarding the nature and content of the social learning process. While Glaser's explanation may be less deterministic than Sutherland's, it is also less sociological. In contrast to Sutherland's focus on variations in the social relationships and cultural meanings to which an individual is actually exposed, Glaser's explanation shifts attention to psychological phenomena—variations in the individual's internal identification with other persons, whether those persons are real or imaginary.

The issues of determinism and psychological explanation also become crucial in the assessment of several more recent attempts to revise Sutherland's theory in accordance with the concepts and principles of psychological theories of behavioral learning (Jeffery, 1965; Burgess & Akers, 1966; Akers, 1977; Adams, 1973). These revisions of differential association theory are inspired by the fact that Sutherland did not present an intensive analysis of the kind of learning involved in individual criminality. Although Sutherland emphasized the social character of criminal learning and its fundamental similarity to noncriminal learning, he did not attempt to specify the psychological details of this learning process.

In the most ambitious attempt to fill in these details, Burgess and Akers (1966) used general principles of learning developed by the psychologist B. F. Skinner (1953) as the basis for a complete reformulation of Sutherland's theory. Terming their revision differential association-reinforcement theory, Burgess and Akers argue that criminal behavior (or any other learned behavior) can be explained as a function of the reinforcement (i.e., rewards) or punishment a person receives from the environment. Put simply, behavior that produces a reward will tend to be performed more frequently in the future, while behavior that is followed by punishment will tend to decrease in frequency. Differential reinforcement occurs when under certain environmental conditions one particular behavior leads to greater or more frequent rewards than does another alternative behavior. The behavior that receives greater environmental reinforcement—for instance, deviant behavior—becomes dominant over the alternative behavior—such as conforming behavior. Therefore, through a process of differential reinforcement, environmental conditions can increase the probability of deviant acts by individuals.

A number of other concepts and general principles of behavior learning are used by Burgess and Akers (1966) to revise or delete each of the original statements in Sutherland's theory. Even more than Sutherland, Burgess and Akers are able to drive home the point that criminal behavior is "normal" in the sense that it is learned in the same way as any other behavior. In later work, Akers (1977) has attempted to show how differential association-reinforcement theory might be used to explain other forms of deviant behavior, such as mental illness, alcoholism, and sexual deviance. Thus, an important contribution of this work has been to extend the social learning tradition to a number of forms of deviant behavior in addition to criminality.

However, as we noted in Chapter 3, behavioristic revisions of Sutherland's theory have been the subject of some controversy within the field of deviance. Objections to the deterministic style of Sutherland's theorizing have been amplified by critics of Burgess and Akers' version of social learning theory. Taylor, Walton, and Young (1973: 133), who favor a more interpretive form of theory, argue that deviant behavior is a meaningful social activity that "cannot be explained in terms of automatons propelled through their lives like Skinnerian rats." These critics agree with Glaser's (1956) position that the social learning tradition should place greater emphasis on subjective interpretations and voluntary decisions that intervene between environmental causes and the norm-violating behavior of human actors. But, as we shall see later, these objections tend to be based on the philosophical or ideological preferences of the critics rather than on empirical evidence against deterministic theories.

Since differential association-reinforcement theory is phrased in the language of psychological learning theory, it might seem obvious that this is a nonsociological explanation of deviant behavior. However, this question is not as clear-cut as it might seem. Unlike some psychological perspectives that explain individual behavior as a function of variations in personality and other internal factors, the body of behavioristic theory on which Burgess and Akers base their work stresses conditions in the environment as the key determinants of human behavior. Burgess and Akers, following Sutherland, are also careful to point out that primary groups are the major source of reinforcement involved in the social learning of deviant behavior. However, as opposed to Sutherland and most other sociologists, Burgess and Akers do not limit their attention to the *social* environment. Differential association-reinforcement theory explicitly includes nonsocial reinforcement and learning without direct contact with other persons as possible sources of deviant behavior (1966; also see Adams, 1973). Only empirical research can determine how essential interpersonal relationships and other social factors are for the learning of deviant behavior, but the inclusion of nonsocial factors in Burgess and Akers' theory carries it beyond the boundaries of a strictly sociological explanation (see Akers et al., 1979).

Despite the criticisms that have been directed at it, Sutherland's differential association theory still represents the best example of sociological analysis within the social learning tradition. The special emphasis Sutherland placed on social relationships and shared cultural meanings has been lost to varying degrees in later revisions of his theory. Yet, as recent developments in this micro-normative tradition would suggest, attention to some nonsociological elements in deviant behavior may provide some useful insights for research. We will now turn to another sociological tradition that has incorporated some psychological viewpoints, control theory.

THE CONTROL TRADITION

Conformity as problematic

So far, this chapter has covered a number of normative theories that are addressed to the same basic question: "Why do *they* do it?" This question treats deviance as problematic. That is, it focuses analytical attention on special pressures or motivations that causes some people (they) to engage in norm-violating behavior. Control theories, however, raise a rather different question for sociological analysis: "Why don't *we* do it?" Here, conformity rather than deviance is treated as problematic, for the latter question shifts attention to social and personal controls that prevent most people (we) from engaging in norm-violating acts. From the viewpoint of the control tradition, deviant behavior is "caused" only in the sense that norm-violating acts are more likely to occur when the controls that cause conformity are weak or absent.

The origins of this theoretical tradition can be traced back to Durkheim (1951) and the work of the Chicago sociologists (see Cohen & Short, 1966: 111–112). Several important statements of control theory also appeared during the normative period (Reiss, 1951; Toby, 1957; Nye, 1958; Reckless, 1961a; 1961b). However, more than with the other normative traditions, active development of the control tradition has continued into the relativistic period (Matza, 1965; Briar & Piliavin, 1965; Hirschi, 1969). Although it is one of the most recent contributions to the control tradition, Hirschi's book, *Causes of Delinquency*, is particularly noteworthy. In this theoretical and empirical work, Hirschi clarifies the basic themes of control theory and provides a convincing demonstration of how an analysis of the problem of conformity can yield useful insights into the phenomenon of deviance.

Hirschi's theory of the social bond

Hirschi (1969) performs a valuable task by beginning his work with a general, critical comparison of the control tradition with other sociological explanations of deviant behavior. Hirschi points out that control theory is similar to anomie theory but dissimilar to differential association theory in its assumption that a common system of values and norms exists within society. But, unlike Merton and the subcultural theorists, control theorists do not feel that powerful environmental pressures or frustrations are necessary to account for the fact that some people engage in behavior that violates this social consensus. Instead, control theorists take the position that people will naturally engage in deviant acts when they lack strong ties or commitments to conventional society. It is not even necessary to require, as does the social learning tradition, that the individual become involved in deviant groups. Control theory simply argues that "a person is *free* to commit (deviant) acts because his ties to the conventional order have been broken" (1969: 3, emphasis added). Again, deviance is unproblematic; what must be explained are the various controls that deny conformers the freedom to deviate.

Hirschi's own version of control theory focuses on several elements of the social bond that ties individuals to conventional society and explains their conforming behavior. Like so many other contemporary ideas in the field of deviance, the notion of a social bond goes back to Durkheim's analysis of different types of suicide (1951). In addition to his examination of anomic suicide, Durkheim distinguished another type of suicide that results from a lack of social integration—the "relaxation of social bonds" between individuals and society (1951: 214). This type of suicide, which Durkheim termed *egoistic* suicide, occurs under conditions where members of society share relatively few common beliefs or where group relationships are weak or lacking. Durkheim describes the egoistic or individualistic way of life encouraged by such conditions as follows (1951: 209):

> The more weakened the groups to which (the individual) belongs, the less he depends on them, the more he consequently depends only on himself and recognizes no other rules of conduct than what are founded on his private interests.

Although individuals are in a sense freer from society under egoistic conditions, they are also less protected from the impact of personal troubles and misfortunes. In the absence of supportive social bonds, suicide rates increase as the isolated "individual yields to the slightest shock of circumstance" (1951: 215).

The concept of a social bond was used by Durkheim for a macro-level explanation of how egoistic conditions contributed to high rates of suicide in certain societies or segments of society. Hirschi, on the other hand, applies this concept in a micro-level analysis of individual conformity and deviance. Hirschi (1969: 16–34) distinguishes four elements of the social bond to conventional society that controls or prevents individual deviant behavior: attachment, commitment, involvement, and belief. The element of *attachment* comes closest to Durkheim's conception of social or group integration. The greater the extent to which the individual is attached to conventional groups, such as the family, the less likely he or she will be free to deviate. *Commitment* is a more rational element of the social bond that refers to the investments a person has in conventional forms of behavior. People committed to conventional educational or occupational careers are unlikely to risk their loss by engaging in deviant behavior. The element of *involvement* is based on the commonsense idea that idle hands are the devil's workshop. That is, people who are highly involved in conventional activities have neither the time nor the energy required for planning and carrying out deviant activities. Whereas these first three elements refer to relationships and activities in the social environment that tie the individual to the conventional social order, Hirschi's final element, *belief*, refers to a more subjective aspect of the social bond. Hirschi assumes that there is a common set of conventional values and norms in society, but he points out that "there is *variation* in the extent to which people believe they should obey the rules of society, and, furthermore, that the less a person believes he should obey the rules, the more likely he is to violate them" (1969: 26).

Hirschi proposes that these four elements can be combined into an interrelated system of variables that together determine the likelihood of conforming or deviant behavior: ". . . the more closely a person is tied to conventional society in any of these ways, the more closely he is likely to be tied in the other ways" (1969: 27). However, it is clear that Hirschi considers *attachment* to be the most important element or variable in his theory of the social bond. He devotes special attention to how close relationships and emotional attachment with conventional groups not only affect one's beliefs in the moral rules of society but also determine one's commitment to conventional educational and occupational pursuits. Commitment to such conventional activities, in turn, determines one's involvement or allocation of time and resources to conforming behavior. Therefore, Hirschi implies that a lack of attachment to the family, to teachers, or to other conventional social relationships is particularly likely to free the individual from the social bond and to increase the probability of deviant behavior.

Like so many other normative theorists, Hirschi applies his theory to juvenile delinquency, although it appears to have implications for other forms of deviant behavior as well (see Stark, 1975). In his book, Hirschi (1969) presents results from a questionnaire survey of a large sample of secondary school students that provide considerable support for predictions from social bonding theory. One finding from this study deserves comment because of its theoretical relevance. Hirschi reports that when a boy has strong bonds to conventional society (as measured by questions relating to family and school), his tendency to engage in delinquent acts is *not* substantially increased by association with delinquent friends (1969: 145–158). This and other findings in Hirschi's study suggest that social bonding theory may be a more adequate explanation of delinquency than the social learning explanation of differential association theory (see, however, Hindelang, 1973). At the very least, Hirschi's work indicates that the social learning tradition, which has long dominated the micro-normative approach to deviance, has some serious competition from the control tradition. Most important, Hirschi's research demonstrates that evaluation of the relative merits of these competing explanations of individual deviant behavior can be pursued on an empirical level as well as on the level of critical analysis.

Earlier contributions to the control tradition

Hirschi's efforts to investigate some empirical implications of his and other theories is exemplary of the healthy respect for research that has characterized the control tradition in general. Many earlier control theorists were also actively involved in research designed to test or demonstrate their explanations of conforming and deviant behavior. As in Hirschi's case, much of this earlier work was concerned with how controls in the social environment, such as a strong family or residence in a "good" neighborhood, could prevent an individual's involvement in deviant behavior. However, particularly in theoretical and empirical work during the normative period, *internal* or psychological controls—such as a strong conscience (Nye, 1958) or a "good" self-concept (Reckless, 1961a; 1961b)—received much greater emphasis than they have in more recent contributions to the control tradition.

This dual focus on psychological and sociological variables in earlier work is illustrated by the title of the initial formulation of control theory by Reiss (1951), "Delinquency as the Failure of Personal and Social Controls." Reiss, who was trained at the University of Chicago, describes the failure of social controls in terms that are reminiscent of the social disorganization period. That is, inadequate social control results from a breakdown or relative weakness in the ability of the family or the community to maintain and enforce the norms of law-abiding society. His description of inadequate personal controls, on the other hand, is based on the psychiatric conception of *personality* as a relatively stable configuration or pattern of psychological dispositions within the individual. Among the inadequate personal controls singled out by Reiss are a weak ego (immature personality) and a weak super-ego (delinquency-oriented personality). Although the development of these internal weaknesses can ultimately be traced back to the social environment and childhood socialization practices, *once established* they are conceptualized as psychological conditions that are *relatively independent* of social conditions in the immediate, ongoing environment. Reiss argues that most cases of delinquency are due to a joint failure of both personal and social controls, but he adds that failure of either type of control by itself might account for some juvenile delinquency.

This dualistic image of personal and social controls, which maintains a rather sharp analytical distinction between individual factors and environmental factors, was abandoned by later control theorists during the relativistic period (Matza, 1964; Briar & Piliavin, 1965). Influenced, perhaps, by the trend away from deterministic theorizing that was emerging in the work of labeling theorists such as Becker (1963), some recent control theorists have presented interpretive analyses of individual conformers or deviants as active participants in ongoing environmental processes. For instance, Briar and Piliavin (1965) point out situational aspects of both the motivation and control of deviant behavior. Rejecting the assumption of other normative theories that persistent pressures or motivations cause norm-violating behavior, Briar and Piliavin take the position "that the motives for such behavior are frequently episodic, oriented to short-term ends, and confined to certain situations" (1965: 36). The question of whether or not an individual will succumb to such "situational inducements" to deviate depends in large part on the strength of one's current "commitments to conformity." Such commitments include "one's attempts to maintain a consistent self image, to sustain valued relationships, and to preserve current and future statuses and activities" (1965: 39). Faced with a situation where these immediate commitments to conformity would be threatened by the performance or discovery of a deviant act, a person with strong commitments will be unlikely to deviate.

However, the clearest example of interpretive theorizing within the control tradition and within the normative perspective on deviance, for that matter, is Matza's (1964) analysis of *Delinquency and Drift*. Earlier in this chapter, we briefly discussed Matza's earlier work (Sykes & Matza, 1957) on subcultural techniques of neutralization that delinquents use to justify or rationalize their deviant conduct in particular situations. In *Delinquency and Drift*, Matza elaborates on his view that deviant behavior by adolescents is not caused in a deterministic sense by the norms of a delinquent subculture or by any other environmental forces. In situations where delinquents neutralize the legal constraints and moral rules of conventional society, deviant behavior becomes a *possibility*—not a forced choice. Matza describes the delinquent as a drifter, who is "committed to neither delinquent nor conventional enterprise" and who "drifts between criminal and conventional action" (1964: 28). However, Matza acknowledges that some critics of his analysis (and of other versions of control theory) object to the idea that a temporary state of drift, a mere absence of moral constraints, is sufficient to account for deviant behavior. He notes that there "is a missing element (in control theory)—an element in the nature of a thrust or an impetus—by which the possibility of delinquency is realized" (1964: 181). True to the nondeterministic stance of his theory, Matza suggests that this impetus is supplied by the deviant's *will* or "decision to commit an infraction" (1964: 183). When a delinquent is drifting between conformity and deviance, the will to choose the latter alternative is activated by past knowledge that the deviant act is easy to do or by a desperate desire to make things happen and overcome the feeling of being pushed around.

But, whether control theories take the interpretive form of Matza's analysis or the more deterministic approach of Hirschi and earlier theorists, we should remember that they are mainly concerned with decisions to conform rather than with decisions to deviate. As Hirschi points out (1969: 34) the question "why do they do it?" is simply not the question these theories are designed to answer.

CONCLUSION

The theories we have considered in this chapter are largely responsible for the continuing vitality of the normative perspective on deviance. In contrast to their growing disenchantment with the broad macro-level frameworks of Merton and the subcultural theorists in recent years, sociologists have stepped up their efforts to determine the influences that differential association, social bonding, and other micro-level processes exert on deviant and nondeviant individuals. Much of the appeal of social learning and control theories lies in their relatively high degree of *testability*. Unlike such empirically elusive notions as a strain toward anomie or the subculture of violence, the central concepts in most of the theories reviewed in this chapter can be readily observed or measured in just about any high school or on any street corner in an urban slum. In the following chapter we will explore three illustrations of how the micro-normative approach has been put to work by researchers interested in the interpersonal context of deviant behavior.

7

Research on interpersonal relationships and deviant behavior

You may have noticed that some of the theories discussed in Chapter 6 bear a strong resemblance to certain commonsense explanations of individual deviant behavior. For instance, doesn't Sutherland's differential association theory essentially repeat what your parents or others have told you about the undesirable influences of bad companions? Don't the arguments of some control theorists about the importance of strong social bonds in the family sound a great deal like the popular belief that broken homes are a leading cause of juvenile delinquency? There is no question that the plausibility of many sociological theories—especially those within the micro-normative approach—is enhanced by their apparent consistency with commonsensical ideas about deviant phenomena.

However, sociologists in the social learning and control traditions have been particularly careful to emphasize that the acceptance of scientific theories, as opposed to commonsense explanations, does not depend on their plausibility but on their consistency with empirical evidence. It is true that the initial inspiration for some theoretical ideas or hypotheses comes from sociologists' personal experiences or from their commonsense understanding of social life; but, ideally, such speculations do not gain full acceptance as verified sociological knowledge until they have been adequately checked out through systematic research.

In the course of their investigations, micro-normative researchers have found that a number of seemingly reasonable ideas about interpersonal relationships and deviant behavior are, in fact, nothing more than common sense. A good case in point is the popular notion that broken homes are a breeding ground of juvenile delinquency. Several studies have found that the presence or absence of an intact household has relatively little effect on the self-reported delinquent behavior of adolescents (Hirschi, 1969; Nye, 1958; Tittle, 1980). For instance, Hirschi's survey revealed that adolescent boys living only with their mother were no more likely to report committing a delinquent act in the past year than were boys whose families were intact (1969: 242). Such results have prompted Hirschi and other control theorists (see Nye, 1958: 41–52) to conclude that the broken home per se is not an important causal factor in delinquent behavior. Nonetheless, Hirschi goes on to observe that "the 'broken-homes-cause-delinquency' hypothesis is so firmly ingrained in . . . common sense that data like those presented here cannot be expected seriously to weaken it" (1969: 243).

Common sense is not always misleading, of course. Another popular belief mentioned above—the bad companions hypothesis—has actually received impressive support in sociological research on a variety of norm-violating behaviors committed by adolescents. A number of studies have found that the greater the extent to which an adolescent's close friends engage in delinquency, alcohol use, or drug use, the greater the likelihood that the young person will report having committed these same acts (see, for example, Jensen, 1972; Kandel, 1980; Akers et al., 1979). Yet, isn't this evidence also consistent with another commonsense hypothesis—birds of a feather flock together? That is, how do we know which comes first, deviant acts or contacts with deviant friends? Here, as in many other cases, common sense offers no clear grounds for deciding between two or more equally reasonable interpretations of the causal links between deviant behavior and interpersonal relationships.

This chapter will focus on the research technique that has typically been used by sociologists to make empirically informed choices among the many plausible explanations for the norm-violating acts of individuals: survey research. The first research illustration by James Short and Fred Strodtbeck (1963) comes from their classic investigation of juvenile delinquency that many sociologists consider to be the high-water mark of empirical work during the normative period. In the full report of their multifaceted research project, *Group Process and Gang Delinquency* (1965), Short and Strodtbeck utilize both survey and observational data to evaluate a number of sociological explanations of various kinds of gang behavior. The article you will read provides a particularly clear illustration of the interpersonal processes that Short and Strodtbeck ultimately found to account best for episodes of violent behavior by gang members. The next research illustration was prepared especially for this book to demonstrate some of the analytical procedures that sociologists use to assess theoretically relevant hypotheses with survey data. Specifically, we will examine some implications of Sutherland's differential association theory using questionnaire data on marijuana use by college students. The final article by Walter Gove and Michael Geerken (1977) represents a departure from the usual concern of micro-normative researchers with criminal or delinquent behavior. Their survey results provide some important evidence on how the interpersonal environments of work and family affect the mental health of women and men. This study not only raises questions about the generality of control theory but also contradicts some commonsense beliefs about the interpersonal stresses and demands placed upon the working wife.

INTRODUCTORY COMMENTS ON SHORT AND STRODTBECK'S RESEARCH

The same phenomenon that inspired romantic musicals like *Grease* and *West Side Story*—lower-class gang delinquency—was viewed as an alarming social problem by the adult public in the United States during the 1950s. As we saw in Chapter 4, sociologists responded to this public concern with a brief flurry of theoretical activity that built the foundation of the subcultural tradition in the field of deviance. Although their respective accounts of the formation and/or content of delinquent subcultures differed in some important respects, all of the subcultural theorists argued that members of lower-class gangs share distinctive norms, values, or focal concerns that encourage or, at least, permit law-violating acts. This proposition not only appeared to be a plausible explanation of gang delinquency but a testable one as well. That is, the subcultural theories generally implied that members of lower-class gangs could be distinguished empirically from non-gang youths or middle-class adolescents by their endorsement of the values and conformity to the expectations of delinquent subcultures.

The following research illustration by Short and Strodtbeck (1963) is based on a project that was initially designed to evaluate this broad subcultural hypothesis. Late in 1958, a group of sociologists including Short, Strodtbeck, and several leading subcultural theorists (Cohen, Ohlin, and Miller) was called upon by the Chicago YMCA for advice in its efforts to reduce gang violence in this urban area. The YMCA was particularly interested in the sociologists' reactions and suggestions regarding a detached workers program that it had recently established in lower-class neighborhoods. Under this program, a number of conflict-oriented juvenile gangs were assigned their own youth worker. This detached worker spent most of his time in the field with gang members, gaining their confidence, steering them away from gang violence and other illegal behavior, and encouraging their participation in more conventional activities such as athletics. During their consultation with YMCA officials, the sociologists recognized the unique research opportunity opened up by the detached worker program. The difficult task of making close contacts with gangs that presumably share a delinquent subculture had already been accomplished by the detached workers. These youth workers were in a good position to observe the day-to-day behavior of lower-class gangs in their natural setting. Furthermore, the detached workers could assist researchers in obtaining gang members' cooperation with efforts to gather survey data on subcultural norms and values.

With the endorsement and support of the Chicago YMCA, Short and Strodtbeck took on the task of developing a research project that could take advantage of this opportunity to explore the nature and influences of delinquent subcultures. They began by considering a basic question of *research design*: if lower-class delinquent gangs share markedly different norms and values than do other adolescent groups, what kinds of group comparisons would be necessary to provide evidence for these differences? For one thing, virtually all the major subcultural theorists implied that middle-class youths would have quite a different cultural outlook on life than would lower-class gang members. Also, *within* the lower class, nongang youths should differ from gang members that have been socialized into delinquent subcultures. Finally, in addition to the variables of social class and gang membership, Short and Strodtbeck believed that comparisons of black and white youths might reveal important racial differences in the endorsement of subcultural norms and values. These three factors were incorporated into Short and Strodtbeck's research design, shown in Figure 7-1, which includes six cells or categories of groups

Figure 7–1
Research design in Short and Strodtbeck's study allowing comparisons by social class, race, and gang status

Race	Social class and gang status		
	Gang	Lower class Nongang	Middle class Nongang
White			
Black			

Source: Adapted from James F. Short, Jr. and Fred L. Strodtbeck, *Group Process and Gang Delinquency* (Chicago: University of Chicago Press, 1965), p. 16.

derived from various combinations of social class, race, and gang status.

Many of the findings reported by Short and Strodtbeck in *Group Process and Gang Delinquency* (1965) are based on comparative analyses of survey data gathered from boys in each cell of the research design. Members of black and white lower-class gangs, of course, were available through the detached workers program. The four nongang cells in the research design were filled with boys recruited from conventional clubs or groups sponsored by the YMCA and similar youth organizations in lower- and middle-class neighborhoods. Interviews and questionnaires administered to all of these boys contained measures of their self-concepts and self-reported delinquent behavior as well as measures of their support for a variety of subcultural and middle-class norms and values. In comparing the responses of the six samples of boys on these survey measures, Short and Strodtbeck were unable to confirm some of the central arguments of the subcultural theorists. For instance, no differences were found between these samples in their endorsement of the values and standards of middle-class culture. Lower-class gang members, both black and white, were just as likely to place a high value on such goals as working for good grades at school or saving money as were middle-class youths (1965: 47–76). Clearly, lower-class gang members *did not reject* the dominant middle-class culture as Cohen (1955) and other theorists contended. On the other hand, when Short and Strodtbeck compared ratings of a number of *subcultural* values across the six samples, the results were more consistent with theoretical expectations. Most notably, gang members of both races placed a higher value on such delinquent goals as being a good fighter with a tough reputation or knowing where to sell what one steals than did other groups in the research design (1965: 47–76). Thus, while gang members hardly appeared to be driven into delinquency by opposition to middle-class society, they did show a greater willingness to reward or, at least, tolerate various deviant activities than did nongang or middle-class youths.

However, Short and Strodtbeck recognized that these systematic comparisons of survey data and the subcultural theories to which they were addressed left many important questions about the *interpersonal* sources of delinquent behavior unanswered. Given the fact that lower-class gangs do share a distinctive subculture, how do these norms and values affect social interaction *within* the gangs? Under what circumstances and through what processes are subcultural expectations translated into delinquent behavior? Which particular members of gangs are most susceptable to these interpersonal influences?

In order to explore these micro-level questions, Short and Strodtbeck focused special attention on the delinquent gangs in the YMCA detached workers program. A particularly valuable source of data on group processes was weekly interviews that the researchers conducted over a three-year period with the youth workers assigned to these gangs. During these unstructured interviews, the YMCA workers were asked to describe in detail the ongoing activities, changing relationships, and, especially, episodes of delinquent behavior that had occurred among gang members throughout the week. By sifting through these rich accounts of gang behavior, Short and Strodtbeck were able to detect some consistent and revealing patterns of social interaction leading to violence and other delinquent acts.

The following research illustration, "The Response of Gang Leaders to Status Threats: An Observation on Group Process and Delinquent Behavior" (Short & Strodtbeck, 1963), is based on incidents reported by youth workers during interviews and requires little additional comment. The cases presented in this article illuminate three basic elements of the group process of status maintenance in conflict-oriented gangs: (1) members in a *leadership position,* (2) when confronted by *interpersonal threats to their status* or prestige within the gang, (3) *respond with subculturally valued behavior*—aggression or violence. As you read Short and Strodtbeck's article, notice how these three elements are represented in the first seven episodes of violence they describe. Then, give special note to their last case of a drug-using group where one of these elements is different. How does this final case shed additional light on the relationship between subcultural values and the process of status maintenance?

Through their flexible use of structured and unstructured survey techniques as well as other data-gathering methods, Short and Strodtbeck made the most of the unusual research opportunity presented by the detached workers program. The results of their multifaceted research project not only provided important evidence relating to existing theories in the subcultural tradition but also opened up some promising new directions for theory and research on group processes and deviant behavior.

RESEARCH ILLUSTRATION 7–A

The response of gang leaders to status threats: An observation on group process and delinquent behavior.[1]

James F. Short, Jr., and Fred L. Strodtbeck

For the explanation of aggressive episodes, group process is seen as an important adjunct both to subcultural and individualistic theories of gang delinquency. Gang leaders are observed to precipitate acts of aggression that are directed outside their group when their status is threatened. This is believed to arise because the leaders' control of internal resources is limited. It also requires the support of aggressive norms within the group for such behavior is not appropriate in a group with "retreatist" norms. The interpretation is based upon instances drawn from observations of a dozen Chicago gangs over a three-year period.

Source: Article reprinted from *American Journal of Sociology* 68 (March 1963): 571–579. Copyright © 1963 by the University of Chicago Press.

[1] This is a revision of a paper read at the annual meeting of the American Sociological Association, August 1961. This investigation was a part of the Youth Studies Re-

This paper describes a particular type of delinquent episode which arises when a gang leader acts to reduce threats to his status by instigating out-group aggression. Our view is that leaders resort to this action because of the limited resources they have for internal control of their group—particularly when their status is attacked.

Unlike other syndrome explanations, such as that of Bloch and Flynn[2] who related delinquency to particular types of parent-child relations, or the various theories that are concerned with the emergence of delinquent subcultures,[3] this paper attempts to provide a clearer understanding of the precipitation of episodes within "delinquent gangs." The focus is on the on-going relations of group members rather than on the boys' family backgrounds or the position of lower-class adolescents within the social structure. The argument is not that family background and social class position are unimportant but, rather, that these factors cannot explain the emergence of particular instances of aggressive delinquency from the on-going, largely non-delinquent, behavior of gang boys.

We decided to develop this paper with liberal use of illustrative instances in order to correct the impression that would exist if William Foote Whyte's superb description of Doc and the Nortons in *Street Corner Society*[4] were permitted to carry the full burden of our need for knowledge about subinstitutionalized elementary social behavior of corner groups.[5] It is almost necessary to protest that Whyte's corner boys were not delinquents, they were older, and they were much more stable as a group than are adolescent delinquent gangs. When one turns to the narrative materials of the delinquency literature, it comes as a surprise to find how little illumination of group process they provide. For any but the most broadly formulated hypotheses concerning the nature of group life among the boys studied, we find these materials inadequate. By contrast, the strength of *Street Corner Society* lies exactly in the fact that the descriptions are given in such a way that the group process is explicit.

---

search Program supported by Research Grant M-3301 from the Behavioral Science Study Section, National Institutes of Health, Public Health Service, and directed by James F. Short, Jr., at the University of Chicago.

[2] Herbert A. Bloch and Frank T. Flynn, *Delinquency: The Juvenile Offender in America Today* (New York: Random House, 1956), pp. 151–75.

[3] See Albert K. Cohen, *Delinquent Boys: The Culture of the Gang* (Glencoe, Ill.: Free Press, 1955); Albert K. Cohen and James F. Short, Jr., "Research in Delinquent Subcultures," *Journal of Social Issues*, XXIV (1958), 20–37; and Richard A. Cloward and Lloyd E. Ohlin, *Delinquency and Opportunity: A Theory of Delinquent Gangs* (Glencoe, Ill.: Free Press, 1960).

[4] *Street Corner Society* (Chicago: University of Chicago Press, 1943); 2d ed., 1955).

[5] See George Homans, *The Human Group* (New York: Harcourt, Brace & Co., 1950); and George Homans, *Social Behavior: Its Elementary Forms* (New York: Harcourt, Brace & Co., 1961).

One notable instance of experimental research specifically related to delinquency is the investigation of Lippitt, Polansky, Redl, and Rosen in which deliberately frustrated camp boys followed in delinquent activity an impulsive boy who was ordinarily given low rank in the group.[6] These authors did not intend to suggest, however, that the mechanism revealed by this ingenious experiment is the typical process for delinquent groups in their natural setting. Similarly, Polsky and Kohn's description of the process by which "delinquency in its collective form" emerges "out of the interaction of a group of youngsters" within a juvenile correctional institution[7] is not meant to serve as the model for collective delinquency outside of a "total institutional" context.[8]

The closest parallel to our concern with group factors in delinquency outside the context of a camp or treatment institution is Jansyn's study of the social system of a gang with whom he worked as a "detached worker."[9] He found that, for this group of boys, delinquent behavior, on both an individual and a group basis, served to increase the solidarity of the group, and that group leadership and membership varied according to specific group goals being implemented. Further, the boys' perceptions of who was and who was not a member of the group, how large the group was, the importance and even the existence of a conception of "turf" or "territory" were responsive to the situation in which the group found itself.

The shifting character of the group structure that Jansyn describes for the white gang he worked with is present in the white gangs contacted in the present project, and in the Negro gangs as well. Central to our present argument is the proposition that flux in membership and amorphous group boundaries reduces the latitude the leader has in dealing with status threats. But, as the case material

---

[6] Ronald Lippitt, Norman Polansky, Fritz Redl, and Sidney Rosen, "The Dynamics of Power: A Field Study of Social Influence in Groups of Children," in *Readings in Social Psychology*, ed. Eleanor Maccoby, Theodore M. Newcomb, and Eugene S. Hartley (New York: Henry Holt & Co., 1958).

[7] See Howard Polsky, "Changing Delinquent Subcultures: A Social Psychological Approach," reprinted from *Social Work* (October, 1959), pp. 1–15; and Howard Polsky and Martin Kohn, "Participant Observation in a Delinquent Subculture," *American Journal of Orthopsychiatry*, XXIX (October, 1959), 737–51.

[8] Erving Goffman, "On the Characteristics of Total Institutions: The Inmate World," and "Staff-Inmate Relations," in *The Prison: Studies in Institutional Organization and Change*, ed. Donald R. Cressey (New York: Holt, Rinehart & Winston, 1961), chaps. i and ii, pp. 15–106.

[9] Leon Jansyn, "Solidarity and Delinquency in a Street Corner Group: A Study of the Relationship Between Changes in Specified Aspects of Group Structure and Variations in the Frequency of Delinquent Activity" (unpublished Master's thesis, University of Chicago, 1960).

illustrates, the disposition of the threatened leader to use out-group aggression to deal with the threat involves further premises about group norms and the required fluctuation in role behavior by the leader. Eight cases, followed by brief interpretative sections, will be presented.

DETACHED WORKER CASE REPORTS

For a three-year period of the research some 8 to 10 detached workers[10] assigned by the YMCA to highly delinquent gangs were interviewed on a weekly basis. These interviews were reviewed by the research staff and representative selections have been made. In proceeding with the selection, we reasoned somewhat as one would in the review of cases in law. The principle is illustrated as it emerges in different form over the range of specific fact situations that might be encountered with street-corner groups.

Case 1. Duke is the leader of the King Rattlers, a conflict-oriented group of approximately 50 Negro boys, aged 15 to 19, who live on the periphery of a commercial area in the inner city. Duke is a good fighter, having risen to his leadership status in the group by being quick and effective with his fists while, at the same time, playing it very cool. Duke does not get caught. The detached worker reaffirmed Duke's status by working through him and was quickly successful in suppressing intergang fighting. Duke's leadership style capitalizes on his coolness and on his ability to both negotiate in intergang councils and to control his boys.

Despite his coolness, Duke did become implicated in a shooting incident that involved other members of the Rattlers and was sent to jail. The boys eventually "beat the rap," but they were held in detention for two and one-half months. While Duke and the others were absent from "the scene," new officers were "elected" by the worker and the group. It was understood that when Duke returned he would be president again. Upon Duke's return, despite the celebrations attending it, no formal recognition was made of his leadership. It was

---

[10] "Detached work" is a form of service currently being practiced by a number of agencies to reach groups of youth who are ordinarily inaccessible through more conventional channels, such as schools and churches, whose families do not send them to the agencies, and who do not themselves voluntarily come to the agencies. Such workers may be either male or female, depending usually on the sex of the client group, and typically they are young adults. In the YMCA project from which the following cases are drawn, workers are males, aged 25–30. Negro gangs have Negro workers, and white gangs have white workers. Our special thanks go to the staff of the Program for Detached Workers of the YMCA of Metropolitan Chicago for their excellent co-operation and stimulating ideas that have contributed much to the research.

shortly after this that the detached worker with the Rattlers made the following observations in a weekly interview:

A: . . . Duke is acting very unusual. It's not the same Duke.
Q: What's happened?
A: I don't know. I feel maybe it's because he's been in jail and he's trying to release a lot of energy. Maybe after a while, he'll settle down. As of yet he hasn't settled down. He is one of the real instigators in fightin'. They say, "You know, Duke is acting like us now." The boys even notice the difference in him. It isn't just me.
Q: Do they appreciate this or don't they like this?
A: They appreciate it because now they have no more problems. All of them like to fight. If Duke chips in, that's better yet. But they notice the change in him. I keep tellin' Duke, "Be careful, boy, you'll be right back in jail."

The worker then described Duke's behavior at a basketball game which had been scheduled with the Jr. Lords.

A. Duke was calling them "mother fucker," and "The Lords ain't shit." Duke walked up to them—Duke doin' all the talkin'—instigator. Bill next to him and Harry listening. Everybody was listening but Duke, and I was having a problem trying to get Duke down there so he could get himself dressed and leave. Duke walked up and said, "you ain't shit. The Jr. Lords ain't shit. Are you a Jr.?" The boys said, "No." And he said, "A fuckin' old Lord, I'm King Rattler." Duke walked all through all of them, "You ain't shit," trying to get a fight. "Come on, Duke," I said, trying to push him down the stairs. But each time he'd get away and go over there, "You Lords ain't shit . . . we're Rattlers. We're Eastside Rattlers."
Q: Was he drunk?
A: No, he's sober but he's changed. Big change. Bill was watchin' him and goin' along. I told Harry to grab him and told Henry to get Duke and take him. I had to grab him—he wouldn't listen. The rest of the Rattlers wanted to fight too. So I had to take Duke downstairs, and while they were getting their clothes on we had a problem with hats. They wanted the new hats of the other team which they could see on the rack. Duke owns a brown hat, but he had worn a gray one over there. By mistake, I gave him a brown hat which belonged to the Lords. When I saw what had happened, I tried to get it back but no one knew where it was.

The prognosis one would make from the hat and fighting incidents would be one of a growing gap between the detached worker and Duke. Such a gap did not, in fact, materialize. Just a week later, the worker took Duke to a large department store where he secured a job as a messengerboy. Duke's behavior was exemplary. His "strange behavior" did not recur, and he resumed a steadying, essentially non-aggressive and non-delinquent influence on the group.

It is to be noted in the detached worker's report quoted above that the boys approved of Duke's aggressiveness, were willing to fight, and, against the express desires of the detached worker, were willing to help Duke conceal the stolen hat. After this brief period of catering to the most broadly held norms of aggressive behavior, Duke resumed the "cool" image that had distinguished him from the group he led. The Duke incident occurred despite the conscious intention of the detached worker to support Duke's leadership.

It is our interpretation that the tough, highly aggressive, behavior was adopted by Duke to clarify the uncertain leadership situation that had arisen as a result of his detention. In the next case, the status threat arises from a detached worker's failure to understand the previously existing leadership structure.

Case 2. A worker who had been successful in reaching, and in reducing the delinquency of a leadership clique known as the "Big Five," suddenly found that a group of his boys were following another boy in predatory and assaultive delinquency. It developed that this new leader had been in jail during the several months that the worker had been with the group. The worker was only dimly aware of the boy's existence and not at all aware of his former leadership position. Upon release from jail, this boy gathered "lower-echelon" boys about himself and led them in a variety of aggressive delinquencies. This situation was well under way before it was understood by the worker but, when he did turn his attention to the errant group, he brought the aggressive behavior of the subgroup under relative control by "capturing" their leader.

Case 3. A contrasting case involves the return from Army duty of a leader of the Midget Lords, a segment of a large conflict-oriented gang complex known as the "Nation of Lords." It resulted in what we call "The Great Train Robbery."

Johnnie was by far the strongest leader of the Lords. When a new worker was assigned to the group, Johnnie was in the service. The worker was told about Johnnie, however, and upon the latter's return to the group late in the summer of 1960, he was introduced to the worker. The worker was not able to "capture" Johnnie immediately and, in fact, found that he was somewhat uncomfortable with Johnnie and the clique of boys who were most directly involved with him. The worker continued, therefore, to spend the majority of his time with the less delinquent boys who were not Johnnie's immediate followers.

One evening Johnnie and his clique asked the worker to take them "out South" to a party. Figuring that this would at least remove a troublesome element from the area, the worker agreed to the request. Rather than staying with the boys, however, the worker returned to the area where he contacted other members of the Midgets.

On their own return trip, Johnnie and his boys made a spur-of-the moment decision to hold up the car on the elevated train on which they were traveling. They beat one man and took cash from passengers.

If this dramatic demonstration of the toughness and daring had been successful, it would have reaffirmed Johnnie's leadership role in his clique, solidified the subgroup, and, in all probability, have drawn the worker into closer work with Johnnie's clique. The interpretation of this incident in terms of status implications is by no means unequivocal but, since the robbery cannot be understood as the actions of boys rationally oriented toward crime as a way of life, the need for an alternative interpretation is clear.

Case 4. The protagonist, Lawrence, was an influential member of a group for which there was no single and most powerful leader. To maintain his position of influence, Lawrence was required to play a central role in many of the varied activities of the group. The incident in question turned around a "quarter party," which Lawrence was "putting down," primarily out of his embarrassment over having no money. Several of the other chiefs were employed at this time, but Lawrence was not. He deprecated the party and urged the Chiefs to join him in "turning it out," that is, in breaking it up.[11] When the other Chiefs refused to go along with the suggestion despite his urging, Lawrence did not pursue the issue further. Instead, he borrowed money from the worker because, we believe, his position in the group made asking for money from another group member untenable.

During the course of the evening, Big Daddy, another member of the Chiefs, started after a member of the Cobras with a hammer. The detached worker grabbed Lawrence and, in recognition of his status and ability to control the other boys, said, "Look, I don't want no crap. What about you?" Lawrence replied, "Don't worry, ain't gonna be no crap," and proceeded to help the worker bring about order.

If we view Lawrence's threat to turn the party out as a way of "saving face" when his financial dilemma further complicated the status ambiguity attendant upon the entry of a new worker into the group, then the resolution of status ambiguity by the loan and the request from the worker for help may be regarded as having prevented the delinquency.

---

[11] Whyte reports Doc's similar plight, though Doc did not suggest a delinquent way out of his dilemma (see Whyte, *op. cit.*).

The next two cases are parallel. They both involve a detached worker's problem in dealing with a highly aggressive boy who had an established role of instigating delinquent episodes.

Case 5. In the first case, the boy, Commando, was known for his daring and for being in the middle of whatever was happening. When the Lords came together as a fighting group, under pressure from a rival gang who were "wolf-packing" in the area, Commando became one of the boys who was most difficult to control. He instigated trouble in a way that captured attention, and he set a style of violence by sometimes carrying a shotgun.

The worker decided to "put down" Commando in front of the rest of the group by telling him that he really was not tough or brave. He concluded by saying, "You ain't nothin'." Commando reacted by being even more reckless in his actions, particularly when members of the rival group were on the scene. He continued to demonstrate to the group that he was not chicken and that he *was* somebody until the worker ceased his public ridicule.

When the worker shifted to a nurturant relation and impressed Commando privately with his responsibility, as a leader, for curbing conflict, the boy became less aggressive and aided the worker. The worker still feels, however, that in a conflict situation, without a worker present, Commando would find it difficult not to "sell wolf tickets" (i.e., challenge) to rival gang members and instigate conflict. Commando appears not to be motivated to convert status won by aggression to a more stabilized rank in the group.

Case 6. A comparable case involved Bill, a tough and influential member of the Pizza Grill Boys. These boys lived in an area where organized crime was firmly intrenched. The boys stole automobiles, auto parts, and many other articles, hot-rodded their cars, and drank excessively. They were not a fighting gang. The worker with these boys had been an intercollegiate boxing champion and had engaged in a brief professional career as a boxer. He taught Bill and others in the group a great deal about boxing. Bill proceeded to employ these skills in beating up on boys in the area. The worker strongly and publicly reprimanded Bill for doing this, indicating that this behavior was stupid and cowardly rather than brave, tough, and skilled. Bill's subsequent action was to drink excessively and then proceed to get into fights that demonstrated how tough he was.

After winning a fight, Bill did not have the skills to convert the advantage to generalized rank. Cases 5 and 6 both involve inflexibility in role shift after aggression, thus suggesting that flexibility is required if a boy is to cope successfully with leadership demands of groups such as these.

The next case is interesting from two perspectives. First, it indicates that the outcome of competitive sports activities, even when supervised, may release a need for status equilibration that results in overt aggression. Second, it provides a commentary on what the participants understand concerning their own motivation.

Case 7. Gary, one of the three top "influentials" among the King Rattlers, was captain of one of the two pool teams from this gang. The other Rattler team won their division play while Gary's team placed second in their division. In the championship playoffs, Gary's team was eliminated in the first round of play, while the other group, which had advanced to the semifinals, wound up in fourth place. Feelings ran high at the playoffs; and individual and team winners received a great deal of praise.

Gary and his team watched first the finals, then the presentation of the individual trophies to the other team from their gang. The trophies, which were proudly displayed upon the return to the Rattler area, re-emphasized Gary's failure in this formal leadership role. The timing was particularly bad because Gary had emerged as one of two major influentials among the Rattlers since the employment and marriage of Duke, the former leader, who was at this time spending less time with the group. But Gary himself had recently obtained a job and had not spent much time on the streets. Gary had been paid on the day of the tournament and, at the tournament, he had the substantial sum of between $50 and $80 in his pocket. For this reason, the gang, which placed a high value on strong-arming, was not clear whether Gary would continue to lead them in this activity.

Although we should like to have more detailed information we know only that, after the tournament sessions were over, Gary and two members of his team strong-armed a man. The team members held the man and Gary hit him; the take was $18. Gary's subsequent comment to the worker was, "Shit, I wasted my time." This was as far as he could go to explain why he had strong-armed with money in his pocket. He told the worker simply, ". . . saw him walking down the street and just got him—for no reason, just got him."

The salient elements in Gary's case are these: (*a*) he was adept at strong-arming, (*b*) strong-arming was status-conferring in the group, and (*c*) Gary played a crucial role in the incident in question. While these facts are not sufficient to establish the relationship, they are all consistent with the interpretation that Gary's action was specifically related to his need for status reaffirmation following the perceived loss in connection with the pool tournament.

Case 8. On a note of caution, we shall close with an observation concerning a drug-using group of white boys who resisted taking up an invitation to aggressive behavior under highly provocative circumstances. The group was oriented primarily around the use of drugs in pill form, though the boys smoked marijuana heavily, drank excessively, and, when they could afford it (and it was available), used heroin. According to the worker, these boys "looked upon fighting as being 'square.'"

The incident to be reported concerns the summer, 1961, "wade-ins" by Negroes and whites at "white" beaches on Chicago's South Side in protest against the segregation of beach facilities. When the possibility of the "wade-ins" became known to a large white gang from the same area as the drug-users, they immediately took up a battle cry and proceeded to plan the co-ordination of groups in opposition to the "wade-ins." Excitement ran high and they admonished the drug-using group to lend support to the cause. The worker reported that the drug-using group "expressed considerable racial hostility" and "talked about getting into the coming battle," but when the "wade-ins" occurred they chose to separate themselves from the milling hostile crowd that gathered on the beach. Instead, they proceeded to get "high" on pills. While six of them did go to the beach, they chose to sit beneath a tree—at the far end of the beach, away from the "wade-in"—and play cards. In the words of the worker, "they could hardly have been less concerned with who was going to occupy the beach."

These boys, in contrast to previous cases cited, had been urged to fight, with clear insinuations that anyone who did not was "chicken," yet they chose to turn away. Their reaction to this threat was withdrawal from the larger group and participation in activity expressive of the norms which distinguished them from the conflict-oriented boys, namely, drug use. This instance does not involve any separate threat to the leader of this group, for all members seemed to agree easily on the course of action. However, this response, in this situation, suggests that, in groups in which the leader's prestige is bound up in competence at enjoying esoteric "kicks," it may well be doubted that status threat would result in aggressive behavior.

From the practical standpoint of understanding of gang functioning, this reservation may not be important, for it is the observation of our group and other workers that individual boys who adopt strong retreatist adaptations (such as drug use) do not continue as prominent members of large gangs. They drift off into small cliques, and in many cases appear to behave as an isolated individual who moves (without developing strong interpersonal ties) into loci of heightened collective emphasis on retreatist norms. From the theoretical standpoint, this instance suggests a possible dependence between group norms and modes of status reaffirmation and, at the same time, reminds us that there was a high evaluation of aggression in the functioning of the groups from which the other examples were collected. By an extension of this thinking, if one doubts that aggression would confer higher status in retreatist groups, it is also plausible to doubt that aggression would confer higher status in middle-class adolescent groups—though for different reasons.

TARGETS AND FUNCTIONS OF AGGRESSION

Miller and his associates suggest in "Aggression in a Boys' Street-Corner Group" that verbal aggression "was an essential element of behavioral mechanisms which operated to delineate standards of personal worth, to facilitate effective collective functioning, to maintain relations of reciprocity and equality, to define attitudes toward those outside the group and their values, to indicate the *limits* of acceptable behavior and to provide effective sanctions against deviation from group-supported standards."[12] For our groups, also, the level of intragroup aggression in such forms as "body-punching" and "signifying" is high but intragroup dominance-seeking aggressive behavior by gang members, including acknowledged leaders, is not supported by group norms and is rarely resorted to by gang leaders.

Leaders we have observed are cautious not to exercise their leadership arbitrarily, and often overtly disavow that they lead the gangs. The percentage of total activities that are formally organized is low, and leaders are, in general, very careful to obtain clearance from other high-status group members before staking their prestige on a given course of action. We do not, in many cases, know how the original hierarchy of status was established, but clearly it is not maintained by aggressive dominance-seeking by leaders.[13] Except when other boys in the gang directly challenge their status, leaders of even the toughest fighting gangs do not engage in dominating, aggressive interpersonal relationships within the gang. Among conflict gangs the leaders are known to have the capacity to function aggressively against other members when necessary to maintain their dominance, but the overwhelming preponderance of their actions are co-ordinating and nurturant.

DISCUSSION

In Cases 5 and 6, the principals, Commando and Bill, made their bids for attention through aggressive behavior but, when the tension was past, they were not able to shift roles. Neither maintained a

---

[12] Walter B. Miller, Hildred S. Geertz, and Henry S. G. Cutter, "Aggression in a Boys' Street-Corner Group," *Psychiatry*, XXIV (November, 1961), 283–98.

[13] Mandel recently discussed the severe sociometric costs of interpersonally aggressive dominance-seeking among the boarding-school boys he studied. See Rudolf Mandel, *Die Aggressivität bei Schulern: Beobachtung und Analyse des Aggressiven Verhaltens einer Knapengruppe im Pubertätsalter* (Bern and Stuttgart: Verlag Hans Huber, 1959); also Miller et al., ibid.

following. The observation that a good suitor may not make a good husband, or a good campaigner a good president, is applicable in other contexts. It is our thought that similar shifts in system requirements occur with great frequency on the corner. The leaders who persist over long periods, like Duke (Case 1), do have aggressive skills as well as the ability to use them selectively.

The quickened tempo of the testing of relationships on corners, in contrast with, for example, work groups, arises in part because leaders do not control important amounts of property, because there are few privileges or immunities they can bestow, and because there are no external institutional pressures that constrain members to accept the discipline of the gang. Gang membership is very fluid,[14] particularly among fringe members. The leader cannot crassly dominate a person who is dissatisfied with the allocation of rewards within the group because of the effectiveness of the threat of splintering away. The result is that the successful gang leader is surprisingly conciliatory in his corner relations.

The recourse to aggressive behavior toward an out-group object is viewed as being a part of the sensitivity to role requirements. Out-group aggression does not undercut the gratification that membership confers and does not expose the relationship to the threat of splintering. The foray provides excitement, a heightened need for leadership, and a non-disruptive way for the leader to exercise his aggressive skills.

We do not mean to imply that all attempts at status re-equilibration through out-group aggression are successful. Sometimes they are not, and when they are not, the consequences can be grave. Kobrin and Finestone describe a case in which a boy withdrew from the gang and began to smoke marijuana,[15] and another case, known to us by correspondence, resulted in suicide. Most failures are unquestionably less dramatic than these, but a social cost is surely involved.

This formulation has specific explanatory implications that may be illustrated by comparisons with Cloward and Ohlin's comment on the reduction of intergang fighting that comes about when detached workers become associated with gangs:

> The reduction in conflict may reflect the skill of the social workers, but another explanation may be that *the advent of the street-gang worker*

---

[14] Our gangs are definitely not the very fluid near-group phenomena which Yablonsky describes, although we can imagine our boys answering as his respondents did after they were picked up (see Lewis Yablonsky, "The Delinquent Gang as a Near-Group," *Social Problems*, VII [Fall, 1959], 108–17; and Harold W. Pfautz, "Near-Group Theory and Collective Behavior," *Social Problems*, IX [Fall, 1961], 167–74).

[15] Solomon Kobrin and Harold Finestone, "Towards a Framework for the Analysis of Juvenile Delinquency" (paper read at the annual meeting of the American Sociological Association, 1958). (Dittoed.)

symbolized the end of social rejection and the beginning of social accommodation. To the extent that violence represents an effort to win deference, one would logically expect it to diminish once that end has been achieved.[16]

Instead of viewing the presence of the worker solely as symbolic of the interest of the larger society, we would also stress that his presence stabilizes what we have come to call "the leadership structure." And, in so doing, we believe it makes less frequent the need for status-maintaining aggressiveness by leaders. We believe that the gang also recognizes its obligation to the worker as a *quid pro quo* for services performed by the worker and for the additional status within the gang world that accrues to a gang by virtue of their having a worker.[17] Both of these points relate to status-maintaining mechanisms within more immediate systems—the gang itself and the gangs of the area—rather than to the "end of rejection" at the hands of a somewhat amorphous middle-class society.

In conclusion, it is to be emphasized that we do not suppose the usual elementary approval and disapproval mechanisms are absent in the gang situation; it is more that we believe gang leaders to be particularly vulnerable when they try to use negative sanctions to maintain their rank. While we view the hypothesis as plausible, we believe it highly desirable to test it by purposive, experimental intervention in the functioning of on-going groups (e.g., by having a detached worker deliberately frustrate a leader). Because of the serious consequences that might follow from the resulting aggressions, we have not made such attempts with the groups presently under observation.

INTRODUCTORY COMMENTS ON ORCUTT'S RESEARCH

Unfortunately, the dynamic view of deviant behavior as an interactional process afforded by Short and Strodtbeck's study is relatively rare in micro-normative research. One other classic example of this kind of empirical analysis is Howard S. Becker's early work, "Becoming a Marihuana User" (1953). Similar to Short and Strodtbeck, Becker drew upon material from unstructured interviews with marijuana users to discover and illustrate how these individuals initially acquired the techniques and motivations for this deviant activity

---

[16] Cloward and Ohlin, *op. cit.*, p. 176. Their italics.

[17] James F. Short, Jr., "Street Corner Groups and Patterns of Delinquency: A Progress Report from National Institute of Mental Health Research Grant M-3301" (March 1, 1961). (Mimeographed.)

through a process of interaction with more experienced users. Although it was not designed as a test or demonstration of Sutherland's differential association theory, Becker's study confirmed the importance of primary group relationships in the development of this pattern of deviant behavior.

The next research illustration builds upon Becker's work to examine further the utility of Sutherland's differential association theory as an explanation of marijuana use. The data for this report were taken from questionnaire surveys conducted among students at two large universities by the author of this book. In addition to its scientific objectives, the following research illustration has been written to introduce you to some of the methods and problems typically encountered in sociological analyses of survey data. We will be particularly concerned with the ways that researchers attempt to gain insight into the operations and outcomes of social processes when they lack the kind of direct, processual evidence on deviant behavior presented in the exceptional studies by Short and Strodtbeck and by Becker.

RESEARCH ILLUSTRATION 7–B

Marijuana use and social relationships

James D. Orcutt

Social research on marijuana use is commonplace today. However, prior to the 1960s, few social scientists considered this activity to be of much importance as a topic for deviance research. As is so often the case, scholarly disinterest in this phenomenon was a reflection of a general lack of public concern with marijuana use as a social problem in the United States. The passage of state and federal laws initially prohibiting the sale and possession of marijuana in the 1930s provoked little controversy or public interest, and received only brief attention in the mass media (Galliher & Walker, 1977). To be sure, prohibitionist propaganda during that time depicting marijuana as a powerful narcotic and killer drug had been widely accepted as fact. But, as long as strict laws appeared to contain the marijuana habit within the shadowy underworld of jazz musicians and urban minorities, the majority of Americans remained apathetic about this distant menace. Researchers were similarly inclined to insulate themselves from the social world of marijuana smokers. Occasional studies were conducted on captive populations of users who had been committed to prisons or federal hospitals for drug treatment. Not surprisingly, most of these studies ignored the social nature of marijuana use and concentrated, instead, on a search for pathological traits or motivations in the personalities of users that drove them to their "habit."

Considering the times in which it was carried out, Howard S. Becker's (1953; 1963) investigation of the process of becoming a marijuana user seems all the more remarkable. Nearly two decades before marijuana use became defined as a controversial and researchable social problem in the Vietnam era, Becker was able to grasp its significance as an intriguing sociological problem. In contrast to prevailing scientific conceptions of the marijuana habit as an expression of individual pathology, Becker provided a sensitive description of marijuana smoking as a fundamentally social activity shared by normal people. Whereas other early studies have long been forgotten, Becker's insights are still theoretically relevant and consistent with recent evidence on marijuana use.

Becker's account of marijuana use as an interpersonal process has particularly clear implications for a theoretical formulation that has likewise survived over the years, Sutherland's differential association theory (1947). Becker's study not only provides support for differential association theory but also offers valuable guidance for further empirical applications of Sutherland's general framework to the specific phenomenon of marijuana use. Based on Becker's novel answer to the seemingly obvious question, "what is a marijuana user?," an attempt will be made here to test some precise predictions derived from Sutherland's theory about marijuana use and social relationships among college students in the 1970s.

BECKER'S STUDY

Even before he began his research, Becker had a far different outlook on the social world of marijuana users than did other investigators during the 1940s and 1950s. An accomplished and active jazz pianist, Becker had an insider's view of a marginal occupation in which marijuana use was a routine activity (see 1963: 79–119). Many of the marijuana smokers interviewed by Becker were, in fact, jazz musicians with whom he had played or was personally acquainted. Clearly, Becker was in a much better position to observe and understand marijuana use as a normal social process than were researchers whose only contacts with their subjects were in hospital or prison settings. From Becker's perspective, marijuana smokers did not appear as inherently pathological individuals set apart from ordinary people by distinctive traits or deviant motives, but as ordinary people who had successfully acquired the ability to use the drug for pleasure. In order to answer the question of how one *becomes* a marijuana user, then, Becker focused on the social experiences of his respondents rather than on their personalities.

Starting with some of his musician acquaintances who then introduced him to other marijuana users, Becker eventually interviewed 50 people about their interpersonal relationships and histories of marijuana use (1963: 45–46). As these interviews progressed, Becker employed the method of *analytic induction* to arrive at a general, uniform description of the process of becoming a marijuana user. Initial hypotheses and impressions suggested by early interviews were checked out and modified, if necessary, on the basis of later interviews. By the completion of his interviewing, Becker had identified three basic steps or stages that *every* person in his sample had undergone when first learning to use marijuana for pleasure. Most importantly, Becker found that social interaction between the new user and more experienced users was essential for the accomplishment of each stage in this learning process.

First, the new user must *learn the technique* of smoking marijuana properly. Becker's respondents usually did not experience any effects from marijuana the first time they tried it. He concluded that one of the main reasons for this is that a novice user does not know how to smoke and inhale the drug "in a way that insures sufficient dosage to produce real symptoms of intoxication" (1963: 46). All of the respondents reported that, either through direct teaching or by observation and imitation, they learned the proper technique from more experienced users.

Second, once new users could smoke marijuana properly, they had to *learn to perceive the effects* of the drug. As Becker points out (1963: 49), the pharmacological actions or "symptoms" produced by marijuana "do not automatically provide the experience of being high." A person must also be able to notice these symptoms, to associate them with the drug, and to interpret them as a high. However, the novice user is initially unable to do this and typically reacts as follows (1963: 49–50):

> His failure to get high worries him, and he is likely to ask more experienced users or provoke comments from them about it. In such conversations he is made aware of specific details of his experience which he may not have noticed or may have noticed but failed to identify as symptoms of being high. . . . The novice . . . picks up from other users some concrete referents of the term "high" and applies these notions to his own experience.

Whereas the first stage in Becker's learning process involved *physical techniques* for smoking marijuana, this stage involves the social acquisition of *subjective techniques* necessary for the perception of effects. Interactionally shared conceptions of the marijuana high function as tools that enable the novice to identify, organize, and give meaning to his or her subjective experiences. In the same sense that a person who cannot smoke the drug properly does not become a marijuana user, a person who cannot learn the subjective techniques for perceiving a high does not succeed in becoming a marijuana user. For Becker's respondents, both of these steps were socially accomplished through participation and interaction in marijuana-using groups.

Finally, having acquired the ability to get something from the drug, the new user must also *learn to enjoy the effects* that are experienced. There is nothing intrinsically pleasurable about sensations of numbness or dizziness; altered perceptions of music or time are not necessarily enjoyable. For many of Becker's respondents, in fact, the newly discovered effects of marijuana were downright frightening. Unless the novice can somehow redefine these ambiguous and anxiety-provoking experiences as pleasurable, the motivation to become a user will be lacking. Becker (1963: 54–55) found that this redefinition occurs socially,

> in interaction with more experienced users who, in a number of ways, teach the novice to find pleasure in this experience which is at first so frightening. They may reassure [the novice] as to the temporary character of the unpleasant sensations and minimize their seriousness, at the same time calling attention to the more enjoyable aspects.

That is, to the extent that "favorable definitions of the experience that one acquires from others" can alter or outweigh feelings of discomfort or anxiety, the novice will become motivated to use marijuana for pleasure (1963: 56). Continued use will be possible as long as the user maintains this positive, socially defined conception of the marijuana high.

What, then, is a marijuana user? For Becker, only a person who has become *able* and *willing* to get high on the drug has reached the point of *being* a user. Use of marijuana for pleasure is not possible for those who have failed to acquire the techniques and motivations necessary for that experience. While pharmacological factors such as the dosage or strength of the drug affect the symptoms of intoxication, Becker makes it clear that the user's ability to fashion an enjoyable marijuana high from these raw materials is essentially a socially acquired skill.

MARIJUANA USE AND DIFFERENTIAL ASSOCIATION THEORY

Viewed within the immediate context of research on marijuana use, Becker's study represented a substantial advance beyond other early work on this topic. However, we will mainly be concerned here with some broader implications of Becker's analysis for sociological theorizing on deviant behavior. Among other things, his three-stage description of the social process of becoming a marijuana user clearly demonstrates the empirical relevance of Sutherland's differential association theory (1947; Sutherland & Cressey, 1974) to at least one form of norm-violating behavior. For instance, Becker's findings are completely in accord with the basic position presented in the first three statements of Sutherland's micro-normative explanation (1974: 75): (1) individual deviant behavior is *learned* (2) through *interpersonal interaction* (3) within *intimate personal groups*. More importantly, Becker provides detailed empirical insights into the two major *products* of social learning that are subsequently distinguished in the fourth statement of Sutherland's theory: (*a*) "techniques of committing" the deviant act and (*b*) "motives, drives, rationalizations, and attitudes" that support the act. On the one hand, the first two stages of Becker's processual model confirm that techniques for getting high must be acquired from other people before one can be a user. On the other hand, Becker shows that the socially learned motive of enjoyment is a distinct but equally necessary requirement for marijuana use.

Additional motives, rationalizations, and attitudes that affect an individual's use of marijuana receive attention in another report from Becker's research, "Marijuana Use and Social Control" (1963: 59–78). A person who has *become* a user must still come to grips with questions of the illegality or immorality of the act in deciding whether to continue doing it. Just like many people who never try the drug in the first place, a beginner may discontinue use out of concern with being caught or because of fears inspired by conventional moral viewpoints on marijuana. Here, too, Becker found that social interaction with other users was the key factor in overcoming these moral and legal barriers (1963: 74):

> In the course of further experience in drug-using groups, the novice acquires a series of rationalizations and justifications with which he may answer objections to occasional use if he decides to engage in it.

The beginner learns to define the risk of arrest or discovery by nonusers as minimal. Moral stereotypes about the dangers of becoming a dope fiend are seen as groundless and are replaced by positive attitudes toward the drug. Becker summarizes the net result of this socially induced change in the individual's attitudes and definitions in the final sentence of his report (1963: 78):

> a person will feel free to use marijuana to the degree that he comes to regard conventional conceptions of it as the uninformed views of outsiders and replaces those conceptions with the "inside" view he has acquired through his experience with the drug in the company of other users.

Thus, Becker reaches a conclusion that seems to confirm the central principle of Sutherland's differential association theory (1974: 75-76): "A person becomes [deviant] because of an excess of definitions favorable to violation of law over definitions unfavorable to violation of law."

Despite the apparent consistency of his evidence with differential association theory, Becker never explicitly links his findings to Sutherland's general explanation of deviance. Becker's disinclination to view his research as a test of differential association might reflect his dissatisfaction with the *deterministic* approach of Sutherland's theory (see Matza, 1969: 101-142). Becker's theoretical goal is to provide an interpretive understanding of marijuana use as a choice that is made possible—not inevitable—by the techniques and social definitions that one learns from others. Becker does imply, of course, that *nonuse* of marijuana is assured or determined by the *absence* of these necessary social and subjective conditions. Can the *use* of marijuana be explained with equal certainty given the *presence* of a sufficient excess of associations and definitions favorable to the act? This is a legitimate and empirically testable implication of Sutherland's theory. We will examine this and other important questions raised by Becker and Sutherland following a brief discussion of the self-report surveys from which the data for this study were taken.

SURVEY METHODS

Samples

The survey data for this report were obtained from questionnaires administered to samples of undergraduate students at two large state universities, University of Minnesota and Florida State University (FSU). The Minnesota survey was conducted during winter quarter 1972 while the FSU survey was carried out during spring quarter 1973.

The procedures for sampling and administering questionnaires to students in the two surveys were similar in many respects. Neither sample was selected randomly or through other probability techniques. Rather, questionnaires were administered to students attending regular meetings of undergraduate courses that had been purposely selected to cover all the major colleges in the universities and to include students at all four class levels. Thus, these samples were diverse, but not necessarily representative, cross sections of the undergraduate populations at the two schools.

To prevent an abnormal drop in attendance on the day that questionnaires were administered to a class, instructors were asked not to make a prior announcement of the survey. However, students attending class on the day of the survey were informed that their participation was voluntary and that their answers would be strictly confidential. Of the undergraduates attending classes on the days questionnaires were administered, 92 percent completed questionnaires at Minnesota while a 97 percent completion rate was obtained at FSU.

At each university, two slightly different versions of the basic questionnaire were distributed alternately to students in each class. Half of the students filled out a version—the Alcohol Form—that dealt with drinking behavior and attitudes toward alcohol. The other half of each class completed the Marijuana Form, which was identical to the first version except for appropriate changes in the wording of items to ask about marijuana use and attitudes toward that drug. Only data from students who completed the Marijuana Form at each school are used in this report. Thus, the analyses below will be based on 460 Minnesota undergraduates and 544 Florida State University undergraduates.

Measures

We will focus on three variables that are crucial to an evaluation of differential association theory: (1) social relationships with users or nonusers of marijuana, (2) definitions favorable or unfavorable to use, and (3) personal use of marijuana to get high. The Minnesota and FSU questionnaires included virtually identical measures of each of these three variables.

The dependent variable for this study, *marijuana use,* was measured by the following item at both schools:

> Which of the following statements best describes the approximate number of times you have gotten "high" on marijuana during the past year?
> 1. I did not use marijuana during the past year.
> 2. I used marijuana during the past year but did not get "high."
> 3. I got "high" on marijuana during the past year but only once or twice.
> 4. I got "high" on marijuana at least 3 times during the past year, but not more than 12 times.
> 5. I got "high" on marijuana more than 12 times during the past year.

An important feature of this item is that it measures a respondent's self-reported ability to get high, which is, for Becker (1953), a defining characteristic of a marijuana user. Therefore, according to Becker's conception, respondents who checked *either* of the first two statements should be classified as *nonusers*. Indeed, for many of the analyses below, responses to this item will be combined or collapsed into two broad categories, nonusers (statements 1 or 2) versus users (statements 3, 4, or 5), distinguishing respondents who did not get high from those who did.

Sutherland, of course, places special emphasis on social relationships or associations in primary groups as a causal or independent variable in deviant behavior. In both the Minnesota and FSU surveys, the following item was used to measure respondents' degrees of participation in deviant or nondeviant relationships: "Of your *four closest friends,* how many would you say use marijuana at least once a month?: (1) One; (2) Two; (3) Three; (4) Four; (5) None." Note that this question measures respondents' *perceptions* of their friends rather than the *actual* extent of marijuana use by friends. Later, we will consider some possible problems that may be involved in the use of this indirect, perceptual measure of respondents' associations with patterns of marijuana use in primary groups.

Finally, to obtain a general measure of the favorable (or unfavorable) definitions that Becker and Sutherland see to be a necessary condition for marijuana use, respondents were asked the following question: "How would you generally characterize your opinions toward marijuana?" Responses to this question were recorded on a five-point scale that ranged from highly positive to highly negative at Minnesota and from positive to negative at FSU. The midpoint of these Likert-type scales was undecided in both surveys. In the analyses below, responses to this item will be collapsed into three categories describing respondents' overall definitions as positive, neutral, or negative.

RESULTS

Response distributions by sample

An appropriate place to begin an analyses of these survey data is by comparing the responses of the Minnesota and FSU students to the items discussed above. Table 1 shows how these samples compare on the dependent variable, marijuana use, as it was originally measured and as it has been collapsed here according to the absence or presence of the marijuana high. Quite clearly, marijuana use was more widespread among the FSU students in 1973 than among the Minnesota students in 1972. Based on responses to the original questionnaire item, slightly more than three out of five (60.8 percent) Minnesota respondents did not even try marijuana during the past year, while less than half of the FSU sample (46.4 percent) fell in this

Table 1
Response distributions by sample for marijuana use as originally measured and as collapsed into a two-category variable

	Marijuana use as originally measured					
Sample	Did not use	Used, but not high	High 1–2 times	High 3–12 times	High 12+ times	Total
Minnesota (1972)	60.8% (278)	5.0% (23)	10.7% (49)	10.9% (50)	12.5% (57)	100.0% (457)
Florida State University (1973)	46.4% (252)	6.1% (33)	8.5% (46)	11.4% (62)	27.6% (150)	100.0% (543)

Somers' $d = .18$

	Marijuana use as collapsed variable		
	First two categories in original measure combined	Last three categories in original measure combined	
Sample	Nonuser	User	Total
Minnesota (1972)	65.9% (301)	34.1% (156)	100.0% (457)
Florida State University (1973)	52.5% (285)	47.5% (258)	100.0% (543)

Somers' $d = .13$

category. At the other extreme, FSU students were twice as likely as Minnesota respondents (27.6 percent versus 12.5 percent) to report having gotten high more than 12 times during the past year. In the bottom half of Table 1 where the first and second categories of the original measure are collapsed into a more general class of nonusers, we find that nearly two thirds of the Minnesota respondents (65.9 percent) did not get high as compared to slightly more than half of the FSU respondents (52.5 percent).

Such comparisons of percentage differences in Table 1 do indicate that there is a statistical relationship between sample and marijuana use—i.e., being an FSU student is associated with increased chances of use. However, some important questions are difficult to answer by simply comparing percentages. How *strong* are the relationships between sample and marijuana use in the two percentage or contingency tables shown in Table 1? Is the statistical relationship between these variables strengthened or weakened when marijuana use is treated as a collapsed, two-category variable? To aid in answering these and other questions about the overall strength and nature of

Table 2
Response distributions by sample for number of respondent's four closest friends who use marijuana

	Number of friends who use marijuana					
Sample	0	1	2	3	4	Total
Minnesota (1972)	46.2% (212)	19.0% (87)	14.2% (65)	8.5% (39)	12.2% (56)	100.0% (459)
Florida State University (1973)	31.4% (171)	17.5% (95)	13.8% (75)	14.3% (78)	23.0% (125)	100.0% (544)
		Somers' $d = .21$				

relationships between variables, survey analysts typically use various *measures of association*. One such measure, Somers' d (see Somers, 1962; Reynolds, 1977), is reported beneath the two sections of Table 1 and in later tables. This measure of association for ranked or ordinal variables will be useful in comparing the relative strengths of relationships in different percentage tables. For instance, the weak to moderate $d = .18$ in the top half of Table 1 decreases in strength (get closer to zero) to $d = .13$ for the relationship where marijuana use is in two categories. Thus, a comparison of these measures of association shows that when some information is lost by collapsing the dependent variable, the statistical relationship between sample and marijuana use is weakened.

Tables 2 and 3 show how the Minnesota and FSU samples compare on responses to the two independent variables: number of friends who use and definition of marijuana. Not surprisingly, Minnesota respondents tend to have fewer friends who use and more negative definitions of the drug than do the FSU respondents. As revealed in Table 2, nearly half of the Minnesota sample (46.2 percent) reported

Table 3
Response distributions by sample for respondent's definition of marijuana

	Definition of marijuana			
Sample	Negative	Neutral	Positive	Total
Minnesota (1972)	47.5% (213)	15.4% (69)	37.1% (166)	100.0% (448)
Florida State University (1973)	38.2% (208)	12.1% (66)	49.6% (270)	100.0% (544)
	Somers' $d = .12$			

having *no* close friends who use, while less than one third of the FSU respondents (31.4 percent) reported a similar lack of close social relationships with marijuana users. At the other extreme, almost twice the proportion of FSU students as Minnesota students (23.0 percent versus 12.2 percent) indicated that *all* of their four closest friends use marijuana at least once a month. Likewise in Table 3, the proportion of respondents endorsing positive definitions of marijuana increases from 37 percent in the Minnesota sample to virtually half (49.6 percent) of the FSU sample.

Relationship between friends' use and respondents' use

The preceding comparisons of responses to single items across samples are of less theoretical interest and importance than are relationships between the independent variables and marijuana use. In this section we will examine one of the major empirical relationships implied by differential association theory: *friends' use of marijuana should be strongly and positively related to one's own use of marijuana*. A number of previous survey investigations have found support for this generalization (see, for example, Goode, 1970; Johnson, 1973; Kandel, 1978; Akers et al., 1979; Andrews & Kandel, 1979). The present study is no exception. Table 4 reveals that as the perceived number of marijuana-using friends increases from 0 to 4 in each sample, the percentages of respondents classified as users according to Becker's criterion also increase dramatically. Of those respondents who reported having *no* close friends who use marijuana, over 9 out of 10 at both Minnesota (95.2 percent) and FSU (91.2 percent) are themselves nonusers. This contrasts markedly with respondents whose four closest friends *all* use marijuana. In the latter category, approximately 88 percent of the Minnesota respondents and 94 percent of the FSU respondents are users. Therefore, in those cases where this pattern of deviant behavior is overwhelmingly *absent or present* among one's primary group associations, the individual's own behavior can be predicted with a high degree of certainty.

The results in Table 4 also point to an interesting and theoretically significant limitation of differential association as an explanation of deviant behavior. As Sutherland himself pointed out (in Cohen et al., 1956: 40), the differential association "hypothesis becomes increasingly uncertain in its operation" as the ratio of associations with deviant and nondeviant patterns "approaches unity." That is, in those cases where a person's associations with patterns of marijuana use are approximately equal to or balanced by associations with patterns of nonuse, Sutherland's theory cannot make a prediction and the chances that the individual will be a user or nonuser should be

Table 4
Marijuana use (collapsed) by number of closest friends who use marijuana within samples

	Sample and number of friends who use marijuana				
	Minnesota (1972)				
Marijuana use (collapsed)	0	1	2	3	4
Nonuser	95.2% (199)	64.4% (56)	46.2% (30)	23.1% (9)	12.5% (7)
User	4.8% (10)	35.6% (31)	53.8% (35)	76.9% (30)	87.5% (49)
Total	100.0% (209)	100.0% (87)	100.0% (65)	100.0% (39)	100.0% (56)
		Somers' d = .47			
	Florida State University (1973)				
	0	1	2	3	4
Nonuser	91.2% (155)	70.5% (67)	42.7% (32)	29.5% (23)	6.4% (8)
User	8.8% (15)	29.5% (28)	57.3% (43)	70.5% (55)	93.6% (117)
Total	100.0% (170)	100.0% (95)	100.0% (75)	100.0% (78)	100.0% (125)
		Somers' d = .48			

roughly 50/50. This argument would apply to respondents in the middle category of Table 4 who have two close friends who use and two who do not use. As the results show, these respondents are, in fact, fairly evenly split between nonusers and users at both Minnesota (46.2 percent versus 53.8 percent) and FSU (42.7 percent versus 57.3 percent).

The overall strength of the relationship between friends' use and respondents' use is indicated within each sample in Table 4 by Somers' d. The values of d within the Minnesota sample (d = .47) and the FSU sample (d = .48) not only reflect a strong, positive relationship in each case but these measures of association are also remarkably similar in magnitude. In other words, the empirical relationship between friends' use and respondents' use that was initially observed in the 1972 Minnesota survey is almost exactly *replicated* in the 1973 FSU survey. The fact that this finding is so consistent or reliable across two surveys conducted at different times in different populations increases confidence in the generality of this relationship and adds further support to Sutherland's theory.

Friends' use, respondents' use, and definitions of marijuana

Although the evidence in Table 4 is important to an assessment of Sutherland's theory, we should remember Cressey's (1960) argument that differential association is not simply a bad companions explanation of deviant behavior. In fact, the variable that Sutherland identifies as the immediate determinant of norm-violating behavior is the ratio of favorable and unfavorable definitions held by the individual toward the deviant act. As Becker's research suggested, once a person has learned from others the necessary techniques for smoking marijuana and perceiving its effects, the decision to put these techniques to use depends ultimately on whether positive meanings are attached to the drug experience. Again, both Becker and Sutherland imply that a person whose general definition of the drug is unfavorable or negative will not become a user no matter how many close social relationships he or she has with marijuana smokers. In contrast, individuals with predominantly positive definitions of marijuana should be more readily influenced by primary group associations with marijuana users. Therefore, according to this line of argument, the empirical relationship between respondents' use and friends' use should *vary in strength within different categories of the mediating variable, definition of marijuana.*

These conditional or contingent relationships and other empirical implications of Sutherland's theory can be examined through the three-way classification of respondents by friends' use, own use, and definition of marijuana presented in Table 5. The Minnesota and FSU samples have been combined in this analysis in order to increase the number of respondents in each cell of the three-variable classification. Percentage comparisons and other results can be very misleading and unreliable when a substantial number of cells in such complex tables are empty or contain very few cases.

The top third of Table 5 shows the relationship between friends' use and own use among those respondents who hold *negative* definitions of marijuana. As expected within this particular category of definition, the percentage of users does not change substantially as number of friends using marijuana increases. Respondents who, coupled with their negative definitions of the drug, have *no* close friends using marijuana do stand out somewhat in that they are virtually certain to be nonusers (97.4 percent). This is not surprising since these particular respondents lack both the favorable definitions and the interpersonal opportunities for learning the techniques that are

Table 5
Marijuana use (collapsed) by number of closest friends who use within categories of respondent's definition of marijuana for Minnesota and FSU samples combined

	Definition of marijuana and number of friends who use				
	Negative definition				
Marijuana use (collapsed)	0	1	2	3	4
Nonuser	97.4% (258)	85.2% (69)	77.5% (31)	81.8% (18)	33.3% (3)
User	2.6% (7)	14.8% (12)	22.5% (9)	18.2% (4)	66.7% (6)
Total	100.0% (265)	100.0% (81)	100.0% (40)	100.0% (22)	100.0% (9)
	Somers' $d = .17$				
	Neutral definition				
	0	1	2	3	4
Nonuser	91.4% (53)	76.3% (29)	50.0% (11)	50.0% (5)	42.9% (3)
User	8.6% (5)	23.7% (9)	50.0% (11)	50.0% (5)	57.1% (4)
Total	100.0% (58)	100.0% (38)	100.0% (22)	100.0% (10)	100.0% (7)
	Somers' $d = .27$				
	Positive definition				
	0	1	2	3	4
Nonuser	74.0% (37)	38.7% (24)	23.0% (17)	10.7% (9)	5.5% (9)
User	26.0% (13)	61.3% (38)	77.0% (57)	89.3% (75)	94.5% (156)
Total	100.0% (50)	100.0% (62)	100.0% (74)	100.0% (84)	100.0% (165)
	Somers' $d = .29$				

necessary to become a marijuana user. However, other respondents who have one, two, or even three close friends who use are only slightly more likely to report behavior that is inconsistent with their own negative definitions, with roughly four out of five students in these three categories being classified as nonusers. A greater tendency to use appears to characterize respondents with four close friends who use; but it is important to note that this category includes a total of only nine respondents holding negative definitions of marijuana and a shift of just three cases could completely reverse the current proportions of users and nonusers. Nonetheless, with this one questionable exception, the results in the top third of Table 5 indicate that a negative definition of marijuana is generally sufficient to deter use even when many friends engage in this pattern of behavior. The relatively weak Somers' $d = .17$ for the relationship between friends' use and own use bears out this conclusion about the overriding influence of negative definitions.

Moving to the bottom third of Table 5 and focusing on respondents who hold *positive* definitions of marijuana, we find further evidence of the contingent relationships predicted by differential association theory. Respondents who have no close friends who use are still unlikely to be users despite their own positive definitions of marijuana. Since persons having no user friends lack the necessary interpersonal opportunities to learn the techniques to get high, the fact that three out of four respondents in this category did not get high is quite consistent with Becker and Sutherland. Significantly, the presence of just one close friend who uses marijuana is associated with a dramatic increase in the proportion of users among respondents with positive definitions of the drug (26.0 percent for zero friends versus 61.3 percent for one friend). That is, students with positive definitions are able to act on their willingness to get high when at least one friend can introduce them to the necessary techniques for smoking and perceiving effects. As expected, each increase in the proportion of one's friends that use is accompanied by an increase in the percentage of marijuana users among respondents with positive definitions, with use being virtually certain (94.5 percent) in the final category of four marijuana using friends. Under the condition of positive definition, then, a rather substantial empirical relationship remains between friends' use and respondents' use of marijuana (Somers' $d = .29$).

Finally, the results in the middle third of Table 5 for respondents with a *neutral* definition (i.e., undecided) of marijuana are very interesting. As was the case with other definitional categories, respondents with no close friends who use are highly unlikely to be users of marijuana (8.6 percent). This finding suggests, again, that the absence of interpersonal opportunities for learning is almost sufficient to insure nonuse of the drug. The presence of one friend who uses does increase the likelihood of use among neutral respondents (23.7 percent), but not nearly to the extent that it did among positive respondents. However, it is the results for respondents with two, three, or four close friends who use that are most intriguing. As long as respondents' personal definitions of marijuana are neutral, their chance of becoming a marijuana user does not appear to increase beyond 50/50, even when every one of their closest friends are users. Although this finding was not anticipated and is based on a relatively small number of cases, it highlights another implication of Sutherland's theory: when there is no excess of favorable or unfavorable definitions, the theory yields no prediction, and the chances of deviant or nondeviant behavior should generally be equiprobable or 50/50. Therefore, as Table 5 indicates, increased social participation with marijuana users beyond the minimum amount necessary for learning techniques will not have an impact as long as the immediate determinant of marijuana use—definition—is neutral or balanced.

DISCUSSION AND CONCLUSION

On the surface, the differences between this study and Becker's (1963) are striking. The data presented here were gathered nearly a quarter of a century after his—a quarter of a century that witnessed dramatic changes in the extent and control of marijuana use in the United States. The middle-class college students surveyed for this research typically move in quite different social worlds than did the jazz musicians and other "outsiders" contacted by Becker. Above all, this quantitative analysis of three questionnaire items stands at the opposite extreme methodologically from Becker's insightful, qualitative analysis of the rich and detailed accounts of marijuana use provided by his informants.

Yet, when viewed from the abstract theoretical perspective of differential association, the differences between these studies become less prominent than do the common implications of their results. Both studies amply justify the emphasis that Sutherland (1947) placed on primary group relationships as the principal source of individual deviant behavior. Less vividly than Becker but, perhaps, more precisely, this study has revealed the particular importance of having at least one close acquaintance from whom one can learn the necessary techniques to get high on marijuana. Of all the students in both samples who reported that none of their close friends were monthly users of marijuana, less than 7 percent indicated that they had gotten high during the past year. This small percentage would undoubtedly have been even lower if the survey measure of friends' use had been more restrictive and had made it possible to identify respondents who were *never* exposed to patterns of marijuana use in their primary group relationships.

The more subjective side of differential association theory—the "motives, drives, rationalizations, and attitudes" discussed by Sutherland as immediate determinants of deviant behavior—emerged as a crucial factor in this study as it did in Becker's work. Just as Sutherland's theory and Becker's analysis of the third stage of enjoyment implied, very few individuals who held a negative definition of marijuana reported having gotten high during the past year. While an excess of negative definitions strongly discouraged use even when a number of one's friends used marijuana, positive definitions of the drug were found to lead to the opposite result. Under the condition that individuals held positive definitions of marijuana, social relationships with other users were clearly associated with increasing chances of getting high.

Perhaps the most impressive demonstration of the predictive power of differential association theory appears in two corner cells of Table 5 where the combined effects of social relationships and subjective definition are strongest. In the upper left-hand corner of this table, over 97 percent of the students holding negative definitions and having zero close friends who use report that they were nonusers of marijuana. However, when these two factors switch to the opposite extreme in the bottom right-hand corner of Table 5—i.e., positive definition and all four closest friends use—nearly 95 percent of the respondents report having been users. The virtually perfect predictions in these two cases would seem to add credence to Sutherland's implicit assumption that deviant (as well as nondeviant) behavior is *determined* by the associations and definitions with which persons come into contact in their social environment. This implication is, of course, inconsistent with Becker's interpretive, insider's conception of marijuana use as a *choice* that one acquires socially but exercises *freely*. This study certainly cannot resolve these alternative views of human nature; however, the results in Table 5 indicate that the choice to use or not to use marijuana is highly predictable, if not strictly determined, under certain conditions specified by Sutherland.

As noted earlier, a number of previous surveys have provided similar evidence for the ability of differential association theory to explain much of the statistical variation in marijuana use among young people (Johnson, 1973; Kandel, 1973; 1974; 1978; Krohn, 1974; Burkett & Jensen, 1975; Griffin & Griffin, 1978; Ginsberg & Greenley, 1978; Thomas et al., 1975). Unlike other investigations in this area, however, the current study has also focused on the special circumstances under which the theory should be *incapable* of yielding a clearcut statistical prediction. Two cases were examined that seem to approximate Sutherland's hypothetical condition of "unity" or balance in the ratio of deviant and nondeviant associations (in Cohen et al., 1956: 30–41). First, when an individual's four closest friends were evenly divided between users and nonusers, the respondent's own chances of being a user were only slightly better than the even odds of 50/50. Second, the odds of being a user remained exactly even among students with a majority of marijuana-using friends as long as their own definition of the drug was undecided or neutral. Thus, in these special cases where there appears to be no excess of deviant or nondeviant associations or definitions, differential association theory predicts an individual's use of marijuana no better than does a random toss of a coin. In short, Sutherland's critical speculation about the limitations of his own theory seems to be born out by these survey data.

Yet, this study itself has some significant limitations that warrant caution in making inferences to Sutherland's theory from results presented here. As in other self-report surveys of drug use, there is reason for concern about the validity and reliability of the single-item indicators used to measure concepts in Sutherland's framework (see Single et al., 1975). In particular, respondents' answers to the question about their best friends' use of marijuana may not only have involved unreliable guesswork but also systematic error introduced by a tendency to make perceptions of others' use consistent with one's own use. Since this systematic perceptual bias could account for at least some of the statistical relationships reported here, additional research measuring the actual use of marijuana among respondents' primary group associates is needed to increase confidence in the findings of this study (see, for example, Kandel, 1973; 1974; 1978).

Inferences about time-order or direction of causality between the variables in this study are unjustified since the data from the two student surveys are *cross-sectional* and the results are merely *correlational*. That is, measures of all three variables were gathered from each student respondent at a single point in time, making it impossible to determine the sequence or timing of changes in those variables. Therefore, to repeat an example used earlier in this chapter, there is no way to determine from these data which came first, marijuana-using "bad companions" or one's personal use of the drug. Several *longitudinal* surveys—that measure these variables at two or more points in time—have tended to support the time order implied by Sutherland's theory: (1) association with marijuana-using friends precedes the onset of one's own use (Kandel, 1978; Ginsberg & Greenley, 1978) and (2) favorable definitions of the drug precede initiation of marijuana use (Andrews & Kandel, 1979). However, other studies in addition to Becker's suggest that this mechanical sequence does not adequately or accurately convey the complex, processual relationships between marijuana use, social definitions, and group participation (Heise, 1977; Zimmerman & Wieder, 1977; also see Britt & Campbell, 1977).

These and other shortcomings of this study can also be found to a greater or lesser degree in virtually all sociological investigations of marijuana use since Becker's groundbreaking work. Taken as a whole, however, research in this area has, despite its imperfections, provided considerable support for Sutherland's general perspective on deviant behavior. As this report has attempted to show, research on marijuana use and social relationships is one area where empirical work can have an important bearing on the growth of theoretical knowledge.

REFERENCES

Akers, Ronald L., Marvin D. Krohn, Lonn Lanza-Kaduce and Marcia Radosevich
    1979 "Social learning and deviant behavior: A specific test of a general theory." *American Sociological Review* 44 (August): 636–655.

Andrews, Kenneth H. and Denise B. Kandel
    1979 "Attitude and behavior: A specification of the contingent consistency hypothesis." *American Sociological Review* 44 (April): 298–310.

Becker, Howard S.
    1963 *Outsiders: Studies in the Sociology of Deviance.* New York: Free Press.
    1953 "Becoming a marihuana user." *American Journal of Sociology* 59 (November): 235–243.

Britt, David W. and Ernest Q. Campbell
    1977 "Assessing the linkage of norms, environments, and deviance." *Social Forces* 56 (December): 532–550.

Burkett, Steven R. and Eric L. Jensen
    1975 "Conventional ties, peer influence, and the fear of apprehension: A study of adolescent marijuana use." *Sociological Quarterly* 16 (Autumn): 522–533.

Cohen, Albert K., Alfred Lindesmith and Karl Schuessler (eds.)
    1956 *The Sutherland Papers.* Bloomington: Indiana University Press.

Cressey, Donald R.
    1960 "Epidemiology and individual conduct: A case from criminology." *Pacific Sociological Review* 3 (Fall): 47–54.

Galliher, John F. and Allynn Walker
    1977 "The puzzle of the social origins of the marihuana tax act of 1937." *Social Problems* 24 (February): 367–376.

Ginsberg, Irving J. and James R. Greenley
    1978 "Competing theories of marijuana use: A longitudinal study." *Journal of Health and Social Behavior* 19 (March): 22–34.

Goode, Erich
    1970 *The Marijuana Smokers.* New York: Basic Books.

Griffin, Brenda S. and Charles T. Griffin
    1978 "Marijuana use among students and peers." *Drug Forum* 7: 155–165.

Heise, David
    1977 "Group dynamics and attitude-behavior relations." *Sociological Methods and Research* 5: 259–288.

Johnson, Bruce D.
    1973 *Marihuana Users and Drug Subcultures.* New York: Wiley.

Kandel, Denise B.
    1978 *Longitudinal Research on Drug Use: Empirical Findings and Methodological Issues.* Washington: Hemisphere-Wiley.

1974 "Inter- and intragenerational influences on adolescent marijuana use." *Journal of Social Issues* 30: 107–135.
1973 "Adolescent marihuana use: Role of parents and peers." *Science* 181 (September 14): 1067–1070.

Krohn, Marvin D.
1974 "An investigation of the effect of parental and peer associations on marijuana use: An empirical test of differential association theory." Pp. 75–89 in Marc Reidel and Terrence P. Thornberry (eds.), *Crime and Delinquency: Dimensions of Deviance.* New York: Praeger.

Matza, David
1969 *Becoming Deviant.* Englewood Cliffs, N.J.: Prentice-Hall.

Reynolds, H. T.
1977 *The Analysis of Cross-Classifications.* New York: Free Press.

Single, Eric, Denise Kandel and Bruce D. Johnson
1975 "The reliability and validity of drug use responses in a large scale longitudinal survey." *Journal of Drug Issues* 5 (Fall): 426–443.

Somers, Robert H.
1962 "A new asymmetric measure for ordinal variables." *American Sociological Review* 27 (October): 799–811.

Sutherland, Edwin H.
1947 *Principles of Criminology* (4th ed.). Philadelphia: Lippincott.

Sutherland, Edwin H. and Donald R. Cressey
1974 *Criminology* (9th ed.). Philadelphia: Lippincott.

Thomas, Charles W., David M. Petersen and Matthew T. Zingraff
1975 "Student drug use: A re-examination of the 'hang-loose ethic' hypothesis." *Journal of Health and Social Behavior* 16 (March): 63–73.

Zimmerman, Don H. and D. Lawrence Wieder
1977 "You can't help but get stoned: Notes on the social organization of marijuana smoking." *Social Problems* 25 (December): 198–207.

INTRODUCTORY COMMENTS ON GOVE AND GEERKEN'S RESEARCH

Over the past 30 years, the sociological literature on crime and delinquency has become heavily populated with analyses of self-report data like Orcutt's or Erlanger's in Chapter 5 (see Tittle et al., 1978). Although critics have pointed out some significant limitations of self-report surveys (Hindelang et al., 1979; Nettler, 1978), there seems to be little doubt that this flexible method for gathering primary data will continue to be a major tool for research on both interpersonal and epidemiological variations in law-violating behavior.

Similarly, the use of survey techniques in the study of mental disorder has advanced well beyond Hollingshead and Redlich's pioneering survey of the "normal" population of New Haven (1953; 1958). Paralleling the growth of self-report research on officially undetected crime and delinquency, sample surveys of self-reported psychiatric "symptoms" have come into widespread use to discover *untreated* cases of mental disorder in urban and rural communities (see Schwab & Schwab, 1978). For example, only a few years after Hollingshead and Redlich's research on treated prevalence, a representative sample of 1,600 adults residing in the Midtown Manhattan area of New York City were interviewed about their mental health (Srole et al., 1962; 1978). Based on two psychiatrists' independent evaluations of respondents' replies to a variety of symptom items and other questions in these household interviews, nearly one fourth of this sample was classified as psychiatrically impaired to the extent that their symptoms interfered with "the necessary functions or roles of adulthood" (Srole et al., 1978: 194). Moreover, only 5 percent of these "impaired" respondents was currently seeing a therapist and nearly three fourths had *never* received psychiatric treatment. These and other striking findings from the Midtown Manhattan survey indicated that treated cases represent only the very tip of a vast iceberg of mental disorder in urban society. Consequently, many other epidemiological researchers have turned to survey techniques to explore hidden variations in the untreated prevalence of psychiatric symptoms (Dohrenwend & Dohrenwend, 1969; Dohrenwend et al., 1980; Schwab & Schwab, 1978).

Survey methods have also proven useful for social psychological investigations of the interpersonal context of mental disorder (Liem & Liem, 1978: 148–153). A good example of micro-level research using self-report measures of psychiatric symptoms is Gove and Geerken's study of "The Effect of Children and Employment on the Mental Health of Married Men and Women" (1977). Many readers will find the questions raised in this research illustration to be intriguing and relevant from a commonsense point of view: Are children hazardous to their parents' mental health? How is the psychological well-being of married women affected by employment outside the home, for better or for worse? In fact, before reading further, you might think about how you would answer these questions based on your own practical knowledge, experiences, and opinions.

However, aside from its bearing on some commonsense conceptions (or misconceptions) about the interpersonal demands placed upon working wives and husbands, Gove and Geerken's analysis implicitly addresses some important issues for the control tradition in deviance theory. Beginning with Durkheim's (1951: 152–216) seminal discussion of egoistic suicide, control theorists have stressed family relationships as one of the most crucial sources of the "social bond" preventing individual deviant behavior. Durkheim specifically argued that the greater the density of family units—that is, the larger the size of families—the greater would be the immunity of individual family members from suicide. As "proof" of this hypothesis, Durkheim presented data showing that the presence of children in a marriage (as opposed to childless marriages) was associated with low rates of suicide for both husbands and wives. Therefore, Durkheim's analysis of egoistic suicide clearly implies that the presence of children strengthens the social bond attaching married people to conventional society. Does the immunity provided by this bond extend beyond suicide to other deviant acts or conditions such as mental disorder? At least a partial answer to this Durkheimian question appears in Table 4 of Gove and Geerken's article, where married respondents' scores on a self-report measure of psychiatric symptoms are related to the number of children they have (if any). Note whether average or mean scores (indicated by the symbol "$\overline{X}$") *increase* as the number of children increases or whether they *decrease* as Durkheim's hypothesis would predict. Gove and Geerken also report the percentages of respondents scoring high on their measure of psychiatric symptoms. Here, as with the mean scores, note whether the presence of children is associated with an increase or decrease in the proportion with high symptom scores.

Table 4 and the other tables presented by Gove and Geerken also divide their respondents into three categories: (1) employed husbands, (2) employed wives, and (3) unemployed wives. The main purpose of this comparison, of course, is to determine how employment affects married women's psychiatric symptoms and other subjective feelings measured in the Chicago survey from which these data are taken. This analytical focus on the employment status of married persons also raises some important questions for control theory. As you may have noticed while reading Chapter 6, most work within the control tradition has focused specifically on the problem of juvenile delinquency (e.g., Nye, 1958; Hirschi, 1969; Hindelang, 1973). Consequently, aside from family relationships, the adolescent's attachment to school has been the only other institutional bond to conventional society that has received much attention from researchers in this tradition. For most adults, however, employment should be far more influential as a source of control than are educational activities. Therefore, an important task for research is to determine whether attachment, commitment, and involvement in a conventional job encourages conformity among adults in much the same way that the school has been found to provide a social bond for younger people.

The first three tables in Gove and Geerken's article allow at least an indirect indication of how employment affects the strength or quality of married people's interpersonal bond to others. If employment *improves* the quality of the social bond as control theorists would predict, then who should be most likely to feel lonely, to desire to be alone, and to perceive others as making excessive demands on them—employed husbands, employed wives, or unemployed wives? The comparisons of mean scores and percentages scoring high on survey measures of these emotional reactions appearing in Tables 1 through 3 present a fairly clear and consistent answer to these questions. In their concluding analyses, Gove and Geerken go on to show that differences in respondents' emotional bonds to others account for much of the variation in psychiatric symptoms reported by these married men and women. Tables 4 and 5 offer some interpersonal answers to the broad epidemiological question raised at the very beginning of Gove and Geerken's article: Why do married women, in general, have higher rates of mental disorder than married men?

We have touched on several implications of Gove and Geerken's study for theoretical questions in the control tradition. Yet, when you read their article, you will find no direct references to Durkheim's analysis of egoism, Hirschi's theory of the social bond, or any other statements of control theory. This is not to fault Gove and Geerken. They do relate their work to theoretical issues and empirical generalizations from research on sex roles and the family. Furthermore, few, if any, other researchers have given serious consideration to whether micro-normative theories such as control theory or differential association theory can be usefully extended to the problem of mental disorder (but see Akers, 1977: 307–339; Eaton, 1980: 35–64). In fact, the point of these comments has been to introduce Gove and Geerken's work as an example of how survey research on mental disorder could potentially expand the scope of knowledge in the control tradition beyond the confines of criminal and delinquent behavior.

RESEARCH ILLUSTRATION 7–C

The effect of children and employment on the mental health of married men and women*

Walter R. Gove and Michael R. Geerken

Gove has proposed that sex differences in psychiatric illness among the married might best be accounted for in terms of differences in the typical roles occupied by married men and married women. The effects of employment, number of children and age of youngest child on the feeling that one (a) confronts incessant demands from others, (b) de-

---

Source: Article reprinted from *Social Forces* 56 (September 1977): 66–76. Reprinted by permission of *Social Forces* and The University of North Carolina Press.

* The research for this paper was supported by grants from NICHD No. 5-R01-HD06911-02 and NSF No. 73-05455A01. We would like to thank Lisa Heinrich and Michael Hughes for their comments on an earlier draft of this paper.

sires to be alone, (c) feels lonely, and (d) manifests psychiatric symptoms support his sex role explanation.

In a recent article, Gove has shown that the evidence consistently indicates that married women tend to be in poorer mental health than married men in modern western industrial nations. As Gove indicates, a survey of the literature suggests a number of possible explanations for this relationship, but there is very little evidence linking these possible explanations to concrete measures of mental health. In the present paper we will be concerned with three factors which may relate to mental health among the married: employment and the presence and age of children. We will first look at three feelings which largely appear to be direct reactions to role situations: (1) a feeling that one is confronting too many demands from others, (2) a desire to withdraw (i.e., to be alone), and (3) a feeling of loneliness. We will then look at a more general measure of mental health, namely, the presence of psychiatric symptoms.

As Gove notes, married persons who hold a job are linked into two major social networks, one at home and one at work. These two networks serve as major sources of gratification for such persons, and as a consequence they have a broader structural base than housewives who remain at home. Such persons, if they find one of their roles unsatisfactory, can focus their interest and concerns on the other role. In contrast, unemployed housewives who find their roles unsatisfactory typically have no major alternative source of gratification. Furthermore, being a housewife does not require a great deal of skill and many of the tasks are repetitive and boring. The housewife also typically spends most of her day isolated from adult interaction. Housewives are likely to find that the tasks associated with a job provide a welcome change and they probably often find them intrinsically more interesting than those they perform at home. An important prediction follows from this analysis: married women who hold a job are apt to be in better mental health than married women who do not.

Most of the evidence (Bernard, a,b; Birnbaum; Cumming et al.; Feld; Langner; Lopata; Myrdal and Klein; Nye, b; Radloff; Rose), but not all (Pearlin; Sharp and Nye), indicates that married women who work are in somewhat better mental health than married women who do not work. Probably one of the reasons that the relationship is not sharper is that married women who work appear to be under greater time and energy demands than either their husbands or unemployed housewives for, in addition to their job, working wives typically perform most of the household chores. (For reviews of the evidence see Bahr; Gove.) Thus, it is likely that working husbands would be in the best mental health, that unemployed housewives would be in the worst, and that the mental health of the employed housewife would fall in between.

In American society rearing children is primarily the responsibility of the mother, particularly when children are young. We would thus expect children to have more effect on the mental health of wives than husbands and that this would be particularly true when the children were young. Although children have traditionally been viewed as a major source of gratification, in modern western industrial society children seem to confine their parents to a narrowly defined domestic role and there is at least some evidence that the presence of children has a negative effect on mental health (Campbell; Radloff; Rollins and Feldman). Furthermore, the evidence presented by Feld and by Nye (a) indicates that employed mothers are somewhat more positive in their attitudes toward children and describe parenthood as less restricting, burdensome and demanding than nonemployed mothers. This is probably true, at least in part, because the unemployed mother is immersed in the world of children while the employed mother has meaningful adult contacts and other sources of gratification which enable her to view her children in a broader perspective.

The data for our analysis were drawn from a survey conducted in Chicago which focused on the effect of household overcrowding on behavior. The sample was comprised of randomly selected individuals residing in randomly sampled households in census tracts that were selected to maximize variation between socioeconomic variables and household crowding. If no one was contacted on the first call, three additional calls were made, for a total of four contact attempts. (For details of the sampling and methodology see Galle and Gove; Gove et al.) We know of no theoretical or pragmatic reason why this method of selection would affect the nature of the observed relationships; nevertheless, we should not generalize the specific values discovered to any population other than the census tracts selected. A second limitation of the sample is that considerably more married women than married men were interviewed. This is probably due to the difficulty of finding employed men at home. Since we treat men separately from women in our analysis, the undersampling of men should not affect the pattern of the observed relationships. However, because of these limitations, the results of our study should be treated as suggestive and not definitive.

Our analysis deals with only married respondents aged 18–60. We look at employed husbands, employed wives, and unemployed wives. Primarily because there are too few cases, unemployed husbands[1] ($n = 24$), husbands who are students ($n = 5$), and wives who are students ($n = 9$) are omitted. The dependent variables vary somewhat (but not greatly) among age groups, so percentages presented have been adjusted for age, using the multiple classification program, a dummy regression program developed by Andrew et al.

DEMANDS

To determine whether or not the respondent felt he or she was constantly confronting demands from others, we developed an additive scale of five items dealing with demands. The five items were: (1) Does it seem as if others are always making demands on you? (2) Do you often feel it is impossible to finish anything? (3) At home does it seem as if you almost never have any peace and quiet? (4) At home does it seem as if you are always having to do something for someone else? and, (5) When you try to do something at home are you almost always interrupted?

As can be seen in Table 1, husbands report fewer demands than employed wives, who in turn report fewer demands than unemployed wives. In all three categories persons with no children report the fewest demands, the rate of demands increases monotonically with the number of children, and the increase is particularly marked among the wives. The number of children has a greater effect on wives than on husbands. Table 1 also presents the relationship between the demands scale and the age of the youngest child. Demands decrease monotonically for both the employed and unemployed housewives as the age of the youngest child increases. In contrast, the age of the youngest child appears to be largely unrelated to the experience of demands among husbands. Of particular interest is the comparison of married men and women who are employed but do not have children, for these men and women can be seen as having very similar roles. Table 1 shows that within this category the two sexes experience almost identical demands.

An analysis of the items in the demand scale shows that three of the items refer specifically to demands in the home and two of the items refer to demands in general. As non-working wives presumably spend more time in the house, it seemed plausible that their high score on the demand scale might be due to the three items referring to the home. Their high score might thus reflect the time they spend in the home and not a greater overall experience of demands (the reference to demands in the home would not account for the greater experience of demands of working wives as compared to working husbands). To check this possibility we created two subscales, one composed of the two general items and one composed of the three items that refer specifically to the home, and replicated the analysis

Table 1
The experience of incessant demands (age adjusted)

	Employed husbands			Employed wives			Unemployed wives			Significance level	
	$\bar{X}$*	% high†	(n)	$\bar{X}$*	% high†	(n)	$\bar{X}$*	% high†	(n)	$\bar{X}$*	% high†
Number of children											
0	.75	23.1	(104)	.80	18.8	(80)	1.08	32.2	(87)		
1–2	1.27	37.4	(91)	1.68	52.2	(69)	1.76	50.3	(157)	.001	.001
3+	1.48	42.9	(49)	2.04	57.5	(47)	2.85	74.7	(95)		
Age of youngest child											
0–4	1.31	37.1	(67)	2.25	66.0	(47)	2.47	64.8	(141)		
5–10	1.40	41.0	(39)	1.60	51.3	(39)	2.11	59.3	(59)	.001	.001
11+	1.11	41.2	(34)	1.37	40.0	(30)	1.61	45.3	(52)		
Total	1.07	32.4	(244)	1.41	39.8	(196)	1.90	52.3	(339)	.001	.001

* Mean number of demands reported.
† Percent reporting two or more demands.

presented in Table 1. Both scales showed a pattern virtually identical to that in Table 1 and all of the comparisons were statistically significant, indicating that the relationships presented reflect an overall experience of demands.

DESIRE TO BE ALONE

To measure the respondents' desire to be alone we developed an additive scale of four items which tapped different aspects of this feeling. The four items were: (1) Do you sometimes find yourself wishing you were all alone? (2) When you are by yourself are you usually glad to be alone? (3) Do you often wish you could get out of the house just to get away from it all? and, (4) At home does it seem as if you can never be by yourself?

As is shown in Table 2, employed husbands were the category least likely to desire to be alone. Employed wives were somewhat more likely and unemployed housewives were much more likely to desire to be alone. Among the employed and unemployed wives, those with no children were the least likely to desire to be alone; the proportion increases monotonically with the number of children, and this increase is particularly large among unemployed wives. There was no clear relationship between desire to be alone and number of children among employed husbands. For both employed and unemployed wives there is a monotonic decrease in the desire to be alone as the age of the youngest child increases. In contrast, husbands are the most likely to desire to be alone when the youngest child is between 5 and 10 years old. Comparing again, employed husbands and wives without children shows that both sexes within this category tend to be very similar on this scale, with there being some tendency for the women to be even less concerned than the men about being alone. Overall, there is a very similar pattern between the desire to be alone and the feeling that incessant demands are made on one.

An analysis of the items in the desire to be alone scale shows that two of the items refer specifically to the home, whereas two do not refer to a specific setting. As with the demands scale we created two subscales, one composed of the two general items and one composed of the two items that specifically referred to the home to see if the unemployed housewives' high scores were due solely to the "at home" items. Both scales showed a pattern very similar to that of Table 2 and all of the comparisons were statistically significant, indicating that the relationships presented reflect an overall desire to be alone and not related specifically to the home.

Table 2
The experience of the desire to be alone (age adjusted)

	Employed husbands			Employed wives			Unemployed wives			Significance level	
	$\bar{X}$*	% high†	(n)	$\bar{X}$*	% high†	(n)	$\bar{X}$*	% high†	(n)	$\bar{X}$*	% high†
Number of children											
0	1.19	34.6	(104)	1.11	25.3	(80)	1.43	39.3	(86)		
1–2	1.11	33.0	(91)	1.46	47.8	(69)	1.57	50.3	(157)	.001	.001
3+	1.59	34.0	(50)	1.64	51.1	(47)	2.03	63.2	(95)		
Age of youngest child											
0–4	1.11	31.3	(67)	1.86	52.4	(47)	2.05	62.0	(141)		
5–10	1.42	40.6	(40)	1.42	48.7	(39)	1.68	55.9	(59)	.001	.001
11+	1.14	29.4	(34)	1.24	36.7	(30)	1.30	35.8	(52)		
Total	1.20	33.9	(245)	1.36	39.5	(196)	1.67	51.0	(338)	.001	.001

* Mean number of desire to be alone reported.
† Percent reporting two or more desires to be alone.

LONELINESS

To measure feelings of loneliness we asked the respondent "do you often feel lonely?" In Table 3 we have presented the proportion of persons who responded positively to this question. Employed hus-

Table 3
Percent lonely (age adjusted)

	(1) Employed husbands		(2) Employed wives		(3) Unemployed wives		Significance level
Number of children							
0	3.7	(104)	13.7	(80)	20.3	(86)	
1–2	6.2	(91)	7.8	(69)	33.6	(157)	.001
3+	8.5	(50)	15.8	(47)	18.0	(95)	
Age of youngest child							
0–4	4.4	(67)	5.0	(47)	27.8	(141)	
5–10	7.2	(40)	13.1	(47)	22.5	(59)	.001
11+	9.5	(34)	15.2	(30)	30.4	(30)	
Total	5.7	(254)	12.1	(196)	25.8	(338)	.001

bands very rarely felt lonely, employed wives were somewhat more likely to feel lonely and unemployed wives were much more likely to feel lonely. There is no clear relationship between loneliness and the presence, number, and age of children. Feelings of loneliness increase slightly for husbands as the number of children increases. Employed wives are the least likely to feel lonely when there are one or two children present, whereas unemployed wives are the most likely to feel lonely when there are one or two children present. For husbands and employed housewives feelings of loneliness increase slightly as the age of the youngest child increases. For the unemployed housewife feelings of loneliness are greatest when there are old or very young children in the household.

In summary, on the measures of these three feelings, employed husbands tend to have the lowest scores and unemployed housewives the highest scores, while employed housewives score between the other two categories. In each case the employed wives' scores are closer to those of the husbands than to those of unemployed wives.

PSYCHIATRIC SYMPTOMS

Next we looked at a more global measure of mental health, psychiatric symptoms. To get a general measure of the respondents' mental health we asked them how often (often, sometimes, never) they had experienced fourteen different psychiatric symptoms during the past

Table 4
The manifestation of psychiatric symptoms (age adjusted)

	Employed husbands			Employed wives			Unemployed wives			Significance level	
	$\bar{X}^*$	% high†	(n)	$\bar{X}^*$	% high†	(n)	$\bar{X}^*$	% high†	(n)	$\bar{X}^*$	% high†
Number of children											
0	5.81	15.3	(102)	7.03	15.6	(77)	7.81	22.0	(86)		
1–2	6.36	15.1	(90)	7.71	26.2	(66)	8.30	30.6	(153)	.001	.001
3+	6.40	15.2	(49)	7.80	29.3	(46)	8.12	30.6	(92)		
Age of youngest child											
0–4	5.95	9.7	(66)	8.48	29.7	(44)	8.53	29.5	(135)		
5–10	6.74	15.1	(39)	7.18	22.3	(39)	7.83	26.2	(59)	.001	.001
11+	6.76	27.6	(34)	7.40	29.7	(30)	7.92	32.8	(51)		
Total	6.13	14.9	(241)	7.46	22.8	(189)	8.12	28.7	(330)	.001	.001

* Mean symptom score.
† Percent of respondents with an arbitrarily chose high score.

few weeks. The symptoms were feeling (1) anxious about something or someone, (2) bothered by special fears, (3) that people were saying all kinds of things behind your back, (4) that it was safer to trust nobody, (5) that you couldn't take care of things because you couldn't get going, (6) so blue or depressed that it interfered with your daily activities, (7) bothered by nervousness, such as being irritable, fidgety or tense, (8) that you were in low spirits, (9) bothered by special thoughts, (10) so restless that you couldn't sit long in a chair, (11) as if nothing turned out the way you wanted it to, (12) somewhat apart or alone even among friends, (13) that personal worries were getting you down, that is, making you physically ill, and (14) that nothing was worthwhile anymore.[2] In making the scale the responses of "often" were assigned a 2, those of "sometimes" a 1 and "never" a 0, and then these values were summed.

The relationships between psychiatric symptoms and the independent variables are presented in Table 4. In all comparisons husbands report the fewest psychiatric symptoms, employed housewives report somewhat more and unemployed housewives report the most. The data are thus consistent with the extensive literature which shows that married women manifest more psychiatric symptoms than men (Gove). Among employed wives, symptoms increase monotonically with an increase in the number of children, and with unemployed wives it is the simple presence of children that increases the rate. For employed husbands the pattern is less clear: the mean scores show a monotonic increase in symptoms occurs with an increase in the number of children, but the percent of respondents with a "high" score does not change with the number of children. Among husbands the manifestation of symptoms is associated with older children. This may be a reflection of husbands becoming more involved with the problems of their children as they grow older. Among employed and unemployed wives there is no clear pattern with age of children, although for both groups the highest mean scores are associated with children in the 0–4 age group, and the lowest scores on both indicators are associated with children in the 5–10 age group.

DISCUSSION

To a large extent we view our first three dependent variables (demands, desire to be alone, and loneliness) as indicators of a person's direct reactions to an immediate situation. These feelings seem to be primarily caused by an immersion in the world of children with its incessant demands and the lack of time for oneself, lack of adult interaction, and lack of opportunity to use instrumental skills (such as are associated with a job). As one would expect there is a moderate to high association between these three variables (the gamma between demands and desires to be alone = .496, the gamma between demands and loneliness = .309, and the gamma between the desire to be alone and loneliness = .397). The fact that persons who desire to be alone are also lonely suggests these are not opposites but that one can wish to be alone and still feel lonely in the presence of others, presumably because one desires the company of a different set of individuals.

Feelings of too many demands, a desire to be alone, and loneliness, which we see as reactions to one's immediate situation, can be viewed to some extent as factors which may contribute to the development of psychiatric symptoms. The items in these scales reflect a fair amount of frustration, alienation, and social isolation, factors which are generally considered to be causally linked to the development of psychiatric symptoms. Furthermore, these feelings appear to be caused by a reaction to a situation (the environment produced by one's home and children) to which one usually has a high degree of normative and pragmatic commitment. The dilemma of a high commitment to a frustrating situation is likely to have a negative effect on one's mental health. (For a review of the evidence relevant to this hypothesis see Nye, b, 209–11.) As we would expect from this reasoning, these three variables have a moderate to high correlation with psychiatric symptoms (the gamma with demands = .308, the gamma with desire to be alone = .333 and the gamma with lonely = .502).

If feelings of too many demands, a desire to be alone, and loneliness are part of the causal link between one's situation and the manifestation of psychiatric symptoms, then controlling for these three variables should reduce the relationship between one's situation and one's psychiatric symptoms. Table 5 presents the relationships between (1) employed husbands, employed wives, and unemployed wives, and (2) psychiatric symptoms, controlling for these three variables. The data suggest that demands, desire to be alone, and loneliness do act as intervening variables; each accounts for some of the differences in the manifestation of psychiatric symptoms. Furthermore, when the three intervening variables are jointly controlled for, the relationship not only becomes statistically nonsignificant but the relationship between employed wives and unemployed wives reverses, with employed wives now manifesting more psychiatric symptoms. This analysis thus suggests that feelings of incessant demands, desire to be alone, and loneliness, which appear to be largely produced by one's role, act as a major link between one's role and the manifestation of psychiatric symptoms. This analysis, however, should be viewed with some caution for it could be argued that the three intervening variables, besides being reactions to an immediate situation, are themselves direct measures of poor mental health.

Table 5
The manifestation of psychiatric symptoms, controlling for demands, desire to be alone and loneliness (all age adjusted)

Controls	Employed husbands	Employed wives	Unemployed wives	Significance level
None				
$\bar{X}$	6.13	7.46	8.12	.001
% high	14.9	27.8	28.7	.001
Demands				
$\bar{X}$	6.60	7.54	7.74	.001
% high	18.5	23.4	25.8	ns
Desire to be alone				
$\bar{X}$	6.42	7.56	7.87	.001
% high	16.8	23.3	27.2	.05
Loneliness				
$\bar{X}$	6.52	7.59	7.78	.01
% high	18.3	24.1	25.6	ns
Demands, alone and loneliness				
$\bar{X}$	6.89	7.70	7.46	ns
% high	21.0	24.8	23.4	ns
n	241	189	330	

In conclusion, we have looked at the effect employment and the number and age of children have on married adults' feelings of facing incessant demands, desire to be alone, loneliness, and the manifestation of psychiatric symptoms. The data indicate that married men who work are in the best mental health, that married women who are unemployed are in the worst mental health, and that the mental health of employed housewives falls in between. Having children in the household generally contributes to poor mental health.

Overall, the data provide fairly strong support for the view that the main reason married women tend to be in poorer mental health than men is because of the roles they typically occupy. However, one cautionary factor should be considered regarding our role explanation of the relationships presented. To some extent employed wives are a self-selected group and it is possible that there is a tendency for wives who seek employment to be in better mental health than those who do not. Of course, self-selection would not account for the overall differences between men and women. Since married women who are employed typically face much greater time and energy demands than their unemployed counterparts, these data, then, suggest that an overload of actual tasks is not the prime cause of the poorer mental health among women, although it may be a contributing factor, especially among employed wives. This indicates that it is the kind of demands found in the home and associated with children (e.g., see LeMasters) which produces a feeling of incessant demands and not simply the number of tasks that must be performed.

NOTES

1. We would note that unemployed husbands manifest slightly more psychiatric symptoms than any other category.
2. As we are concerned with poor mental health and not specific forms of mental illness (there are simply too few cases of real mental illness to be picked up in a study such as ours) we have asked questions tapping a wide variety of symptoms (e.g., anxiety, depression, psychosis). In contrast to mental illness, which is viewed by some in terms of discrete "cases," mental health is probably best viewed as a continuum ranging from good to poor. In recent years the three most popular psychiatric symptoms scales have been the Langner Scale, the Health Opinion Survey (HOS) (MacMillan), and the Gurin et al. scale. By now there is very extensive literature on the validity of these scales and, as is indicated by the reviews by Seiler and by Tousignant et al., and the empirical analysis by Schwartz et al., the scales are not adequate as general measures of mental illness or psychiatric impairment. As is noted in detail in Gove and Geerken, considerable effort was put into choosing the items used in the present study and, as we demonstrate in that paper, the results presented are not affected by problems of response bias.

REFERENCES

Andrew, F. M., J. N. Morgan, and J. A. Songuist. 1967. *Multiple Classification Analysis*. Ann Arbor: Institute for Social Research, University of Michigan.
Bahr, S. 1974. "Effects on Power and Division of Labor in the Family." In Lois W. Hoffman and F. Ivan Nye (eds.), *Working Mothers*. San Francisco: Jossey-Bass.
Bernard, Jessie. a:1971. *Women and the Public Interest*. New York: Aldine- Atherton.
—————. b:1971. "The Paradox of the Happy Housewife." In Vivian Gornick and Barbara Moran (eds.), *Women in Sexist Society: Studies in Power and Powerlessness*. New York: Basic Books.
Birnbaum, J. 1971. "Life Patterns, Personality Style, and Self-Esteem in Gifted Family Oriented and Career Committed Women." *Dissertation Abstracts International* 32(September):1834b.
Campbell, A. 1975. "The American Way of Mating: Marriage Si, Children Only Maybe." *Psychology Today* 8(May):37–43.
Cumming, E., C. Lazer, and L. Chisolm. 1975. "Suicide as an Index of Role Strain among Employed and Not Employed Married Women in British Columbia." *Canadian Review of Sociology and Anthropology* 12(4):462–70.
Feld, S. 1963. "Feelings of Adjustment." In F. Ivan Nye and Lois W. Hoffman (eds.), *The Employed Mother in America*. Chicago: Rand McNally.
Galle, Omer, and Walter Gove. 1977. "Crowding and Behavior in Chicago, 1940–1970." *Human Ecology* (forthcoming).
Gove, W. 1972. "The Relationship between Sex Roles, Marital Status and Mental Illness." *Social Forces* 51(September):34–44.
Gove, W., and M. Geerken. 1977. "Response Bias in Surveys of Mental Health: An Empirical Investigation." *American Journal of Sociology* (in press).
Gove, W., M. Hughes, and O. Galle. 1976. "Overcrowding in the Home: An Empirical Investigation of Some of Its Possible Pathological Consequences." Paper presented at a meeting of the American Public Health Association in Miami, Fla.
Gurin, Gerald, Joseph Veroff, and Sheila Feld. 1960. *Americans View their Mental Health*. New York: Basic Books.
Langner, T. 1962. "A Twenty-Two Item Screening Score of Psychiatric Symptoms Indicating Impairment." *Journal of Health and Human Behavior* 3(Winter):269–76.

LeMasters, E. E. 1974. *Parents in Modern America*. Homewood: Dorsey.
Lopata, Helena. 1971. *Occupation Housewife*. New York: Oxford University Press.
MacMillan, A. 1957. "The Health Opinion Survey Technique for Estimating Prevalence of Psychoneurotic and Related Types of Disorder in Communities." *Monograph Supplement 7, Psychological Report* 3(September):325–39.
Myrdal, Alva, and Viola Klein. 1956. *Women's Two Roles: Home and Work*. Boston: Routledge & Kegan Paul.
Nye, F. Ivan. a:1963. "Adjustment to Children." In F. Ivan Nye and Lois W. Hoffman (eds.), *The Employed Mother in America*. Chicago: Rand McNally.
———. b:1974. "Effects on the Mother." In Lois W. Hoffman and F. Ivan Nye (eds.), *Working Mothers*. San Francisco: Jossey-Bass.
Pearlin, L. 1975. "Sex Roles and Depression." *Proceedings of the Fourth Life-Span Developmental Psychology Conference: Normative Life Crises:* 191–207.
Radloff, L. 1975. "Sex Differences in Depression: The Effects of Occupation and Marital Status." *Sex Roles* 1(3):249–65.
Rollins, B., and H. Feldman. 1970. "Marital Satisfaction over the Family Life-Cycle." *Journal of Marriage and the Family* 32(February):20–28.
Rose, A. M. 1955. "Factors Associated with the Life Satisfaction of Middle-Aged Persons." *Marriage and Family Living* 17(February):15–19.
Schwartz, C., J. Myers, and B. Astrachan. 1973. "Comparing Three Measures of Mental Status: A Note on the Validity of Estimates of Psychological Disorder in the Community." *Journal of Health and Social Behavior* 14(September):265–73.
Seiler, L. 1973. "The 22-Item Scale Used in Field Studies of Mental Illness: A Question of Method, A Question of Substance, and A Question of Theory." *Journal of Health and Social Behavior* 14(September):252–64.
Sharp, L., and F. I. Nye. 1963. "Maternal Mental Health." In F. Ivan Nye and Lois W. Hoffman (eds.), *The Employed Mother in America*. Chicago: Rand McNally.
Tousignant, M., G. Denis, and R. Lachapelle. 1974. "Some Considerations Concerning the Validity and Use of the Health Opinion Survey." *Journal of Health and Social Behavior* 15(September): 241–52.

CONCLUSION

Having reached the end of four chapters on normative theory and research, we should take one last look at the master question of this perspective: Why do they do it? Most of the sociologists whose work we have reviewed above have attempted to answer this question by pointing to particular *motivations* for deviant behavior. We have touched on a number of efforts to identify certain values, frustrations, environmental pressures, or attitudes that push or pull individuals in the direction of deviance. Researchers and theorists in the anomie, subculture, and social learning traditions have all tended to use motivational explanations, especially in the study of crime and delinquency (see Kornhauser, 1978; Empey, 1982).

In the introductory comments on Short and Strodtbeck's (1963; 1965) research as well as in Chapters 4 and 5, we noted that some serious questions have been raised about the adequacy of motivational explanations of macro-level phenomena such as crime rates. Aside from the issue of whether rates of crime and delinquency actually vary by social class, Short and Strodtbeck, Erlanger (1976), and many other survey researchers (e.g., Voss, 1966; Hirschi, 1969; Berger & Simon, 1974; Johnson, 1979) have failed to find support for the propositions that frustrated ambitions or distinctive subcultural values are important motives for deviant behavior in the lower class or elsewhere in society.

Not surprisingly, motivational explanations have proven more successful in micro-level research on individual deviant behavior. As the second research illustration in this chapter suggested, Sutherland's development of the principle of differential association to account for the "specific direction of motives and drives" (Sutherland & Cressey, 1974: 75) has been particularly pertinent to the study of drug and alcohol use among adolescents. Primary group associations and favorable attitudinal definitions have emerged as the key causal factors in many recent investigations of these forms of deviant behavior (see, for example, the reviews by Glynn, 1981; Kandel, 1980; and Radosevich et al., 1979; 1980; also see Akers et al., 1979; Clayton & Lacy, 1982; Huba & Bentler, 1980; Jaquith, 1981; Stafford & Ekland-Olson, 1982; Strickland, 1982). While studies of other forms of adolescent and adult crime (e.g., Johnson, 1979; Tittle, 1980: 187–191) have also yielded results consistent with Sutherland's approach, his emphasis on rationally motivated, law-violating behavior has discouraged efforts to extend the social learning tradition in sociology to the area of mental disorder (but see Akers, 1977; Krohn & Akers, 1977).

The control tradition, on the other hand, tends to *avoid* motivational explanations and might be more readily applied to seemingly "irrational" forms of deviance. The Gove and Geerken (1977) study provides just one illustration of this possibility. An even more direct parallel between control theory and research on psychiatric disorders is evident in recent work on the relationship between social supports and mental health (see the reviews by Goldstein, 1979; Henderson, 1980; and Mueller, 1980; also see Lin et al., 1979; Turner, 1981; Williams et al., 1981). As Henderson points out, this research tends to agree with the general hypothesis that strong social bonds of primary group attachment and support are associated with relatively low levels of psychiatric symptoms. In moving toward the view that "social bonds are . . . necessary in themselves for mental health" (Henderson, 1980: 64), these researchers have arrived at a position that bears a close family resemblance to Hirschi's (1969) account of adolescent conformity.

Paradoxically, then, some researchers have attempted to breath new life into the normative perspective by declining to answer its traditional motivational question. However, as we turn to the work of relativistic theorists and researchers in the next four chapters, we will encounter even less regard for the question of why "they" do it and much greater concern with social control as a problem in itself.

The micro-relativistic approach: Labeling theory

8

Relativistic theories of deviance are in some ways easier and in other ways more difficult to describe than are the normative theories discussed in the preceding chapters. Whereas at least four major theoretical traditions have developed within the normative perspective, relativistic theorizing can be generally divided into two traditions: labeling theory and conflict theory. However, as we review the work of relativistic theorists included within these two broad categories, we will find much greater diversity in their ideas and analytical emphases than was the case with the normative approaches to deviance.

Whatever the differences between them, the theories discussed in this and the following chapters are all based to a great extent on the following principle (Erikson, 1962: 308, emphasis in original):

> Deviance is not a property *inherent in* certain forms of behavior; it is a property *conferred upon* these forms by the audiences which directly or indirectly witness them. Sociologically, then, the critical variable in the study of deviance is the social *audience*.

Depending on the particular relativistic theory under consideration, a social audience may consist of a small group or a social class, ordinary citizens or formal agents of social control. But the crucial point here is that audiences *create deviance* by defining or reacting to certain persons or forms of behavior as deviant.

Beginning with this basic insight, relativistic theorists depart on two separate analytical paths in their efforts to understand how deviance is created by audience definitions. As we saw in Chapter 1, labeling theorists have focused on micro-level phenomena—the interactional processes through which individuals are singled out and labeled deviant by others. Conflict theorists, on the other hand, have taken a much broader view of the creation of deviance in present and past societies. Approaching this problem on a macro level of analysis, these theorists have attempted to understand the processes of political and economic conflict that underly the historical development of law and of systems of social control.

The present chapter will focus on labeling theory and the theoretical developments that preceded and followed its rise as the major micro-relativistic approach to deviance. We will give special attention to the early work of Edwin M. Lemert (1951), a theorist who is sometimes considered to be the father of labeling theory, but who has more recently become one of its most outspoken critics (1972; 1974).

As we shall see, Lemert was responsible for the first comprehensive discussion of two analytical problems—the problem of audience reactions and the problem of secondary deviance—that became central themes in the work of mainstream labeling theorists during the early 1960s (Becker, 1963; Kitsuse, 1962; Erikson, 1962). Although this chapter will also touch on some criticisms of labeling theory voiced by Lemert and other sociologists, discussion of some recent attacks on the ideological biases of this and other theories of deviance will be reserved for a later chapter focusing on conflict theory—the macrorelativistic approach that has made some of its most important contributions by analyzing critically the current state of the field of deviance.

INTELLECTUAL FOUNDATIONS OF THE LABELING TRADITION

Sociologists have yet to agree on a single label to use when referring to this micro-relativistic tradition. The term most frequently seen in the deviance literature, and the one used throughout this book, is *labeling* (or *labelling*) *theory*. However, the terms *societal reaction theory* or *social reaction theory* are often applied to this same line of theoretical development. Still other names relate more directly to the intellectual background of this approach than to its central concepts. Matza (1969), for instance, characterizes the labeling theorists as neo-Chicagoans. Becker (1973: 181) has expressed his preference for the phrase "interactionist theory of deviance" (also see Rubington & Weinberg, 1978). These latter two terms identify the labeling tradition with an earlier and much broader perspective on social behavior known as *symbolic interactionism* or *interactionist social psychology*. Interactionist social psychology emerged a number of years ago in the work of scholars at the University of Chicago. Many of the basic ideas of labeling theorists, as well as their distinctive orientation toward theory and research, reflect the intellectual impact of symbolic interactionism.

The influence of interactionist social psychology

As the term *symbolic interactionism* suggests, interactionist social psychology involves the study of how language or symbolic meanings are used in the process of social interaction. Being social psychologists, theorists within this perspective have been almost exclusively concerned with such micro-level phenomena as face-to-face relationships, parent-child interaction, or social influences on the self-concepts of individuals. Several sociologists at the University of Chicago during the social pathology and social disorganization periods, including Charles H. Cooley and W. I. Thomas, made important contributions to the early development of interactionist thought. However, the principal architect of symbolic interactionism at Chicago was not a sociologist but a social philosopher, George Herbert Mead.

The best-known statement of Mead's ideas is *Mind, Self, and Society* (1934), a book published posthumously by his students from lecture notes. As the title of this work indicates, Mead's philosophical analyses provide significant insights into the nature of human thought and decision making (mind), the social origin of one's sense of identity (self), and the processes by which individuals share meanings and engage in organized social action (society). Essential to all these phenomena is the human ability to use language, to learn, and manipulate symbolic meanings. Mead argues that while lower animals merely *react* deterministically to environmental stimuli, human action depends on the subjective meanings that individuals attach to their environment, to themselves, and to other people. This does not imply that human behavior is completely unpredictable. Through the process of social interaction, people are able to share their subjective meanings and intentions with one another, and to anticipate how the other person is planning to act. The way we act is influenced to a great extent by our subjective appraisal of how others view us and expect us to act. According to Mead, then, social action takes the form of a complex, interpretive process. Human acts are *constructed from* subjective definitions and shared meanings rather than *determined by* environmental conditions.

As a philosopher, Mead was not greatly concerned with the implications of his analysis for sociological theory and research. However, Mead's ideas had an immediate impact on many of his sociological colleagues and students at the University of Chicago. The work of Herbert Blumer (1969), who studied under Mead, has been particularly instrumental in the development of symbolic interactionism as a sociological perspective. Blumer has been highly critical of deterministic theorizing by sociologists. Consistent with Mead, he points out that theories based on simple cause-and-effect relationships cannot hope to grasp the complex and dynamic character of social interaction. Instead, Blumer argues that sociologists should develop theory in much the same way that ordinary people approach their daily encounters with others—by attempting to interpret and understand the shared meanings that guide social interaction. In order to construct theories that accurately reflect the meanings that social actors attach to their behavior, the sociologist must attempt to see their world as they themselves see it. Therefore, interactionist theorizing is based on "*direct* examination of the actual empirical social world" as it is experienced and interpreted by social actors (Blumer, 1969: 48, emphasis in original).

The interpretive form of theorizing advocated by Blumer and other interactionist social psychologists is highly compatible with some of the research techniques employed by Chicago sociologists during the social disorganization period. Direct observation of social interaction in natural settings, used effectively by urban ethnographers in the 1920s, became the preferred mode of research by symbolic interactionists in later years.

The links between labeling theory and interactionist social psychology are direct and clear. Most of the leading labeling theorists were trained by Blumer or other symbolic interactionists. For better or for worse, labeling theorists have adopted the interpretive form of theorizing and the emphasis on the direct observation of interactional processes that have been the hallmarks of the Mead-Blumer perspective. Deviant labels are analyzed as shared meanings that are applied to certain persons in the course of social interaction. The task for labeling theory, as for interactionist social psychology in general, is to work toward an understanding of how meanings (such as criminal or psychotic or queer) influence both the actions and subjective views of social audiences as well as the actions and self-concepts of persons to whom those meanings are applied. Following the methodological lead of symbolic interactionism, labeling theorists typically propose that this search for understanding begin with direct observation of the social worlds of deviants and their audiences.

It should be emphasized that labeling is not the only approach to deviance that has drawn upon interactionist ideas. The influence of this broad social psychological orientation is also apparent in social learning theory (Glaser, 1956; 1962; Cressey, 1962) and other work within the normative perspective on deviance (Cohen, 1965). But, beginning with early work by Edwin Lemert (1951), labeling theory has become increasingly deserving of its title as *the* interactionist theory of deviance.

Lemert: Societal reaction and secondary deviation

By all accounts, the year 1951, the publication date of Lemert's *Social Pathology*, should mark the origin of the relativistic perspective in general and the labeling tradition in particular. Even though earlier writings had applied some relativistic ideas to the analysis of deviance and social problems (Tannenbaum, 1938; Waller, 1936; Fuller & Myers, 1941a), Lemert's work represented the first attempt to develop a systematic, comprehensive theory of deviance and audience reaction processes. *Social Pathology* is referenced by all of the major labeling theorists in the 1960s as a source of their relativistic focus on deviant phenomena (Kitsuse, 1962; Becker, 1963; Erikson, 1966; Schur, 1969).

Yet, as we noted in Chapter 2, one of the many ironies associated with Lemert's contributions to the labeling tradition is that *Social Pathology* did not have an immediate impact on the field of deviance. Overshadowed especially by the rise of subcultural theory during the 1950s, Lemert's unique insights were not rediscovered until the following decade. Furthermore, Lemert is reluctant to define himself as a labeling theorist and has, in fact, been highly critical of the work of other sociologists in this tradition. For instance, he has objected to the "extreme relativism" of some versions of labeling theory that deemphasize the objective reality of deviant behavior and imply "that almost any meaning can be assigned to human attributes and actions" (1972: 22). Elsewhere, he has pointed out a number of shortcomings of labeling theory that stem from its close relationship to symbolic interactionism (1974). These and other considerations have generated a good deal of confusion as to where Lemert's work fits into the labeling tradition (see Becker, 1973; 177–212; Kitsuse, 1975; Rains, 1975).

Neither Lemert's vital role in the development of the relativistic perspective nor his recent criticisms of labeling theory can be adequately understood unless we look to his early theoretical position in *Social Pathology* (1951). Despite its title, this text was quite critical of the conceptions of social problems and deviance that prevailed during the earlier social pathology and social disorganization periods. Lemert (1951: 22) used the term *sociopathic behavior* to refer to "behavior which at a given time and place is socially disapproved" or, in other words, deviant.

Social Pathology stands apart from later theoretical work in the labeling tradition in its concern with the objective, norm-violating aspects of certain forms of behavior. In a chapter on "Deviation and Differentiation," Lemert uses the latter term to refer generally to the infinite number of ways in which people differ from one another, including differences in biological and social attributes as well as differences in behavior. However, only some of these differences will bring "people . . . into public focus as deviants" (1951: 30). The concept of *deviation*, as distinguished from the notion of normal differentiation between people, "can only have value if there are adequate means of describing and delimiting social norms" (1951: 30). Norms vary considerably across time and place, particularly in complex, urban-industrial societies. Members of society typically become aware of norms only in retrospect; i.e., *after* these standards of conduct have been violated. Despite the difficulties inherent in the identification and classification of social norms, Lemert maintains that they are useful for the sociological study of deviance. The extent and amount of deviation in a particular social situation can be *objectively* determined by comparing the observed behavior against normative standards (1951: 51):

> the sum total of deviation in a given situation will consist of the variance of the actions from prescribed social norms multiplied by the number of persons who engage in such actions.

Lemert clearly distinguishes this normative conception of deviation from another important concept in his theory, *societal reaction*. Generally, the societal reaction is defined as the "over-all responses of persons and groups of a society to deviation" (1951: 449). Lemert appears to apply this concept not only to behavioral responses, such as verbal expressions of disapproval or efforts at social control, but also to subjective feelings and attitudes that people hold in response to norm-violating behavior. Whatever the exact ways in which the societal reaction is expressed, Lemert contends that its intensity or severity will tend to correspond closely to "the degree, amount, and visibility of the deviation" (1951: 54), other things being equal. That is, the extent to which behavior objectively departs from social norms as well as the importance placed upon those norms by a group or community will be major factors contributing to the societal reaction.

At this point, Lemert seems to be more intent on developing a theory of audience reactions than a theory of sociopathic deviation. He goes on to analyze how the societal reaction may sometimes take on a spurious (erroneous) quality, being either much more or less severe than is warranted by the objective seriousness of the norm-violating behavior. Lemert notes, for example, that "cases are easily discovered in which a somewhat minor violation of legal rules has provoked surprisingly stringent penalties" (1951: 55). In such cases, societal definitions of the deviant are, in part, *putative*—distorted or exaggerated views or stereotypes which have no foundation in objective fact. Among the factors that bring about spurious reactions and misimpressions about deviation "is the rivalry or conflict of groups . . . as they aspire to power or struggle to maintain their position" of power in a community (1951: 56). Therefore, Lemert suggests that analyses of political conflict are particularly relevant in those instances where societal reactions appear to be inconsistent with the objective characteristics of deviants and their norm-violating behavior. This idea, of course, became a central theme in later relativistic theorizing by conflict theorists.

Lemert's analysis of the nature and determinants of the societal reaction is an important theoretical contribution in itself. However, his early work is best known today for its analysis of a distinction between *primary and secondary deviation* (1951: 75–78). Primary deviation refers to those common instances where individuals commit norm-violating acts without viewing themselves as being involved in a deviant social role. Lemert points out that "deviations remain primary deviations . . . as long as they are rationalized or otherwise dealt with as functions of a socially acceptable role" (1951: 75). People who use alcohol heavily, for example, may view themselves as social drinkers rather than as alcoholics. Or, a teenage boy might rationalize his theft of an automobile as borrowing the car for a while.

But, what if there is a societal reaction to such acts of primary deviation? Especially when primary deviation is highly visible and repeated frequently, the individual will tend to be penalized or rejected by others. Perhaps as a show of hostility or resentment to these punishments, the individual may engage in further deviant behavior that, in turn, is met by increasingly severe societal reactions, etc. One likely outcome of this progressive, interactional process is secondary deviation (1951: 76):

> When a person begins to employ his deviant behavior or a role based upon it as a means of defense, attack, or adjustment to the . . . problems created by the consequent societal reaction to him, his deviation is secondary.

Rather than denying the "name calling, labeling, or stereotyping" involved in societal reactions (1951: 77), the individual adjusts by personally identifying with the deviant role signified by those reactions. The deviant reorganizes his or her self-concept around this stigmatized social role, with secondary deviation being a behavioral expression of this new personal identity.

Lemert emphasizes that the processes through which secondary deviation emerges as an individual response or adjustment to societal reactions by no means follow a fixed or predetermined course. Drawing heavily upon symbolic interactionist imagery, Lemert argues that the deviant "must be understood as a dynamic, creative, choice-making" actor (1951: 78). While avoiding a deterministic theory of secondary deviation, Lemert does specify certain limits that societal reactions place on the range of social roles and behavioral choices that is available to actors who are defined as deviant. Societal reactions tend to "erect barriers" between the deviant and the "socially respectable community" that narrow the actor's opportunities for social participation to deviant roles or to deviant groups (1951: 78–98). In general, then, Lemert singles out the interrelated processes of change in the actor's *self-concept* and change in the actor's *social participation* as crucial phenomena for sociological analyses of secondary deviation.

Lemert's theory of secondary deviation became a model for later contributions to the labeling tradition. However, we are now in a position to see why Lemert has objected (1972; 1974) to the treatment that this and other aspects of his early work has received at the hands of labeling theorists during the relativistic period.

First, while Lemert incorporated both normative and relativistic conceptions of deviance into the overall framework of *Social Pathology* (1951), later interpretations tended to focus selectively on the more subjective, relativistic implications of his theorizing. Lemert's contention that the severity of societal reactions will generally correspond to the objective seriousness of norm-violating behavior was replaced by the position that "(d)eviant labels are applied without regard to (or independent of) the behaviors or acts of those labelled" (Kitsuse, 1975: 275). Here, the lack of correspondence between objective behavior and societal reaction, which Lemert touched on in his discussion of spurious reactions, is treated by Kitsuse as a central analytical principle of labeling theory (see Rains, 1975). As we noted earlier, Lemert (1972) has branded as extreme relativism this tendency of labeling theorists to deemphasize the importance of norm-violating behavior as a factor in audience reaction processes.

Second, Lemert has characterized later attempts to analyze deviance as a more or less inevitable outcome of labeling and social control as "crude sociological determinism" (1972: 16). In particular, Lemert (1967: 51) feels that his complex, symbolic interactionist theory of secondary deviation has been oversimplified by Becker's conception of career deviance:

> A career denotes a course to be run, but the delineation of fixed sequences or stages through which persons move from less to more serious deviance is difficult to reconcile with an interactional theory. . . . A more defensible conception of deviant career is that of recurrent or typical contingencies and problems awaiting someone who continues in a course of action.

Third, Lemert has argued that labeling theorists, in their preoccupation with the problem of secondary deviation, have failed to come to grips with the other major theoretical concern of *Social Pathology*—societal reaction. In making this criticism, Lemert (1974) has pointed out some of the limitations of symbolic interactionist thought. Whatever its advantages for micro-level analyses of how individuals are stigmatized by deviant labels, this social psychological orientation provides little guidance for analyses of how political power and group conflict affect legislative and organizational reactions to deviance. Thus, Lemert appears to join contemporary conflict theorists in calling for a macro-level approach to societal reaction processes.

Finally, however, Lemert puts himself at odds with both the labeling theorists and the conflict theorists on the issue of values in the study of deviance. As we noted earlier, Lemert (1972: 24) has accused labeling theorists of generating "more social criticism than science" in their efforts to present value-engaged, humanistic portraits of deviants as underdogs. Similarly, he has described as doctrinaire the more recent critical analyses of capitalist society and social control appearing in the work of conflict theorists (1974: 462). In leveling these criticisms at more recent contributions to the relativistic perspective, Lemert has remained consistent with the essentially value-free, scientific orientation to the study of deviance that he laid out in the opening pages of *Social Pathology* (1951: 3–6). There, after pointing out that science itself is based on the value of free inquiry and that the study of deviance is influenced by public opinion and practical concerns, he goes on to ask (1951: 5):

> do these admissions mean that the sociologist must break out his colors and show whose side he is on in public controversies? We think not . . . there is nothing (in scientific inquiry) which demands that the scientist advocate or condemn the discoveries he makes.

Whereas many relativistic sociologists in recent years have come to agree with Becker's (1967) suggestion that they should take sides, Lemert has continued to hold the position that, above all, the "sociology of deviance must be a science of deviance" (1972: 25).

The continuities and tensions between Lemert's work and other contributions to the labeling tradition illustrate in microcosm the current state of deviance theory in general. Written before clear-cut boundaries emerged between the normative and relativistic perspectives, *Social Pathology* (1951) combined major elements of both viewpoints on deviant phenomena. While this unique marriage of ideas has made Lemert's work the subject of considerable confusion and controversy, it also suggests the possibility of an eventual synthesis or integration of conflicting viewpoints within the contemporary field of deviance. Be that as it may, we will now move on to consider how the problems of societal reaction and secondary deviance were approached by later theorists within the labeling tradition.

BECKER, KITSUSE, AND ERIKSON: THE MAINSTREAM OF LABELING THEORY

You have already been introduced in earlier chapters to some of the central ideas presented in three theoretical analyses by Becker (1963), Kitsuse (1962), and Erikson (1962) that marked the beginning of the relativistic period. Sociologists typically turn to these three works for quotations or examples that illustrate the distinctive insights which labeling theory and the relativistic perspective have contributed to the study of deviant phenomena. Here, we will not only be interested in the common features which identify the works of Becker, Kitsuse, and Erikson as the mainstream of labeling theory but also in some important differences in their respective analyses of audience reactions and secondary deviance.

Next to Lemert's early work (1951), Becker's book *Outsiders* (1963; 1973) presents the most comprehensive treatment of the problems of audience reactions and secondary deviance. In Chapter 1, of course, we focused on Becker's analysis of the latter phenomenon, which he conceptualized as career deviance. For the moment, then, let us turn to Becker's discussion of the initial question of how social audiences define and react to deviance.

Early in his book, Becker introduces the basic relativistic theme that deviance is created by audience reactions (1963: 9, emphasis deleted): "social groups create deviance by making the rules whose infraction constitutes deviance, and by applying those rules to particular people and labeling them as outsiders." Note, here, that Becker refers to three analytically distinct aspects of group reactions: the *making* of rules, the *application* of rules, and the *labeling* of particular people as deviants or outsiders. Becker's use of the word *rules* rather than *norms* in conjunction with the first two aspects of group reactions is deliberate and wholly consistent with his relativistic point of view. In contrast to the image of cultural consensus and uniformity brought to mind by the term *norm*, Becker emphasizes that "society has many groups, each with its own set of rules" (1963: 8). In such a diverse, pluralistic society, the interesting question is not whether people break rules, but, rather, how some groups are able to impose their rules on others. Therefore, analytical attention is focused on the activities of those who Becker calls "moral entrepreneurs" (1963: 147–163)—social audiences engaged in the business of creating and enforcing moral rules.

However, it is the third element in Becker's conception of audience reactions—labeling—that is most crucial to his overall formulation. Without denying the importance of rules and their creation, Becker argues that the question of who is deviant and who is not ultimately depends on the outcome of labeling processes rather than on infractions of rules. Whereas Lemert emphasized that societal reactions are generally contingent on the seriousness of norm-violating behavior, Becker emphasizes circumstances where rule-breaking behavior in itself is a poor predictor of whether individuals will actually be labeled as deviant by social audiences. For instance, Becker (1963: 13) points out that the law is differentially applied to Negroes and whites. It is well known that a Negro believed to have attacked a white woman is much more likely to be punished than a white man who commits the same offense . . . a Negro who murders another Negro is much less likely to be punished than a white man who commits murder.

Using these and other examples, Becker attempts to demonstrate how the processes through which individuals are categorically labeled as criminal, delinquent, or otherwise deviant depend as much or more on *who* is being labeled and *who* is doing the labeling than on the nature of the rules or behaviors involved. Therefore, we really "cannot know whether a given act (or actor) will be categorized as deviant until the response of others has occurred" (1963: 14). This implies that it is most useful for the sociologist to define and analyze deviance *relativistically*—i.e., by using as a criterion the deviant labels which social audiences actually attach to certain acts and actors through interactional processes.

Kitsuse's (1962) analysis of societal reactions takes an even more radically relativistic position. While Becker (1963: 14) grants that audience reactions may be based *in part* on the fact that a given act violates the rules shared by a particular group, Kitsuse completely avoids using the concepts of norm or rule as even partial standards for defining behavior as deviant. For Kitsuse, "deviance" *is* the interactional process by which audiences define and react to others as deviant. As we noted in Chapter 1, Kitsuse specifically argues that audiences create deviance by *interpreting* behavior as deviant, by *defining* persons who so behave as a certain kind of deviant, and by *treating* them in ways that are considered appropriate for this kind of deviant.

In his discussion of the first stage of this process, Kitsuse suggests that the subjective interpretation of behavior as deviant involves much more than a simple matter of comparing an individual's actions against some shared rule or norm. Audiences assign deviant meanings to behavior through a complex, subjective process that draws upon indirect evidence, such as rumors, as well as direct observations of how people act in certain situational settings. Depending on how behavior is interpreted, an audience may then subjectively define or classify the actor according to some deviant category such as criminal or homosexual. Even after reaching this second stage in Kitsuse's model, the audience may continue to engage in a process of "retrospective interpretation," where the actor's *past behavior is reinterpreted* as further evidence that he or she always has been a criminal, homosexual, etc. (1962: 253). However, Kitsuse contends that an individual is not sociologically deviant until the audience reaches the third stage in the general process and, reacting in accord with subjective interpretations and definitions, actually begins to treat the individual as deviant through verbal or physical expressions of rejection or disapproval. Thus, at all three stages in Kitsuse's relativistic conception of deviance, analytical attention is almost totally focused on the subjective and behavioral reactions of social audiences.

The work of the third mainstream labeling theorist, Erikson (1962; 1966), presents an interesting contrast to the strong themes of interactionist social psychology that run through the work of Becker and Kitsuse. Erikson's analysis of societal reactions owes a much greater debt to Durkheim, Parsons, and other sociological theorists usually associated with the macro-normative approach to deviance. Although Erikson's work is premised on the relativistic definition of deviance quoted at the beginning of this chapter, he does not elaborate much on the subjective or interactional processes by which some individuals define other individuals as deviant. Instead, he attempts to reveal some broader insights into the positive functions or benefits which deviants provide for entire communities or social systems.

Challenging the conventional view that deviance is a wholly undesirable or destructive element in social life, Erikson argues that deviants actually help to strengthen the moral boundaries of organized society. By singling out and reacting to certain individuals as deviant through such formal ceremonies as criminal trials, a community provides its nondeviant members with a clear, public demonstration of where the invisible line between moral and immoral behavior is drawn. Those persons who have been publicly excluded from the community as deviant outsiders (to use Becker's term) become concrete, living examples to the rest of us of "what *not* to do and what *not* to be." Based on his functional analysis of boundary maintenance, Erikson (1962: 310) contends that "deviance cannot be dismissed as behavior which *disrupts* stability in society, but is itself . . . an important condition for *preserving* stability."

But, returning to a more micro-level question, how are particular individuals initially selected by a community for public censure as deviants? Erikson introduces the notion of a community screening device to express the relativistic idea that social control is selectively applied to certain persons for reasons other than their objective behavior. He points out (1962: 308) that the selective screen of social control

> takes a number of factors into account which are not directly related to the deviant act itself: it is concerned with the actor's social class, his past record as an offender, the amount of remorse he manages to convey, and many other similar concerns.

Erikson implies that this screening process is guided as much by whether the individuals will serve as a "good" example of a typical deviant as it is by the nature of the act that this individual may have committed.

Becker, Kitsuse, and Erikson's analyses of deviance as a social definition created by audience reaction processes constitute an important part of the labeling tradition. Each theorist, in his own way, has attempted to develop more fully the relativistic implications of Lemert's earlier analysis of deviation and societal reaction by emphasizing *discrepancies* rather than *linkages* between objective behavior and audience definitions. However, there is a second sense in which the creation of deviance has been conceptualized and explored in the labeling tradition (see Hawkins & Tiedeman, 1975: 43–50), the sense in which Lemert referred to secondary deviance as a possible outcome or product of societal reactions. The proposition that labeling and social control processes create the very phenomena that they presumably are intended to eliminate—stable patterns of deviant activity—has become the most celebrated and most controversial contribution of the labeling tradition.

Of the three labeling theorists we are discussing in this section, only Becker and Erikson (and not Kitsuse) deal extensively with the problem of secondary deviance. It is important to point out that neither of these theorists bases his analysis of this problem strictly on Lemert's early, symbolic interactionist analysis of secondary deviation (1951). In fact, Lemert's more recent criticism of labeling theory as "crude sociological determinism" (1972: 16) appears to have been inspired primarily by differences between his treatment and the Becker-Erikson treatment of this particular analytical problem.

Becker (1963), in addition to citing Lemert's *Social Pathology* (1951) as a source of his ideas, acknowledges his debt to an even earlier textbook on crime by Tannenbaum (1938). Tannenbaum began his book by attempting to show how the social control of crime can often create more problems than it solves. In the following passage, Tannenbaum (1938: 19–20) presents a dramatic portrait of the undesirable and unanticipated consequences that await young boys who happen to be arrested and "tagged" as delinquent by police:

> The boy arrested . . . is singled out in specialized treatment. This boy, no more guilty than the other members of his group, discovers a world of which he knew little. His arrest suddenly precipitates a series of institutions, attitudes, and experiences which the other children do not share. . . . In this entirely new world he is made conscious of himself as a different human being than he was before his arrest. He becomes classified as a thief, perhaps, and the entire world about him has sud-

denly become a different place for him and will remain different for the rest of his life. . . . The process of making the criminal, therefore, is a process of tagging, defining, identifying, segregating, emphasizing, making conscious and self-conscious; it becomes a way of stimulating, suggesting, emphasizing, and evoking the very traits that are complained of. . . . The person becomes the thing he is described as being. . . . The child's isolation forces him into companionship with other children similarly defined, and the gang becomes his means of escape, his security. The life of the gang gives it special mores . . . and makes it the source of a new series of experiences that lead directly to a criminal career.

Clearly, Tannenbaum's view of the impact of social control on the individual is much more deterministic in nature than was Lemert's later conception of secondary deviation as a complex process of adjustment by a choice-making actor. Tannenbaum seems to imply that once a boy has been arrested and tagged, he has little choice but to move passively toward the career of crime dictated by the stigmatizing reactions of others.

Most important, Tannenbaum's brief discussion of tagging presents in skeletal form the steps in the process of progressive involvement in deviance which Becker later described as a deviant career (1963: 19–39). Both writers begin by emphasizing the crucial event of arrest and formal labeling. Each goes on to stress the subsequent impact of this event on the individual's self-concept and participation in conventional groups. Finally, these two theorists reach a common conclusion where the individual turns to deviant groups for social support and becomes committed to deviance as a way of life.

To be sure, Becker takes pains to avoid the heavily deterministic tone of Tannenbaum's rendition of this process. Becker acknowledges that "everyone caught in one deviant act and labeled a deviant does not move inevitably toward greater deviance" (1963: 36). Particularly if arrest or other formal reactions occur "at a point where (the individual) can still choose between alternate lines of action . . . he may decide that he does not want to take the deviant road" (1963: 37). But even here, Becker seems to leave the labeled individual with fewer options and with less control over the choice of those options than does Lemert's analysis of secondary deviation. By arguing that the career deviant's fate "depends not so much on what he does as on what other people do" (1963: 31), Becker portrays the individual more as a victim than as a voluntary actor.

Erikson (1962: 312) essentially shares Becker's (1963: 34) view of the labeling process as a self-fulfilling prophecy where the individual's behavior eventually confirms the initial deviant label. Like Becker, Erickson argues that formal labels imposed by official agencies of social control are especially likely to cast individuals into stabilized deviant roles. Underlying Erikson's analysis of the secondary deviance process is his functionalist assumption that communities or social systems "need" a steady volume of deviants to maintain the moral boundaries of organized society. Therefore, community agencies of social control function to meet this need by placing people *irreversibly* into deviant roles. Trials and other commitment ceremonies make it clear to all, including the suspect, that a person has been officially judged to be deviant. Such official deviants are then gathered together in special institutions (prisons and mental hospitals) that "give them an opportunity to teach one another the skills and attitudes of a deviant career." (1962: 311). Furthermore, a person who is unceremoniously released from prison or a mental hospital comes back to a community which is "suspicious that he will return to deviant activity upon a moment's provocation" (1962: 312). With the mechanisms of public labeling, institutionalization, and community distrust working against them, it is virtually inevitable that many individuals will "respond to this uncertainty by resuming deviant activity" (1962: 312). Thus, the official prophecy of deviance is confirmed and the community is assured of a steady flow of deviant behavior to mark its moral boundaries.

The deterministic orientation of Becker and Erikson's analyses of the problem of secondary deviance should not necessarily be considered as a defect of those formulations. In fact, when compared to Lemert's more complex analysis, these two versions of labeling theory may have the virtue of being more readily testable through empirical research. Lemert's conception of secondary deviation, with its emphasis on the dynamic and voluntary nature of human action, provides little "guidance in predicting which outcome is likely to occur" as the individual adjusts to societal reactions (Hawkins and Tiedeman, 1975: 48). By taking a strong position that formal labeling is indeed a major cause of patterned deviant activity, Becker and Erikson not only suggest an alternative to normative explanations of deviant behavior but also raise important practical and political questions about the unanticipated, problematic consequences of societal reactions and social control.

LATER DEVELOPMENTS IN THE LABELING TRADITION

Since the appearance of the initial statements by Becker, Kitsuse, and Erikson, the theoretical, empirical, and critical literature on labeling theory has grown at a tremendous rate. However, despite all of the attention focused on this micro-relativistic approach to deviance during the late 1960s and 1970s, surprisingly little in the way of new theoretical developments have been forthcoming. Lemert and the three mainstream labeling theorists have continued to publish actively; but these works largely represent efforts to extend or clarify their original theoretical positions (Lemert, 1964; 1967; 1972; 1974; 1981; Becker, 1973; Kitsuse, 1972; 1975; Erikson, 1966). Neither have collections of readings on labeling theory (Becker, 1964; Rubington & Weinberg, 1978) nor books devoted to evaluation and criticism of this approach (Schur, 1971; Gove, 1980) carried it much beyond the early work of the four theorists discussed above. At least one commentator has taken this lack of new breakthroughs in labeling theory as an indication of the exhaustion of this approach to deviance (Manning, 1973).

Although current theoretical work lacks the sense of excitement and vitality that accompanied the emergence of labeling theory and the relativistic perspective in the early 1960s, many sociologists disagree that the labeling tradition is exhausted (see Goode, 1975). As is typically the case following the introduction of a new theoretical perspective on empirical phenomena, labeling theorists now appear to be engaged in "mopping-up operations" (Kuhn, 1970) aimed at filling in gaps in the original formulations or at applying those formulations to specific kinds of deviance.

One area in the field of deviance where the application of labeling theory has led to particularly important developments is the study of mental disorder. Early in the 1960s, a psychiatrist, Thomas Szasz (1960; 1961) began to raise serious questions about the utility of the medical model of mental illness that had long dominated both psychiatric and sociological knowledge in this area. Similarly, a sociologist, Erving Goffman (1961) dramatically described the dehumanizing and stigmatizing effects of "total institutions," such as mental hospitals or asylums, upon their inmates. The relativistic argument running through these works—that mental disorders are actually created or intensified by psychiatric treatment—was more systematically developed in a later book by Thomas Scheff, *Being Mentally Ill* (1966). Drawing heavily on both Lemert and Becker, Scheff conceptualized mental illness as a label imposed upon certain individuals by psychiatrists and other agents of social control. Furthermore, Scheff viewed chronic patterns of bizarre behavior or disordered thought not as symptoms of some underlying disease, but as secondary deviance—the performance of stereotyped deviant roles adopted as the result of labeling processes. In this and other applications of labeling theory to psychiatric diagnosis and treatment, micro-relativistic sociologists such as Scheff have broadened the boundaries of the field of deviance by developing a general perspective on mental disorder and crime as socially defined phenomena.

In addition to mental disorder, the labeling approach has been applied theoretically and empirically to such diverse phenomena as blindness (Scott, 1969) and other physical disabilities (Freidson, 1966), mental retardation (Mercer, 1973), problem drinking (Roman and Trice, 1968), and the so-called victimless crimes of abortion, homosexuality, and drug addiction (Schur, 1965). Most of this work has focused on the problem of secondary deviance and how formal labeling affects the self-concepts and social participation of individuals as they are channeled into various deviant roles. By moving in this direction, labeling theory has increasingly taken the labeled deviant and his or her social world as its object of analysis. Ironically, this tendency to devote greater analytical attention to deviants rather than to the social audiences that label them is similar in many ways to the earlier analytical focus of normative theories of deviant behavior. This development has been criticized by a number of sociologists who have pointed out the need for more attention to the problem of audience reactions and to the phenomenon of social control (Lemert, 1974; Orcutt, 1973; Davis, 1972; Liazos, 1972; Mankoff, 1971).

Much of the later theoretical work on the problem of audience reactions is more properly considered as part of the conflict tradition rather than of the labeling tradition. Following the path suggested in Lemert's (1951) early analysis of group conflict and societal reaction, conflict theorists have pursued macro-level questions pertaining to the nature and sources of social control in complex, industrial societies. However, some sociologists have continued to develop the micro-level approach to audience interpretations, definitions, and reactions introduced by Kitsuse (1962).

One group of theorists, usually identified as *ethnomethodologists* or *phenomenological sociologists,* have argued that the mainstream labeling theorists have failed to provide an adequate description of the commonsense procedures that social audiences use in everyday life to recognize and interpret various kinds of deviance. Douglas (1970: 12), for instance, points out that labeling theorists, being preoccupied with the effects of different categorical labels upon secondary deviants, "never saw the need to determine the conditions under which one category would be applied rather than another." For ethnomethodologists and related theorists, the search for these conditions must begin with detailed analyses of the ways social audiences think about and talk about deviance in concrete social situations. The meaning assigned to a given act, whether deviant or not, can only be understood *relative to situational circumstances:* "Almost any behavior, such as taking one's clothes off, is appropriate or acceptable in some situational context, but not in most others" (Douglas, 1971: 138). Therefore, ethnomethodologists appear to arrive at an even more relativistic position than do labeling theorists by proposing that audience definitions of deviance fundamentally depend on the particular situational contexts within which acts are perceived to have occurred (also see Blum, 1970; Orcutt, 1975).

However, some ethnomethodologists have gone on to analyze the general procedures, processes, or rules that audiences use to assign deviant meanings to situational behavior. For example, McHugh (1970) has specified two basic procedures that audiences use to determine whether an actor is morally responsible for an act, thereby determining whether the act is deviant. On the one hand, audiences attempt to assess the *conventionality* of an act that has occurred; that is, they attempt to determine whether it was indeed *possible* for the actor to have acted differently or to have not performed the act at all. On the other hand, audiences also concern themselves with the *theoreticity* of the act; that is, did the actor *knowingly intend* to commit the act? In general, an audience will conclude that the actor is morally responsible and that the act is deviant if the actor is perceived to have been *free* to behave differently (conventionality) and to have *intentionally chosen* the act in question (theoreticity). Both of these questions depend on evidence provided by the situational context of the act.

While McHugh's analysis is mainly concerned with informal reactions to deviance by ordinary members of society, other ethnomethodologists have focused on how situational features of deviance figure into the processing of "offenders" by official agencies of social control (Sudnow, 1965; Cicourel, 1968). Police, public defenders, or probation officers employ information about the environmental background of individuals or about the circumstances under which an act is committed to construct "reasonable" explanations of deviant activity and to provide documentation that certain offenders are "typical" of the kind of people who commit such acts.

The idea that situational factors play a crucial part in interpretations and definitions of deviance has also been central to efforts to apply *attribution theory* to the problem of audience reactions (Hawkins & Tiedeman, 1975; Prus, 1975; Orcutt, 1973). Attribution theory was originally developed by social psychologists interested in the general question of how people perceive the causes of other people's behavior (Heider, 1958; Jones & Davis, 1965; Kelley, 1967). Similar to McHugh's (1970) ethnomethodological formulation, attribution theory proposes that an individual will tend to be perceived as personally responsible for committing an act only when situational causes for that behavior can be ruled out. For example, we are unlikely to attribute deviant motives to a person who, through accidental circumstances or because of overwhelming situational pressures, has harmed another person. However, when a person repeatedly does violence to others across a variety of situational circumstances, audiences will tend to use this evidence as grounds for attributing violent or criminal motives to the individual. Thus, both ethnomethodology and attribution theory stress the intimate, relativistic relationship between situational contexts and audience definitions of deviance.

CONCLUSION

In this chapter we have traced the development of the labeling tradition from its intellectual foundations in Chicago symbolic interactionism, through its formative stages in the works of Lemert, Becker, Kitsuse, and Erikson, to its current state of less dramatic growth or, perhaps, exhaustion. As in earlier chapters on the normative theories, we have focused on the cumulative efforts of various theorists to come to grips with central analytical problems that characterize this particular approach to deviance. These efforts have opened up some new and promising avenues for research in the field of deviance. By conceptualizing deviance as a subjective phenomenon that is created by audience reactions, labeling theorists have highlighted the importance of research on definitional processes that were virtually ignored by the normative perspective. Furthermore, by proposing that secondary deviance is a product of labeling and social control processes, some labeling theorists directly confronted the normative theorists with an alternative explanation of patterned deviant behavior—a confrontation which seems to invite empirical assessment. In the next chapter, we will look at several examples of the innovative research that has been inspired by the labeling tradition.

However, the impact of labeling theory on the field of deviance cannot be measured in strictly scientific terms alone. The work of the labeling theorists not only portrayed the definition and control of deviance as analytically problematic but also as morally and politically problematic. Becker's work, in particular, was instrumental in making sociologists conscious of the moral and political dilemmas which infuse the study of deviance (1963; 1964; 1967). As we noted in earlier chapters, of course, Becker argued against the position that sociologists could remain morally detached or value-neutral in their investigations of encounters between labeled deviants and agents of social control. In identifying with the moral viewpoint of the outsider, Becker was also able to shed some light on the political nature of the labeling process. Viewed from the perspective of the underdog, the question of who is deviant and who is not hinges on the question of who has the *power* to create and enforce rules and to apply stigmatizing labels to others. This relativistic conception of labeling as a power game provides the basic ingredient for a political critique of the uses and abuses of social control by certain dominant groups in modern, complex societies.

The rapid acceptance of labeling theory in the 1960s may have been due as much to Becker's articulate advocacy of this value-engaged orientation as it was to the more purely theoretical insights offered by him and his fellow labeling theorists. Certainly, Becker's moral sympathies with deviant underdogs and his critical portrait of the political process by which moral entrepreneurs impose their rules on others struck a resonant chord with sociologists and students during those years of civil rights activism and antiwar protest.

Yet, it was not the labeling theorists but the conflict theorists who have most fully developed the implications of the relativistic perspective for critical, value-engaged analyses of deviance and social control. In fact, conflict theorists and Marxist sociologists have been highly critical of the failure of Becker and other micro-relativistic theorists to use the study of deviance to raise broader, macro-level questions about basic, structural inequalities in capitalist society (Liazos, 1972; Thio, 1973; Gouldner, 1968; also see Becker, 1973: 177–208). Therefore, discussion of the importance of value-engaged theory and critical analysis within the relativistic perspective will take place in Chapters 10 and 11 where we will examine the recent theoretical, empirical, and critical contributions to the conflict tradition.

Research on interpersonal reactions to deviance

9

Before reading past this sentence, take half a minute to list as many different forms of deviant behavior as you can.

Now, take another 30 seconds to list as many different kinds of social control as you can bring to mind.

If you did attempt this seemingly pointless exercise, you would probably find that the first task is much easier than the second. Virtually all of us can quickly generate a long and relatively systematic list of felonies, misdemeanors, sexual acts, mental disorders, and other assorted violations of social norms. For most people, however, it would take a good deal of thought to get beyond a few obvious examples of social control such as arrest, imprisonment, psychiatric treatment, or scolding. The point is that our commonsense knowledge about deviance and social control is extremely lopsided. Whereas we have learned to make subtle and detailed distinctions between specific kinds of deviant behavior, our ability to perceive and describe the various ways people react to deviance is far more limited. We tend to be much more aware of what deviants might do to "us" than we are of what agents of social control might do to "them."

In the early 1960s, labeling theorists were able to point to a similar imbalance in sociological work on deviance. Kitsuse, for instance, observed that "theory and research in the area . . . have been concerned primarily with the classification and analysis of *deviant forms of behavior* and relatively little attention has been given to societal reactions to deviance" (1962: 247). After years of inattention to the topic of social control, sociologists in the labeling tradition have just begun the difficult task of describing and classifying the complex processes through which individuals are labeled and treated as deviant.

Most sociological research on interpersonal reactions to deviance is designed to meet this need for descriptive knowledge about basic mechanisms and patterns of social control. In particular, many microrelativistic studies have been based on various techniques for *direct observation* of encounters between social audiences and the individuals that they define as deviant. Unlike other sources of data such as surveys or official records, observational research allows the investigator to see social control in action; data can be gathered on the actual processes rather than the mere products of interpersonal reaction. The unique insights provided by direct observation have enabled researchers to fill in some important gaps in sociological knowledge about the ways that different social control processes work.

Observational data on interpersonal reactions to deviance have been gathered through a number of methods and in a wide variety of settings. The research illustrations presented in this chapter will give you a good sample of the diversity of studies in this general category. The first study by Rosenhan (1973) is based on *participant observation* conducted by researchers who had themselves admitted as inpatients in psychiatric hospitals. This work, which is already recognized as a classic contribution to the deviance literature, dramatically reveals the self-sustaining power of psychiatric labeling as seen from the standpoint of innocent victims of this social control process. Whereas Rosenhan's observers were complete participants in the hospital setting, Lundman's (1974) study of police arrest practices illustrates the use of partial participant observation. Here, neutral observers riding with officers in patrol cars utilized special recording equipment to gather data on a variety of social factors affecting the process of police reaction to public drunkenness offenders. Finally, we will turn from these participant observation studies of formal social control processes to an innovative study of informal reactions to shoplifting. Steffensmeier and Terry (1973) depart from the naturalistic approach of most observational work in the labeling tradition and present data from a *field experiment*, where an interpersonal encounter between ordinary shoppers and a rule-breaking actor was not merely observed but actually created by the investigators.

INTRODUCTORY COMMENTS ON ROSENHAN'S RESEARCH

In his book *Outsiders* (1963), Howard Becker presented a hypothetical example of a law-abiding boy who was falsely accused and arrested as a delinquent to illustrate a central conceptual principle of labeling theory: it's not what you do, but how others define you that makes you socially deviant. Becker speculated that if such "bum raps" can occur in the legal system where rules of evidence and due process protect the accused, then cases of false accusation "probably occur much more frequently in nonlegal settings where procedural safeguards are not available" (1963: 20). The following study by Rosenhan, "On Being Sane in Insane Places" (1973), offers some compelling empirical support for Becker's speculation. Among other things, this remarkable observational study demonstrates that false accusations of deviance—or, rather, false diagnoses—are, indeed, a very real possibility in psychiatric settings.

This and other discoveries came about through the novel but effective strategy Rosenhan's participant observers used to gain new insights into psychiatric social control: they put themselves on the receiving end of it. Rosenhan, a psychologist, and eight other normal people (including three psychologists, a pediatrician, a psychiatrist, a painter, a housewife, and a graduate student) individually went to the admissions offices of 12 different psychiatric hospitals and complained of hearing voices that said "empty," "hollow," and "thud." It is important to note that this particular set of "symptoms" was completely contrived and had never been reported in the psychiatric literature. Nonetheless, *in every case* these pseudopatients were falsely diagnosed as having a severe mental disorder and were admitted to the hospitals on a voluntary basis. Once the pseudopatients were taken to a psychiatric ward, they ceased reporting any symptoms and behaved just as they normally would. To be discharged from the hospital, each pseudopatient had to convince the staff that he or she was really sane.

Some of the results of this study might strike you as startling, even nightmarish. Despite their apparently normal behavior following admission as voluntary patients, Rosenhan and his collaborators were held in these institutions for an average of 19 days. In one case, a pseudopatient was hospitalized for nearly two months! Even though they eventually succeeded in gaining discharges, none of the pseudopatients was certified to be truly normal or sane upon release. In all 12 instances, the observers left the institutions with the psychiatric label "schizophrenia in remission" entered into their permanent records.

Rosenhan's dramatic findings on the ease of admission and the difficulty of discharge in psychiatric institutions became the subject of considerable controversy as we shall see later. However, observational data gathered by the researchers during the course of their hospitalization are of even greater significance for a sociological understanding of psychiatric treatment as a process of social control. The pseudopatients took detailed field notes on routine patterns of activity as well as unusual incidents they observed on the psychiatric wards. Most of Rosenhan's descriptive analysis of the experience of psychiatric hospitalization is based on *qualitative* data taken from these notes. Throughout his article, Rosenhan uses specific anecdotes from field notes to typify or illustrate general observations and common impressions reported by the pseudopatients. For instance, consider the following "conversation" between a pseudopatient and a psychiatrist:

Pseudopatient: Pardon me, Dr. X. Could you tell me when I am eligible for grounds privileges?

Physician: Good morning, Dave. How are you today? [Moves off without waiting for a response.]

If, as Rosenhan indicates, this type of encounter was observed frequently on the hospital wards, what would you conclude about the nature or quality of social interaction between patients and staff? Rosenhan's conclusion, which he attempts to document with this and other anecdotal evidence, is that hospital staff tend to "depersonalize" patients and avoid meaningful social contacts with them. Rosenhan's skillful presentation of these qualitative data not only provides a rich description of the peculiar features of the process of interpersonal avoidance but also conveys to the reader a subjective sense or feel for its dehumanizing impact on patients. By encouraging an understanding of social control from the underdog's point of view, Rosenhan's qualitative analyses serve as an excellent example of the humanistic approach to deviance research advocated by Becker and many other sociologists within the labeling tradition.

Despite the intuitive appeal of qualitative insights from participant observation studies, hard-nosed researchers often object that impressionistic or "*soft*" data can all too readily be slanted or selected to fit the preconceived biases of the investigator. Specifically, isn't it possible that Rosenhan chose to emphasize a relatively few, shocking incidents of depersonalization and that he could just as easily have cited numerous anecdotes portraying warm and therapeutic relationships between staff and patients? Or, when vague and implicitly statistical terms like *frequently* or *rarely* are used to describe certain activities, isn't it reasonable to ask exactly *how frequently* or *how rarely* these actions were observed to occur? Apparently anticipating such objections, Rosenhan instructed his observers to gather *quantitative* data on a variety of routine behaviors and events that occurred during their hospitalization. Thus, Rosenhan was able to buttress many of his generalizations about interpersonal reactions to patients with explicit statistical evidence. For example, Table 1 in Rosenhan's article is based on data from four hospitals where pseudopatients kept a count of the responses they received after approaching members of the staff with simple requests for information. Look at the percentages of encounters in Table 1 in which staff did not even stop to make eye contact with pseudopatients and judge for yourself whether Rosenhan is justified in characterizing staff-patient relationships as depersonalized.

At this point, however, it will probably come as no surprise to you that many psychiatrists do not believe that Rosenhan's conclusions are justified by his evidence. His article became the subject of almost unprecedented controversy following its publication in the prestigious journal *Science*. In no less than 15 letters to the editor of *Science* (Fleischman et al., 1973) and seven critical essays prepared for the *Bulletin of the Menninger Clinic* (Wiedeman et al., 1973; Holzman et al., 1973), psychiatrists voiced their particular concern with Rosenhan's conclusion that "we cannot distinguish the sane from the insane in psychiatric hospitals" (1973: 257). Rosenhan's critics attacked his findings on the false diagnoses of 12 pseudopatients and defended the ability of the psychiatric profession to distinguish various forms of psychoses from "nonpsychotic" (normal?) behavior. At least one critic implied that the pseudopatients may not, in fact, have acted nor been as normal as Rosenhan indicated in his article! At the other extreme, several psychiatrists attempted to account for his findings on admissions and discharges by arguing that the pseudopatients had by chance encountered 12 hospitals with unusually incompetent diagnostic procedures.

Whatever the scientific merits of Rosenhan's observational research, the intense critical reaction to the issues he raised about the validity and reliability of psychiatric diagnoses highlights a crucial ideological implication of his work. By questioning the credibility of diagnostic labels, Rosenhan, in effect, challenges the legitimacy of the medical model of deviance upon which psychiatric social control is based. Indeed, the goal of Rosenhan's analysis is not only to describe the uses of social control in psychiatric settings but to raise the more troublesome issue of whether individuals *should* be subject to the potential abuses of being labeled as mentally ill. In this respect as well as in many others, Rosenhan's study falls squarely in the humanistic, value-engaged tradition of Becker and other labeling theorists.

RESEARCH ILLUSTRATION 9–A

On being sane in insane places

*David L. Rosenhan**

If sanity and insanity exist, how shall we know them?

The question is neither capricious nor itself insane. However much we may be personally convinced that we can tell the normal from the abnormal, the evidence is simply not compelling. It is commonplace, for example, to read about murder trials wherein eminent psychiatrists for the defense are contradicted by equally eminent psychiatrists for the prosecution on the matter of the defendant's sanity.

Source: Article reprinted from *Science* 179 (January 19, 1973), pp. 250–258. Copyright 1973 by the American Association for the Advancement of Science.

* The author is professor of psychology and law at Stanford University, Stanford, California 94305. Portions of these data were presented to colloquiums of the psychology departments at the University of California at Berkeley and at Santa Barbara; University of Arizona, Tucson; and Harvard University, Cambridge, Massachusetts.

More generally, there are a great deal of conflicting data on the reliability, utility, and meaning of such terms as "sanity," "insanity," "mental illness," and "schizophrenia" (1). Finally, as early as 1934, Benedict suggested that normality and abnormality are not universal (2). What is viewed as normal in one culture may be seen as quite aberrant in another. Thus, notions of normality and abnormality may not be quite as accurate as people believe they are.

To raise questions regarding normality and abnormality is in no way to question the fact that some behaviors are deviant or odd. Murder is deviant. So, too, are hallucinations. Nor does raising such questions deny the existence of the personal anguish that is often associated with "mental illness." Anxiety and depression exist. Psychological suffering exists. But normality and abnormality, sanity and insanity, and the diagnoses that flow from them may be less substantive than many believe them to be.

At its heart, the question of whether the sane can be distinguished from the insane (and whether degrees of insanity can be distinguished from each other) is a simple matter: do the salient characteristics that lead to diagnoses reside in the patients themselves or in the environments and contexts in which observers find them? From Bleuler, through Kretchmer, through the formulators of the recently revised *Diagnostic and Statistical Manual* of the American Psychiatric Association, the belief has been strong that patients present symptoms, that those symptoms can be categorized, and, implicitly, that the sane are distinguishable from the insane. More recently, however, this belief has been questioned. Based in part on theoretical and anthropological considerations, but also on philosophical, legal, and therapeutic ones, the view has grown that psychological categorization of mental illness is useless at best and downright harmful, misleading, and pejorative at worst. Psychiatric diagnoses, in this view, are in the minds of the observers and are not valid summaries of characteristics displayed by the observed (3–5).

Gains can be made in deciding which of these is more nearly accurate by getting normal people (that is, people who do not have, and have never suffered, symptoms of serious psychiatric disorders) admitted to psychiatric hospitals and then determining whether they were discovered to be sane and, if so, how. If the sanity of such pseudopatients were always detected, there would be prima facie evidence that a sane individual can be distinguished from the insane context in which he is found. Normality (and presumably abnormality) is distinct enough that it can be recognized wherever it occurs, for it is carried within the person. If, on the other hand, the sanity of the pseudopatients were never discovered, serious difficulties would arise for those who support traditional modes of psychiatric diagnosis. Given that the hospital staff was not incompetent, that the pseudopatient had been behaving as sanely as he had been outside of the hospital, and that it had never been previously suggested that he belonged in a psychiatric hospital, such an unlikely outcome would support the view that psychiatric diagnosis betrays little about the patient but much about the environment in which an observer finds him.

This article describes such an experiment. Eight sane people gained secret admission to 12 different hospitals (6). Their diagnostic experiences constitute the data of the first part of this article; the remainder is devoted to a description of their experiences in psychiatric institutions. Too few psychiatrists and psychologists, even those who have worked in such hospitals, know what the experience is like. They rarely talk about it with former patients, perhaps because they distrust information coming from the previously insane. Those who have worked in psychiatric hospitals are likely to have adapted so thoroughly to the settings that they are insensitive to the impact of that experience. And while there have been occasional reports of researchers who submitted themselves to psychiatric hospitalization (7), these researchers have commonly remained in the hospitals for short periods of time, often with the knowledge of the hospital staff. It is difficult to know the extent to which they were treated like patients or like research colleagues. Nevertheless, their reports about the inside of the psychiatric hospital have been valuable. This article extends those efforts.

PSEUDOPATIENTS AND THEIR SETTINGS

The eight pseudopatients were a varied group. One was a psychology graduate student in his 20s. The remaining seven were older and "established." Among them were three psychologists, a pediatrician, a psychiatrist, a painter, and a housewife. Three pseudopatients were women, five were men. All of them employed pseudonyms, lest their alleged diagnoses embarrass them later. Those who were in mental health professions alleged another occupation in order to avoid the special attentions that might be accorded by staff, as a matter of courtesy or caution, to ailing colleagues (8). With the exception of myself (I was the first pseudopatient and my presence was known to the hospital administrator and chief psychologist and, so far as I can tell, to them alone), the presence of pseudopatients and the nature of the research program was not known to the hospital staffs (9).

The settings were similarly varied. In order to generalize the findings, admission into a variety of hospitals was sought. The 12 hospitals in the sample were located in five different states on the East and

West coasts. Some were old and shabby, some were quite new. Some were research-oriented, others not. Some had good staff-patient ratios, others were quite understaffed. Only one was a strictly private hospital. All of the others were supported by state or federal funds or, in one instance, by university funds.

After calling the hospital for an appointment, the pseudopatient arrived at the admissions office complaining that he had been hearing voices. Asked what the voices said, he replied that they were often unclear, but as far as he could tell they said "empty," "hollow," and "thud." The voices were unfamiliar and were of the same sex as the pseudopatient. The choice of these symptoms was occasioned by their apparent similarity to existential symptoms. Such symptoms are alleged to arise from painful concerns about the perceived meaninglessness of one's life. It is as if the hallucinating person were saying, "My life is empty and hollow." The choice of these symptoms was also determined by the *absence* of a single report of existential psychoses in the literature.

Beyond alleging the symptoms and falsifying name, vocation, and employment, no further alterations of person, history, or circumstances were made. The significant events of the pseudopatient's life history were presented as they had actually occurred. Relationships with parents and siblings, with spouse and children, with people at work and in school, consistent with the aforementioned exceptions, were described as they were or had been. Frustrations and upsets were described along with joys and satisfactions. These facts are important to remember. If anything, they strongly biased the subsequent results in favor of detecting sanity, since none of their histories or current behaviors were seriously pathological in any way.

Immediately upon admission to the psychiatric ward, the pseudopatient ceased simulating *any* symptoms of abnormality. In some cases, there was a brief period of mild nervousness and anxiety, since none of the pseudopatients really believed that they would be admitted so easily. Indeed, their shared fear was that they would be immediately exposed as frauds and greatly embarrassed. Moreover, many of them had never visited a psychiatric ward; even those who had, nevertheless had some genuine fears about what might happen to them. Their nervousness, then, was quite appropriate to the novelty of the hospital setting, and it abated rapidly.

Apart from that short-lived nervousness, the pseudopatient behaved on the ward as he "normally" behaved. The pseudopatient spoke to patients and staff as he might ordinarily. Because there is uncommonly little to do on a psychiatric ward, he attempted to engage others in conversation. When asked by staff how he was feeling, he indicated that he was fine, that he no longer experienced symptoms. He responded to instructions from attendants, to calls for medication (which was not swallowed), and to dining-hall instructions. Beyond such activities as were available to him on the admissions ward, he spent his time writing down his observations about the ward, its patients, and the staff. Initially these notes were written "secretly," but as it soon became clear that no one much cared, they were subsequently written on standard tablets of paper in such public places as the dayroom. No secret was made of these activities.

The pseudopatient, very much as a true psychiatric patient, entered a hospital with no foreknowledge of when he would be discharged. Each was told that he would have to get out by his own devices, essentially by convincing the staff that he was sane. The psychological stresses associated with hospitalization were considerable, and all but one of the pseudopatients desired to be discharged almost immediately after being admitted. They were, therefore, motivated not only to behave sanely, but to be paragons of cooperation. That their behavior was in no way disruptive is confirmed by nursing reports, which have been obtained on most of the patients. These reports uniformly indicate that the patients were "friendly," "cooperative," and "exhibited no abnormal indications."

THE NORMAL ARE NOT DETECTABLY SANE

Despite their public "show" of sanity, the pseudopatients were never detected. Admitted, except in one case, with a diagnosis of schizophrenia (10), each was discharged with a diagnosis of schizophrenia "in remission." The label "in remission" should in no way be dismissed as a formality, for at no time during any hospitalization had any question been raised about any pseudopatient's simulation. Nor are there any indications in the hospital records that the pseudopatient's status was suspect. Rather, the evidence is strong that, once labeled schizophrenic, the pseudopatient was stuck with that label. If the pseudopatient was to be discharged, he must naturally be "in remission"; but he was not sane, nor, in the institution's view, had he ever been sane.

The uniform failure to recognize sanity cannot be attributed to the quality of the hospitals, for, although there were considerable variations among them, several are considered excellent. Nor can it be alleged that there was simply not enough time to observe the pseudopatients. Length of hospitalization ranged from 7 to 52 days, with an average of 19 days. The pseudopatients were not, in fact, carefully observed, but this failure clearly speaks more to traditions within psychiatric hospitals than to lack of opportunity.

Finally, it cannot be said that the failure to recognize the pseudopatients' sanity was due to the fact that they were not behaving sanely. While there was clearly some tension present in all of them, their daily visitors could detect no serious behavioral consequences—nor, indeed, could other patients. It was quite common for the patients to "detect" the pseudopatients' sanity. During the first three hospitalizations, when accurate counts were kept, 35 of a total of 118 patients on the admissions ward voiced their suspicions, some vigorously. "You're not crazy. You're a journalist, or a professor [referring to the continual note-taking]. You're checking up on the hospital." While most of the patients were reassured by the pseudopatient's insistence that he had been sick before he came in but was fine now, some continued to believe that the pseudopatient was sane throughout his hospitalization (*11*). The fact that the patients often recognized normality when staff did not raises important questions.

Failure to detect sanity during the course of hospitalization may be due to the fact that physicians operate with a strong bias toward what statisticians call the type 2 error (*5*). This is to say that physicians are more inclined to call a healthy person sick (a false positive, type 2) than a sick person healthy (a false negative, type 1). The reasons for this are not hard to find: it is clearly more dangerous to misdiagnose illness than health. Better to err on the side of caution, to suspect illness even among the healthy.

But what holds for medicine does not hold equally well for psychiatry. Medical illnesses, while unfortunate, are not commonly pejorative. Psychiatric diagnoses, on the contrary, carry with them personal, legal, and social stigmas (*12*). It was therefore important to see whether the tendency toward diagnosing the sane insane could be reversed. The following experiment was arranged at a research and teaching hospital whose staff had heard these findings but doubted that such an error could occur in their hospital. The staff was informed that at some time during the following three months, one or more pseudopatients would attempt to be admitted into the psychiatric hospital. Each staff member was asked to rate each patient who presented himself at admissions or on the ward according to the likelihood that the patient was a pseudopatient. A 10-point scale was used, with a 1 and 2 reflecting high confidence that the patient was a pseudopatient.

Judgments were obtained on 193 patients who were admitted for psychiatric treatment. All staff who had had sustained contact with or primary responsibility for the patient—attendants, nurses, psychiatrists, physicians, and psychologists—were asked to make judgments. Forty-one patients were alleged, with high confidence, to be pseudopatients by at least one member of the staff. Twenty-three were considered suspect by at least one psychiatrist. Nineteen were suspected by one psychiatrist *and* one other staff member. Actually, no genuine pseudopatient (at least from my group) presented himself during this period.

The experiment is instructive. It indicates that the tendency to designate sane people as insane can be reversed when the stakes (in this case, prestige and diagnostic acumen) are high. But what can be said of the 19 people who were suspected of being "sane" by one psychiatrist and another staff member? Were these people truly "sane," or was it rather the case that in the course of avoiding the type 2 error the staff tended to make more errors of the first sort—calling the crazy "sane"? There is no way of knowing. But one thing is certain: any diagnostic process that lends itself so readily to massive errors of this sort cannot be a very reliable one.

THE STICKINESS OF PSYCHODIAGNOSTIC LABELS

Beyond the tendency to call the healthy sick—a tendency that accounts better for diagnostic behavior on admission than it does for such behavior after a lengthy period of exposure—the data speak to the massive role of labeling in psychiatric assessment. Having once been labeled schizophrenic, there is nothing the pseudopatient can do to overcome the tag. The tag profoundly colors others' perceptions of him and his behavior.

From one viewpoint, these data are hardly surprising, for it has long been known that elements are given meaning by the context in which they occur. Gestalt psychology made this point vigorously, and Asch (13) demonstrated that there are "central" personality traits (such as "warm" versus "cold") which are so powerful that they markedly color the meaning of other information in forming an impression of a given personality (14). "Insane," "schizophrenic," "manic-depressive," and "crazy" are probably among the most powerful of such central traits. Once a person is designated abnormal, all of his other behaviors and characteristics are colored by that label. Indeed, that label is so powerful that many of the pseudopatients' normal behaviors were overlooked entirely or profoundly misinterpreted. Some examples may clarify this issue.

Earlier I indicated that there were no changes in the pseudopatient's personal history and current status beyond those of name, employment, and, where necessary, vocation. Otherwise, a veridical description of personal history and circumstances was offered. Those circumstances were not psychotic. How were they made consonant with the diagnosis of psychosis? Or were those diagnoses modified in such a way as to bring them into accord with the circumstances of the pseudopatient's life, as described by him?

As far as I can determine, diagnoses were in no way affected by the relative health of the circumstances of a pseudopatient's life. Rather, the reverse occurred: the perception of his circumstances was shaped entirely by the diagnosis. A clear example of such translation is found in the case of a pseudopatient who had had a close relationship with his mother but was rather remote from his father during his early childhood. During adolescence and beyond, however, his father became a close friend, while his relationship with his mother cooled. His present relationship with his wife was characteristically close and warm. Apart from occasional angry exchanges, friction was minimal. The children had rarely been spanked. Surely there is nothing especially pathological about such a history. Indeed, many readers may see a similar pattern in their own experiences, with no markedly deleterious consequences. Observe, however, how such a history was translated in the psychopathological context, this from the case summary prepared after the patient was discharged.

> This white 39-year-old male . . . manifests a long history of considerable ambivalence in close relationships, which begins in early childhood. A warm relationship with his mother cools during his adolescence. A distant relationship to his father is described as becoming very intense. Affective stability is absent. His attempts to control emotionality with his wife and children are punctuated by angry outbursts and, in the case of the children, spankings. And while he says that he has several good friends, one senses considerable ambivalence embedded in those relationships also. . . .

The facts of the case were unintentionally distorted by the staff to achieve consistency with a popular theory of the dynamics of a schizophrenic reaction (15). Nothing of an ambivalent nature has been described in relations with parents, spouse, or friends. To the extent that ambivalence could be inferred, it was probably not greater than is found in all human relationships. It is true the pseudopatient's relationships with his parents changed over time, but in the ordinary context that would hardly be remarkable—indeed, it might very well be expected. Clearly, the meaning ascribed to his verbalizations (that is, ambivalence, affective instability) was determined by the diagnosis: schizophrenia. An entirely different meaning would have been ascribed if it were known that the man was "normal."

All pseudopatients took extensive notes publicly. Under ordinary circumstances, such behavior would have raised questions in the minds of observers, as, in fact, it did among patients. Indeed, it seemed so certain that the notes would elicit suspicion that elaborate precautions were taken to remove them from the ward each day. But the precautions proved needless. The closest any staff member came to questioning these notes occurred when one pseudopatient asked his physician what kind of medication he was receiving and began to write down the response. "You needn't write it," he was told gently. "If you have trouble remembering, just ask me again."

If no questions were asked of the pseudopatients, how was their writing interpreted? Nursing records for three patients indicate that the writing was seen as an aspect of their pathological behavior. "Patient engages in writing behavior" was the daily nursing comment on one of the pseudopatients who was never questioned about his writing. Given that the patient is in the hospital, he must be psychologically disturbed. And given that he is disturbed, continuous writing must be a behavioral manifestation of that disturbance, perhaps a subset of the compulsive behaviors that are sometimes correlated with schizophrenia.

One tacit characteristic of psychiatric diagnosis is that it locates the sources of aberration within the individual and only rarely within the complex of stimuli that surrounds him. Consequently, behaviors that are stimulated by the environment are commonly misattributed to the patient's disorder. For example, one kindly nurse found a pseudopatient pacing the long hospital corridors. "Nervous, Mr. X?" she asked. "No, bored," he said.

The notes kept by pseudopatients are full of patient behaviors that were misinterpreted by well-intentioned staff. Often enough, a patient would go "berserk" because he had, wittingly or unwittingly, been mistreated by, say, an attendant. A nurse coming upon the scene would rarely inquire even cursorily into the environmental stimuli of the patient's behavior. Rather, she assumed that his upset derived from his pathology, not from his present interactions with other staff members. Occasionally, the staff might assume that the patient's family (especially when they had recently visited) or other patients had stimulated the outburst. But never were the staff found to assume that one of themselves or the structure of the hospital had anything to do with a patient's behavior. One psychiatrist pointed to a group of patients who were sitting outside the cafeteria entrance half an hour before lunchtime. To a group of young residents he indicated that such behavior was characteristic of the oral-acquisitive nature of the syndrome. It seemed not to occur to him that there were very few things to anticipate in a psychiatric hospital besides eating.

A psychiatric label has a life and an influence of its own. Once the impression has been formed that the patient is schizophrenic, the expectation is that he will continue to be schizophrenic. When a sufficient amount of time has passed, during which the patient has done nothing bizarre, he is considered to be in remission and available for discharge. But the label endures beyond discharge, with the unconfirmed expectation that he will behave as a schizophrenic again. Such labels, conferred by mental health professionals, are as influential on the patient as they are on his relatives and friends, and it should not surprise anyone that the diagnosis acts on all of them as a self-fulfilling prophecy. Eventually, the patient himself accepts the diagnosis, with all of its surplus meanings and expectations, and behaves accordingly (5).

The inferences to be made from these matters are quite simple. Much as Zigler and Phillips have demonstrated that there is enormous overlap in the symptoms presented by patients who have been variously diagnosed (16), so there is enormous overlap in the behaviors of the sane and the insane. The sane are not "sane" all of the time. We lose our tempers "for no good reason." We are occasionally depressed or anxious, again for no good reason. And we may find it difficult to get along with one or another person—again for no reason that we can specify. Similarly, the insane are not always insane. Indeed, it was the impression of the pseudopatients while living with them that they were sane for long periods of time—that the bizarre behaviors upon which their diagnoses were allegedly predicated constituted only a small fraction of their total behavior. If it makes no sense to label ourselves permanently depressed on the basis of an occasional depression, then it takes better evidence than is presently available to label all patients insane or schizophrenic on the basis of bizarre behaviors or cognitions. It seems more useful, as Mischel (17) has pointed out, to limit our discussions to *behaviors*, the stimuli that provoke them, and their correlates.

It is not known why powerful impressions of personality traits, such as "crazy" or "insane," arise. Conceivably, when the origins of and stimuli that give rise to a behavior are remote or unknown, or when the behavior strikes us as immutable, trait labels regarding the *behaver* arise. When, on the other hand, the origins and stimuli are known and available, discourse is limited to the behavior itself. Thus, I may hallucinate because I am sleeping, or I may hallucinate because I have ingested a peculiar drug. These are termed sleep-induced hallucinations, or dreams, and drug-induced hallucinations, respectively. But when the stimuli to my hallucinations are unknown, that is called craziness, or schizophrenia—as if that inference were somehow as illuminating as the others.

THE EXPERIENCE OF PSYCHIATRIC HOSPITALIZATION

The term "mental illness" is of recent origin. It was coined by people who were humane in their inclinations and who wanted very much to raise the station of (and the public's sympathies toward) the psychologically disturbed from that of witches and "crazies" to one that was akin to the physically ill. And they were at least partially successful, for the treatment of the mentally ill *has* improved considerably over the years. But while treatment has improved, it is doubtful that people really regard the mentally ill in the same way that they view the physically ill. A broken leg is something one recovers from, but mental illness allegedly endures forever (*18*). A broken leg does not threaten the observer, but a crazy schizophrenic? There is by now a host of evidence that attitudes toward the mentally ill are characterized by fear, hostility, aloofness, suspicion, and dread (*19*). The mentally ill are society's lepers.

That such attitudes infect the general population is perhaps not surprising, only upsetting. But that they affect the professionals—attendants, nurses, physicians, psychologists, and social workers—who treat and deal with the mentally ill is more disconcerting, both because such attitudes are self-evidently pernicious and because they are unwitting. Most mental health professionals would insist that they are sympathetic toward the mentally ill, that they are neither avoidant nor hostile. But it is more likely that an exquisite ambivalence characterizes their relations with psychiatric patients, such that their avowed impulses are only part of their entire attitude. Negative attitudes are there too and can easily be detected. Such attitudes should not surprise us. They are the natural offspring of the labels patients wear and the places in which they are found.

Consider the structure of the typical psychiatric hospital. Staff and patients are strictly segregated. Staff have their own living space, including their dining facilities, bathrooms, and assembly places. The glassed quarters that contain the professional staff, which the pseudopatients came to call "the cage," sit out on every dayroom. The staff emerge primarily for caretaking purposes—to give medication, to conduct a therapy or group meeting, to instruct or reprimand a patient. Otherwise, staff keep to themselves, almost as if the disorder that afflicts their charges is somehow catching.

So much is patient-staff segregation the rule that, for four public hospitals in which an attempt was made to measure the degree to which staff and patients mingle, it was necessary to use "time out of the staff cage" as the operational measure. While it was not the case that all time spent out of the cage was spent mingling with patients (attendants, for example, would occasionally emerge to watch television in the dayroom), it was the only way in which one could gather reliable data on time for measuring.

The average amount of time spent by attendants outside of the cage was 11.3 percent (range, 3 to 52 percent). This figure does not represent only time spent mingling with patients, but also includes time spent on such chores as folding laundry, supervising patients while they shave, directing ward cleanup, and sending patients to off-ward activities. It was the relatively rare attendant who spent time talking with patients or playing games with them. It proved impossible to obtain a "percent mingling time" for nurses, since the amount of time they spent out of the cage was too brief. Rather, we counted instances of emergence from the cage. On the average, daytime nurses emerged from the cage 11.5 times per shift, including instances when they left the ward entirely (range, 4 to 39 times). Late afternoon and night nurses were even less available, emerging on the average 9.4 times per shift (range, 4 to 41 times). Data on early morning nurses, who arrived usually after midnight and departed at 8 A.M., are not available because patients were asleep during most of this period.

Physicians, especially psychiatrists, were even less available. They were rarely seen on the wards. Quite commonly, they would be seen only when they arrived and departed, with the remaining time being spent in their offices or in the cage. On the average, physicians emerged on the ward 6.7 times per day (range, 1 to 17 times). It proved difficult to make an accurate estimate in this regard, since physicians often maintained hours that allowed them to come and go at different times.

The hierarchical organization of the psychiatric hospital has been commented on before (20), but the latent meaning of that kind of organization is worth noting again. Those with the most power have least to do with patients, and those with the least power are most involved with them. Recall, however, that the acquisition of role-appropriate behaviors occurs mainly through the observation of others, with the most powerful having the most influence. Consequently, it is understandable that attendants not only spend more time with patients than do any other members of the staff—that is required by their station in the hierarchy—but also, insofar as they learn from their superiors' behavior, spend as little time with patients as they can. Attendants are seen mainly in the cage, which is where the models, the action, and the power are.

I turn now to a different set of studies, these dealing with staff response to patient-initiated contact. It has long been known that the amount of time a person spends with you can be an index of your significance to him. If he initiates and maintains eye contact, there is reason to believe that he is considering your requests and needs. If he pauses to chat or actually stops and talks, there is added reason to infer that he is individuating you. In four hospitals, the pseudopatient approached the staff member with a request which took the following form: "Pardon me, Mr. [or Dr. or Mrs.] X, could you tell me when I will be eligible for grounds privileges?" (or ". . . when I will be presented at the staff meeting?" or ". . . when I am likely to be discharged?"). While the content of the question varied according to the appropriateness of the target and the pseudopatient's (apparent) current needs the form was always a courteous and relevant request for information. Care was taken never to approach a particular member of the staff more than once a day, lest the staff member become suspicious or irritated. In examining these data, remember that the behavior of the pseudopatients was neither bizarre nor disruptive. One could indeed engage in good conversation with them.

The data for these experiments are shown in Table 1, separately for physicians (column 1) and for nurses and attendants (column 2). Minor differences between these four institutions were overwhelmed by the degree to which staff avoided continuing contacts that patients had initiated. By far, their most common response consisted of either a brief response to the question, offered while they were "on the move" and with head averted, or no response at all.

The encounter frequently took the following bizarre form: (pseudopatient) "Pardon me, Dr. X. Could you tell me when I am eligible for grounds privileges?" (physician) "Good morning, Dave. How are you today?" (Moves off without waiting for a response.)

It is instructive to compare these data with data recently obtained at Stanford University. It has been alleged that large and eminent universities are characterized by faculty who are so busy that they have no time for students. For this comparison, a young lady approached individual faculty members who seemed to be walking purposefully to some meeting or teaching engagement and asked them the following six questions.

1. "Pardon me, could you direct me to Encina Hall?" (at the medical school: ". . . to the Clinical Research Center?").
2. "Do you know where Fish Annex is?" (there is no Fish Annex at Stanford).
3. "Do you teach here?"
4. "How does one apply for admission to the college?" (at the medical school: ". . . to the medical school?").
5. "Is it difficult to get in?"
6. "Is there financial aid?"

Without exception, as can be seen in Table 1 (column 3), all of the questions were answered. No matter how rushed they were, all respondents not only maintained eye contact, but stopped to talk. Indeed, many of the respondents went out of their way to direct or take the questioner to the office she was seeking, to try to locate "Fish Annex," or to discuss with her the possibilities of being admitted to the university.

Table 1
Self-initiated contact by pseudopatients with psychiatrists and nurses and attendants, compared to contact with other groups

	Psychiatric hospitals		University campus (nonmedical)	University medical center Physicians	
Contact	(1) Psychiatrists	(2) Nurses and attendants	(3) Faculty	(4) "Looking for a psychiatrist"	(5) "Looking for an internist"	(6) No additional comment
Responses:						
Moves on, head averted (%)	71	88	0	0	0	0
Makes eye contact (%)	23	10	0	11	0	0
Pauses and chats (%)	2	2	0	11	0	10
Stops and talks (%)	4	0.5	100	78	100	90
Mean number of questions answered (out of 6)	*	*	6	3.8	4.8	4.5
Respondents (No.)	13	47	14	18	15	10
Attempts (No.)	185	1283	14	18	15	10

* Not applicable.

Similar data, also shown in Table 1 (columns 4, 5, and 6), were obtained in the hospital. Here too, the young lady came prepared with six questions. After the first question, however, she remarked to 18 of her respondents (column 4), "I'm looking for a psychiatrist," and to 15 others (column 5), "I'm looking for an internist." Ten other respondents received no inserted comment (column 6). The general degree of cooperative responses is considerably higher for these university groups than it was for pseudopatients in psychiatric hospitals. Even so, differences are apparent within the medical school setting. Once having indicated that she was looking for a psychiatrist, the degree of cooperation elicited was less than when she sought an internist.

POWERLESSNESS AND DEPERSONALIZATION

Eye contact and verbal contact reflect concern and individuation; their absence, avoidance and depersonalization. The data I have presented do not do justice to the rich daily encounters that grew up around matters of depersonalization and avoidance. I have records of patients who were beaten by staff for the sin of having initiated verbal contact. During my own experience, for example, one patient was beaten in the presence of other patients for having approached an attendant and told him, "I like you." Occasionally, punishment meted out to patients for misdemeanors seemed so excessive that it could not be justified by the most radical interpretations of psychiatric canon. Nevertheless, they appeared to go unquestioned. Tempers were often short. A patient who had not heard a call for medication would be roundly excoriated, and the morning attendants would often wake patients with, "Come on, you m——f——s, out of bed!"

Neither anecdotal nor "hard" data can convey the overwhelming sense of powerlessness which invades the individual as he is continually exposed to the depersonalization of the psychiatric hospital. It hardly matters *which* psychiatric hospital—the excellent public ones and the very plush private hospital were better than the rural and shabby ones in this regard, but, again, the features that psychiatric hospitals had in common overwhelmed by far their apparent differences.

Powerlessness was evident everywhere. The patient is deprived of many of his legal rights by dint of his psychiatric commitment (21). He is shorn of credibility by virtue of his psychiatric label. His freedom of movement is restricted. He cannot initiate contact with the staff, but may only respond to such overtures as they make. Personal privacy is minimal. Patient quarters and possessions can be entered and examined by any staff member, for whatever reason. His personal history and anguish is available to any staff member (often including the "grey lady" and "candy striper" volunteer) who chooses to read his folder, regardless of their therapeutic relationship to him. His personal hygiene and waste evacuation are often monitored. The water closets may have no doors.

At times, depersonalization reached such proportions that pseudopatients had the sense that they were invisible, or at least unworthy of account. Upon being admitted, I and other pseudopatients took the initial physical examinations in a semipublic room, where staff members went about their own business as if we were not there.

On the ward, attendants delivered verbal and occasionally serious physical abuse to patients in the presence of other observing patients, some of whom (the pseudopatients) were writing it all down. Abusive behavior, on the other hand, terminated quite abruptly when other staff members were known to be coming. Staff are credible witnesses. Patients are not.

A nurse unbuttoned her uniform to adjust her brassiere in the presence of an entire ward of viewing men. One did not have the sense that she was being seductive. Rather, she didn't notice us. A group of staff persons might point to a patient in the dayroom and discuss him animatedly, as if he were not there.

One illuminating instance of depersonalization and invisibility occurred with regard to medications. All told, the pseudopatients were administered nearly 2,100 pills, including Elavil, Stelazine, Compazine, and Thorazine, to name but a few. (That such a variety of medications should have been administered to patients presenting identical symptoms is itself worthy of note.) Only two were swallowed. The rest were either pocketed or deposited in the toilet. The pseudopatients were not alone in this. Although I have no precise records on how many patients rejected their medications, the pseudopatients frequently found the medications of other patients in the toilet before they deposited their own. As long as they were cooperative, their behavior and the pseudopatients' own in this matter, as in other important matters, went unnoticed throughout.

Reactions to such depersonalization among pseudopatients were intense. Although they had come to the hospital as participant observers and were fully aware that they did not "belong," they nevertheless found themselves caught up in and fighting the process of depersonalization. Some examples: a graduate student in psychology asked his wife to bring his textbooks to the hospital so he could "catch up on his homework"—this despite the elaborate precautions taken to conceal his professional association. The same student, who had trained for quite some time to get into the hospital, and who had looked forward to the experience, "remembered" some drag races that he had wanted to see on the weekend and insisted that he be discharged by that time. Another pseudopatient attempted a romance with a nurse. Subsequently, he informed the staff that he was applying for admission to graduate school in psychology and was very likely to be admitted, since a graduate professor was one of his regular hospital visitors. The same person began to engage in psychotherapy with other patients—all of this as a way of becoming a person in an impersonal environment.

THE SOURCES OF DEPERSONALIZATION

What are the origins of depersonalization? I have already mentioned two. First are attitudes held by all of us toward the mentally ill—including those who treat them—attitudes characterized by fear, distrust, and horrible expectations on the one hand, and benevolent intentions on the other. Our ambivalence leads, in this instance as in others, to avoidance.

Second, and not entirely separate, the hierarchical structure of the psychiatric hospital facilitates depersonalization. Those who are at the top have least to do with patients, and their behavior inspires the rest of the staff. Average daily contact with psychiatrists, psychologists, residents, and physicians combined ranged from 3.9 to 25.1 minutes, with an overall mean of 6.8 (six pseudopatients over a total of 129 days of hospitalization). Included in this average are time spent in the admissions interview, ward meetings in the presence of a senior staff member, group and individual psychotherapy contacts, case presentation conferences, and discharge meetings. Clearly, patients do not spend much time in interpersonal contact with doctoral staff. And doctoral staff serve as models for nurses and attendants.

There are probably other sources. Psychiatric installations are presently in serious financial straits. Staff shortages are pervasive, staff time at a premium. Something has to give, and that something is patient contact. Yet, while financial stresses are realities, too much can be made of them. I have the impression that the psychological forces that result in depersonalization are much stronger than the fiscal ones and that the addition of more staff would not correspondingly improve patient care in this regard. The incidence of staff meetings and the enormous amount of record-keeping on patients, for example, have not been as substantially reduced as has patient contact. Priorities exist, even during hard times. Patient contact is not a significant priority in the traditional psychiatric hospital, and fiscal pressures do not account for this. Avoidance and depersonalization may.

Heavy reliance upon psychotropic medication tacitly contributes to depersonalization by convincing staff that treatment is indeed being conducted and that further patient contact may not be necessary. Even here, however, caution needs to be exercised in understanding the role of psychotropic drugs. If patients were powerful rather than powerless, if they were viewed as interesting individuals rather than diagnostic entities, if they were socially significant rather than social lepers, if their anguish truly and wholly compelled our sympathies and concerns, would we not *seek* contact with them, despite the availability of medications? Perhaps for the pleasure of it all?

THE CONSEQUENCES OF LABELING AND DEPERSONALIZATION

Whenever the ratio of what is known to what needs to be known approaches zero, we tend to invent "knowledge" and assume that we understand more than we actually do. We seem unable to acknowledge that we simply don't know. The needs for diagnosis and remediation of behavioral and emotional problems are enormous. But rather than acknowledge that we are just embarking on understanding, we continue to label patients "schizophrenic," "manic-depressive," and "insane," as if in those words we had captured the essence of understanding. The facts of the matter are that we have known for a long time that diagnoses are often not useful or reliable, but we have nevertheless continued to use them. We now know that we cannot distinguish insanity from sanity. It is depressing to consider how that information will be used.

Not merely depressing, but frightening. How many people, one wonders, are sane but not recognized as such in our psychiatric institutions? How many have been needlessly stripped of their privileges of citizenship, from the right to vote and drive to that of handling their own accounts? How many have feigned insanity in order to avoid the criminal consequences of their behavior, and, conversely, how many would rather stand trial than live interminably in a psychiatric hospital—but are wrongly thought to be mentally ill? How many have been stigmatized by well-intentioned, but nevertheless erroneous, diagnoses? On the last point, recall again that a "type 2 error" in psychiatric diagnosis does not have the same consequences it does in medical diagnosis. A diagnosis of cancer that has been found to be in error is cause for celebration. But psychiatric diagnoses are rarely found to be in error. The label sticks, a mark of inadequacy forever.

Finally, how many patients might be "sane" outside the psychiatric hospital but seem insane in it—not because craziness resides in them, as it were, but because they are responding to a bizarre setting, one that may be unique to institutions which harbor nether people?

Goffman (4) calls the process of socialization to such institutions "mortification"—an apt metaphor that includes the processes of depersonalization that have been described here. And while it is impossible to know whether the pseudopatients' responses to these processes are characteristic of all inmates—they were, after all, not real patients—it is difficult to believe that these processes of socialization to a psychiatric hospital provide useful attitudes or habits of response for living in the "real world."

SUMMARY AND CONCLUSIONS

It is clear that we cannot distinguish the sane from the insane in psychiatric hospitals. The hospital itself imposes a special environment in which the meanings of behavior can easily be misunderstood. The consequences to patients hospitalized in such an environment—the powerlessness, depersonalization, segregation, mortification, and self-labeling—seem undoubtedly countertherapeutic.

I do not, even now, understand this problem well enough to perceive solutions. But two matters seem to have some promise. The first concerns the proliferation of community mental health facilities, of crisis intervention centers, of the human potential movement, and of behavior therapies that, for all of their own problems, tend to avoid psychiatric labels, to focus on specific problems and behaviors, and to retain the individual in a relatively nonpejorative environment. Clearly, to the extent that we refrain from sending the distressed to insane places, our impressions of them are less likely to be distorted. (The risk of distorted perceptions, it seems to me, is always present, since we are much more sensitive to an individual's behaviors and verbalizations than we are to the subtle contextual stimuli that often promote them. At issue here is a matter of magnitude. And, as I have shown, the magnitude of distortion is exceedingly high in the extreme context that is a psychiatric hospital.)

The second matter that might prove promising speaks to the need to increase the sensitivity of mental health workers and researchers to the *Catch 22* position of psychiatric patients. Simply reading materials in this area will be of help to some such workers and researchers. For others, directly experiencing the impact of psychiatric hospitalization will be of enormous use. Clearly, further research into the social psychology of such total institutions will both facilitate treatment and deepen understanding.

I and the other pseudopatients in the psychiatric setting had distinctly negative reactions. We do not pretend to describe the subjective experiences of true patients. Theirs may be different from ours, particularly with the passage of time and the necessary process of adaptation to one's environment. But we can and do speak to the relatively more objective indices of treatment within the hospital. It could be a mistake, and a very unfortunate one, to consider that what happened to us derived from malice or stupidity on the part of the staff. Quite the contrary, our overwhelming impression of them was of people who really cared, who were committed and who were uncommonly intelligent. Where they failed, as they sometimes did painfully, it would be more accurate to attribute those failures to the environment in which they, too, found themselves than to personal callousness. Their perceptions and behavior were controlled by the situation, rather than being motivated by a malicious disposition. In a more benign environment, one that was less attached to global diagnosis, their behaviors and judgments might have been more benign and effective.

REFERENCES AND NOTES

1. P. Ash, *J. Abnorm. Soc. Psychol.* **44,** 272 (1949); A. T. Beck, *Amer. J. Psychiat.* **119,** 210 (1962); A. T. Boisen, *Psychiatry* **2,** 233 (1938); N. Kreitman, *J. Ment. Sci.* **107,** 876 (1961); N. Kreitman, P. Sainsbury, J. Morrisey, J. Towers, J. Scrivener, *ibid.,* p. 887; H. O. Schmitt and C. P. Fonda, *J. Abnorm. Soc. Psychol.* **52,** 262 (1956); W. Seeman, *J. Nerv. Ment. Dis.* **118,** 541 (1953). For an analysis of these artifacts and summaries of the disputes, see J. Zubin, *Annu. Rev. Psychol.* **18,** 373 (1967); L. Phillips and J. G. Draguns, *ibid.* **22,** 447 (1971).
2. R. Benedict, *J. Gen. Psychol.* **10,** 59 (1934).
3. See in this regard H. Becker, *Outsiders: Studies in the Sociology of Deviance* (Free Press, New York, 1963); B. M. Braginsky, D. D. Braginsky, K. Ring, *Methods of Madness: The Mental Hospital as a Last Resort* (Holt, Rinehart & Winston, New York, 1969); G. M. Crocetti and P. V. Lemkau, *Amer. Sociol. Rev.* **30,** 577 (1965); E. Goffman, *Behavior in Public Places* (Free Press, New York, 1964); R. D. Laing, *The Divided Self: A Study of Sanity and Madness* (Quadrangle, Chicago, 1960); D. L. Phillips, *Amer. Sociol. Rev.* **28,** 963 (1963); T. R. Sarbin, *Psychol. Today* **6,** 18 (1972); E. Schur, *Amer. J. Sociol.* **75,** 309 (1969); T. Szasz, *Law, Liberty and Psychiatry* (Macmillan, New York, 1963); *The Myth of Mental Illness: Foundations of a Theory of Mental Illness* (Hoeber-Harper, New York, 1963). For a critique of some of these views, see W. R. Gove, *Amer. Sociol. Rev.* **35,** 873 (1970).
4. E. Goffman, *Asylums* (Doubleday, Garden City, N.Y., 1961).
5. T. J. Scheff, *Being Mentally Ill: A Sociological Theory* (Aldine, Chicago, 1966).
6. Data from a ninth pseudopatient are not incorporated in this report because, although his sanity went undetected, he falsified aspects of his personal history, including his marital status and parental relationships. His experimental behaviors therefore were not identical to those of the other pseudopatients.
7. A. Barry, *Bellevue Is a State of Mind* (Harcourt Brace Jovanovich, New York, 1971); I. Belknap, *Human Problems of a State Mental Hospital* (McGraw-Hill, New York, 1956); W. Caudill, F. C. Redlich, H. R. Gilmore, E. B. Brody, *Amer. J. Orthopsychiat.* **22,** 314 (1952); A. R. Goldman, R. H. Bohr, T. A. Steinberg, *Prof. Psychol.* **1,** 427 (1970); unauthored, *Roche Report* **1** (No. 13), 8 (1971).
8. Beyond the personal difficulties that the pseudopatient is likely to experience in the hospital, there are legal and social ones that, combined, require considerable attention before entry. For example, once admitted to a psychiatric institution, it is difficult, if not impossible, to be discharged on short notice, state law to the contrary notwithstanding. I was not sensitive to these difficulties at the outset of the project, nor to the personal and situational emergencies that can arise, but later a

writ of habeas corpus was prepared for each of the entering pseudopatients and an attorney was kept "on call" during every hospitalization. I am grateful to John Kaplan and Robert Bartels for legal advice and assistance in these matters.

9. However distasteful such concealment is, it was a necessary first step to examining these questions. Without concealment, there would have been no way to know how valid these experiences were; nor was there any way of knowing whether whatever detections occurred were a tribute to the diagnostic acumen of the staff or to the hospital's rumor network. Obviously, since my concerns are general ones that cut across individual hospitals and staffs, I have respected their anonymity and have eliminated clues that might lead to their identification.

10. Interestingly, of the 12 admissions, 11 were diagnosed as schizophrenic and one, with the identical symptomatology, as manic-depressive psychosis. This diagnosis has a more favorable prognosis, and it was given by the only private hospital in our sample. On the relations between social class and psychiatric diagnosis see A. deB. Hollingshead and F. C. Redlich, *Social Class and Mental Illness: A Community Study* (Wiley, New York, 1958).

11. It is possible, of course, that patients have quite broad latitudes in diagnosis and therefore are inclined to call many people sane, even those whose behavior is patently aberrant. However, although we have no hard data on this matter, it was our distinct impression that this was not the case. In many instances, patients not only singled us out for attention, but came to imitate our behaviors and styles.

12. J. Cumming and E. Cumming, *Community Ment. Health* **1,** 135 (1965); A. Farina and K. Ring, *J. Abnorm. Psychol.* **70,** 47 (1965); H. E. Freeman and O. G. Simmons, *The Mental Patient Comes Home* (Wiley, New York, 1963); W. J. Johannsen, *Ment. Hygiene* **53,** 218 (1969); A. S. Linsky, *Soc. Psychiat.* **5,** 166 (1970).

13. S. E. Asch, *J. Abnorm. Soc. Psychol.* **41,** 258 (1946); *Social Psychology* (Prentice-Hall, New York, 1952).

14. See also I. N. Mensh and J. Wishner, *J. Personality* **16,** 188 (1974); J. Wishner, *Psychol. Rev.* **67,** 96 (1960); J. S. Bruner and R. Tagiuri, in *Handbook of Social Psychology,* G. Lindzey, Ed. (Addison-Wesley, Cambridge, Mass., 1954), vol. 2, pp. 634–654; J. S. Bruner, D. Shapiro, R. Tagiuri, in *Person Perception and Interpersonal Behavior,* R. Tagiuri and L. Petrullo, Eds. (Stanford Univ. Press, Stanford, Calif., 1958), pp. 277–288.

15. For an example of a similar self-fulfilling prophecy, in this instance dealing with the "central" trait of intelligence, see R. Rosenthal and L. Jacobson, *Pygmalion in the Classroom* (Holt, Rinehart & Winston, New York, 1968).

16. E. Zigler and L. Phillips, *J. Abnorm. Soc. Psychol.* **63,** 69 (1961). See also R. K. Freudenberg and J. P. Robertson, *A.M.A. Arch. Neurol. Psychiatr.* **76,** 14 (1956).

17. W. Mischel, *Personality and Assessment* (Wiley, New York, 1968).

18. The most recent and unfortunate instance of this tenet is that of Senator Thomas Eagleton.

19. T. R. Sarbin and J. C. Mancuso, *J. Clin. Consult. Psychol.* **35,** 159 (1970); T. R. Sarbin, *ibid.* **31,** 447 (1967); J. C. Nunnally, Jr., *Popular Conceptions of Mental Health* (Holt, Rinehart & Winston, New York, 1961).

20. A. H. Stanton and M. S. Schwartz, *The Mental Hospital: A Study of Institutional Participation in Psychiatric Illness and Treatment* (Basic, New York, 1954).

21. D. B. Wexler and S. E. Scoville, *Ariz. Law Rev.* **13,** 1 (1971).

22. I thank W. Mischel, E. Orne, and M. S. Rosenhan for comments on an earlier draft of this manuscript.

INTRODUCTORY COMMENTS ON LUNDMAN'S RESEARCH

In the next illustration of observational research on interpersonal reactions to deviance, the scene shifts from Rosenhan's mental hospitals to the streets of a large midwestern city. Lundman's (1974) analysis of "Routine Police Arrest Practices" provides a close look at the social control of public drunkenness in an urban area. Although it is not typically viewed as a major crime by the public or by criminologists, the offense of public drunkenness has for years loomed as the largest single category in U.S. arrest statistics. FBI estimates for 1977 indicated that over 1,300,000 arrests occurred nationally for public drunkenness (not to mention over a million additional arrests for related charges such as vagrancy or disorderly conduct; see Webster, 1977). Even so, urban police officers overlook or release the vast majority of intoxicated persons with whom they come into contact during their patrols. As you will see below, Lundman reports that less than one third (31 percent) of the encounters observed between police and intoxicated citizens resulted in arrest. Clearly, police exercise considerable discretion when reacting to persons who are technically in violation of laws against public drunkenness.

From a practical standpoint, it is apparent that selective enforcement of these laws functions to keep the flow of drunkenness offenders through the legal system within manageable limits. However, the crucial issue for Lundman and other labeling researchers is this: If the law is not applied uniformly in police encounters with public drunks, then what additional, *nonlegal* factors or contingencies influence officers' use of their power of arrest? In other words, how does the process of selective enforcement actually operate? The kinds of situational insights that are required to answer these sociological questions cannot be obtained by sorting through official records or by conducting interviews at times and places far removed from events that transpire on city streets. Therefore, following the lead of several previous researchers in the labeling tradition, Lundman approaches the issue of selective enforcement through an analysis of observational data gathered during routine police patrols.

The use of observers riding in police cars to gather firsthand descriptions of encounters between officers and citizens was pioneered in the 1960s by Piliavin and Briar (1964) and by Black and Reiss (1970; Black, 1970; Reiss, 1971). The Piliavin and Briar study, which was discussed in Chapter 1, presented mostly qualitative data on 66 encounters between adolescents and juvenile officers in Oakland, California. Whereas Piliavin and Briar spent much of nine months gathering their own data from the backseats of patrol cars, Black and Reiss employed a team of 36 observers riding (or, occasionally, walking the beat) with police officers in three different metropolitan areas. Well over 5,000 encounters between uniformed officers and citizens were recorded in "event reports" completed by these observers following patrol shifts. One notable conclusion reached in both of these projects was that the general *demeanor* of citizens while interacting with officers was an important contingency in police reactions. That is, citizens who were observed to be uncooperative or disrespectful during encounters with officers were more likely to be arrested than were civil, cooperative citizens.

Lundman's data come from a later, more sophisticated observational project designed and directed by Richard E. Sykes and John P. Clark (1975). As Lundman (1974) indicates in the following article, this particular phase of Sykes and Clark's research utilized a team of seven observers who were randomly assigned to routine patrol shifts in "Midwest City" (Minneapolis). However, Lundman only briefly mentions the technological innovation that allowed these observers to reproduce a far more detailed and dynamic record of police-citizen encounters than was possible in earlier studies. Observers carried an electronic device developed by Sykes (1977) that resembled an adding machine keyboard attached to a battery-operated portable tape recorder. Each key on this device, when pressed, recorded a distinctive signal on a cassette tape. The observers in Sykes and Clark's study were taught to record their observations in the field using a complex code, in which a wide variety of acts, events, or items of information could be represented by pressing different sequences of numbered keys (e.g., 5-1-0 or 1-3-4-5). At the completion of a patrol shift, these coded observations were transferred from the cassette tape to computer storage for subsequent editing, processing, and analysis.

The advantages of this methodology over conventional pencil-and-paper techniques for gathering observational data are considerable. After three months of intensive training and practice with the equipment and coding system, Sykes and Clark's (1975) observers were able to provide a direct, "blow-by-blow" account of interactional exchanges between police and citizens. As opposed to a written event report where a citizen might be globally characterized as disrespectful toward an officer, Sykes and Clark's observational records could specify the exact number, timing, and nature of various disrespectful acts that might occur during an encounter. More important, as Brent and Sykes (1979) have more recently shown, these data can be used to study the complex *interactional linkages* between acts of citizens and preceding or subsequent acts of officers. In short, this observational methodology is uniquely capable of preserving the processual quality of police-citizen encounters.

As one of the earliest analyses of Sykes and Clark's data, the following research illustration focuses mainly on outcomes rather than on interactional dynamics of encounters between police and publicly intoxicated citizens. Even so, Lundman takes good advantage of the richness of those data by examining a host of factors that could be expected on the basis of relativistic theories to distinguish arrests from other, less serious outcomes. Before you read Lundman's article, you might give some thought to the process of selective enforcement and to some of the situational circumstances or social characteristics of citizens that might affect it. You will find that Lundman's analysis provides a few surprises as well as a good deal of confirmation for some assertions of labeling theorists about nonlegal contingencies in arrest decisions.

RESEARCH ILLUSTRATION 9–B

Routine police arrest practices: A commonweal perspective*

Richard J. Lundman

> Employing a commonweal conception of police organizations, the central aim of the present study was to determine the extent to which routine police arrest practices suggest police abuse of the societal delegated privilege to exercise non-negotiable coercive force. Public drunkenness encounters occurring in a large midwestern city were analyzed; and it was found that significantly higher rates of arrest were associated with offense conspicuousness, offender powerlessness, and offender disrespect. The major conclusion drawn is that the police abuse this societal delegated privilege. The implications of this conclusion for the commonweal conception of the police are discussed.

Modern police departments are generally viewed as commonweal organizations serving the public at large. Unlike mutual benefit organizations serving memberships, business concerns responsive to owners, or service organizations serving specific clientele, the police ostensibly serve and protect the interests of the public at large (Blau and Scott, 1962: 45–54).

One of the problems associated with all commonweal organizations is that of external democratic control. In democratic societies, the actions of commonweal organizations are to be monitored to insure that the ends being served are those intended. In the absence of effective monitoring and control, the possibility of organizational

---

Source: Article reprinted from *Social Problems* 22 (October 1974), pp. 127–141.

* Research support was provided by a grant from the United States Public Health Service, National Institute of Mental Health, Center for the Studies of Crime and Delinquency. Grant No. R01 MH17917-02, "Quantitative Studies of Police Encounters." Data analysis support was partially provided by grants from the Department of Sociology and the Office of Research, University of Delaware. The author wishes to thank Kenneth W. Eckhardt, James C. Fox, Paul T. McFarlane, and Frank R. Scarpitti for their critical readings of earlier versions of this paper.

abuse (Remington and Rosenblum, 1960: 497) of societal delegated privileges emerges.

The police, however, pose unique monitoring and control problems in American society in that they have been granted the unique privilege to exercise non-negotiable coercive force (Bittner, 1970: 36–47). During a working shift, police officers confront a variety of problems: barking dogs, automobile accidents, groups of juveniles, husband-wife disputes, noisy parties, and drunken citizens. In each of these situations forceful actions are taken by the police: owners are warned, traffic rerouted, juveniles dispersed, husbands sent, parties quieted, and infrequently, citizens arrested. What lends unity to the infinite variety of police actions, in short, is police exercise of a societal delegated privilege to exercise non-negotiable coercive force.

The specific problem this privilege poses for external democratic control is that its exercise is essentially unrestricted. With the exceptions of restrictions on the use of deadly force, the use of force for personal rather than public interests, and the requirement that force not be used maliciously, few legal boundaries surround police exercise of this privilege. This privilege is further unrestricted in the sense of not being subject to systematic examination by individuals and agencies outside the police. Citizens in many communities find the red tape and/or indifference which stand between them and the agencies responsible for dealing with complaints of police abuse of this privilege reason enough not to pursue their complaints (Bayley and Mendelsohn, 1969: 129 ff.). Moreover, since the majority of police-citizen encounters do not end in arrest (Black 1968), routine police actions are not subject to examination by the courts. Finally, even when arrest and arraignment occur, mass "trials" (Milewski, 1971) and plea bargaining (Sudnow, 1965) restrict the possibility of detailed court examination of police arrest practices.

The position of the police in American society, therefore, emerges as logically contradictory: on the one hand the police are a commonweal organization ostensibly subject to external democratic control, while on the other they have been granted an essentially unrestricted privilege to exercise non-negotiable coercive force. The threat which this privilege poses for external democratic control is clear, if not necessarily automatic. We can, for example, imagine a society in which the pressures which promote isolation of the police (Clark, 1965) are such that the police act in ways which the general public would have them act were it to exercise its right (Bittner, 1973) to external democratic control.

The central aim of the present study is to determine the extent to which routine police arrest practices suggest abuse of the societal delegated privilege to exercise non-negotiable coercive force. A secondary aim is to assess the adequacy of the commonweal conception of the police. Specifically, the focus of the present study is on the factors which influence the dispositional decisions made by police officers in their encounters with public drunkenness offenders. Public drunkenness was selected for analysis because it is the single most frequent offense for which citizens are annually arrested (U.S. Department of Justice, 1969: 110–111). Public drunkenness is a problem regularly encountered by the police and it is suggested that examination of the factors which relate to the exercise of police arrest discretion in this circumstance allows partial determination of the extent to which the police routinely operate outside the rule of law (Skolnick, 1966).

METHOD[1]

During the 15 months beginning in June, 1970, a quantitative participant-as-observer study of police-citizen encounters was undertaken in "Midwest City," which had a 1970 population of over one-half million and is located in a SMA of over two million. A group of seven observers trained in the use of an interaction code (Sykes, 1973) travelled with the police on a random time sample basis. Without prior notice, observers appeared at a precinct station with directions to ride on a randomly selected patrol car for a full shift. Which car they were to ride on was not known to the police in advance.

Among the factors coded were: whether it was a police or citizen initiated contact; the nature of the problem; the location of the encounter; and a wide variety of interaction and action codes pertaining to politeness and impoliteness, the giving and compliance with orders, displays of temper and violence, and the outcome of the encounter. Demographic data on citizen participants were also coded including: sex, age, race, and class status.

The data were recorded by observers using portable electronic field encoding equipment (Sykes, 1969). The final data base consists of 2,835 *potential* police-citizen contacts. When such contacts involved police-citizen interaction they were defined as encounters (n=1,978). To isolate public drunkenness offenses, encounters selected for analysis in this study met the following three criteria: (1) an alledged offender was present; (2) the alledged offender was drunk; and (3) the problem which gave rise to the encounter was not a felony or moving traffic violation. Of the 1,978 encounters, 195 or approximately 10 percent met these three criteria.

---

[1] This description of the field method borrows, with some exceptions, from Richard E. Sykes and John P. Clark, "A Preliminary Theory of Low Visibility Enforcement Decisions by Police," Minneapolis: Minnesota Systems Research, Inc., 1973 (mimeo).

The data, therefore, consist of 195 non-felony *arrest discretionary* encounters wherein the major issue confronting the police officer is the drunkenness of the offender. The logic employed in the analysis of the data is that of Rosenberg (1968) and the manner of data presentation that of Black (1971). The dependent variable is percent of encounters ending in arrest and a (Z) score difference of proportions test is used to determine initially the presence or absence of statistically significant differences (Blalock, 1960: 176ff.).

RESULTS

The police are lenient in their encounters with drunkenness offenders. Of the 195 encounters which could have ended in arrest, only 31 percent did. It appears that the police are aware of the stigmatizing effects of formal action (Piliavin and Briar, 1964; Bittner, 1967b) and are reluctant to employ arrest in the majority of these encounters. Moreover, the courts and jails already crowded with drunkenness offenders (Milewski, 1971; Spradley, 1970; Wiseman, 1970) exert pressure on the police to hold down drunkenness arrests.

A basic initial observation, then, is that it is not the criminal offense of public drunkenness which leads to the arrest of drunkenness offenders. The police are aware of large numbers of eligible offenders and select only a minority for formal processing.

A. Initiator

A-1. MOST DRUNKENNESS ENCOUNTERS ARISE THROUGH CITIZEN RATHER THAN POLICE INITIATIVE

The police are primarily a reactive social control agency dependent upon citizens for basic organizational inputs (Reiss, 1971: 64). Row A of Table 1 shows that the vast majority of these drunkenness encounters (143 or 73 percent) arose through citizen rather than police initiative. An implication of this finding is that involvement in the criminal justice system for the offense of public drunkenness is primarily a result of lay rather than professional labeling (Mechanic, 1962). In the absence of citizen inputs the police would be aware of significantly fewer public drunkenness offenses.

A-2. WHEN THE POLICE DO INITIATE AN ENCOUNTER WITH A DRUNKENNESS OFFENDER, THE PROBABILITY OF ARREST IS SIGNIFICANTLY GREATER

Despite police dependence upon citizen inputs, uniformed patrol officers are expected to devote their non-call time to proactive cruising. Row A of Table 1 shows that when this proactive policing results

Table 1
Percent of police-citizen encounters ending in arrest according to selected conditions of the encounter

Condition	Number	Percent ending in arrest
A. Initiator		
Police	52	42
Citizen	143	27
B. Location		
1. Area of the city		
Downtown	54	43
Non-downtown	141	27
2. Place		
Open, public	127	31
Closed, public	14	71
Private	51	23
C. Complainant configuration		
Complainant	73	27
No complainant	122	34
D. Demographic characteristics		
1. Sex of offender(s)*		
Male	160	34
Female	15	20
2. Age of offender(s)*		
<25	66	24
≥25	123	37
3. Race of offender(s)*		
White American	141	26
Afro-American	12	33
Native American	32	53
4. Class status of offender(s)*		
White collar	15	20
Blue collar	132	25
Declassified	44	52
Totals	195	31

*Encounters were excluded in this analysis if the offenders present displayed mixed demographic characteristics (i.e., male and female (n = 20), mixed racial characteristics (n = 10), mixed class characteristics (n = 4), or mixed age characteristics (n = 6).

in contact with a drunkenness offender, the probability of arrest is significantly greater: 42 percent of police initiated encounters ended in arrest as compared to 27 percent of citizen initiated ($Z = 2.00$, $p < .05$).[2] This higher rate of arrest appears to reflect the greater conspicu-

---

[2] It was also found that police initiated encounters were "blocked" (Rosenberg, 1968: 26ff.) with encounters occurring in the downtown area of Midwest City. Since downtown encounters also ended significantly more frequently in arrest, I controlled

ousness of offenses discovered by the police. Uniformed patrol officers are legally constrained from routine proactive policing of closed private places and consensually constrained from proactive observation of closed public places. As a consequence, the offenses patrol officers proactively discover are the most conspicuous: offenders on sidewalks, streets, alleys, parks, and doorways.

B. Location

The police are sensitive to the locations of the encounters in which they are involved. Bittner (1967a), for example, has suggested that police practices in skidrow areas reflect the relative isolation of these areas: the police are freer to develop and employ peace keeping techniques apart from legal mandates. Petersen (1971) reported that downtown drunkenness offenders were arrested more frequently because of the effort involved in taking offenders home. Black (1968) reported that the type of place to which the police are called allows prediction of the type of problem which gave rise to the call.

B-1. DRUNKENNESS OFFENDERS ENCOUNTERED IN DOWNTOWN LOCATIONS ARE ARRESTED SIGNIFICANTLY MORE FREQUENTLY THAN OFFENDERS IN OTHER LOCATIONS

Row B-1 of Table 1 shows that encounters occurring in downtown locations ended significantly more frequently in arrest than encounters located elsewhere (43 percent versus 27 percent, $Z = 2.17$, $p < .05$).[3] In part, the higher rate of arrest reflects the greater effort involved in returning downtown offenders home. A neglected dimension, however, would appear to be the greater conspicuousness of downtown offenses. Many urban areas confront the problem of maintaining viable center city areas, and public drunkenness offenders pose esthetic, if not criminal, problems. As Chambliss (1966) pointed out in the context of vagrancy laws, it appears that public drunkenness laws are also employed to clear downtown streets of unsightly citizens.

---

for the effects of location. The result was that the relationship remained essentially unchanged: 50 percent of police-initiated downtown encounters ended in arrest as compared to 40 percent of citizen-initiated downtown encounters.

[3] As previously noted, downtown location is blocked with police initiation. When initiator is controlled, however, location continues to exert an independent effect on arrest. It is clear, at the same time, that interactive or cojoint effects emerge: 1) 50 percent of police initiated downtown encounters ended in arrest as compared to 40 percent of citizen initiated downtown encounters; 2) 38 percent of police initiated non-downtown encounters ended in arrests compared to 24 percent of citizen initiated non-downtown encounters.

B-2. DRUNKENNESS OFFENDERS ENCOUNTERED IN CLOSED PUBLIC PLACES ARE ARRESTED SIGNIFICANTLY MORE FREQUENTLY THAN OFFENDERS IN OTHER TYPES OF PLACES

Row B-2 of Table 1 shows that encounters occurring in closed public places such as libraries and bus depots ended in arrest significantly more frequently than encounters occurring in open public places such as sidewalks (71 percent versus 31 percent, $Z = 3.42$, $p < .01$) or closed private places such as apartments (71 percent versus 23 percent, $Z = 3.42$, $p < .01$).[4] Here again, the dimension of offense conspicuousness would appear to play a determining role. Encounters occurring on sidewalks or private residences are, respectively, likely to have large unfocussed audiences or small focussed audiences. Encounters in closed, public places, in contrast, are likely to have large focussed audiences consisting, for example, of customers and a proprietor. In this latter instance, the offense is likely to be significantly more conspicuous.

C. Complainants

C-1. THE PRESENCE OF COMPLAINANTS IS NOT ONE OF THE CONDITIONS RELATING TO POLICE ARREST OF DRUNKENNESS OFFENDERS

A number of recent studies have suggested the importance of citizen complaints insofar as police actions are concerned. Black and Reiss (1970: 70), for example, attributed the higher rate of arrest of Afro-American juveniles to the presence of citizen complainants who successfully lobby for arrest. Black (1970: 738ff.) similarly reported that the police are sensitive to citizen preferences regarding the writing of a formal report of a criminal incident. Row C-1 of Table 1 shows, however, that 27 percent of the encounters with a complainant present ended in arrest as compared to 34 percent with no complainant present ($Z = 1.91$, $p > .05$).

Although the data are not directly comparable, this was the obverse of what was expected, and additional analysis was undertaken to determine whether the relationship was distorted. Of the possible distorting variables, initiator appeared most logical, since in police initiated encounters complainants are rarely present. The relationship between complainant presence and arrest was, therefore, elaborated by controlling for initiator. It was found that 27 percent of citizen initiated encounters with a complainant present ended in arrest as

---

[4] Detailed elaborative analysis revealed no evidence which leads me to conclude that the relationship is spurious.

compared to 28 percent with no complainant. It would appear that in drunkenness encounters, exercise of police arrest discretion is not related to the presence or absence of citizen complainants.

D. Offender demographic characteristics

D-1. THE SEX OF THE DRUNKENNESS OFFENDER IS NOT ONE OF THE CONDITIONS RELATING TO THE EXERCISE OF POLICE ARREST DISCRETION

A number of previous studies (Goldman, 1963) have indicated that female offenders are infrequently involved in the criminal justice system via police arrest. The explanation has been that women commit fewer legally sanctionable acts; and when they do, the police are reluctant to arrest them. The data in Row D-1 of Table 1 provide some support for both propositions showing that drunkenness offenders are infrequently women and when they are, arrest is not likely. Thus, the police arrested 34 percent of male offenders are compared to 20 percent of female offenders. The difference, however, is not statistically significant ($Z = 1.10$, $p > .05$).

D-2. AGE IS NOT ONE OF THE CONDITIONS RELATING TO THE EXERCISE OF POLICE ARREST DISCRETION

Row D-2 of Table 1 shows that arrest of drunkenness offenders occurs more frequently when the offender is over 25 years of age. The difference, however, is not statistically significant: 24 percent of encounters wherein the offender was under the age of 25 ended in arrest as compared to 37 percent of over 25 encounters ($Z = 1.83$, $p > .05$).

D-3. THE POLICE DISCRIMINATE AGAINST NATIVE AMERICAN DRUNKENNESS OFFENDERS ON THE BASIS OF RACE

The question of whether the police discriminate against certain citizens on the basis of race has repeatedly been addressed by students of the police. Piliavin and Briar (1964), for example, reported that Afro-American juveniles were arrested more frequently than white American juveniles and argued that police surveillance tactics resulting in greater encounter hostility accounted for this difference. Black and Reiss (1970: 70) attributed the higher rates of arrest of Afro-American juveniles to the presence of complainants who successfully lobby for arrest. Wilson (1968) suggested that the higher rate of arrest of Afro-American juveniles in "Eastern City" was due to an absence of police professionalism. The essential interpretation, then, seems to be that while minority arrest is more frequent, it is for reasons other than racial prejudice. As is clear, however, the reference is to Afro-American citizens.

Row D-3 of Table 1 shows that Native American drunkenness offenders were arrested significantly more frequently than white American drunkenness offenders (53 percent versus 26 percent, $Z = 3.08$, $p < .01$) and more frequently, but not significantly so, than Afro-American offenders (53 percent versus 33 percent, $Z = 1.21$, $p > .05$). Afro-American offenders were *not* arrested significantly more frequently than white American offenders (33 percent versus 26 percent, $Z = .54$, $p > .05$).[5] It appears that one of the conditions of the relationship between race and arrest is the specific racial identity of the offender. That is, while no evidence of racial discrimination against Afro-American citizens exists, evidence of racial discrimination against Native American citizens does.

D-4. THE POLICE DISCRIMINATE AGAINST DECLASSIFIED DRUNKENNESS OFFENDERS ON THE BASIS OF CLASS STATUS

As with race, class status has previously been identified as one of the conditions relating to the exercise of police arrest discretion (Petersen, 1971; Quinney, 1970; Skolnick, 1966; Silver, 1967; Spradley, 1970; Werthman and Piliavin, 1967). The assertion has been that powerless citizens are arrested more frequently by the police than the relatively powerful. Row D-4 of Table 1 shows that for the offense of public drunkenness, arrest is significantly reserved for declassified citizens such as chronic drunkenness offenders and others on the fringes of the dominant culture. Thus, 52 percent of declassified offenders were arrested by the police as compared to 25 percent of blue-collar offenders ($Z = 3.32$, $p < .01$) and 20 percent of white-collar offenders ($Z = 2.15$, $p < .05$). Blue-collar offenders were *not* arrested significantly more frequently than white-collar offenders (25 percent versus 20 percent, $Z = .42$, $p > .05$).[6]

---

[5] Elaborating upon the significantly higher rate of arrest of Native American drunkenness offenders, it was found that Native American encounters occurred more frequently in downtown locations, involved more complainants, and involved more declassified offenders. As a consequence additional analysis introducing appropriate controls was undertaken. The results were as follows: 1) when location was controlled, Native American offenders continued to be arrested more frequently; 2) when complainant presence was controlled, Native American offenders continued to be arrested more frequently; and 3) when class status was controlled, Native American offenders were arrested more frequently. Within the limits of this analysis, it appears that the police discriminate against Native American public drunkenness offenders.

[6] Elaborating upon the significantly higher rate of arrest of declassified offenders it was found that declassified encounters occurred more frequently in downtown locations and more frequently involved Native American offenders. As a consequence additional analysis introducing appropriate controls was undertaken. The results were

E. Disrespect

E-1. THE PROBABILITY OF ARREST INCREASES AS PUBLIC DRUNKENNESS OFFENDERS ARE DISRESPECTFUL IN THEIR INTERACTION WITH THE POLICE

As numerous others have found (cf., Piliavin and Briar, 1964; Black and Reiss, 1970), the police are sensitive to the demeanor of the citizens with whom they interact and more frequently arrest those who evidence disrespect for the police. In this section the frequencies of displays of temper, violence, impoliteness, and non-compliance are examined as they relate to the exercise of police arrest discretion. The data substantiate previous findings indicating that police selection of drunkenness offenders relates to the level of disrespect shown the police (see Table 2).

Row A of Table 2 shows that citizens who evidence "high" ($X_i > \bar{X}$) levels of temper[7] in their interaction with the police are arrested more

Table 2
Percent of encounters ending in arrest according to indicators and level of disrespect

Indicator and level* of disrespect	Number	Percent ending in arrest
A. Temper		
Low	157	29
High	38	42
B. Violence		
Low	188	31
High	7	(4)
C. Impoliteness		
Low	132	26
High	63	44
D. Non-compliance		
Low	159	28
High	36	44

* Low = $0 \leq X_i \leq \bar{X}$
High = $X_i > \bar{X}$

as follows: (1) when location was controlled, declassified encounters continued to end more frequently in arrest; (2) when race was controlled, declassified class status continued to exert an independent effect on arrest.

[7] Temper was considered displayed whenever a citizen raised his/her voice above a normal conversational level, when anger or hostility was present in an actor's voice, and/or when a verbal statement contained a threat to normal freedom.

frequently than offenders with "low" ($0 \leq X_i \leq \bar{X}$) levels of temper. The difference, however, is not statistically significant (42 percent versus 29 percent, $Z = 1.63$, $p > .05$).

Row B of Table 2 shows that acts of potential or actual physical violence[8] by drunkenness offenders play so small a role in these encounters as to be nearly invisible. Thus, only seven encounters involved citizen violence and four ended in arrest while 31 percent of the violence free encounters ended in arrest. The role of violence in police selection of drunkenness offenders, in short, is negligible.

Row C of Table 2 shows that citizens who are impolite[9] in their interaction with the police are arrested significantly more frequently than offenders who are less impolite. Thus, 44 percent of drunkenness offenders with high levels of impoliteness were arrested as compared to 26 percent of drunkenness offenders with low levels of impoliteness ($Z = 2.57$, $p < .01$).

Row D of Table 2 shows that citizens who fail to comply with the orders given them by the police are arrested significantly more frequently than citizens who comply with those orders. The police arrested 44 percent of drunkenness offenders with high levels of noncompliance as compared to 28 percent with low levels of noncompliance ($Z = 2.00$, $p < .05$).

The data in Table 2, in short, confirm the oft reported observation that police selection of citizens for formal processing by the criminal justice system relates to the level of disrespect shown the police. Drunkenness offenders who evidence disrespect by being impolite in their interaction with the police or by failing to comply with police orders are more likely to be arrested; offenders who evidence respect are arrested significantly less frequently.

At this point it becomes necessary to deviate from the procedure followed thus far of footnoting results of elaborative analyses. The reason is clear in light of the data just presented: it is possible that the higher rates of arrest of Native American and declassified public drunkenness offenders are attributable to higher levels of disrespect. Piliavin and Briar (1964) and Black (1970), as noted previously, found that the higher rates of arrest of Afro-American juveniles were a function of the higher levels of disrespect evidenced by these offenders. Elaborative analysis permits rejection of this rival explanation.

---

[8] Potential or actual acts of physical violence included verbal threats of physical attack, efforts at territorial or physical restraint, fighting, making weapons ready for use, and/or the use of weapons.

[9] A verbal statement was considered impolite if it deviated from polite middle-class interaction in the directions of aggressive non-compliance, embarrassment, heated argument, name calling, ridicule, and/or personal vituperation.

E-2. THE HIGHER RATE OF ARREST OF NATIVE AMERICAN OFFENDERS IS NOT ATTRIBUTABLE TO THE LEVELS OF DISRESPECT SHOWN THE POLICE

The data in Section A of Table 3 show that when level of disrespect is held constant, Native American offenders are arrested more frequently than white American offenders. The small number of "Afro-

Table 3
Percent of encounters ending in arrest according to the race and class status of the offender, by level of disrespect

		Indicator and level* of disrespect			
		Impoliteness		Non-compliance	
Condition		Low	High	Low	High
A. Race					
	White American	20	41	24	38
		(99)	(41)	(114)	(26)
	Afro-American	(3)	(3)	27	(1)
		(7)	(5)	(11)	(1)
	Native American	42	69	38	(5)
		(19)	(13)	(15)	(7)
B. Class status					
	White collar	31	(0)	28	(0)
		(13)	(2)	(14)	(1)
	Blue collar	21	38	23	39
		(92)	(39)	(108)	(23)
	Declassified	41	71	48	64
		(27)	(17)	(33)	(11)

* Low = $0 \leq X_i \leq \bar{X}$
High = $X_i < \bar{X}$

American cases" precludes meaningful comparison. Thus:

1. 42 percent of Native American offenders with low levels of impoliteness were arrested as compared to 20 percent of white American offenders with low levels of impoliteness;
2. 60 percent of Native American offenders with high levels of impoliteness were arrested as compared to 41 percent of white American offenders with high levels of impoliteness;
3. 38 percent of Native American offenders with low levels of non-compliance were arrested as compared to 24 percent of white American offenders with low levels of non-compliance; and
4. five of seven Native American offenders with high levels of non-compliance were arrested as compared to 38 percent of white American offenders with high levels of non-compliance.

E-3. THE HIGHER RATE OF ARREST OF DECLASSIFIED OFFENDERS IS NOT ATTRIBUTABLE TO THE LEVELS OF DISRESPECT SHOWN THE POLICE

The data in Section B of Table 3 show that when level of disrespect is held constant, declassified offenders are arrested more frequently than blue-collar offenders. The small number of "white-collar cases" precludes meaningful comparison. Thus:

1. 41 percent of declassified offenders with low levels of impoliteness were arrested as compared to 21 percent of blue-collar offenders with low levels of impoliteness;
2. 71 percent of declassified offenders with high levels of impoliteness were arrested as compared to 38 percent of blue-collar offenders with high levels of impoliteness;
3. 48 percent of declassified offenders with low levels of non-compliance were arrested as compared to 23 percent of blue-collar offenders with low levels of non-compliance; and
4. 64 percent of declassified offenders with high levels of non-compliance were arrested as compared to 39 percent of blue-collar offenders with high levels of non-compliance.

These data, then, support the earlier specifications of the relationships between class status, race, and the exercise of police arrest discretion. That is, within the limits of this elaborative analysis it appears that the police discriminate against declassified and Native American public drunkenness offenders.

DISCUSSION

The central aim of the present study has been to determine the extent to which the police abuse the societal delegated privilege to exercise coercive force. The specific focus was on the factors which relate to police arrest of public drunkenness offenders; and it appears that two comments are in order. *First,* if we look at these findings as a whole, it appears that three factors relate most directly to police selection of certain drunkenness offenders for formal processing by the criminal justice system: (1) offense conspicuousness; (2) offender powerlessness; and (3) offender disrespect.

The data provide three indicators of the importance of offense conspicuousness. If the police, given their limited resources, happen upon an offense, arrest is more likely than if a citizen reports an offense to the police. Further, down-town offenders and those encountered in closed, public places were also arrested more frequently.

In drunkenness encounters, then, one of the factors which determines whether or not an offender will be treated formally is the conspicuousness of the offense. Offenders who confine their drunkenness to locations and places not easily observed by the police and/or other citizens are not likely to be arrested—even though involved in an encounter with the police. Offenders, on the other hand, who are encountered by the police in conspicuous locations stand a significantly greater chance of being arrested.

The role of offender powerlessness is suggested by two of these findings: (1) the higher rate of arrest of Native American offenders; and (2) the higher rate of arrest of declassified offenders. Until very recently Native Americans have been among the least powerful of American minority groups (Marden and Meyer, 1962: 326ff.). Declassified citizens constitute an equally powerless minority within the dominant American culture (Spradley, 1970). Why, then, do the police discriminate against certain citizens on the basis of their perceptions of powerlessness?

Arrest decisions must be made quickly by police officers and in the absence, therefore, of careful evaluation of the fragmentary information immediately available. Moreover, the decision to arrest generally evokes vocal and, occasionally, physical opposition by the citizen being arrested. As a consequence, the possibility of making a "mistake" (Chambliss and Liell, 1966) by arresting someone who will make a scene, draw attention to the officer via a false arrest suit, or draw attention to the department via community publicity of the arrest, looms large in the mind of many police officers. To protect themselves against potential mistakes, police officers classify arrests along a continuum from safe to risky. An arrest is considered safe if the offense is minor and the offender is not likely to have the resources to cause the arrest to be a mistake. Stated simply: it appears that Native American and declassified public drunkenness offenders are arrested significantly more frequently because the probability of making a mistake is significantly less.

The role of offender disrespect, finally, has been documented in numerous other studies; and it was hardly surprising, therefore, that the probability of arrest for the offense of public drunkenness also increases as an offender is disrespectful towards the police. Despite the frequency of this finding, it is necessary to remind ourselves that it is not illegal or criminal to be disrespectful to the police. Police officials have recognized this in theory, if not in fact: "The officer must remember that there is no law against making a policeman angry and that he cannot charge a man with making him angry" (Wilson, 1963: 117). As this and numerous other studies make clear, however, citizens are routinely arrested for the offense of being disrespectful.

The second point follows from the observation on the relationship between offender disrespect and arrest: *all of the above factors are clearly non-legal in nature.* As compared to legal seriousness or questions of evidence, for example, nowhere are offense conspicuousness, offender powerlessness, or offender disrespect recognized as legal grounds for arrest. These and other (Black, 1970; Black and Reiss, 1970; Goldman, 1963; Petersen, 1971; Piliavin and Briar, 1964; Skolnick, 1966; Spradley, 1970; Wilson, 1968) findings document the extent to which the police routinely operate outside the rule of the law. In a society ostensibly committed to "equal justice under the law" it has been demonstrated that police arrest of public drunkenness offenders reflects the influence of nonlegal factors. From the perspective of the police as a commonweal organization, the conclusion which of necessity must be drawn is that the police are currently abusing the privilege delegated by society to exercise non-negotiable coercive force.

A secondary aim, however, has been to assess the adequacy of the commonweal conception of the police. It appears that these findings contain at least two implications insofar as this issue is concerned. First, assuming the adequacy of the commonweal view, these findings imply that societal monitoring and control of the police is less than effective. As noted previously, the actions of commonweal organizations are monitored to insure that societal ends are being served. In the presence of evidence that intended ends are not being served, control is initiated such that routine practices reflect intended ends. These data indicate that society has failed in its right of mastery over its police (Bittner, 1973: 223).

A second implication directly concerns the adequacy of the commonweal conception of the police. An alternative conception of the police suggests that from their inception the police were an agent of the power elite, intended to protect and serve the interests of but a small segment of society (cf., Lane, 1961; Silver, 1966). Recent sociological writing has extended this interpretation to contemporary police organizations (Liazos, 1972; Quinney, 1970; Thio, 1972). With data such as these, however, it is not possible to assess the validity of alternative conceptions; and it is clear, therefore, that additional research is in order. Knowledge of routine police practices has rapidly accumulated, and it is now necessary to concentrate attention on the implications of these practices for the organizational position and role of the police in democratic society. This study represents a step in that direction.

REFERENCES

Bayley, David H. and Harold Mendelsohn
    1969   Minorities and the Police. New York: The Free Press.

Bittner, Egon
    1967a "The police on skid row: A study of peace keeping." American Sociological Review 32 (October): 699–715.
    1967b "Police discretion in emergency apprehension of mentally ill persons." Social Problems 14: 3 (Winter): 278–292.
    1970   The Functions of the Police in Modern Society. Chevy Chase, Maryland: National Institute of Mental Health, Center for Studies of Crime and Delinquency.
    1973   Die Politzei: Soziologische Studien und Forschungsbevicte. Edited by Johannes Feest and Rudiger Lautman (book review). American Journal of Sociology 79:1 (July): 221–224.

Black, Donald J.
    1968   "Police encounters and social organization: An observation study." Unpublished Ph.D. Dissertation. University of Michigan.
    1970   "Production of crime rates." American Sociological Review 34:4 (August): 733–748.
    1971   "The social organization of arrest." Stanford Law Review 23:6 (June): 1104–1110.

———— and Albert J. Reiss, Jr.
    1970   "Police control of juveniles." American Sociological Review 35:1 (February): 63–77.

Blalock, Hubert M., Jr.
    1960   Social Statistics. New York: McGraw-Hill Book Company, Inc.

Blau, Peter M. and W. Richard Scott
    1962   Formal Organizations. San Francisco: Chandler Publishing Company.

Chambliss, William J.
    1964   "A sociological analysis of the law of vagrancy." Social Problems 12:1 (Summer): 67–77.

———— and Liell, John T.
    1966   "The legal process in the community setting." Crime and Delinquency 12 (October): 310–317.

Clark, John P.
    1965   "Isolation of the police: a comparison of the British and American situations." Journal of Criminal Law, Criminology and Police Science 56 (September): 307–319.

Lane, Roger
    1967   Policing the City: Boston, 1822–1885. Cambridge: Harvard University Press.

Liazos, Alexander
    1972   "The poverty of the sociology of deviance: Nuts, Sluts, and Perverts." Social Problems 20:1 (Summer): 103–120.

Marden, Charles F. and Gladys Meyer
    1962   Minorities in American Society. Second Edition. New York: American Book Club.

Mechanic, David
    1962   "Some factors in identifying and defining mental illness." Mental Hygiene 46: 66–74.

Mileski, Maureen
    1971   "Courtroom encounters: An observation study of a lower criminal court." Law and Society Review 5:4 (May): 473–538.

Petersen, David M.
    1971   "Police disposition of the petty offender." Department of Sociology, The Ohio State University (mimeo).

Piliavin, Irving and Scott Briar
    1964 "Police encounters with juveniles." American Journal of Sociology 70 (September): 206–214.

Quinney, Richard
    1970 The Social Reality of Crime. Boston: Little, Brown and Company.

Reiss, Albert J., Jr.
    1971 The Police and the Public. New Haven, Connecticut: Yale University Press.

Remington, Frank J. and Victor G. Rosenblum
    1960 "The criminal law and the legislative process." Current Problems in Criminal Law (Winter): 481–499.

Rosenberg, Morris
    1968 The Logic of Survey Analysis. New York: Basic Books.

Silver, Allan
    1967 "The demand for order in civil society: A review of some themes in the history of urban crime, police, and riot," in David J. Bordua (ed.). The Police: Six Sociological Essays. New York: John Wiley and Sons, Inc.

Skolnick, Jerome H.
    1966 Justice Without Trial: Law Enforcement in Democratic Society. New York: John Wiley and Sons, Inc.

Spradley, James P.
    1970 You Owe Yourself a Drunk: An Ethnography of Urban Nomads. Boston: Little, Brown and Company.

Sudnow, David
    1965 "Normal crime: Sociological features of the penal code in a public defender office." Social Problems 12:3 (Winter): 255–276.

Sykes, Richard E.
    1973 "A social systems perspective on the police-citizen encounter." Minneapolis: Minnesota Systems Research, Inc. (mimeo).

_____ and John P. Clark
    1973 "A preliminary theory of low visibility enforcement decisions by police." Minneapolis: Minnesota Systems Research, Inc. (mimeo).

_____ and Fraine Whitney
    1969 "Systematic observation utilizing the Minnesota Interaction Data Coding and Reduction System." Behavior Science (March)

Thio, Alex
    1973 "Class bias in the sociology of deviance." American Sociologist 8:1 (February): 1–12.

U.S. Department of Justice
    1969 Uniform Crime Reports.

Werthman, Carl and Irving Piliavin
    1967 "Gang members and the police," in David J. Bordua (ed.). The Police: Six Sociological Essays. New York: John Wiley and Sons, Inc.

Wilson, James Q.
    1968 "The police and the delinquent in two cities," in Stanton Wheeler (ed.). Controlling Delinquents. New York: John Wiley and Sons, Inc.

Wilson, Orlando W.
    1963 Police Administration. New York: McGraw-Hill Book Company.

Wiseman, Jacqueline P.
    1970 Stations of the Lost: The Treatment of Skid Row Alcoholics. Englewood Cliffs, New Jersey: Prentice-Hall, Inc.

INTRODUCTORY COMMENTS ON STEFFENSMEIER AND TERRY'S RESEARCH

Despite its title, "Deviance and Respectability: An Observational Study of Reactions to Shoplifting," the final research illustration takes a rather different methodological approach to interpersonal reaction processes than did the previous two studies. In contrast to most observational researchers, Darrell Steffensmeier and Robert Terry (1973) employ an experimental design to achieve an unusual degree of control over a number of variables that are relevant to labeling theory. As was evident in Lundman's (1974) analysis, a host of interrelated factors and contingencies affect the reactions of social audiences to a given rule-breaking act. A glance at Lundman's Table 1, for instance, reveals that the probability of arrest for public intoxication not only depends on various social characteristics of the offender or actor, but on several audience and situational variables as well. Obviously, some of these factors are more influential in police reactions than are others. However, it is difficult to isolate the effects of particular variables or to demonstrate causal relationships in data such as Lundman's which reflect naturally occurring, uncontrolled events. Experimental research, on the other hand, allows the investigator to *create* specific events that are of theoretical interest and to *control* the influences of other extraneous or confounding factors that might confuse the results (see Campbell & Stanley, 1963). Let us briefly consider how this was accomplished in the following study, which is based on Steffensmeier's dissertation research.

Steffensmeier and Terry (1973) begin their article by noting four general classes of variables that they (and others in the labeling tradition) consider important for understanding audience reactions to deviance: (1) variations in the deviant act, (2) characteristics of the actor and (3) audience, and (4) situational factors. However, you should recall from Chapter 8 that mainstream labeling theorists such as Becker (1963) and Kitsuse (1962) directed attention away from the first set of variables—characteristics of the rule-breaking act—to emphasize the actor, audience, and situation as crucial sources of variation in reactions to deviance. Accordingly, labeling researchers have often attempted to show that the deviant labels or meanings attached to the *same rule-breaking act* vary markedly depending on who is performing the act or on who is observing this performance. Lundman (1974) made an effort to control variation in the act, of course, by restricting his analysis to cases of public drunkenness. Yet, consider the many ways in which behaviors generally classified as drunken by officers or observers might differ from one encounter to the next. Could some of the arrests that Lundman attributed to officers' biases against males, Native Americans, and declassified offenders actually be due to subtle, unmeasured aspects of behavior that are particularly characteristic of these groups? Data presented in Table 3 of Lundman's article indicate that uncontrolled differences in behavior cannot be ignored when interpreting the results of this and other observational studies of naturally occurring processes.

In contrast, the deviant act in Steffensmeier's experiment was completely staged. Hired accomplices performed over 200 acts of shoplifting in plain view of ordinary shoppers in several retail stores. Most of these shoppers reported the shoplifting incident to store personnel, but a large number of these unwitting experimental subjects did absolutely nothing about the rule-breaking act they witnessed. Now, could these variations in audience reaction be caused by variations in the deviant act? Probably not. As Steffensmeier and Terry describe it below, the shoplifters' behavior always followed a prescribed sequence and usually involved theft of items worth less than $3. For all practical purposes, then, this deviant act was indeed the same or *constant* across all encounters between shoppers and shoplifters.

With the act held constant and, therefore, ruled out as a possible source of variation in audience reactions, Steffensmeier and Terry are able to concentrate on theoretically relevant effects of actor and audience variables that were built into the research design shown in Figure 1 of their article. Pertaining to the labeling issue of who performs the act, two actor characteristics—appearance ("hippie" versus "straight") and sex—were systematically and independently varied through the use of four different accomplices in the role of shoplifter. The audience characteristic of sex was also varied, with approximately half of the shoplifting incidents being staged in front of males and half in front of female shoppers. Which of these three variables do you suppose had the strongest influence on the reporting of the deviant act? The results of this carefully controlled investigation provide a clear answer to this question and shed light on some subtle, combined effects of actor and audience characteristics.

A fourth potential source of variation in interpersonal reactions mentioned earlier—characteristics of the situation—is not prominently featured in Steffensmeier and Terry's analysis; nonetheless, it did figure in to Steffensmeier's initial choice of research sites. You will read that the shoplifting incidents were staged in three different stores, which ranged from a small neighborhood grocery to a large discount department store. Contrary to Steffensmeier's expectations, this situational variation had little effect on shoppers' reporting levels and did not alter relationships involving other experimental variables. Yet, the very fact that the basic findings of this study were not derived from only one experimental setting but were replicated in several rather different contexts increases confidence in the *generality* of those results. Also note that these stores all represent *natural field situations*, with the subjects being unaware (at least initially) that they were participating in an experiment. What advantages (or disadvantages) might there be in a field experiment such as this as compared to the typical social psychological experiment conducted in a special laboratory with college students recruited as subjects? (see Wuebben et al., 1974; Martin & Sell, 1979; Aronson & Carlsmith, 1968).

While Steffensmeier and Terry's work highlights several advantages of experimental techniques (also see Steffensmeier & Terry, 1975), this methodological approach has some obvious limitations in certain areas of deviance research. Ethical considerations preclude experimentation on many theoretical questions within the normative perspective dealing with the causes of deviant behavior. We could not, for instance, randomly assign 12-year-olds to delinquent gangs or to nondelinquent peer groups as an experimental test of differential association theory (however, see McCord & McCord, 1959). Similarly, a relativistic study of secondary deviance employing a random experimental assignment of deviant labels would raise serious ethical questions (cf. Freedman & Doob, 1968). Some researchers in the labeling tradition might also object to experimentation on methodological grounds, arguing that deterministic analyses of cause-and-effect relationships are inappropriate or irrelevant to the study of interactional processes such as audience reactions to deviance. Be that as it may, you should judge for yourself whether the methodological strategy illustrated by Steffensmeier and Terry's article is a useful alternative to purely observational approaches to research on interpersonal reactions to deviance.

RESEARCH ILLUSTRATION 9–C

Deviance and respectability: An observational study of reactions to shoplifting*

Darrell J. Steffensmeier and Robert M. Terry

In general, observational field studies dealing with reactions to deviance have lacked the kind of control that allows for experimental manipulation of variables and the systematic examination of posited relationships. In addition, there are few studies dealing with public reactions to deviance. The research reported here consisted of a field experiment in which *rigged* shoplifting events were enacted in the presence of store

---

Source: Article reprinted from *Social Forces* 51 (June 1973): 417–426. Reprinted by permission of *Social Forces* and the University of North Carolina Press.

* The authors are grateful for financial assistance provided by the Center for Research in Interpersonal Behavior and the Graduate College of the University of Iowa. We would also like to thank Renee Steffensmeier for critical readings of earlier drafts of this paper and Larry Rhoades for helpful suggestions regarding final editing.

customers who were in a position to observe and react to the shoplifting incidents. Three variables were varied as part of the field experiment: (1) appearance of shoplifter, (2) sex of shoplifter, and (3) sex of store customer. Major findings were that sex of shoplifter and sex of store customer had little effect on reporting levels whereas appearance of shoplifter exerted a major independent effect on reporting levels.

The interactionist-labeling perspective in deviance asserts that audience responses to deviant acts are crucial to the understanding of deviant behavior. Furthermore, to understand audience response—reactions toward various types of deviance—investigators need to discover the meaning these behaviors have for potential reactors. These meanings may vary with the deviant's other social identities, with situational factors such as social support and social setting, and the characteristics of potential reactors. Although some research relates these variables to audience reactions, few studies have manipulated such variables within a field setting.

A growing body of observational field studies treats the reactions of official control agents such as the police (e.g., Black, 1970; Piliavin and Briar, 1964) and courts to deviant actors (Emerson, 1969). But such research has generally lacked the kind of control that allows for experimental manipulation of variables and the systematic examination of posited relationships. In addition, studies examining the reactions of the general public have been largely ignored. With few exceptions (e.g., Darley and Latane, 1968; Denner, 1968; Freed et al., 1955; Lefkowitz et al., 1955), there is a dearth of experimental field research that systematically examines posited relationships between reactions of the general public and deviant behavior.

Current thinking in sociology indicates that the study of deviant behavior must overcome problems in the validity of official statistics (see, especially, Douglas, 1971a; Kitsuse and Cicourel, 1963; Wheeler, 1967), must recognize that while official control agents are important it is the general public that usually initiates responses to deviant behavior (e.g., Black, 1970), and must study deviance in its natural setting rather than as mediated through the official reports and actions of formal control agents (e.g., Douglas, 1971b; Humphreys, 1970).

This research attempts to shed some light on the nature and basis of reactions to a particular kind of deviance and, in doing so, tries to overcome the aforementioned problems by (1) using field research methods, (2) ascertaining responses of the general public to instances of deviant behavior in real life situations, and (3) making direct observations of behavior of members of the social audience. Specifically, appearance and sex of the deviant are varied systematically in order to assess their effects upon the responses of the general public to observed instances of shoplifting.[1]

There is much theoretical support for the notion that the actor's social identity is a crucial determinant of reactions to deviant behavior (Douglas, 1970; Goffman, 1963; Lemert, 1951; Lofland, 1969). Two important aspects of social identity considered in this research are those of appearance and sex, both of which can be subsumed under the more abstract rubric of respectability.

Much of the literature in the interactionist-labeling perspective has argued that differential treatment is accorded persons with poor social backgrounds, less than perfect social identities, or "bad" reputations. Many analyses of deviant categories are founded on the assumption that particular classes of people are more likely to perform deviant acts and to be particular types of deviant persons (Hughes, 1945; Kitsuse, 1962; Lofland, 1969; Scheff, 1966; Simmons, 1965; Sudnow, 1965). Such studies are highly consistent in arguing that respectability decreases the likelihood of deviant imputations, whereas "unrespectability" has the opposite effect.

In this research, appearance and sex are used as indicators of respectability. Reports by Ball (1970) and Cameron (1964) have noted that a respectable appearance serves as a buffer against a deviant imputation. Lefkowitz *et al.* (1955) found that a respectable appearance was influential in inducing others to engage in deviant behavior (jaywalking). In a field experiment, Bickman (1971) found that persons who appeared to be of low status were treated more dishonestly by experimental subjects than were those of apparently higher status. It has been noted that one's appearance (kinds of clothing, hair style, and the like) is part and parcel of being a particular kind of person and also indicates, in a general sense, an individual's attitude toward community norms (Carey, 1968; Stone, 1962). In the current scene, commonsense distinctions between hippie and straight appearances are especially noteworthy.

Another of actor's social identities thought to affect reactions to deviance in one's sex. Consistent research findings show that females are less severely dealt with by formal control agents than are males and some evidence exists to support the notion that public attitudes

---

[1] Theoretically the choice of shoplifting is predicated on the assumption that it is a form of deviant behavior which elicits variable social reactions that are usually mild to moderate. Moreover, shoplifting is a sufficiently problematic form of deviance to allow for other deviant identities to influence reactions to it. Several practical considerations also determined the selection of shoplifting as the object of investigation. It was a behavior around which a field experiment could readily be constructed and that in turn allowed for the observation of a large number of subjects within a limited time period and simultaneously permitted the control and manipulation of the independent variables.

and reactions toward the sexes tend to favor females (Pollak, 1961; Reckless, 1961; Ward and Kassebaum, 1965). Schur (1969) has argued that the greater attitude of protectiveness taken toward women in our society and more generally the nature of their social roles and situations permit women to exploit their sex for criminal purposes and to engage in various kinds of criminal behavior with relatively little fear of detection or prosecution.

The effect of sex status on deviant imputation can be fitted into Goffman's discussion of social identities and more specifically into the rubric of respectability. Goffman (1963) argues that an individual's biography is composed of both past and present events and characteristics which function so as to establish an individual's social identity. The latter refers to those attributes others can observe, providing thereby a basis for classifying an actor as a particular kind of person. Such attributes as age and sex are of primary importance in making such categorizations. Although none of these variables is inherently bound to the notion of respectability, the deviant behavior literature rather clearly indicates that being a male tends to be viewed as an unfavorable attribute by social control agents and increases a person's vulnerability to the imputation of deviance.

Our third independent variable, sex of subject, is ambiguously grounded in research that generally indicates that females are less tolerant of deviance than are males (Phillips, 1964; Westie and Martin, 1959; Williams, 1964); although there is conflicting evidence (Whatley, 1959). Traditional sex role differences, theoretically at least, have emphasized more support of stability and the ongoing system among females than among males. Thus, females should be less accepting of nonconforming behavior than males (Parsons and Bales, 1955) and therefore should be more likely to report deviant acts.

HYPOTHESES

On the basis of the foregoing, the following hypotheses are the targets of inquiry:

1. *Store customers will be more likely to report a shoplifting incident when the shoplifter has a hippie rather than a straight appearance.*
2. *Store customers will be more likely to report a shoplifting incident when the shoplifter is male rather than female.*
3. *Female store customers will be more likely to report a shoplifting incident than male store customers.*

METHODS

This research sought to discover factors related to reactions to shoplifting. "Reactions" was defined in terms of variation in the willingness of store customers to report behavior (shoplifting) which was blatantly illegal and deviant. In order to observe the reactions of a wide variety of subjects and simultaneously maintain some degree of control over the frequency of occurrence and consistency of the deviant behavior, a natural field experiment was designed. While this approach assured a rather high degree of external validity it presented some difficulties in settling on the variables determining societal reactions. For the experimental situation allowed us to investigate only those independent variables that were amenable to immediate observation in fleeting encounters: hence, sex and appearance.

The study was conducted in three preselected stores in a midwestern university city of 50,000. The experiment can best be described as a rigged shoplifting incident—i.e., its occurrence was prearranged. The store's manager and personnel had complete knowledge of the experiment and the researchers had their full cooperation in staging the shoplifting incidents.

A. Shoplifting sequence

The man concern of this research was the extent to which customers were willing to report shoplifting to store personnel. In order to control the frequency and consistency of the shoplifting situation three accomplices were employed. One accomplice played the part of a shoplifter and two more accomplices layed the parts of store employees. The experimental procedure is best understood through a discussion of the roles played by the accomplices.

The first accomplice played the part of a shoplifter. This accomplice was to place himself under the direct observation of a customer (the subject), and then steal some item of merchandise in an obvious and deliberate manner.[2] Having done his shoplifting, the first accomplice moved to another location where he remained out of hearing distance but within eyesight of the subject. This procedure avoided the possible intimidation of the subject and simultaneously eased identification of the shoplifter if the subject showed a willingness to report the incident. The appearance and sex of the shoplifter were varied systematically.

The second and third research accomplices played the parts of store employees.[3] The principal task of the second accomplice or first

---

[2] In the course of pretesting, we found that for subjects to be aware of the shoplifting as well as for them to be reasonably certain that it was shoplifting, our shoplifters had to be quite blatant and aggressive in their shoplifting. At least one member of the research team had to be reasonably certain that the subject saw the shoplifting.

[3] The research accomplices who were assigned the roles of store employees were all males who appeared to be about 25–30 years old. To give as much credibility as possible to the experiment, these accomplices wore the same apparel as the regular store employees. In Stores A and B, long white aprons made the accomplices easily

store employee was to make himself readily available should the subject wish to report the shoplifting incident. As soon as the shoplifter moved away to another location (after he had shoplifted) the first store employee had instructions to move into the immediate vicinity of the subject and act as though he were arranging merchandise on the shelves or counters. The accomplice remained in the area for a brief period of time in order to allow the subject ample opportunity to report. If the subject reported, then the store employee was instructed to "apprehend" the shoplifter and both of them moved backstage.[4] If the subject did not report the shoplifting, the accomplice left the area and signaled to a third accomplice to intervene.

The third accomplice played the part of a second store employee. He was instructed to act more directly and vigorously in order to increase the likelihood of reporting. He asked the subject for assistance in identifying a possible shoplifter by prompting the subject in two different ways. The first prompting was as follows: "Good afternoon (evening), sir (madam), we have been watching so-and-so (identifying description) for shoplifting. Did you happen to see anything?" If, in response to this first prompting the subject reported the shoplifter, then the employee "apprehended" him and they moved backstage. If the subject did not respond to the first prompting, the same store employee was instructed to intervene more forcefully to elicit reporting from the subject. The second prompting was as follows: "Gee, I was quite sure I saw him (her) take something (specify item) and put it down his coat. You didn't happen to see anything suspicious, did you?" If the subject still did not report, the accomplice left the vicinity and there was no further prompting of the subject.

After the experiment was completed each subject was immediately debriefed by another research assistant. Every conceivable effort was made to clarify to the subject the nature and the purpose of the deception. In addition, an attempt was made to interview the subject briefly as to his perception of and reaction to the experiment.[5]

---

identifiable. However in Store C regular employees were less well differentiated and thus some minor modifications were introduced in our accomplices in order to ensure their proper identification by subjects. These modifications did not seem to create any noticeable differences in the experimental situation that would affect our interpretation of the data.

[4] Backstage refers to an area of the store reserved for store personnel where the researcher and his associates were able to record each event as it happened and plan for the next event without being observed by subjects.

[5] Studying behavior in the natural environment raises ethical questions about the deception of subjects and the invasion of their privacy. Should people be used in a social-psychological experiment without their permission or awareness? The question is difficult to answer. We feel that in the case of this study the permission of the subjects was not crucial. None of the subjects expressed hostility toward the experiment and most were highly cooperative. Note, for example, that *178* of the *191* adult

B. Operationalization of the dependent variable

The dependent variable in this research is willingness to report a shoplifting incident. On a higher theoretical level we are getting at the willingness of potential reactors to impute a deviant label to presumably deviant actors. The use of prompting as a device to obtain variation in the dependent variable was suggested by the previous research of Latane and Darley (1969) and Denner (1968). As operationalized in this research, willingness to report could achieve four possible values:

1. If the subject reported the shoplifting incident to the first store employee this response was assigned a value of *high* willingness to report. As will be recalled, the first store employee took a passive stance toward the subject and made no direct attempt to encourage reporting. No prompting was used at this point.

2. If the subject reported the shoplifting incident to the second store employee in response to the first prompting, this behavior was held to indicate *medium high* willingness to report.

3. If the subject reported the shoplifting incident to the second store employee in response to the second prompting, this behavior was assigned a value of *medium low* willingness to report.

4. The category of *low* willingness to report consisted of all subjects who did not report the shoplifting incident.

Table 1 gives the distributions obtained for the sample on the dependent variable, willingness to report. As can be seen, we got good variance in type of response. A good deal of reporting took place even without prompting.

Table 1
Frequency distribution of respondent reporting levels

Reporting	Total sample (n = 212)	Adults (n = 191)	Students (n = 21)
High	62(29.2)	61(31.9)	1 (4.8)
Medium high	73(34.4)	71(37.2)	2 (9.5)
Medium low	28(13.2)	25(13.1)	3(14.3)
Low	49(23.1)	34(17.8)	15(71.4)

subjects completed the postexperimental interview, and 171 of these 178 consented either to a mailed questionnaire or home interview. Careful and thorough pretesting enabled us to avoid numerous problems.

C. Research sites

Stores were selected on the basis of several criteria. We thought it important to use stores of differing size and degree of bureaucratization.[6] Also, the stores had to retail merchandise that would be easy and obvious to steal. We also sought stores that had customers who represented the nonstudent population of a university-dominated city.

After considering these matters, we approached several store managers to determine their willingness to participate in the project. Some were encouraging and enthusiastic. Out of necessity, then, the stores finally selected as research sites were those at which most cooperation was offered. Fortunately, these stores varied along the relevant dimensions of size and bureaucratization. In addition, each store had certain unique features.

Store A was a small, older chain grocery store, located close to the downtown area. Patrons consisted largely of persons living in the immediate neighborhood, older people, and university students. Store B was a relatively new, large chain grocery store located in a fringe area shopping center. The patrons consisted chiefly of housewives. Store C was a very large discount department store located on the edge of the city. For a number of reasons (location, prices, variety of merchandise, store hours, etc.) this store was more likely to attract out-of-town customers than the other stores.[7]

We tried to get approximately equal numbers of subjects in each store. Except for persons later identified as college students, this aim was achieved, with 67 subjects exposed to shoplifting in Store A, 69 in Store B, and 55 in Store C. Since the stores differed in size and therefore in the number of customers during any given time period, trial runs were conducted on four separate occasions in Store A, on two separate occasions in Store B, and on one occasion in Store C. In addition, Store A was used to conduct all pretests for the experiment.

D. Experimental design

A primary justification for the study of contrived rather than real shoplifting is the greater ability to manipulate the independent variables. Two identities of the shoplifters were systematically varied—appearance and sex. In addition, sex of the subject (shopper) was also varied across experimental events. Each variable is dichotomized,

---

[6] Subsequent reports will deal with the effects on reporting levels of size of store and degree of bureaucratization of the store. In general, these variables had little effect on reporting levels and did not affect the relationships between reporting levels and the three variables discussed in this article.

[7] Since two of the stores studied were grocery stores, most things stolen were food items. The remainder consisted of articles of clothing, small appliances, cosmetics, etc. The items shoplifted were of relatively small value, most retailing for less than $3.00.

resulting in an overall research design of the 2 × 2 × 2 variety. Figure 1 illustrates the eight comparison groups produced by this design. Approximately 25 subjects are represented in each cell, with a total sample size of 212. Each subject was exposed to only one combi-

Figure 1
Representation of the research design

	Sex of shoplifter	
	Male	Female
	Appearance of shoplifter	Appearance of shoplifter
Sex of subject	Hippie Straight	Hippie Straight
Male Female		

nation of the independent variables, sex of shoplifter and appearance of shoplifter. We tried to include proportionate numbers of male and female subjects from various age categories and backgrounds and to exclude persons who appeared to be college students. Of the total of 212 subjects, 191 were classifiable as nonstudent adults. All future tabulations of experimental data are based on these 191 subjects.[8]

E. **Operationalizing the independent variables**

The major independent variables in this research were appearance and sex. Appearance was varied: hippie vs. straight. Sex was varied by using male and female shoplifters. Attributes of the shoplifter presentation types are as follows:

(1) *Hippie shoplifter:*

(a) *Male:* He wore soiled patched blue jeans, blue workman's shirt, and blue denim jacket; well-worn scuffed shoes with no socks. He had long and unruly hair with a ribbon tied around his forehead. He was unshaven and had a small beard.

(b) *Female:* She wore soiled patched blue jeans, blue workman's shirt, and dirty blue denim jacket; well-worn ragged tennis shoes with no socks. She had long unruly and ratted hair. She wore no makeup.

(2) *Straight shoplifter:*

(a) *Male:* He wore neatly pressed dress slacks, sport shirt and tie,

---

[8] A subject was operationally defined as a student if he/she indicated that he/she attended the university full- or part-time and was less than 26 years old. Pretesting indicated that students were highly unlikely to report, irrespective of prompting.

sport jacket, shined shoes. He had short, trimly cut hair and was clean shaven.

(b) *Female:* She wore a dress, shined shoes or boots, a fur coat. Her hair was well-styled. She wore makeup and was well groomed.

Other than the induced differences of grooming and dress, the shoplifters were about the same age, same height and build, and attractiveness.

RESULTS

Tables 2 and 3 analyze the effects on reporting levels of our three independent variables. Table 2 also shows the interaction effects among our three independent variables. The tests of hypotheses, which are treated separately below, are derived from the information presented in Tables 2 and 3.

Table 2
Three-way analysis of variance of reporting levels and tests for interaction effects for appearance of shoplifter, sex of shoplifter, and sex of subject*

Source	SS	DF†	MS	F	Prob.
Total	235.1296	$(npqr - 1) = 190$			
Main effects					
Appearance of shoplifter (A)	46.9782	$(q - 1) = 1$	46.9782	48.1186	<.001
Sex of shoplifter (B)	.0048	$(p - 1) = 1$	.0048	.0049	>.05 N.S.
Sex of subject (C)	2.7066	$(r - 1) = 1$	2.7066	2.7723	>.05 N.S.
Interactions					
AB interaction	.1688	$(q - 1)(p - 1) = 1$	.1688	.1728	>.05 N.S.
AC interaction	.5145	$(q - 1)(r - 1) = 1$	.5145	.5269	>.05 N.S.
BC interaction	4.6232	$(p - 1)(r - 1) = 1$	4.6232	4.7354	$.01 < p < .05$
ABC interaction	1.4594	$(q - 1)(p - 1)(r - 1) = 1$	1.4594	1.4948	>.05 N.S.
Error					
Error SS (W. cell)	178.6741	$pqr(\bar{n} - 1) = 183$	.9763		

* The analysis of variance procedures used in Table 2 were based on the "method of expected equal frequencies." According to this procedure, if cell Ns do not differ markedly, a fairly simple weighting procedure can be used to estimate what the cell sums and sums of squared scores would be if all Ns had been the same. (See Kohout, forthcoming; Schuessler, 1971, for cogent discussions of the procedure involved.)
† In computing the degrees of freedom, q = levels of A, p = levels of B, r = levels of C, and $\bar{n}$ = the average cell frequency.

Appearance and reporting

Our hypothesis predicts that the level of reporting of a shoplifting incident will be higher for the hippie than for the straight shoplifter. The hypothesis is clearly supported in that the relationship ($r = .465$) is large and in the expected direction and the F-test results are highly

Table 3
Summary correlation table*

Zero-order	First-order	Second-order
$r_{wy} = .465$	$r_{wy.x} = .465$	$r_{wy.xz} = .471$
(appearance of shoplifter)	$r_{wy.z} = .471$	
$r_{xy} = .012$	$r_{xy.w} = .016$	$r_{xy.wz} = .018$
(sex of shoplifter)	$r_{xy.z} = 0.14$	
$r_{zy} = .096$	$r_{zy.w} = .127$	$r_{zy.wx} = .127$
(sex of subject)	$r_{zy.x} = .096$	

* The measure of association reported is Pearson's coefficient of correlation.
    z = sex of subject
    x = sex of shoplifter
    w = appearance of shoplifter
    y = reporting level

significant. In line with previous arguments, the shoplifter's appearance provides the potential reactor with information that enables him to locate the actor on a high-low evaluative continuum. Apparently a hippie appearance constitutes a negative identity that results in a greater willingness on the part of subjects to report the hippie over the straight shoplifter and, by extension, a greater willingness to impute a deviant label to a hippie rather than a straight actor. The effects of shoplifter's appearance on reporting levels is discussed in greater detail following presentation of other results.

Sex of shoplifter and reporting

Our hypothesis as to the effect of shoplifter's sex on reporting levels is not supported in the data. The relationship ($r = .012$) is in the expected direction but is so small as to be nonexistent. In addition, F-test results are not significant.

Explanations for this finding are easy to come by, although such explanations are speculative. First, the findings may be limited to shoplifting and may not be generalizable to other deviance. Also, the trend toward sexual equality may be narrowing sex differentials in attitudes and actions toward offenders and the protectiveness argument may be no longer feasible. Finally, findings of differential reactions to offenders on the basis of sex have focused upon the reactions of formal control agents rather than the general public. It may be that control agents discriminate whereas the public does not.

Sex of subject and reporting levels

Our hypothesis asserts that females will be more likely to report than will males. The data offer little support for the hypothesis. As indicated in Tables 2 and 3, relationship ($r = .096$) is in the expected direction, but it is so small that we reject the hypothesis. In addition, F-test results are not significant. Again, it is possible that changing cultural definitions of female social roles and the increasing equalitarianism of women in general has had the effect of narrowing sexual differentials in reactions to deviance. Williams (1964) has argued that this is occurring with racial prejudice and discrimination, and a similar process might have produced these results with respect to deviance.

Interaction effects

Table 2 shows the interaction effects on reporting levels of various combinations of our independent variables. Only the interaction effect between sex of shoplifter and sex of subject proved to be significant (BC Interaction: $.01 < p < .05$). This interaction effect can be explained ex post facto by means of further analyses. The cell means for combinations of the independent variables were used to rank-order reporting levels for various categories of shoplifters and subjects. In addition, a new variable was derived by combining the sex of subject and sex of shoplifter. The derived variable yields a dichotomy—opposite sex vs. same sex reporting. The results are presented in Table 4, a table which neatly summarizes the results of this research.

Table 4
Mean reporting levels for combinations of independent variables

Rank order	Sex of subject	Sex of shoplifter	Sex of subject and sex of shoplifter	Appearance of shoplifter	Mean reporting level
1	Female	Male	Opposite	Hippie	1.4347
2	Female	Female	Same	Hippie	1.5217
3	Male	Female	Opposite	Hippie	1.7173
4	Male	Male	Same	Hippie	1.9130
5	Female	Male	Opposite	Straight	2.2962
6	Male	Female	Opposite	Straight	2.5000
7	Female	Female	Same	Straight	2.8518
8	Male	Male	Same	Straight	2.9166

First, the appearance of the shoplifter has the strongest and most clear-cut effect on reporting levels. Hippie shoplifters are always more likely to be reported than straight shoplifters. Second, for hippie shoplifters, female subjects report more than male subjects, irrespective of sex of shoplifter. For straight shoplifters, subject's willingness to report is greater when the shoplifter is of the opposite, rather than the same sex. According to these rank orders, straight shoplifters who are the same sex as the subject-witness are the least likely of all shoplifters to be reported.

Within categories of shoplifter's appearance we have a case of specification. For the hippie shoplifter, sex of subject has an independent effect on reporting: females report more often than males. In the case of the straight shoplifter, the interaction of sex of subject and sex of shoplifter clearly affects the level of reporting. The simple finding of interaction between these two independent variables becomes more complicated than it at first appeared to be in Table 2.

This specification of different levels of reporting requires us to try to explain the results for each category, separately. For straight shoplifters, same sex reporting may be less than opposite sex reporting because subjects are more able to empathize with persons of the same sex. Another possibility is that subjects are more likely to report a member of the opposite sex because they feel less threatened. That is, subjects may feel that they are less likely to be attacked (physically or verbally) in a highly visible public situation by a member of the opposite sex than by a member of the same sex.

On the other hand, female subjects are more likely than male subjects to report the shoplifter who is a hippie because they are probably more offended by the overt violation of community norms and are more threatened by such attacks on the social order of the community. Females therefore are more likely than males to sanction persons with a nonrespectable appearance. The possibility that female subjects are more concerned with the appearance of respectability and with maintenance of social order explains the differential in reporting between male and female subjects when the shoplifter is a hippie.

DISCUSSION

The major results of this research are that sex of shoplifter and sex of subject had little effect on reporting levels, whereas appearance of shoplifter exerted a major independent effect on reporting levels. The importance of appearance merits further discussion: How to account for its significance?

The evidence presented clearly indicates that a hippie appearance constituted a highly salient basis for social differentiation. From the perspective of "middle class" America, hippies and other beatnik types are viewed as basically unstable, as lacking in ambition and ability, and as marginal contributors to the social system. By the mere fact of being a hippie the person has demonstrated his lack of moral worth, his unrespectability, from the dominant cultural perspective.

As such, a hippie label represents a stigma, an extreme negative identity. Such an identity has been variously dealt with as a "master status" by Becker (1963), a "pivotal category" by Lofland (1969), or a "central trait" by Asch (1946). All of these concepts refer to a similar phenomenon: an extreme negative identity can exercise a disproportionate influence in structuring perceptions and behaviors and, in terms of this research, the reactions to shoplifting. A hippie identity or label constitutes, for many subjects in this research, a master status, a pivotal category, or a central trait, which greatly increases the individual's vulnerability to stigmatization as a deviant.[9]

Some anecdotal observations illustrate these notions. These observations also depict the less conscious, less deliberate reactions of the subjects to the hippie identity than to the straight identity. In general, most subjects appeared to be inclined *not* to report the shoplifting incident and to avoid getting involved. When they witnessed the incident and the shoplifter gave off no other negative cues or stimuli they were apt to hesitate. Hesitation of this sort was likely to result in disengagement and failure to report.

Subjects were more likely to hesitate when the shoplifter was straight rather than hippie. A number of subjects, for instance, indicated that they considered reporting the straight shoplifter but thought twice or hesitated before proceeding with a course of action. This "thinking twice" or hesitating then often resulted in their deciding simply to ignore the incident.

But in the case of hippie shoplifters, this hesitation was less likely to occur. That is, when witnessing a hippie shoplifting the subject was not only more likely to consider reporting but he was also less likely to think twice about it and thus in reality he was more likely to proceed to report. The hippie appearance seemed to tip the scales in the direction of increased reporting.

Further support for the importance of appearance comes from the level of enthusiasm in reporting. In reporting the hippie shoplifter

---

[9] Related notions have been dealt with in exchange theory wherein perceived statuses or identities are characterized in terms of positive and negative credits. In dealing with reactions to deviance the reasoning is as follows: the higher the perceived status of an individual the greater his "stock" of esteem, or accumulation of credits. Being involved in visibly deviant behaviors, such as shoplifting, reduces the absolute level of these accumulated credits. However, if a high- (straight-appearing actor) and low- (hippie-appearing actor) status individual commit the same deviant act the high-status person can retain some level of positive credits while the low-status person can go to zero or minus quantity of credits (Alvarez, 1968; Hollander, 1958; Homans, 1961). Thus having a high status or respectable identity served to "protect" the actor from being reported for shoplifting whereas having a low-status or less-than-respectable identity increases the likelihood of being reported. That is, a hippie appearance reduces actor's level of positive credits to a considerable degree, with the effect that when such an actor engages in deviant behavior, more positive credits are lost and his chances for being reported are greatly increased.

some subjects were very excited—even enthusiastic. Although not true of all subjects, reporting of hippie shoplifters (without prompting) frequently included such comments as "That hippie thing took a package of lunchmeat," or "That son of a bitch hippie over there just stuffed a banana down his coat." For these subjects, the high levels of reporting of hippie shoplifters must be viewed within a particular situational context wherein his undoing was not simply a result of his being a shoplifter, but because he was both shoplifter *and* hippie.

CONCLUSIONS

Via the use of field research techniques combined with an experimental design we have provided clear support for the basic interactionist-labeling contention that the imputation of deviance resides not only in the *fact* of deviance per se; it also depends heavily on the meanings that the audience attach to the behavior and the actor. Willingness to report deviant acts can be assumed to depend on the "deviant's" other social identities, a significant clue to identity being provided by his appearance.

At the same time, however, some other identities that may seem to be important at first glance may actually prove to be unimportant aspects of the interpersonal relationships between offender and audience. This seemed to be the case with sex of shoplifter and sex of subject, although it is apparent that the complexity of the relationships involved necessitates additional research. Further research should also focus upon other aspects of the social identities of the offender, the situational contexts in which deviant acts occur, and the backgrounds and relevant identities of members of the social audience. At the very least we have demonstrated that in order to get at such problems it is possible and fruitful to utilize experimental field research techniques.

REFERENCES

Alvarez, R. 1968. "Informational Reactions to Deviance in Simulated Work Organizations: A Laboratory Experiment." *American Sociological Review* 33 (December):895–911.

Asch, S. E. 1946. "Forming Impressions of Personality." *Journal of Abnormal and Social Psychology* 41:258–90.

Ball, D. W. 1970. "The Problematics of Respectability." In Jack Douglas (ed.), *Respectability and Deviance*. New York: Basic Books.

Becker, Howard S. 1963. *Outsiders: Studies in the Sociology of Deviance*. New York: Free Press.

Bickman, L. 1971. "The Effect of Social Class on the Honesty of Others." *Journal of Social Psychology* 85:87–92.

Black, D. J. 1970. "Production of Crime Rates." *American Sociological Review* 35 (August):733–48.

Black, D. J., and A. J. Reiss, Jr. 1970. "Police Control of Juveniles." *American Sociological Review* 35(February):63–77.

Cameron, Mary O. 1964. *The Booster and the Snitch*. Glencoe: Free Press.
Carey, James T. 1968. *The College Drug Scene*. Englewood Cliffs: Prentice-Hall.
Darley, J. M., and B. Latane. 1968. "Bystander Intervention in Emergencies: Diffusion of Responsibility." *Journal of Personality and Social Psychology* 8:377–83.
Denner, B. 1968. "Did a Crime Occur? Should I Inform Anyone? A Study of Deception." *Journal of Personality* 36:454–68.
Douglas, Jack (ed.). 1970. *Respectability and Deviance*. New York: Basic Books.
─────────. 1971a. *American Social Order*. New York: Free Press.
─────────. 1971b. (ed.). *Research on Deviance*. New York: Random House.
Emerson, Robert M. 1969. *Judging Delinquents*. Chicago: Aldine.
Freed, A., P. J. Chandler, R. R. Blake, and J. S. Mouton. 1955. "Stimulus and Background Factors in Sign Violation." *Journal of Personality* 23:499.
Goffman, Erving. 1963. *Stigma: Notes on the Management of Spoiled Identity*. Englewood Cliffs: Spectrum Books.
Hollander, E. P. 1958. "Conformity, Status, and Idiosyncrasy Credit." *Psychological Review* 65:117–27.
Homans, George C. 1961. *Social Behavior: Its Elementary Forms*. New York: Harcourt, Brace & World.
Hughes, E. C. 1945. "Dilemmas and Contradictions of Status." *American Journal of Sociology* 50(March):353–9.
Humphreys, Laud. 1970. *Tearoom Trade*. Chicago: Aldine.
Kitsuse, J. I. 1962. "Societal Reaction to Deviant Behavior: Problems of Theory and Method." *Social Problems* 9:247–56.
Kitsuse, J. I., and A. Cicourel. 1963. "A Note on the Uses of Official Statistics." *Social Problems* 11:131–9.
Kohout, Frank, J. 1972. *Applied Statistics*. Forthcoming.
Latane, B., and J. Darley. 1969. "Bystander Apathy." *American Scientist* 57:244–68.
Lefkowitz, M., R. R. Blake, and J. S. Mouton. 1955. "Status Factors in Pedestrian Violation of Traffic Signals." *Journal of Abnormal and Social Psychology* 51:704–705.
Lemert, Edwin. 1951. *Social Pathology*. New York: McGraw-Hill.
Lofland, John. 1969. *Deviance and Identity*. Englewood Cliffs: Prentice-Hall.
Parsons, Talcott, and Robert F. Bales. 1955. *Family Socialization and Interaction Process*. Glencoe: Free Press.
Phillips, D. L. 1964. "Rejection of the Mentally Ill: The Influence of Behavior and Sex." *American Sociological Review* 29(October):679–87.
Piliavin, I., and S. Briar. 1964. "Police Encounters with Juveniles." *American Journal of Sociology* 70(November):206–14.
Pollak, Otto. 1961. *The Criminality of Women*. New York: Perpetua Books.
Reckless, Walter. 1961. *The Crime Problem*. New York: Appleton-Century-Crofts.
Scheff, Thomas J. 1966. *Being Mentally Ill: A Sociological Theory*. Chicago: Aldine.
Schuessler, Karl. 1971. *Analyzing Social Data*. Boston: Houghton Mifflin.
Schur, E. M. 1969. "Reactions to Deviance: A Critical Assessment." *American Sociological Review*.
Simmons, J. L. 1965. "Public Stereotypes of Deviants." *Social Problems* 13:223–32.
Stone, G. P. 1962. "Appearance and the Self." In Arnold Rose (ed.), *Human Behavior and Social Processes*. Boston: Houghton Mifflin.
Sudnow, D. 1965. "Normal Crimes: Sociological Features of the Penal Code in a Public Defender Office." *Social Problems* 12:255–76.
Ward, David A., and Gene Kassebaum. 1965. *Women's Prison: Sex and Social Structure*. Chicago: Aldine.
Westie, F. R., and J. C. Martin. 1959. "The Tolerant Personality." *American Sociological Review* 24(August):521–28.
Whatley, C. D. 1959. "Social Attitudes Toward Discharged Mental Patients." *Social Problems* 6:313–20.
Wheeler, S. 1967. "Criminal Statistics: A Reformulation of the Problem." *Journal of Criminal Law, Criminology, and Police Science* 58:317–24.
Williams, Robin M., Jr. 1964. *Strangers Next Door*. Englewood Cliffs: Prentice-Hall.

CONCLUSION

The research illustrations in this chapter offer a flattering view of the labeling tradition. Many of the central tenets of this relativistic approach to deviance appear to be borne out in these three studies. For instance, the strategy of relativistic description discussed in Chapter 3 is executed effectively by Rosenhan (1973). He builds his analysis of psychiatric labeling on the premise that there was absolutely nothing wrong with the pseudopatients and nothing crazy or even unusual about their behavior following admission. Against this neutral backdrop of ordinary people acting in presumably normal ways, the stigmatizing and depersonalizing reactions of hospital staff take on an especially vivid and harsh appearance. By showing that these reactions were essentially *independent* of the behavior of the pseudopatients, Rosenhan invites his readers to view psychiatric social control as both empirically and morally problematic.

Of course, this general strategy of attempting to neutralize or hold constant the behavior of labeled actors also underlies the research methods employed by Lundman (1974), Steffensmeier and Terry (1973), and many other investigators in the labeling tradition. However, an increasing number of sociologists are taking a somewhat broader, multivariate approach to the study of audience reaction processes by including *variations in deviant behavior* among the potential influences they examine. Specifically, some of these researchers have found that social definitions and reactions to mental disorder are more strongly influenced by the severity or disruptiveness of the actor's symptoms than by other factors emphasized in labeling theory (for example, Bord, 1971; Kirk, 1974; Larkin & Loman, 1977; Rushing & Esco, 1977; Greenley, 1979). Evidence such as this has helped fuel a lengthy and often heated debate over whether labeling theory or the disease model of psychiatric medicine provides a better explanation of the onset and treatment of mental disorder. Known as the Scheff-Gove controversy after its two main protagonists, this debate has centered on Scheff's (1966) claim that labeling is the "single most important cause" of stable careers of mental disorder. Gove, for his part, contends that most of the research in this area fails to support Scheff's claim, showing instead that "a substantial majority of the persons who are hospitalized have a serious psychiatric disturbance quite apart from any secondary deviance" produced by labeling experiences (1970: 882). Over the course of numerous exchanges with Gove (1975a; 1975b; 1976; 1979) and other critics (Chauncey, 1975; Imershein & Simons, 1976; Horwitz, 1979), Scheff has attempted to clarify his position by stating that *both* rule-breaking behavior (i.e., psychiatric symptoms) and labeling variables (e.g., the power or status of the actor) should be analyzed as contingencies of audience reactions, with the *relative importance* of these two sets of factors being "the central issue in labeling theory" (1975; also see 1974; 1976; 1979). Thus, it would appear that Scheff has joined his critics in calling for multivariate analysis of various causes and consequences of reactions to mental disorder (for example, see Link, 1982). This deterministic strategy represents a distinct movement away from the more interpretive style of labeling research illustrated by the Rosenhan article.

A similar methodological trend is apparent in recent investigations of audience reactions to criminal behavior at various points in the legal control system. A good example here is a study by Smith and Visher (1981) that examines the same phenomenon as did Lundman (1974)—police arrest practices. Whereas Lundman's observational data were restricted to cases of public drunkenness—a minor misdemeanor—Smith and Visher's data covered a wide array of police-citizen contacts, in which suspected offenses ranged from serious felonies to routine misdemeanors. Consequently, they included a two-category variable of *offense seriousness* (felony versus misdemeanor) among a number of other predictors in a multivariate analysis of arrest decisions observed in three urban areas. Like Lundman, Smith and Visher found that several nonlegal variables, such as the suspect's race or demeanor toward the officer (antagonistic versus civil), influenced arrest decisions. In addition, offense seriousness emerged as one of the strongest predictors of police reactions. All other factors being equal, felony suspects were much more likely to be arrested than misdemeanor suspects. Similar investigations of decision making at other points in the legal control system (e.g., sentencing) have revealed that offense seriousness plays a major, and sometimes predominant, part in legal reactions (Bernstein et al., 1977a; 1977b; Cohen & Kluegel, 1978; Hagan et al., 1979; 1980; LaFree, 1981; Myers, 1979).

Does this recent evidence for the heavy impact of rule-breaking behavior on legal and psychiatric outcomes refute labeling theory? While many critics answer "Yes!" (see the essays in Gove, 1980), sociologists viewing this issue from the relativistic perspective would hardly agree. First, some labeling theorists, especially Lemert (1951; 1972), have always included objective aspects of the actor's behavior among the contingencies to be considered in research on audience reactions to deviance. More generally, labeling theory is fundamentally concerned with the *interactional processes* through which acts or actors are interpreted, defined, and reacted to as deviant (Kitsuse, 1962) rather than with the *outcomes* or products of social control. As Lemert (1981: 298) had recently argued, process has been "ignored or paid lip service" in multivariate analyses that provide only a static, cross-sectional view of particular stages or consequences of control, such as arrest or hospitalization (also see Petrunik, 1980; Short and Meier, 1981). Efforts to illuminate the *processual* nature of interpersonal reactions in institutions (Rosenhan, 1973), on the street (Sykes and Clark, 1975) or in experimental laboratories (Neff & Orcutt, 1978) are still in an early stage of development. If interest in labeling theory has declined in recent years, this is probably due less to an abundance of negative evidence than to a shift of attention to macro-level questions raised by the tradition examined in the next chapter, conflict theory.

10

The macro-relativistic approach: Interest group and neo-Marxist conflict theory

This book began by pointing out that the sociological field of deviance is currently beset by a number of important theoretical, methodological, and ideological controversies. Here, in the last of the chapters reviewing theoretical approaches to deviance, we will examine a tradition that has played a major part in most of these contemporary controversies—conflict theory. The fact that many conflict theorists identify themselves as "radical deviance theorists" or as "critical criminologists" is testimony to the self-conscious concern with sociological and political criticism that infuses much of the work within this macro-relativistic approach. However, as with the labeling tradition, we will find considerable diversity in the ideas and analytical goals of the various sociologists who have contributed to the development of modern conflict theories of deviance.

To help you understand some important differences between the theories falling within this macro-relativistic tradition, it will be useful to distinguish between *neo-Marxist* and *interest group* versions of conflict theory (see Akers, 1977: 13–20; Taylor, Walton, & Young, 1973: 237–267). Theories in the former category, which are based on the ideas of Karl Marx, have been primarily responsible for the recent critical thrust of the conflict tradition. Although Marx, himself, did not develop a systematic theory of deviance or crime, the neo-Marxists have attempted to extend his view that the legal and political systems of capitalist societies are products of an underlying, historical process of conflict between opposing economic classes. Therefore, neo-Marxist theories focus particular attention on the economic structure of society and on the relationship of societal definitions of deviance to the process of class conflict.

Theories of interest group conflict, on the other hand, tend to be based on the pluralistic assumption that all modern societies contain a number of groups with conflicting or competing interests and values. Working with a broader conception of the political process than the neo-Marxists, interest group theorists contend that changes in the law or in systems of social control may be generated by conflicts between various cultural, religious, or ethnic groups as well as by conflict between groups with divergent economic interests. In general, interest group theorists fit more in the mold of conventional scientific investigators and manifest less concern with social criticism and political activism than do the neo-Marxists. Nonetheless, all conflict theorists share a sociological interest in the large-scale, political processes through which societal definitions of deviance are created and maintained.

First, we will look briefly at early work on conflict that preceded and facilitated the emergence of relativistic versions of conflict theory in the 1960s. In addition to Marx, a number of other early European and American theorists have had an impact on the contemporary conflict tradition. Second, we will discuss interest group versions of conflict theory, focusing particularly on the work of Joseph Gusfield (1963; 1967) as a prime example of a non-Marxist analysis of historical changes in the law produced by conflict processes. Finally, we will turn to several recent theoretical contributions that have been instrumental in shifting the conflict approach in a more critical, neo-Marxist direction.

INTELLECTUAL FOUNDATIONS OF THE CONFLICT TRADITION

Marx and class conflict

Even though most of Karl Marx's major works were written prior to the American Civil War, his ideas continue to have a profound impact on contemporary social and political thought. Within sociology, Marx's work has traditionally had a far greater influence on European sociologists than on their counterparts in the United States. One reason for this, of course, has been ideological hostility in the United States toward the political implications of Marx's writings. In addition, Marx's sweeping, macro-level focus on the structure of capitalist society was inconsistent with the theoretical emphases on normative consensus and on social psychological phenomena that dominated American sociology in earlier years. Like Durkheim, Marx possessed the sociological vision referred to in Chapter 4—the ability to grasp the broad societal and historical forces that transcend individual members of society. But, in contrast to Durkheim, Marx's view of society emphasized *conflict* rather than *consensus* as the fundamental social fact. Therefore, it would appear that the recent popularity of Marxist thought in the field of deviance and elsewhere is yet another indication of important changes in the theoretical and political climate of American sociology during the relativistic period.

Marx wrote extensively, but relatively clear and concise statements of his sociological position can be found in two works he coauthored with Friedrich Engels in the 1840s, the *Manifesto of the Communist Party* (1955) and *The German Ideology* (1947; also see 1969–1970). In this brief review, we will focus selectively on those aspects of Marx's analytical framework that have figured most heavily into recent neo-Marxist theories of deviance.

The single most important element in Marx's sociological theorizing is the concept of *class*. Whereas contemporary sociologists sometimes use the term *social class* loosely to refer to the relative ranking of individuals on such dimensions as education or income, class for Marx referred to basic structural components of society as a whole. The class structure of a particular society is determined by the system of economic production that exists in that society at a given point in history. That is, the division of different segments of the population into classes ultimately depends on their respective relationships of *ownership* versus *nonownership* of the existing means of production. In the case of capitalist economies, the means of production are the factories, machines, and financial resources used in the manufacture of material goods to be sold for profit. As capitalist society develops historically, Marx argued that it "is more and more splitting up into two great hostile camps, into two great classes directly facing each other—bourgeoisie and proletariat" (Marx & Engels, 1955: 10). The *bourgeoisie* or *capitalist class* are the owners of the manufacturing system who reap the profits from the sale of material goods. The *proletariat* or *working class* are nonowners of capital who are forced to exchange their labor for wages paid by capitalist employers.

Class conflict originates from the opposing interests of these two major classes. On the one hand, it is in the interest of the capitalist class to expand its control over the economic apparatus of society, to maximize profits, and, therefore, to keep the wages of laborers as low as possible. On the other hand, the working class, denied ownership and control of the products of its own labor, becomes alienated from the entire productive process. As the dominant, bourgeois class pursues its interests and strengthens its monopolistic control over the economic order, it becomes increasingly in the interest of the working class to overthrow the capitalist system that holds it captive and exploits its labor.

However, before the proletariat can exercise its historical role in the abolition of the capitalist system, workers must develop a *class consciousness* or collective awareness of their objective interests as a revolutionary class. Not only is the working class internally divided by competition for the meager wages paid by capitalist employers but workers are also subject to the false consciousness of bourgeois ideology. Based on its control of the economic foundation of social life, the bourgeoisie also dominates the cultural and political superstructure of capitalist society. Marx held that the "ideas of the ruling class are in every epoch the ruling ideas" (1947: 39). Thus, all segments of society, including workers, fall under the cultural influence of an ideology that justifies and supports the interests of the capitalist class. Furthermore, the political superstructure of capitalist society—the state—"is nothing more than the form of organization which the bourgeois necessarily adopt . . . for the mutual guarantee of their property and interests" (1947: 59). The laws and armies of the capitalist state are political tools that protect the interests of the ruling class and suppress the efforts of workers to rise up against it.

Marx argued that the historical process of class conflict would be advanced by critical theorists, such as himself, who identified with the proletariat and who attempted to make workers conscious of their true class interests. By exposing the economic underpinnings of bourgeois ideology and by bringing the working class to a realization of who its real enemy was, Marx worked to hasten the inevitable fall of the capitalist system through a revolution by the working class. Only then, after ownership of private property was abolished, could a communist society emerge—a society free of classes and, therefore, free of oppression and conflict.

Throughout all of his writings, Marx had little to say specifically about deviance (Taylor, Walton, & Young, 1973: 209–221). He commented on the criminal tendencies of the *lumpenproletariat*—the social scum at the very bottom of capitalist society beneath the organized working class. He also made ironic reference to the functions of crime, pointing out that such occupational groups as the police, judges, and professors of criminal law would not exist were it not for criminals. Far more significant for the conflict tradition are the powerful analytical tools and the macro-level frame of reference that Marx developed in his general critique of capitalist society. Even though Western capitalism has developed in some directions not anticipated by Marx, contemporary neo-Marxist theories have found his conceptions of class, structural conflict, and ideology to be readily applicable to analyses of the definition and control of deviance by the advanced capitalist state (see Quinney, 1977).

Above all, Marx stands out in the history of sociology as the foremost advocate and example of how the critical social analyst can actively influence the course of human events. Like many contemporary neo-Marxists, Marx would have evaluated the success of his theorizing not according to its ability to explain social phenomena—the criterion of bourgeois science—but according to the practical criterion of its actual impact on historical developments. By Marx's own standards, then, his theoretical work must indeed be judged a success.

Other sources of the conflict tradition

While Marx's ideas have recently been raised to a central position within the conflict tradition, the emergence of this general approach to deviance was stimulated as much or more by other early perspectives on social conflict. Another early German theorist, Georg Simmel, also viewed conflict as a ubiquitous feature of social life (1955; also see Coser, 1956; Wolff, 1950). As opposed to Marx's singular focus on class conflict as a structural characteristic of capitalist society as a whole, Simmel analyzed conflict as a general form of social relationship that is manifested in a variety of group or societal contexts. Simmel contributed some keen insights into how the conflicts and hostilities that inevitably arise between various groups in organized societies can have such positive functions as strengthening group boundaries and uniting group members together in a common cause.

Simmel's work on group conflict had an immediate impact on American sociologists during the social pathology period and, more importantly, during the social disorganization period. Conflict and competition were among the four basic social processes specified in an influential textbook by Park and Burgess (1921), leading theorists of the Chicago School who were greatly indebted to Simmel. As we noted in Chapter 2, the concept of conflict became especially prominent in analyses of crime and delinquency by Chicago sociologists during the 1930s. For example, high rates of crime among immigrant populations in urban areas were thought to be caused by cultural conflict between the legal rules of American society and the traditional conduct norms of the immigrants' native cultures (Sellin, 1938). Well into the normative period, Vold's (1958) attempt to explain criminal behavior as an outcome of various forms of group conflict continued to draw explicitly from the early perspectives of Simmel and the Chicago sociologists.

During the same time that group or cultural conflicts were being studied as causes of deviant behavior in complex urban societies, a few American theorists began to suggest that social definitions of crime and social problems could also be understood as products of conflict processes. One of the clearest statements of this relativistic idea was presented in 1929 by Sutherland in a paper titled "Crime and the Conflict Process" (1956c). As the following passages from this paper indicate, Sutherland anticipated many of the basic themes of interest group conflict theory (1956c: 99–100, 103):

> In opposition to . . . many scientific explanations (of criminal behavior) it seems to be desirable to attempt to describe crime as part of a process, and that process seems to be essentially a process of conflict. . . . This process seems to go on somewhat as follows: A certain group of people feel that one of their values—life, property, beauty of landscape, theological doctrine—is endangered by the behavior of others. If the group is politically influential, the value important, and the danger serious, the members of the group secure the enactment of a law and thus win the co-operation of the State in the effort to protect their value. The law is a device of one party in conflict with another party.

In contrast to Marx's singular focus on economic factors in class conflict, Sutherland argued that "all kinds of interests and . . . conflicting ideals" exist as points of possible opposition between groups in modern, heterogenous societies (1956c: 107).

An approach similar to Sutherland's was developed by other sociologists who treated the public definition of social problems as a process of value conflict (Waller, 1936; Fuller & Myers, 1941a; 1941b; also see Spector & Kitsuse, 1977). These theorists pointed out that objective conditions or behaviors that some groups define as social problems—such as abortion, for example—are often accepted and encouraged by the values of other groups. Even when groups agree that a certain condition is a problem, value conflicts may lead to disagreement over the appropriate solution to the problem. Therefore, the particular ways that communities define and react to social problems depend on the relative ability of various interest groups to translate their respective values into public policy.

Developing more or less independently of Marxist theory, this early work on conflict in American sociology devoted relatively little attention to economic issues and class divisions. Much greater stress was placed on cultural interests—the distinctive norms, values, and lifestyles of various groups in a complex, pluralistic society—as primary sources of conflict, deviant behavior, and political action. Throughout the 1940s and early 1950s, little additional progress was made beyond this early work, as American sociology turned away from the concept of conflict and became dominated by consensus models of society. However, by the late 1950s, several important theoretical works in general sociology (Coser, 1956; Dahrendorf, 1959) and in the field of deviance (Vold, 1958; Miller, 1958) signaled a renewed interest in conflict theory, an interest which mushroomed during the relativistic period.

Given the early importance of the Chicago School in American work on conflict, it is not surprising that the initial macro-level analysis of deviance and conflict during the relativistic period was presented by a sociologist trained at the University of Chicago, Joseph Gusfield (1963). Gusfield's work has provided new insights into the old idea of cultural conflict and has become a classic example of the non-Marxist, interest group conflict approach to deviance.

INTEREST GROUP CONFLICT THEORIES

Gusfield and status politics

In American society, no body of law is so exalted and so final as is the Constitution of the United States. In January 1919, the following statement was formally added to this body of law as part of the 18th Amendment:

> After one year from the ratification of this article the manufacture, sale or transportation of intoxicating liquors within, the importation thereof into, or the exportation thereof from the United States and all territory subject to the jurisdiction thereof for beverage purposes is hereby prohibited.

In short, the distribution and sale of alcoholic beverages was *constitutionally defined as deviant*. The Prohibition Amendment, focusing as it does on the rather mundane question of alcohol use, today seems curiously out of place in a legal document concerned with such fundamental issues as human rights and the basic structure of American government. How and why was this remarkable definition of deviance created?

Gusfield attempts to answer this question in *Symbolic Crusade* (1963), a relativistic analysis of the Temperance or Prohibition movement that climaxed with the passage of the 18th Amendment. According to Gusfield, the driving force behind the Temperance movement was cultural conflict between rural, Protestant, native Americans, and a newer population in the United States around the turn of the century—urban, Catholic immigrants from Europe. The parties to this conflict were not sharply divided by class distinctions, i.e., by the ownership and nonownership of property. Far from being an economic elite, the native Americans who supported the Temperance movement were members of the old middle class whose economic position was not too far above that of the immigrant groups they opposed. Neither were class interests or economic issues at the center of the political struggle over Prohibition. Rather, Gusfield interprets the Temperance movement as an effort of native Americans to preserve their status interests—their position as a highly prestigious and respected cultural group in American society—against the growing threat of alien cultures introduced by a vast wave of European immigrants.

Gusfield develops a theory of status politics as a framework for understanding these aspects of the Temperance movement and other "symbolic crusades" aimed at the moral reform of public policy (1963: 12–35, 166–188). Gusfield points out that complex societies, in addition to being divided into various classes in an economic order, are also stratified according to a *status order*, in which the values, norms, and lifestyles of some groups have greater prestige than those of other groups. Prestige is symbolically conferred upon a given group when its moral viewpoint is reflected in the policies and actions of government, schools, and other societal institutions. The law is a particularly useful instrument for maintaining status dominance. A group whose cultural norms and values are backed by the authority of the law can command the respect or, at least, the obedience of other groups. Thus, moral issues, such as Prohibition, civil liberties, or abortion, are the arena of status politics, where conflicting cultural groups struggle for public recognition and legal endorsement of their respective ways of life. The ultimate goal of status politics is clear: "Victory in issues of status is the symbolic conferral of respect upon the norms of the victor and disrespect upon the norms of the vanquished" (1963: 174).

Gusfield applies this theoretical framework in a historical analysis of the development of the Temperance movement based on documents and records of various Temperance organizations. He found that reformers in the early and middle 1800s viewed drinkers as repentant deviants who could be encouraged to change their errant ways through moral persuasion. Although drunkenness was an offense against the value placed on sobriety and hard work by rural, middle-class Americans, neither drinkers nor their behavior posed a significant threat to the dominance of that group in the status order of small-town American society.

However, this situation changed markedly toward the end of the 19th century. A massive influx of European immigrants swelled the populations of major cities in the United States. This rapid urbanization of American society "threatened the social position of those (native groups) who strongly identified their social status with dominance in the small-town image of the community" (1963: 80). Furthermore, the adherence of most immigrants to the Catholic religion was a direct affront to the traditional dominance and prestige of Protestantism in American life. Superimposed upon one another, these dramatic social changes represented a substantial threat to the old status order of American society.

According to Gusfield, the political issue of Prohibition became symbolic of the struggle between immigrant and native groups for cultural dominance in the early 20th century. Drinking was an accepted part of everyday life for many immigrants. Therefore, through the creation of laws that prohibited this practice, native Americans could publicly reassert their moral superiority over the immigrants. During this period, Temperance organizations that represented middle-class status interests defined drinkers as enemy deviants who must be coerced rather than persuaded to stop the use of alcohol. Consistent with Gusfield's thesis, rural sections of the country—the stronghold of the native, middle-class culture—led the way with local and state laws banning the sale of alcohol. Not only did Temperance forces have a solid power base in rural areas but they were also far better organized for their war against demon rum than were the opponents of Prohibition. The regional strength and organizational superiority of the Temperance movement were decisive factors in its eventual success on a national level. As viewed from the context of Gusfield's theory of status politics, the Prohibition Amendment "was the high point of the struggle to assert the public dominance of old middle-class values. It established the victory of Protestant over Catholic, rural over urban, tradition over modernity" (1963: 7).

In focusing on conflicting status interests of different cultural groups as a central element in the Temperance movement, Gusfield does not deny the possible relevance of class conflict and economic issues for understanding other historical changes in the definition of deviance. In fact, he argues that the repeal of the Prohibition Amendment during the Depression of the 1930s was precipitated by the economic demand "for increased employment and tax revenues which a reopened beer and liquor industry would bring" (1963: 127). However, Gusfield contends that in American society, where class lines are not so sharply drawn as in many European societies, status interests are an especially important source of political conflicts. According to Gusfield (1963: 166–188; also see 1967), a purely Marxist approach fails to appreciate the significance of cultural prestige and other symbolic goals in the efforts of some groups to impose their moral definitions of deviance on other segments of American society.

Later work on interest group conflict

For a brief period following the publication of *Symbolic Crusade* (1963), a number of other sociologists shared Gusfield's concern with interest group conflict and status politics. In a historical analysis of vagrancy laws in England and the United States, Chambliss (1964) attempted to show that statutes requiring vagrants to work or defining them as criminal were created to protect the status interests of wealthy landowners and merchants. Platt's book, *The Child Savers* (1969), argued that the invention of the deviant label juvenile delinquent and the associated movement to establish juvenile courts in the United States around the turn of the century "may be understood as a crusade which served symbolic and ceremonial functions for native, middle-class Americans" (1969: 98). Although both Chambliss (1973) and Platt (1975) later became leading spokesmen for the neo-Marxist approach, their early historical analyses of societal definitions of deviance were more closely linked to a broader, interest group conception of status politics.

However, the most notable example of a deviance theorist whose work evolved from an interest group approach in the 1960s to a critical, neo-Marxist approach in the 1970s is Richard Quinney. Quinney based his earliest theoretical overview of the political definition of crime on the following pluralistic conception of interest group activity (1964: 20):

> Basic to the shaping of public policy is the activity of *political groups*. Cultural diversity and social differentiation create diverse groups with special interests. Some of these groups become organized to such an extent that they are in a position to influence public policy. Interest groups exert their influence at any level and branch of government in order to have their values represented in policy decisions. The ability of any interest group to influence public policy, in turn, is dependent upon the group's position in the political power structure.

Going on to apply this framework specifically to legal policy, Quinney pointed out that "*any* interest group with the ability to get in a strategic position can determine" both the *content* and *enforcement* of criminal law (1964: 20, emphasis added). Thus, the activities of less powerful groups that threaten the values and interests of politically dominant groups will tend to be defined and reacted to as criminal.

In 1970, Quinney offered a more formal statement of interest group conflict theory in his influential textbook, *The Social Reality of Crime*. There he characterized the criminal law as a set of "definitions (which) describe behaviors that conflict with the interests of the segments of society that have the power to shape public policy" (1970: 16). In addition to restating his earlier position regarding the political determination of the content and enforcement of the law, Quinney went on to imply that the public's *subjective* conceptions of crime and criminals are shaped by powerful interest groups that control the mass media.

Although *The Social Reality of Crime* (1970) was instrumental in popularizing the macro-relativistic approach, in general, and interest group conflict theory, in particular, Quinney soon abandoned his pluralistic conception of interest group politics in favor of a more radical, Marxist orientation. Only a few years later, Quinney critically observed that his and other versions of interest group conflict theory "could account for merely the surface phenomena of social and political life, ignoring the dynamic forces that make conflict possible" (1973: 591). As we saw in Chapter 1, Quinney's 1975 revision of his theory of the social reality of crime substituted the Marxist concept of dominant class for his earlier concept of powerful segments of society.

Despite the defections of Quinney and other neo-Marxist theorists, interest group conflict theory continues to have a number of contemporary advocates. For instance, a recent textbook by McCaghy, *Devi-*

ant Behavior: Crime, Conflict, and Interest Groups (1976), adopts essentially the same theoretical position that was taken by Quinney in the early 1960s. Central to the general framework of McCaghy's book are the propositions that American "society contains many diverse groups whose interests are antagonistic to one another" and that "the application of law is a method by which more powerful interest groups can exert control over the less powerful" (1976: 102).

In a more recent theoretical work, Spector and Kitsuse (1977) attempt to combine elements of labeling theory with elements of the old value-conflict approach to social problems into a general macro-relativistic theory of group "claims-making activities." The concept of claims making refers to the process by which certain groups publically claim or allege that some condition or form of behavior should be defined and treated as a social problem. Spector and Kitsuse (1977: 85–96) make a valuable distinction between two types of claims-making groups. On the one hand, they restrict the term *interest group* to those groups that claim to be the *victims* of the conditions defined as problems. Such groups claim to have a direct stake—i.e., something to gain or lose—in the alleged social problem. On the other hand, a *value-oriented group* refers to humanitarian reformers or moral crusaders who "set out to improve the lot of disadvantaged others " (1977: 87). With no direct stake or material interest in the alleged problem, value-oriented groups appear to base their claims on moral ideals and on value judgments about the undesirability of certain conditions or patterns of behavior.

However, the deviance theorist who has persisted longest in an effort to develop a non-Marxist framework for the analysis of conflict processes is Austin Turk. In contrast to most interest group theorists, Turk has focused primarily on variations in official crime rates as a relativistic phenomenon rather than on historical changes in the law. In an early paper, Turk (1964a) criticized the tendency of normative theorists to assume that high rates of official crime in the lower class and in minority groups were a direct reflection of a high incidence of actual law-violating behavior in those relatively powerless segments of the population. Instead, he emphasized the need for theories which explored "the possibility that the more powerful can use the legal process to ascribe the status of criminal to members of the less powerful categories of a population *irrespective of actual behavior*" (1964a: 458). Turk identified this theoretical issue as the problem of "illegitimation" (1964b) or, later, "criminalization" (1966; 1969)—i.e., the relative probability that members of various groups in a society will be legally defined as criminal.

Although Turk's theory of criminalization has gone through several revisions (1964b; 1966; 1969), the concepts of *power* and *conflict* have always played a central part in his general framework. The phenomenon of criminalization takes place within a power structure, where authorities exercise varying degrees of political control over subjects. Both the cultures and the behavior patterns of groups occupying different positions in the power structure of a society—as, for example, whites versus blacks in America—often differ to the extent that they conflict. Since authorities dominate the legal system, they are able to use the law to their advantage in conflict situations. Thus, the greater the power of authorities and the greater the significance of the conflict for their cultural and behavioral norms, the greater the likelihood that members of the opposing group of subjects will be defined and punished as criminals.

Particularly in his most extended treatment of his theory, *Criminality and Legal Order* (1969), Turk discusses a number of other factors that affect the nature of authority-subject conflicts and the probability of criminalization. More recently, he has gone on to consider other facets of his general view of law as a weapon or source of power in social conflicts (1976a; 1976b). Although Turk stands out as the most complex and unique theorist within the conflict tradition, his work is clearly more consistent with interest group theory than with neo-Marxist theory. Turk does not restrict his concept of authority-subject relationships to the narrower Marxist notion of class relationships (1969). Nor does he assign any special theoretical priority to economic power as opposed to power based on the control of other resources such as knowledge or physical violence (1976a). Rather, Turk views conflict and struggles for power as ubiquitous features of all "interactions and relations between people and others not of their own kind" (1976b: 285). However, it is Turk's continuing advocacy of a scientific, value-free orientation to conflict theory that most sharply distinguishes his work from that of the neo-Marxists. Throughout the 1960s, Turk argued that theoretical analyses of deviance and conflict should be phrased "in the neutral, testable language of science instead of the partisan, value-oriented language of involvement" (1969: 58). As Turk has more recently pointed out (1976b), this position puts both his version of conflict theory and the work of other interest group theorists at odds with the radical, value-engaged theorizing of contemporary neo-Marxists.

NEO-MARXIST CONFLICT THEORIES

With the exception of Durkheim's early contributions to the anomie and control traditions, all of the theoretical approaches to deviance we have reviewed thus far have developed within the confines of American sociology. However, neo-Marxist theory represents a significant departure from this long-standing pattern. The recent development of radical versions of conflict theory has been an international enterprise, shared by American and European sociologists alike. Therefore, it is particularly appropriate to begin this section with a discussion of the work of three British sociologists who have played a major part in this contemporary theoretical movement—Ian Taylor, Paul Walton, and Jock Young.

Taylor, Walton, and Young: The new criminology

Not since Durkheim's *Suicide* has a book on deviance by European sociologists been so widely read in the United States as has Taylor, Walton, and Young's *The New Criminology: For a Social Theory of Deviance* (1973). Despite its title, this work devotes far less attention to the formulation of a new theory of deviance than it does to trenchant criticism of old sociological theories of crime and deviance. But, for Taylor, Walton, and Young (as well as for most other neo-Marxists), critical analysis of the philosophical, methodological, and ideological limitations of existing theories is a necessary and integral part of the process of advancing deviance theory beyond those limitations. Even though no single existing theory provides an adequate understanding of crime and social control in contemporary society, critical analysis of earlier approaches can, at least, reveal the "formal requirements of a fully social theory of deviance" which will serve as a blueprint for the construction of a new criminology (1973: 268–282).

Taylor, Walton, and Young's critique essentially takes the form of a *dialectical analysis.* Using this distinctively Marxist method of analysis, they focus on a number of contradictory themes (i.e., the thesis and the antithesis) that have emerged in the course of the historical development of deviance theory. For instance, the contradictory ideas of *freedom* versus *constraint* appeared early in the history of social thought on deviance as a dominant theme in the philosophical conflict between the classical and positivist schools of criminology in 19th century Europe (Taylor, Walton, & Young, 1973: 1–66). Whereas classical criminologists such as Beccaria and Bentham viewed criminal acts as freely willed, deliberate choices made by rational individuals, positivist criminologists such as Lombroso contended that criminal behavior was determined or constrained by various biological and psychological causes.

A second dialectical theme—*individualism* versus *structuralism*—emerged in Durkheim's work and represented a major step toward a fully social theory of deviance. Durkheim attempted to avoid the clash between the classical and positivist conceptions of individual action by moving above it to a macro-level, societal perspective on deviance. By conceptualizing rates of crime and suicide as distinctively social phenomena produced by structural conditions external to individuals, "Durkheim urged a confrontation between sociologists, concerned with social facts, and those who would engage in individualistic" explanations of deviant behavior (Taylor, Walton, & Young, 1973: 67).

Finally, Taylor, Walton, and Young view the recent emergence of the theme of *consensus* versus *diversity* in the work of the labeling theorists as "a remarkable advance towards a fully social theory of deviance" (1973: 139). Labeling theorists, of course, rejected Merton's assumptions that the norms and values of American society are based on cultural consensus and that deviant behavior can be objectively defined as acts which violate this consensus. Instead, social diversity became the keynote of labeling theory's relativistic position that "what is deviant for one person may not be deviant for another" (1973: 140).

However, sociologists such as Durkheim or the labeling theorists, in rejecting the one-sided theoretical positions of earlier work on deviance, have themselves been guilty of developing only one side of the dialectical themes they introduced. Despite Durkheim's sophisticated understanding of the wider structural origins of deviance, he inadequately conceptualized individual deviance as a meaningless expression of biological impulses and appetites (Taylor, Walton, & Young, 1973: 89). Labeling theory's attack on the assumption of the normative perspective that certain behaviors are consensually and objectively deviant often "lapses into a relativistic idealism, where it is almost as if without labels there would be no deviance" (1973: 145). A fully social theory of deviance, on the other hand, would render as topics for sociological analysis *both sides* of the contradictory themes of freedom versus constraint, individualism versus structuralism, and consensus versus diversity. Furthermore, these contradictory elements "must all appear in the theory, as they do in the real world, in a complex, dialectical relationship to one another" (1973: 277).

Taylor, Walton, and Young admit that considerable work is needed before a theory which encompasses all of these dialectical themes can be formulated. However, in the concluding chapter of *The New Criminology* (1973: 268–282), they discuss a list of formal requirements—a set of analytical objectives or directions—that should guide further work toward a fully social theory of deviance.

Taylor, Walton, and Young emphasize that an adequate theory of deviance must combine the normative and relativistic perspectives in order to account for the social origins of deviant acts as well as audience reactions to those acts. At the broadest, macro level of analysis, such a theory would require both a *political economy of crime* and a *political economy of social reaction*. To meet these requirements, deviance theory must draw heavily from Marx's general analysis of the political and economic structure of advanced capitalism. The structural constraints that contribute to criminal activity can only be understood within "the overall social context of inequalities of power, wealth and authority in the developed industrial society" (1973: 270). Similarly, the political economy of social reaction would "lay bare the structured inequalities in power and interest which underpin the processes whereby the laws are created and enforced" by the capitalist state (1973: 168).

However, a purely macro-level theory cannot do justice to the dialectical relationship between structural constraints and individual responses to those constraints. Therefore, two additional, micro-level requirements for a fully social theory of deviance are a *social psychology of crime* and a *social psychology of social reaction*. The former requirement calls for explanation of "the different ways in which structural demands are interpreted, reacted against, or used by (individuals) in such a way that an essentially deviant choice is made" (1973: 271). The latter requirement emphasizes a parallel need for "an account of the contingencies and the (immediate) conditions which are crucial to the decision to act against the deviant" (1973: 272–273). In short, the actions of both deviants and their audiences must be understood on a social psychological level as conscious, meaningful choices.

The comprehensive analytical framework outlined in these and other formal requirements is not merely aimed at a fuller theoretical understanding of the dialectics of deviance and social control in existing capitalist societies. In addition, the new criminology envisioned by Taylor, Walton, and Young would be ideologically committed to fundamental *changes* in those existing structural arrangements which give some segments of society the power to criminalize others. In making this commitment, Taylor, Walton, and Young view themselves and other neo-Marxists as parties to still another dialectical conflict which is now emerging in the field of deviance, *radicalism* versus *correctionalism* (1973: 278–282; also see, 1975: 6–57). The limitations of previous, correctional theories of deviance can be traced, in part, to their unquestioning ideological acceptance of the prevailing capitalist social order. For instance, the narrow, deterministic focus on causes of deviant behavior within the normative perspective reflects an underlying concern with the reform or correction of those subordinate members of society who trespass against the existing order. Even the labeling theorists and the interest group conflict theorists—with their vague, pluralistic conceptions of social order—failed to expose or question the structural bases of power in capitalist society. Taylor, Walton, and Young argue that any theory that is not inspired by a radical commitment "to the abolition of inequalities of wealth and power . . . is inevitably bound to fall into correctionalism" (1973: 281).

In rejecting correctional theories of deviance and the capitalist system to which they are ideologically committed, radical neo-Marxists work toward a society where the contradictions of capitalism no longer exist—where individual freedom is no longer shackled by the structural constraints of economic inequality and political domination, where it is no longer necessary to maintain a forced consensus by criminalizing actions which are expressions of human diversity. In the following passage from a later collection of essays titled *Critical Criminology* (1975: 24), Taylor, Walton, and Young make it clear that the far-reaching goals of radicalism will require practical action (praxis) as well as critical and theoretical analysis:

> Radical theory cannot rest content with the description of existing social arrangements. . . . It has to develop methodologies for the realization of the societies its own critique would necessitate, for . . . a revolutionary theory . . . will gain acceptance only if the nature of the social relationships embodied in the theory are actualized in the real world.

In short, Taylor, Walton, and Young concur with Marx that social change stands as the ultimate criterion for judging the success of radical theory.

Taylor, Walton, and Young's work is largely responsible for the strong emphasis on critical analysis in contemporary neo-Marxist theorizing. Although, as we shall soon see, they were not the first to use radical criticism as a basis for theoretical development, no other critique has equaled the comprehensiveness of their broad-ranging analysis of deviance theory. Furthermore, *The New Criminology* introduced many American sociologists to the potential utility of the dialectical method as a tool for critical inquiry and as a principle for theory construction in the field of deviance. However, we can more fully grasp the significance of Taylor, Walton, and Young's contribution by placing it in the context of related work which preceded and followed it. Therefore, we will turn now to some earlier radical critiques of deviance theory by American sociologists; then, we will consider some more recent efforts to formulate neo-Marxist theories of the political economy of deviance and social control in capitalist societies.

Radical criticism in the United States

Unlike European scholars such as Taylor, Walton, and Young, radical critics in the United States were initially influenced more by the critical works of an American sociologist, C. Wright Mills, than they were by the writings of Marx. Mills, who died in 1962, was an authority on the Marxist literature (see Mills, 1962). However, his hard-hitting attacks on the bureaucratic mentality of middle-class society (1951), on the political control of the United States by a power elite (1956), and on the lack of intellectual imagination in American sociology (1959) represented a brand of critical scholarship that was uniquely his own. In Chapter 2, we referred to an early paper by Mills on "The Professional Ideology of Social Pathologists" (1942). This classic analysis of how the theoretical conception of urban pathology was ideologically linked to the rural, middle-class world view of early American sociologists became a model for radical critiques of deviance theory published in the late 1960s and early 1970s.

In an apparent effort to distinguish their own political position from the "liberal" viewpoint of Becker and other micro-relativistic theorists, American radicals focused their initial critical attention on labeling theory. The first of several articles on the ideological biases and limitations of the labeling tradition was written by Alvin W. Gouldner (1968), who has been described as "Mills' successor as this country's leading 'radical' sociologist" (Timasheff & Theodorson, 1976: 286). In the spirit of Mills's critique of the social pathologists, Gouldner attempts to lay bare the professional ideology implicit in Becker's value-engaged, underdog viewpoint on deviance. Gouldner sees Becker as representative of the liberal Establishment that dominates American sociology and serves the interests of the American administrative class—a national elite of high-level bureaucratic officials. Labeling theory, in its expression of sympathy with underdog deviants who are victimized by *low level* officials (such as the police and prison wardens) and mismanaged by *local* caretaking institutions (such as jails and mental hospitals), is wholly consistent with the ideology of *high level* officials in *national* welfare bureaucracies. That is, by discrediting local officials as bigoted or incompetent in their treatment of deviants, labeling theory "legitimates the claims of the higher administrative classes in Washington" that deviance can be managed more effectively through the national bureaucracies of the liberal welfare state (Gouldner, 1968: 110). In return for this ideological support, labeling theorists and other liberal sociologists are assured of recognition and, more importantly, research funding from "their friends in high places."

The key point of Gouldner's analysis is that Becker's ideological preoccupation with low-level officials is responsible for a huge blind spot in the critical scope of labeling theory. Neither the master institutions of society, which ultimately produce the suffering of deviants and other underdogs, nor the high-level officialdom controlling these institutions are subjected to critical scrutiny. It is here that Gouldner identifies the crucial difference between the radical and liberal viewpoints on deviance (1968: 111):

> I think that *radical* sociologists differ from liberals in that, while they take the standpoint of the underdog, they apply it to the study of overdogs. Radical sociologists want to study "power elites," the leaders, or masters, of men; liberal sociologists focus their efforts upon underdogs and victims and their immediate bureaucratic caretakers.

Following the lead of Mills and Gouldner, other radical sociologists criticized labeling theory in the early 1970s for its failure to draw attention to the activities of power elites. Alexander Liazos (1972) argued that the exclusive concern of labeling theory with "nuts, sluts and 'preverts' " has led to neglect of two important theoretical problems. First, little attention has been paid to *covert institutional violence*—"the unethical, illegal, and destructive actions of powerful individuals, groups, and institutions . . . carried out quietly in the normal course of events" (1972: 111). Many more human lives are destroyed by poverty, racism, and other conditions caused by the normal "institutional workings of a profit-oriented society and economy" than by the dramatic and predatory acts of violent deviants who typically capture the attention of sociologists (1972: 112). Second, Liazos contends that the labeling literature lacks "an extensive discussion of how power operates in the designation of deviance" (1972: 115). Here, Liazos agrees with Gouldner that sociologists must look beyond the lower and middle levels of power and examine the manipulation of law and social control by elite groups at the top of the power hierarchy in American society.

Liazos' arguments were closely paralleled by Alex Thio's critical analysis of "Class Bias in the Sociology of Deviance" (1973). Thio contends that a power elite is "primarily responsible for creating and shaping the social and cultural structure" of the United States (1973: 2). This powerful class is able to influence societal definitions of deviance through its ideological control of the mass media and educational institutions, its political clout in legislatures, and its dominance of systems of social control. Labeling theory, like earlier approaches to deviance in sociology, reflects this dominant ideological bias in its tendency "to focus on powerless deviants" (1973: 5). Deviance by the powerful—"political skulduggery, wanton militarism or illegal warmaking, and misuse of policymaking power by top governmental leaders"—is neglected and unexplained by the labeling theorists (1973: 9). Thio goes on to argue that such activities by the powerful class are actually encouraged by the widespread belief that only the powerless are really deviant. Seen by themselves and others as respectable citizens, powerful people are induced to engage in various illegal acts that are rarely recognized as deviant.

However, in the same year that Thio published his critique, other American sociologists began to express dissatisfaction with the theoretical potential of the power elite model of society. In an important analysis of "Functional and Conflict Theories of Crime," Chambliss (1973) observed that neither the interest group nor the power elite approaches to conflict theory could provide the general, historical perspective on social order and social control which is offered by a Marxist approach. Other American sociologists were responsive to Taylor, Walton, and Young's (1973) call for dialectical analyses of the political economy of deviance and social control which go beyond mere description of existing power arrangements. For instance, in a book review of *The New Criminology*, Quinney (1973) was inspired to write the following confession on behalf of conflict theorists and radical critics in the United States:

> we found injustice in bureaucratic authority, big and corrupt business, and inequality of life chances. However, without a class-historical analysis, our critique of American society was necessarily inadequate. The conflict process was not understood dialectically. Conflict failed to be viewed in terms of the dynamics and contradictions of concrete historical conditions and processes.

Thus, Quinney and other American conflict theorists joined with Taylor, Walton, and Young's effort to move beyond these theoretical limitations by returning to the classic insights of Marx.

Recent trends in neo-Marxist theory

Whereas Taylor, Walton, and Young (1973) provided only a general sketch of the formal requirements for neo-Marxist theorizing, a number of other theorists have now begun the task of filling in the substance of this developing branch of the conflict tradition (Quinney, 1974; 1975; 1977; Spitzer, 1975; Davis, 1980; Hepburn, 1977; also see the essays in Taylor, Walton, & Young, 1975). The major analytical trends in contemporary neo-Marxist thought are particularly apparent in two works: Quinney's recent book, *Class, State and Crime* (1977), and Spitzer's article, "Toward a Marxist Theory of Deviance" (1975).

First and most important, Quinney and Spitzer base their work on critical, macro-level analyses of the *political economy of advanced capitalist society*. Both theorists contend that existing forms of deviance and social control can only be understood within the larger context of historically specific relations of economic production and class conflict which characterize late capitalism. Two developments in industrial production are particularly prominent in advanced capitalism: (1) increasing technological complexity (e.g., greater use of sophisticated machinery) and (2) increasing monopoly control of industry by a small but powerful capitalist class (see Quinney, 1977: 63–105). However, rather than simply strengthening the position of the capitalist class, these historical developments must be understood dialectically as conditions which also threaten the very survival of the capitalist system. Certain contradictions and crises have become increasingly apparent in advanced capitalism as the gap between the capitalist class and other segments of the class structure has widened.

This brings us to the second major concern of Quinney and Spitzer. One of the crucial contradictions of advanced capitalism is its inherent tendencies toward the *production of problem populations*. According to Spitzer, the definitive characteristic of problem populations "is the fact that their behavior, personal qualities and/or position threaten the *social relations of production* in capitalist societies" (1975: 642, emphasis in original). Capitalist relations of production would be threatened, for example, when the poor steal from the rich, when people refuse or are unable to work, or when radical groups question the ideology which supports the capitalist system. Both Quinney and Spitzer point out that a significant source of such threats is the surplus population of unskilled and unemployed people produced by advanced capitalism. In an economy which increasingly demands highly skilled workers and is subject to severe fluctuations in the market for unskilled labor, millions of people are forced into a marginal, impoverished position at the bottom of the class structure.

Drawing upon Marx and Engels' view of the lumpenproletariat (1969–1970), Quinney argues that the surplus population tends to respond to their oppressed position through "crimes of accommodation" (1977: 52–60). By engaging in predatory crimes (e.g., burglary, robbery, or drug dealing) or personal crimes (e.g., assault, rape, or murder), members of the surplus population create problems for the capitalist system which produced their marginal and brutalizing conditions of existence. Spitzer, on the other hand, implies that much of the surplus population is transformed by the capitalist state into a relatively harmless but costly grouping which he terms "social junk" (1975: 645). Unproductive segments of the surplus population, which represent only a passive threat to capitalist relations of production, are generally controlled and processed by welfare and "therapeutic" agencies. However, the costs of institutions and programs to contain and regulate social junk such as the mentally ill, the aged, or the welfare poor place a heavy financial burden on the capitalist state.

Other problem populations discussed by Quinney and Spitzer

pose more direct, political threats to the capitalist order. Quinney, again following Marx, notes that the expansion of mass production in advanced capitalism has generated growing alienation of the employed working class from its work situation. As a defensive reaction to the exploitation of its labor, the working class engages in "crimes of resistance" such as sabotage of automobiles on assembly lines and other actions directed against employers (1977: 54–55). Reflecting an inherent contradiction of capitalism, crimes of resistance will become more common and politically organized as this alienating system of production expands. In a similar vein, Spitzer argues that the capitalist institution of mass education has produced a problem population of young people who are both alienated and politically active (1975: 644). The state responds to the acute problems posed by student radicals and other political deviants by treating them as "social dynamite." In contrast to social junk, social dynamite is typically processed through the legal system which has the capacity for direct and active intervention (1975: 646).

Quinney and Spitzer's analyses of the contradictions that generate problem populations lead into their third area of interest, *the transformation of state controls*. Since the production of all of these problem populations is dialectically related to the development of the underlying political economy, the threats and costs they represent will inevitably *increase* with the future expansion of capitalist production. Existing forms and systems of social control, which may have been adequate in earlier phases of capitalist development, are already unable to cope with this "growing crisis—the overproduction of deviance" (Spitzer, 1975: 648). Therefore, the means of social control used by the capitalist state are also transformed in an effort to contain this advancing threat.

Quinney believes that the state, in its increasingly important "role in securing the capitalist system," (1977: 85) is now turning to more oppressive forms of social control. As a prime example of this emerging pattern, he presents an extensive critique of the programs and ideology of the contemporary criminal justice movement (1977: 1–29, 107–144). Under the ideological banner of a national war on crime, millions of dollars have been spent to expand and modernize law-enforcement agencies. This federally coordinated movement has for the first time in American history linked together "all levels of the state . . . in a nationwide system of criminal justice" (1977: 112). In Quinney's view, the criminal justice movement has transformed the legal system into a more repressive and "modern means of controlling (the) surplus population produced by late capitalist development" (1977: 131).

However, Spitzer offers a rather different picture of the new forms of state control that are currently emerging in late capitalism (1975: 647–649). He argues that the state will explore less expensive and less oppressive methods of managing problem populations as the costs of older, segregative controls (such as institutionalization in prisons or mental hospitals) skyrocket. He suggests four alternative forms of control that are likely to be favored by the state in the future. The first of these, *normalization,* simply involves a reduction in the processing and institutionalization of deviants. Here, problem populations are essentially swept under the rug. An example of this approach is the contemporary decarceration movement that has led to the direct release of inmates of prisons and mental hospitals back into the community (see Scull, 1977). A second way of cutting state expenses is *conversion,* where potential troublemakers or "rehabilitated" deviants are recruited as lower-level agents of social control (e.g., as counselors, psychiatric aids, or parole officers). A third and broader alternative, *containment,* involves the geographic segregation of problem populations. For instance, various formal or informal measures can be used to restrict deviant groups to certain areas of cities where they "can be ignored or managed passively as long as they remain in their place" (Spitzer, 1975: 649). Finally, *support of criminal enterprise* can be used as a means of opening up alternative sources of income and services for problem populations that would otherwise be dependent on state resources. Given the freedom to operate by the state, organized crime "provides goods and services which ease the hardships and deflect the energies of the underclass" (1975: 649). The central element in all of these approaches, of course, is a reduction of state expenses for the management of expanding problem populations.

The differences between Spitzer's and Quinney's predictions for future transformations in state controls may be due, in part, to a difference in their respective conceptions of the general goals of neo-Marxist theorizing. Spitzer addresses his complex analysis of alternative forms of state control to a conventional goal of scientific theory: to guide "the accumulation of evidence to refine our understanding of the relationships" between deviance, class conflict, and social control (1975: 650). For Quinney, on the other hand, the fundamental goal of neo-Marxist theorizing is ideological in nature: "to develop a political consciousness among all people who are oppressed by the capitalist system" (1977: 104). Accordingly, Quinney's theoretical emphasis on the oppressive growth of the criminal justice movement can be seen as an effort to promote a dialectical movement of political resistance among working-class people. By providing "people with an understanding of their alienation and oppressed condition," neo-Marxist theory can, in Quinney's view, become "a means of expression that is the beginning of socialist revolution" (1977: 164).

Aside from this and other differences in orientation and emphasis, the works of Quinney and Spitzer manifest a common concern with the three analytical problems discussed above—the political economy of advanced capitalist society, the production of problem populations, and the transformation of state controls. All of these analytical trends signal a return to *macro-level* issues in deviance and social control which had been largely overlooked by labeling theory and other social psychological approaches during the 1960s and early 1970s. Furthermore, neo-Marxist theorists have begun to take a renewed interest in the *causation of deviant behavior* (i.e., production of problem populations), a question which was pushed into the background by the heavily relativistic emphasis of labeling theory and interest group conflict theory. In fact, by focusing on the structural origins of both deviant behavior and social definitions of deviance, neo-Marxist theorists are now attempting to develop a comprehensive viewpoint that transcends the boundaries currently separating the normative and relativistic perspectives.

CONCLUSION

Not surprisingly, theoretical work within the conflict tradition, particularly neo-Marxist theorizing, has been the subject of intense controversy. For instance, the appearance of Taylor, Walton, and Young's *The New Criminology* (1973) stimulated an almost unprecedented barrage of critical commentary. Non-Marxists have attacked these authors for subordinating the objective standards of scientific inquiry to their ideological biases (Turk, 1974) and for exhibiting an excessive intolerance for other, less radical approaches to deviance (Jensen, 1974). But, ironically, more orthodox Marxists have accused Taylor, Walton, and Young of distorting Marx's views of crime and of basing their work on moralism rather than on Marxism (Hirst, 1975; Mugford, 1974; Bankowski, Mungham, & Young, 1977).

It should be obvious from these examples that much, if not most recent criticism in the sociology of deviance focuses on political and ideological issues, a development for which the conflict tradition is largely responsible. This critical emphasis has clearly had some positive effects on a field which generally ignored such questions prior to the 1960s. However, as critical analysis has become increasingly important in the field of deviance, the empirical relevance of deviance theories has received relatively less attention than in the past. Perhaps this is because conflict theories are very difficult to evaluate empirically. Some of these theories are so vague and so deficient in specific empirical implications that it is unclear what kinds of evidence would be required for their assessment. This is particularly the case with some earlier theories of interest group conflict.

Although the mechanisms involved in processes of conflict and social control have been more clearly specified in recent neo-Marxist theorizing, major questions remain about the implications of these abstract, macro-level formulations for empirical research on deviance. Micro-level phenomena—so important in Taylor, Walton, and Young's stress on the dialectic of individualism versus structuralism—are virtually ignored, except for some rather simplistic observations by Quinney (e.g., individual predatory crime is caused by the brutalizing effects of capitalism). However, recent neo-Marxist theorizing has also been characterized as untestable in macro-level research as well (Horwitz, 1977). As Horwitz points out, for example, when neo-Marxist theories are used to account for the particular forms of social control that exist in contemporary American society, the resulting explanations tend to be circular or tautological. No matter what form of control is observed, oppressive or not, it is explained as fulfilling the needs of the capitalist system. Since any system of control must, by definition, serve the needs of the ruling capitalist class, there are no empirical conditions which can refute the theory.

Spitzer's response (1977) to the latter criticism reveals some of the basic requirements for empirical research on neo-Marxist theory and within the macro-relativistic approach in general. Spitzer argues that it is inappropriate to examine the implications of his and other Marxist formulations in one society at one point in time. The very strength of neo-Marxist theory is its *historical* focus on how changes in the underlying political economy "call into being specific forms of social control at particular points in their development" (1977: 364). In other words, since the economic and political organization of the entire society is the crucial unit of analysis, historical or cross-national evidence is required to examine the variations in deviance and social control that are produced by changes or variations in societal organization. Therefore, the proposals of some neo-Marxists that, in socialist societies, social control will be in the hands of the working class rather than in the hands of the state (Quinney, 1977: 159) or that various forms of crime would be abolished (Taylor, Walton, & Young, 1975: 20) can be assessed empirically by comparing societies at a socialist state of development with those at a capitalist stage of development (cf. Akers, 1977: 14–16; Beirne, 1979; 1980; Jacobs, 1980).

The kinds of historical and cross-national data that are necessary for evaluating neo-Marxist or interest group versions of conflict theory are generally lacking in the research literature on deviance (but see Newman, 1976). It is significant that one particular interest group conflict theory, Gusfield's theory of status politics (1963), has become widely accepted largely because it was supported by a thorough historical investigation of the American Temperance movement. In Chapter 11 we will turn to several other historical studies that illustrate both the potential and the problems of research in the emerging conflict tradition.

Research on societal definitions and reactions to deviance

11

The three research illustrations presented in this chapter are distinguished by their use of historical evidence to gain insight into societal definitions and reactions to deviance. The historical focus of these studies places them in a venerable research tradition that stretches back to classic works of the founders of sociology. Marx, Weber, and Durkheim—who are typically labeled as "theorists" by contemporary sociologists—were all accomplished historical researchers. Historical forces were integral, of course, to Marx's dialectical vision of social change. Throughout his writings, he made abundant use of historical materials to document the class struggles and internal contradictions emerging at various stages in the development of feudal and capitalist societies (see Marx & Engels, 1969–1970). Weber's brilliant case study of *The Protestant Ethic and the Spirit of Capitalism* (1958) is counted as a classic by historians and sociologists alike. *The Protestant Ethic* was just a brief segment of a tremendous body of historical research that Weber conducted on religion and society (see Bendix, 1960). More closely related to the main theme of this chapter, Durkheim (1933) examined ancient laws as "social facts" reflecting the underlying development of the division of labor in society. Although he was unsuccessful in his attempt to show that the law becomes less repressive as societal complexity increases, his evolutionary approach to social control continues to interest macro-relativistic researchers (see Jones, 1981).

The methodological precedent set by Marx, Weber, and Durkheim had its most enduring impact on European sociology. In comparison, American sociologists have not shown a great deal of respect for the historical orientation of their founding fathers. Particularly during the 1940s and 1950s, Marxist perspectives encountered considerable ideological resistance on this side of the Atlantic. Historical methods, in general, were frequently dismissed as "soft" or nonscientific by quantitative researchers. The field of deviant behavior, like many other branches of American sociology during the normative period, devoted more attention to short-term, social psychological phenomena than to the broad historical themes and processes that intrigued European scholars.

However, the ideas and historical methods of Marx and company found new life in the 1960s. A major contribution that we reviewed in the last chapter—Gusfield's (1963) historical analysis of the Temperance movement as a case of status politics—owed a considerable intellectual debt to the work of Max Weber. The first research illustration in this chapter, "A Sociological Analysis of the Law of Vagrancy" by William Chambliss (1964), also applies Weber's concept of status groups in a case study of legal change. In addition to researchers in the conflict tradition like Gusfield and Chambliss, a few labeling researchers helped to bring a renewed respect for history to the study of societal reactions to deviance. The work of Durkheim figured prominently in Kai Erikson's (1966) functionalist interpretation of community reactions to witchcraft and other heresies in colonial New England. Another mainstream labeling theorist, Howard Becker, presented a more controversial analysis of historical materials in his book, *Outsiders* (1963). Becker departed from the classical socio-historical views of Marx, Weber, and Durkheim by arguing, it seemed, that major changes in the law could be brought about by activities of *individual* reformers or moral entrepreneurs. By portraying the passage of the Marijuana Tax Act as the personal crusade of one man, Becker's historical work drew attention away from broader structural or cultural bases of legal change (see Taylor, Walton, & Young, 1973: 166–171).

The two concluding research illustrations attempt, in part, to refute Becker's conclusion. Patricia Morgan (1978) turns to some of the first antidrug laws in the United States—early California legislation against opium—to determine if either Becker's or Gusfield's conception of societal definition processes can provide an adequate account of still another case of legal change. In a sense, Morgan attempts to test the Becker and Gusfield frameworks in a different set of historical data. Galliher and Walker (1977), on the other hand, return to events in the 1930s that Becker had originally analyzed to see if the historical "facts" in the case of national marijuana prohibition are actually consistent with the interpretations that Becker and other researchers have imposed upon them. Galliher and Walker's paper not only offers a look at some of the sources of data that are available to historical researchers but also some of the limitations and problems of scientific inference inherent in this research method. It is as true for Becker as it was for Durkheim that history often did not happen exactly the way the historical investigator thinks it should have happened!

INTRODUCTORY COMMENTS ON CHAMBLISS' RESEARCH

In Chapter 9 you read an illustration of experimental research in which a dramatic event—a blatant act of shoplifting—was created intentionally to provoke a strong punitive response from onlookers. In contrast to social psychologists like Steffensmeier and Terry (1973), of course, macro-level researchers cannot intervene directly in the phenomena they study. Political processes cannot be manipulated; class conflicts cannot be created experimentally. However, for some macro-level questions, it is possible to let history be the experimenter. Looking backward, investigators can see how past societies have responded to the natural stimuli of powerful or unusual historical events. For instance, as we saw in Chapter 4, Durkheim (1951: 241–254) observed that periodic economic crises in 19th-century Europe were followed by sharp increases in suicide rates, a societal response that he attributed to acute effects of anomie. The strategy of the natural experiment is also apparent in the following research illustration by Chambliss (1964), which focuses on some far-reaching societal consequences of another, more terrible kind of crisis that struck Europe in an earlier historical period.

What would happen to a society that lost one third of its population in less than two years? This is the sort of conjecture that one might only expect to hear from science fiction writers or military planners. Nonetheless, such a catastrophic loss of population actually did occur in medieval Europe during the Black Death of the mid-14th century. This and later epidemics of bubonic plague had profound effects on the cultural and structural foundations of feudal society, and undoubtedly contributed to its decline during the late Middle Ages (see Tuchman, 1978; McNeill, 1976). Chambliss (1964) examines one immediate response of feudal England to the social and economic impact of the Black Death in 1349: the creation of the first laws against vagrancy. The original purpose of these laws was, quite literally, to keep the labor force of this agricultural society in its place. As you will see, Chambliss attributes this societal reaction mainly to an *economic* crisis—a severe labor shortage—produced by the plague.

While Chambliss builds a strong case for his economic interpretation of the law of vagrancy, you should be aware that this natural experiment, like other historical analyses, may be based on selective or unreliable views of past events. For instance, most historians now question the mortality rate of 50 percent during the Black Death that Chambliss cites in his article (Shrewsbury, 1970; Bean, 1963; Morris, 1977). In fact, Shrewsbury has estimated that the English death rate during the plague of 1948–49 did not exceed $\frac{1}{20}$ of the population (1970: 123). It appears, then, that the economic stimulus of labor force mortality *may* have been much weaker than Chambliss indicates. The lack of adequate records on vital statistics during the 14th century makes it difficult if not impossible to resolve this issue.

One aspect of the Great Pestilence (as contemporary writers called it) that is not in doubt is the sense of terror and despair that it aroused among the population of England. Today, the bubonic plague is known to have been transmitted from rats to humans by flea bites.

However, during the 14th century, people had no understanding of this invasion that seemed to spread mysteriously and chaotically from village to village, choosing its victims almost at random. One common reaction to the appearance of the symptoms of the pestilence among one's neighbors was to flee out of fear of contagion, leaving behind home, work, and social obligations, at least temporarily (see Shrewsbury, 1970). Therefore, it is possible that *collective panic and flight* among serfs and free laborers, rather than their sheer mortality, was the initial stimulus for laws defining vagrancy as deviant. As you read Chambliss' article, see if he presents any historical evidence that would allow him to rule out this alternative interpretation of the legal changes wrought by the Black Death. Here as elsewhere, think critically about the empirical evidence!

Chambliss' analysis does not stop with the origin of vagrancy laws in the plague years of the 14th century, but it follows the evolution of this societal definition through less troubled times in England and the United States. Sweeping across six centuries, his analysis demonstrates how a historical perspective can reveal slowly emerging patterns and shifts in social control that are imperceptible to a contemporary observer. In this respect, Chambliss' work exemplifies the classic use of historical materials by Marx and Weber to clarify major underlying themes of social change and conflict (Chirot, 1976). By providing a long-range view of legal evolution as well as a dramatic natural experiment on societal reactions to a unique crisis, the following article illustrates well the flexibility and richness of historical data for macro-level research on deviance and social control.

RESEARCH ILLUSTRATION 11–A

A sociological analysis of the law of vagrancy*

William J. Chambliss

With the outstanding exception of Jerome Hall's analysis of theft[1] there has been a severe shortage of sociologically relevant analyses of the relationship between particular laws and the social setting in

---

Source: Article reprinted from *Social Problems* 12 (Summer 1964), pp. 67–77.

* For a more complete listing of most of the statutes dealt with in this report the reader is referred to Burn, *The History of the Poor Laws*. Citations of English statutes should be read as follows: 3 Ed. 1. c. 1. refers to the third act of Edward the first, chapter one, etc.

[1] Hall, J., *Theft, Law and Society*, Bobbs-Merrill, 1939. See also, Alfred R. Lindesmith, "Federal Law and Drug Addiction," *Social Problems* Vol. 7, No. 1, 1959, p. 48.

which these laws emerge, are interpreted, and take form. The paucity of such studies is somewhat surprising in view of widespread agreement that such studies are not only desirable but absolutely essential to the development of a mature sociology of law.[2] A fruitful method of establishing the direction and pattern of this mutual influence is to systematically analyze particular legal categories, to observe the changes which take place in the categories and to explain how these changes are themselves related to and stimulate changes in the society. This paper is an attempt to provide such an analysis of the law of vagrancy in Anglo-American Law.

LEGAL INNOVATION: THE EMERGENCE OF THE LAW OF VAGRANCY IN ENGLAND

There is general agreement among legal scholars that the first full fledged vagrancy statute was passed in England in 1349. As is generally the case with legislative innovations, however, this statute was preceded by earlier laws which established a climate favorable to such change. The most significant forerunner to the 1349 vagrancy statute was in 1274 when it was provided:

> Because that abbies and houses of religion have been overcharged and sore grieved, by the resort of great men and other, so that their goods have not been sufficient for themselves, whereby they have been greatly hindered and impoverished, that they cannot maintain themselves, nor such charity as they have been accustomed to do; it is provided, that none shall come to eat or lodge in any house of religion, or any other's foundation than of his own, at the costs of the house, unless he be required by the governor of the house before his coming hither.[3]

Unlike the vagrancy statutes this statute does not intend to curtail the movement of persons from one place to another, but is solely designed to provide the religious houses with some financial relief from the burden of providing food and shelter to travelers.

The philosophy that the religious houses were to give alms to the poor and to the sick and feeble was, however, to undergo drastic change in the next 50 years. The result of this changed attitude was the establishment of the first vagrancy statute in 1349 which made it a crime to give alms to any who were unemployed while being of

---

[2] See, for example, Rose, A., "Some Suggestions for Research in the Sociology of Law," *Social Problems* Vol. 9, No. 3, 1962, pp. 281–283, and Geis, G., "Sociology, Criminology, and Criminal Law," *Social Problems* Vol. 7, No. 1, 1959, pp. 40–47.

[3] 3 Ed. 1. c. 1.

sound mind and body. To wit:

> Because that many valiant beggars, as long as they may live of begging, do refuse to labor, giving themselves to idleness and vice, and sometimes to theft and other abominations; it is ordained that none, upon pain of imprisonment shall, under the colour of pity or aims, give anything to such which may labour, or presume to favour them towards their desires; so that thereby they may be compelled to labour for their necessary living.[4]

It was further provided by this statute that:

> . . . every man and woman, of what condition he be, free or bond, able in body, and within the age of threescore years, not living in merchandize nor exercising any craft, nor having of his own whereon to live, nor proper land whereon to occupy himself, and not serving any other, if he in convenient service (his estate considered) be required to serve, shall be bounded to serve him which shall him require . . . And if any refuse, he shall on conviction by two true men, . . . be commited to gaol till he find surety to serve.
>
> And if any workman or servant, of what estate or condition he be, retained in any man's service, do depart from the said service without reasonable cause or license, before the term agreed on, he shall have pain of imprisonment.[5]

There was also in this statute the stipulation that the workers should receive a standard wage. In 1351 this statute was strengthened by the stipulation:

> An none shall go out of the town where he dwelled in winter, to serve the summer, if he may serve in the same town.[6]

By 34 Ed 3 (1360) the punishment for these acts became imprisonment for 15 days and if they "do not justify themselves by the end of that time, to be sent to gaol till they do."

A change in official policy so drastic as this did not, of course, occur simply as a matter of whim. The vagrancy statutes emerged as a result of changes in other parts of the social structure. The prime-mover for this legislative innovation was the Black Death which struck England about 1348. Among the many disastrous consequences this had upon the social structure was the fact that it decimated the labor force. It is estimated that by the time the pestilence had run its course at least 50 percent of the population of England had died from the plague. This decimation of the labor force would necessitate rather drastic innovations in any society but its impact

---

[4] 35 Ed. 1. c. 1.
[5] 23 Ed. 3.
[6] 25 Ed. 3 (1351).

was heightened in England where, at this time, the economy was highly dependent upon a ready supply of cheap labor.

Even before the pestilence, however, the availability of an adequate supply of cheap labor was becoming a problem for the landowners. The crusades and various wars had made money necessary to the lords and, as a result, the lord frequently agreed to sell the serfs their freedom in order to obtain the needed funds. The serfs, for their part, were desirous of obtaining their freedom (by "fair means" or "foul") because the larger towns which were becoming more industrialized during this period could offer the serf greater personal freedom as well as a higher standard of living. This process is nicely summarized by Bradshaw:

> By the middle of the 14th century the outward uniformity of the manorial system had become in practice considerably varied . . . for the peasant had begun to drift to the towns and it was unlikely that the old village life in its unpleasant aspects should not be resented. Moreover the constant wars against France and Scotland were fought mainly with mercenaries after Henry III's time and most villages contributed to the new armies. The bolder serfs either joined the armies or fled to the towns, and even in the villages the free men who held by villein tenure were as eager to commute their services as the serfs were to escape. Only the amount of 'free' labor available enabled the lord to work his demense in many places.[7]

And he says regarding the effect of the Black Death:

> . . . in 1348 the Black Death reached England and the vast mortality that ensued destroyed that reserve of labour which alone had made the manorial system even nominally possible.[8]

The immediate result of these events was of course no surprise: Wages for the "free" man rose considerably and this increased, on the one hand, the landowners problems and, on the other hand, the plight of the unfree tenant. For although wages increased for the personally free laborers, it of course did not necessarily add to the standard of living for the serf, if anything it made his position worse because the landowner would be hard pressed to pay for the personally free labor which he needed and would thus find it more and more difficult to maintain the standard of living for the serf which he had heretofore supplied. Thus the serf had no alternative but flight if he chose to better his position. Furthermore, flight generally meant both freedom and better conditions since the possibility of work in the new weaving industry was great and the chance of being caught small.[9]

---

[7] Bradshaw, F., *A Social History of England*, p. 54.
[8] *Ibid.*
[9] *Ibid.*, p. 57.

It was under these conditions that we find the first vagrancy statutes emerging. There is little question but that these statutes were designed for one express purpose: to force laborers (whether personally free or unfree) to accept employment at a low wage in order to insure the landowner an adequate supply of labor at a price he could afford to pay. Caleb Foote concurs with this interpretation when he notes:

> The anti-migratory policy behind vagrancy legislation began as an essential complement of the wage stabilization legislation which accompanied the breakup of feudalism and the depopulation caused by the Black Death. By the Statutes of Labourers in 1349–1351, every able-bodied person without other means of support was required to work for wages fixed at the level preceding the Black Death; it was unlawful to accept more, or to refuse an offer to work, or to flee from one country to another to avoid offers of work or to seek higher wages, or go give alms to able-bodied beggars who refused to work.[10]

In short, as Foote says in another place, this was an "attempt to make the vagrancy statutes a substitute for serfdom."[11] This same conclusion is equally apparent from the wording of the statute where it is stated:

> Because great part of the people, and especially of workmen and servants, late died in pestilence; many seeing the necessity of masters, and great scarcity of servants, will not serve without excessive wages, and some rather willing to beg in idleness than by labour to get their living: it is ordained, that every man and woman, of what condition he be, free or bond, able in body and within the age of threescore years, not living in merchandize, (etc.) be required to serve. . .

The innovation in the law, then, was a direct result of the aforementioned changes which had occurred in the social setting. In this case these changes were located for the most part in the economic institution of the society. The vagrancy laws were designed to alleviate a condition defined by the lawmakers as undesirable. The solution was to attempt to force a reversal, as it were, of a social process which was well underway; that is, to curtail mobility of laborers in such a way that labor would not become a commodity for which the landowners would have to compete.

Statutory dormancy: A legal vestige

In some time, of course, the curtailment of the geographical mobility of laborers was no longer requisite. One might well expect that

---

[10] Foote, C., "Vagrancy Type Law and Its Administration," *Univ. of Pennsylvania Law Review* (104), 1956, p. 615.

[11] *Ibid.*

when the function served by the statute was no longer an important one for the society, the statutes would be eliminated from the law. In fact, this has not occurred. The vagrancy statutes have remained in effect since 1349. Furthermore, as we shall see in some detail later, they were taken over by the colonies and have remained in effect in the United States as well.

The substance of the vagrancy statutes changed very little for some time after the first ones in 1349–1351 although there was a tendency to make punishments more harsh than originally. For example, in 1360 it was provided that violators of the statute should be imprisoned for 15 days[12] and in 1388 the punishment was to put the offender in the stocks and to keep him there until "he finds surety to return to his service."[13] That there was still, at this time, the intention of providing the landowner with labor is apparent from the fact that this statute provides:

> and he or she which use to labour at the plough and cart, or other labour and service of husbandry, till they be of the age of 12 years, from thenceforth shall abide at the same labour without being put to any mistery or handicraft: and any covenant of apprenticeship to the contrary shall be void.[14]

The next alteration in the statutes occurs in 1495 and is restricted to an increase in punishment. Here it is provided that vagrants shall be "set in stocks, there to remain by the space of three days and three nights, and there to have none other sustenance but bread and water; and after the said three days and nights, to be had out and set at large, and then to be commanded to avoid the town."[15]

The tendency to increase the severity of punishment during this period seems to be the result of a general tendency to make finer distinctions in the criminal law. During this period the vagrancy statutes appear to have been fairly inconsequential in either their effect as a control mechanism or as a generally enforced statute.[16] The processes of social change in the culture generally and the trend away from serfdom and into a "free" economy obviated the utility of these statutes. The result was not unexpected. The judiciary did not apply the law and the legislators did not take it upon themselves to change the law. In short, we have here a period of dormancy in which the statute is neither applied nor altered significantly.

---

[12] 34 Ed. 3 (1360).

[13] 12 R. 2 (1388).

[14] *Ibid*.

[15] 11 H. & C. 2 (1495).

[16] As evidenced for this note the expectation that ". . . the common gaols of every shire are likely to be greatly pestered with more numbers of prisoners than heretofore . . ." when the statutes were changed by the statute of 14 Ed. c. 5 (1571).

A SHIFT IN FOCAL CONCERN

Following the squelching of the Peasant's Revolt in 1381, the services of the serfs to the lord ". . . tended to become less and less exacted, although in certain forms they lingered on till the 17th century . . . By the 16th century few knew that there were any bondmen in England . . . and in 1575 Queen Elizabeth listened to the prayers of almost the last serfs in England . . . and granted them manumission."[17]

In view of this change we would expect corresponding changes in the vagrancy laws. Beginning with the lessening of punishment in the statute of 1503 we find these changes. However, instead of remaining dormant (or becoming more so) or being negated altogether, the vagrancy statutes experienced a shift in focal concern. With this shift the statutes served a new and equally important function for the social order of England. The first statute which indicates this change was in 1530. In this statute (22 H. 8. c. 12 1530) it was stated:

> If any person, being whole and mighty in body, and able to labour, be taken in begging, or be vagrant and can give no reckoning how he lawfully gets his living; . . . and all other idle persons going about, some of them using divers and subtle crafty and unlawful games and plays, and some of them feigning themselves to have knowledge of . . . crafty sciences . . . shall be punished as provided.

What is most significant about this statute is the shift from an earlier concern with laborers to a concern with *criminal* activities. To be sure, the stipulation of persons "being whole and mighty in body, and able to labour, be taken in begging, or be vagrant" sounds very much like the concerns of the earlier statutes. Some important differences are apparent, however, when the rest of the statute includes those who ". . . can give no reckoning how he lawfully gets his living"; "some of them using divers subtil and unlawful games and plays." This is the first statute which specifically focuses upon these kinds of criteria for adjudging someone a vagrant.

It is significant that in this statute the severity of punishment is increased so as to be greater not only than provided by the 1503 statute but the punishment is more severe than that which had been provided by *any* of the pre-1503 statutes as well. For someone who is merely idle and gives no reckoning of how he makes his living the offender shall be:

> . . . had to the next market town, or other place where they [the constables] shall think most convenient, and there to be tied to the end of a cart naked, and to be beaten with whips throughout the same

---

[17] Bradshaw, *op. cit.*, p. 61.

> market town or other place, till his body be bloody by reason of such whipping.[18]

But, for those who use "divers and subtil crafty and unlawful games and plays," etc., the punishment is " . . . whipping at two days together in manner aforesaid."[19] For the second offense, such persons are:

> . . . scourged two days, and the third day to be put upon the pillory from nine of the clock till eleven before noon of the same day and to have one of his ears cut off.[20]

And if he offend the third time " . . . to have like punishment with whipping, standing on the pillory and to have his other ear cut off."

This statute (1) makes a distinction between types of offenders and applies the more severe punishment to those who are clearly engaged in "criminal" activities, (2) mentions a specific concern with categories of "unlawful" behavior, and (3) applies a type of punishment (cutting off the ear) which is generally reserved for offenders who are defined as likely to be a fairly serious criminal.

Only five years later we find for the first time that the punishment of death is applied to the crime of vagrancy. We also note a change in terminology in the statute:

> and if any ruffians . . . after having been once apprehended . . . shall wander, loiter, or idle use themselves and play the vagabonds . . . shall be eftfoons not only whipped again, but shall have the gristle of his right ear clean cut off. And if he shall again offend, he shall be committed to gaol till the next sessions; and being there convicted upon indictment, he shall have judgment to suffer pains and execution of death, as a felon, as an enemy of the commonwealth.[21]

It is significant that the statute now makes persons who repeat the crime of vagrancy a felon. During this period then, the focal concern of the vagrancy statutes becomes a concern for the control of felons and is no longer primarily concerned with the movement of laborers.

These statutory changes were a direct response to changes taking place in England's social structure during this period. We have already pointed out that feudalism was decaying rapidly. Concomitant with the breakup of feudalism was an increased emphasis upon commerce and industry. The commercial emphasis in England at the turn of the 16th century is of particular importance in the development of vagrancy laws. With commercialism came considerable traffic bearing

---

[18] 22 H. 8. c. 12 (1530).
[19] Ibid.
[20] Ibid.
[21] 27 H. 8. c. 25 (1535).

valuable items. Where there were 169 important merchants in the middle of the 14th century there were 3,000 merchants engaged in foreign trade alone at the beginning of the 16th century.[22] England became highly dependent upon commerce for its economic support. Italians conducted a great deal of the commerce of England during this early period and were held in low repute by the populace. As a result, they were subject to attacks by citizens and, more important, were frequently robbed of their goods while transporting them. "The general insecurity of the times made any transportation hazardous. The special risks to which the alien merchant was subjected gave rise to the royal practice of issuing formally executed covenants of safe conduct through the realm."[23]

Such a situation not only called for the enforcement of existing laws but also called for the creation of new laws which would facilitate the control of persons preying upon merchants transporting goods. The vagrancy statutes were revived in order to fulfill just such a purpose. Persons who had committed no serious felony but who were suspected of being capable of doing so could be apprehended and incapacitated through the application of vagrancy laws once these laws were refocused so as to include " . . . any ruffians . . . [who] shall wander, loiter, or idle use themselves and play the vagabonds . . . "[24]

The new focal concern is continued in 1 Ed. 6. c. 3 (1547) and in fact is made more general so as to include:

> Whoever man or woman, being not lame, impotent, or so aged or diseased that he or she cannot work, not having whereon to live, shall be lurking in any house, or loitering or idle wandering by the highway side, or in streets, cities, towns, or villages, not applying themselves to some honest labour, and so continuing for three days; or running away from their work; every such person shall be taken for a vagabond. And . . . upon conviction of two witnesses . . . the same loiterer (shall) be marked with a hot iron in the breast with the letter V, and adjudged him to the person bringing him, to be his slave for two years . . .

Should the vagabond run away, upon conviction, he was to be branded by a hot iron with the letter S on the forehead and to be thenceforth declared a slave forever. And in 1571 there is modification of the punishment to be inflicted, whereby the offender is to be "branded on the chest with the letter V" (for vagabond). And, if he is convicted the second time, the brand is to be made on the forehead. It is worth noting here that this method of punishment, which first

---

[22] Hall, *op. cit.*, p. 21.
[23] *Ibid.*, p. 23.
[24] 27 H. 8. c. 25 (1535).

appeared in 1530 and is repeated here with somewhat more force, is also an indication of a change in the type of person to whom the law is intended to apply. For it is likely that nothing so permanent as branding would be applied to someone who was wandering but looking for work, or at worst merely idle and not particularly dangerous *per se*. On the other hand, it could well be applied to someone who was likely to be engaged in other criminal activities in connection with being "vagrant."

By 1571 in the statute of 14 El. c. 5 the shift in focal concern is fully developed:

> All rogues, vagabonds, and sturdy beggars shall . . . be committed to the common gaol . . . he shall be grievously whipped, and burnt thro' the gristle of the right ear with a hot iron of the compass of an inch about; . . . And for the second offense, he shall be adjudged a felon, unless some person will take him for two years in to his service. And for the third offense, he shall be adjudged guilty of felony without benefit of clergy.

And there is included a long list of persons who fall within the statute: "proctors, procurators, idle persons going about using subtil, crafty and unlawful games or plays; and some of them feigning themselves to have knowledge of . . . absurd sciences . . . and all fencers, bearwards, common players in interludes, and minstrels . . . all juglers, pedlars, tinkers, petty chapmen . . . and all counterfeiters of licenses, passports and users of the same." The major significance of this statute is that it includes all the previously defined offenders and adds some more. Significantly, those added are more clearly criminal types, counterfeiters, for example. It is also significant that there is the following qualification of this statute: "Provided also, that this act shall not extend to cookers, or harvest folks, that travel for harvest work, corn, or hay."

That the changes in this statute were seen as significant is indicated by the following statement which appears in the statute:

> And whereas by reason of this act, the common gaols of every shire are like to be greatly pestered with more number of prisoners than heretofore hath been, for that the said vagabonds and other lewd persons before recited shall upon their apprehension be committed to the said gaols; it is enacted . . .[25]

And a provision is made for giving more money for maintaining the gaols. This seems to add credence to the notion that this statute was seen as being significantly more general than those previously.

It is also of importance to note that this is the first time the term

---

[25] 14 Ed. c. 5. (1571).

rogue has been used to refer to persons included in the vagrancy statutes. It seems, *a priori*, that a "rogue" is a different social type than is a "vagrant" or a "vagabond"; the latter terms implying something more equivalent to the idea of a "tramp" whereas the former (rogue) seems to imply a more disorderly and potentially dangerous person.

The emphasis upon the criminalistic aspect of vagrants continues in Chapter 17 of the same statute:

> Whereas divers *licentious* persons wander up and down in all parts of the realm, to countenance their *wicked behavior;* and do continually assemble themselves armed in the highways, and elsewhere in troops, *to the great terror* of her majesty's true subjects, *the impeachment of her laws*, and the disturbance of the peace and tranquility of the realm; and whereas many outrages are daily committed by these dissolute persons, and more are likely to ensue if speedy remedy be not provided (Italics added)

With minor variations (*e.g.*, offering a reward for the capture of a vagrant) the statutes remain essentially of this nature until 1743. In 1743 there was once more an expansion of the types of persons included such that "all persons going about as patent gatherers, or gatherers of alms, under pretense of loss by fire or other casualty; or going about as collectors for prisons, gaols, or hospitals; all persons playing of betting at any unlawful games; and all persons who run away and leave their wives or children . . . all persons wandering abroad, and lodging in alehouses, barns, outhouses, or in the open air, not giving good account of themselves," were types of offenders added to those already included.

By 1743 the vagrancy statutes had apparently been sufficiently reconstructed by the shifts of concern so as to be once more a useful instrument in the creation of social solidarity. This function has apparently continued down to the present day in England and the changes from 1743 to the present have been all in the direction of clarifying or expanding the categories covered but little has been introduced to change either the meaning or the impact of this branch of the law.

We can summarize this shift in focal concern by quoting from Halsbury. He has noted that in the vagrancy statutes:

> ". . . elaborate provision is made for the relief and incidental control of destitute wayfarers. These latter, however, form but a small portion of the offenders aimed at by what are known as the Vagrancy Laws, . . . many offenders who are in no ordinary sense of the word vagrants, have been brought under the laws relating to vagrancy, and the great number of the offenses coming within the operation of these laws have

little or no relation to the subject of poor relief, but are more properly directed towards the prevention of crime, the preservation of good order, and the promotion of social economy."[26]

Before leaving this section it is perhaps pertinent to make a qualifying remark. We have emphasized throughout this section how the vagrancy statutes underwent a shift in focal concern as the social setting changed. The shift in focal concern is not meant to imply that the later focus of the statutes represents a completely new law. It will be recalled that even in the first vagrancy statute there was reference to those who "do refuse labor, giving themselves to idleness and vice and sometimes to theft and other abominations." Thus the possibility of criminal activities resulting from persons who refuse to labor was recognized even in the earliest statute. The fact remains, however, that the major emphasis in this statute and in the statutes which followed the first one was always upon the "refusal to labor" or "begging." The "criminalistic" aspect of such persons was relatively unimportant. Later, as we have shown, the criminalistic potential becomes of paramount importance. The thread runs back to the earliest statute but the reason for the statutes' existence as well as the focal concern of the statutes is quite different in 1743 than it was in 1349.

VAGRANCY LAWS IN THE UNITED STATES

In general, the vagrancy laws of England, as they stood in the middle 18th century, were simply adopted by the states. There were some exceptions to this general trend. For example, Maryland restricted the application of vagrancy laws to "free" Negroes. In addition, for *all* states the vagrancy laws were even more explicitly concerned with the control of criminals and undesirables than had been the case in England. New York, for example, explicitly defines prostitutes as being a category of vagrants during this period. These exceptions do not, however, change the general picture significantly and it is quite appropriate to consider the U.S. vagrancy laws as following from England's of the middle 18th century with relatively minor changes. The control of criminals and undesirables was the *raison de etre* of the vagrancy laws in the U.S. This is as true today as it was in 1750. As Caleb Foote's analysis of the application of vagrancy statutes in the Philadelphia court shows, these laws are presently applied indiscriminately to persons considered a "nuisance." Foote suggests that " . . . the chief significance of this branch of the criminal law lies

---

[26] Earl of Halsbury, *The Laws of England*, Butterworth & Co., Bell Yard, Temple Bar, 1912, pp. 606–607.

in its quantitative impact and administrative usefulness."[27] Thus it appears that in America the trend begun in England in the 16th, 17th, and 18th centuries has been carried to its logical extreme and the laws are now used principally as a mechanism for "clearing the streets" of the derelicts who inhabit the "skid roads" and "Bowerys" of our large urban areas.

Since the 1800s there has been an abundant source of prospects to which the vagrancy laws have been applied. These have been primarily those persons deemed by the police and the courts to be either actively involved in criminal activities or at least peripherally involved. In this context, then, the statutes have changed very little. The functions served by the statutes in England of the late 18th century are still being served today in both England the the United States. The locale has changed somewhat and it appears that the present-day application of vagrancy statutes is focused upon the arrest and confinement of the "down and outers" who inhabit certain sections of our larger cities but the impact has remained constant. The lack of change in the vagrancy statutes, then, can be seen as a reflection of the society's perception of a continuing need to control some of its "suspicious" or "undesirable" members.[28]

A word of caution is in order lest we leave the impression that this administrative purpose is the sole function of vagrancy laws in the U.S. today. Although it is our contention that this is generally true it is worth remembering that during certain periods of our recent history, and to some extent today, these laws have also been used to control the movement of workers. This was particularly the case during the Depression years and California is of course infamous for its use of vagrancy laws to restrict the admission of migrants from other states.[29] The vagrancy statutes, because of their history, still contain germs within them which make such effects possible. Their main purpose, however, is clearly no longer the control of laborers but rather the control of the undesirable, the criminal and the "nuisance."

DISCUSSION

The foregoing analysis of the vagrancy laws has demonstrated that these laws were a legislative innovation which reflected the socially

---

[27] Foote, *op. cit.*, p. 613. Also see in this connection, Irwin Deutscher, "The Petty Offender," *Federal Probation*, XIX, June, 1955.

[28] It is on this point that the vagrancy statutes have been subject to criticism. See for example, Lacey, Forrest W., "Vagrancy and Other Crimes of Personal Condition," *Harvard Law Review* (66), p. 1203.

[29] Edwards *vs* California. 314 S: 160 (1941).

perceived necessity of providing an abundance of cheap labor to landowners during a period when serfdom was breaking down and when the pool of available labor was depleted. With the eventual breakup of feudalism the need for such laws eventually disappeared and the increased dependence of the economy upon industry and commerce rendered the former use of the vagrancy statutes unnecessary. As a result, for a substantial period the vagrancy statutes were dormant, undergoing only minor changes and, presumably, being applied infrequently. Finally, the vagrancy laws were subjected to considerable alteration through a shift in the focal concern of the statutes. Whereas in their inception the laws focused upon the "idle" and "those refusing to labor" after the turn of the 16th century and emphasis came to be upon "rogues," "vagabonds," and others who were suspected of being engaged in criminal activities. During this period the focus was particularly upon "roadmen" who preyed upon citizens who transported goods from one place to another. The increased importance of commerce to England during this period made it necessary that some protection be given persons engaged in this enterprise and the vagrancy statutes provided one source for such protection by re-focusing the acts to be included under these statutes.

Comparing the results of this analysis with the findings of Hall's study of theft we see a good deal of correspondence. Of major importance is the fact that both analyses demonstrate the truth of Hall's assertion that "The functioning of courts is significantly related to concomitant cultural needs, and this applies to the law of procedure as well as to substantive law."[30]

Our analysis of the vagrancy laws also indicates that when changed social conditions create a perceived need for legal changes that these alterations will be effected through the revision and refocusing of existing statutes. This process was demonstrated in Hall's analysis of theft as well as in our analysis of vagrancy. In the case of vagrancy, the laws were dormant when the focal concern of the laws was shifted so as to provide control over potential criminals. In the case of theft the laws were re-interpreted (interestingly, by the courts and not by the legislature) so as to include persons who were transporting goods for a merchant but who absconded with the contents of the packages transported.

It also seems probable that when the social conditions change and previously useful laws are no longer useful there will be long periods when these laws will remain dormant. It is less likely that they will be officially negated. During this period of dormancy it is the judiciary which has principal responsibility for *not* applying the statutes. It is

---

[30] Hall, *op. cit.*, p. XII.

possible that one finds statutes being negated only when the judiciary stubbornly applies laws which do not have substantial public support. An example of such laws in contemporary times would be the "Blue Laws." Most states still have laws prohibiting the sale of retail goods on Sunday yet these laws are rarely applied. The laws are very likely to remain but to be dormant unless a recalcitrant judge or a vocal minority of the population insist that the laws be applied. When this happens we can anticipate that the statutes will be negated.[31] Should there arise a perceived need to curtail retail selling under some special circumstances, then it is likely that these laws will undergo a shift in focal concern much like the shift which characterized the vagrancy laws. Lacking such application the laws will simply remain dormant except for rare instances where they will be negated.

This analysis of the vagrancy statutes (and Hall's analysis of theft as well) has demonstrated the importance of "vested interest" groups in the emergence and/or alteration of laws. The vagrancy laws emerged in order to provide the powerful landowners with a ready supply of cheap labor. When this was no longer seen as necessary and particularly when the landowners were no longer dependent upon cheap labor nor were they a powerful interest group in the society the laws became dormant. Finally a new interest group emerged and was seen as being of great importance to the society and the laws were then altered so as to afford some protection to this group. These findings are thus in agreement with Weber's contention that "status groups" determine the content of the law.[32] The findings are inconsistent, on the other hand, with the perception of the law as simply a reflection of "public opinion" as is sometimes found in the literature.[33] We should be cautious in concluding, however, that either of these positions are necessarily correct. The careful analysis of other laws, and especially of laws which do not focus so specifically upon the "criminal," are necessary before this question can be finally answered.

In conclusion, it is hoped that future analyses of changes within the legal structure will be able to benefit from this study by virtue of

---

[31] Negation, in this instance, is most likely to come about by the repeal of the statute. More generally, however, negation may occur in several ways including the declaration of a statute as unconstitutional. This later mechanism has been used even for laws which have been "on the books" for long periods of time. Repeal is probably the most common, although not the only, procedure by which a law is negated.

[32] M. Rheinstein, *Max Weber on Law in Economy and Society,* Harvard University Press, 1954.

[33] Friedman, N., *Law in a Changing Society,* Berkeley and Los Angeles: University of California Press, 1959.

(1) the data provided and (2) the utilization of a set of concepts (innovation, dormancy, concern and negation) which have proved useful in the analysis of the vagrancy law. Such analyses should provide us with more substantial grounds for rejecting or accepting as generally valid the description of some of the processes which appear to characterize changes in the legal system.

INTRODUCTORY COMMENTS ON MORGAN'S RESEARCH

As a preface to the next two research illustrations, which deal with certain landmark events in the history of U.S. drug laws, let us consider some more recent evidence about societal definitions of drug-related deviance. In 1972, a team of researchers led by Peter Rossi asked a sample of 200 adult residents of Baltimore, Maryland, to rate the seriousness of 140 illegal acts on a scale ranging from 9 (most serious) to 1 (least serious). After calculating an average (i.e., mean) rating for each crime, Rossi and his associates ranked all 140 offenses according to their overall perceived seriousness. Table 11–1 shows selected segments of this ranking that include drug- and alcohol-related offenses (adapted from Rossi et al., 1974: 228–229).

It is immediately apparent in Table 11–1 that acts involving the opiate drug *heroin* were viewed as extraordinarily serious forms of deviant behavior by the Baltimore respondents. Selling heroin ranks virtually at the top of this list of offenses (3), with an average seriousness rating of 8.293. As you look down the rankings in this table, you will find that the act of selling heroin is defined as more serious than several forms of premeditated murder (6 and 7), forcible rape (4 and 13), and armed robbery (9, 30, 32, and 35). Similarly, the personal act of using heroin (28) is ranked ahead of a number of violent interpersonal acts including beating up a child (31) and, ironically, two examples of *homicide closely related to alcohol use* (33 and 36). Whatever their other effects might be, the sale and use of heroin certainly seem to have possessed the power to evoke a strong, hostile reaction in this sample of the general public in the early 1970s.

Perhaps the societal definitions of heroin reflected in Table 11–1 do not surprise you as much as the relatively high degree of seriousness that the respondents attached to other drug-related acts. Would you perceive selling LSD (10) as more serious than kidnapping for ransom (12) or assassination of a public official (15)? Would you put the act of selling marijuana (49) in the same league with father-daughter incest (50) or causing the death of an employee by neglecting to repair

Table 11–1
Ranking of selected offenses according to average seriousness ratings in Baltimore survey conducted by Rossi et al.

Rank	Crime*	Mean rating
1	Planned killing of a policeman	8.474
2	Planned killing of a person for a fee	8.406
3	*Selling heroin*	8.293
4	Forcible rape after breaking into a home	8.241
5	Impulsive killing of a policeman	8.214
6	Planned killing of a spouse	8.113
7	Planned killing of an acquaintance	8.093
8	Hijacking an airplane	8.072
9	Armed robbery of a bank	8.021
10	*Selling LSD*	7.949
11	Assault with a gun on a policeman	7.938
12	Kidnapping for ransom	7.930
13	Forcible rape of a stranger in a park	7.909
14	Killing someone after an argument over a business transaction	7.898
15	Assassination of a public official	7.888
. . .		
28	*Using heroin*	7.520
29	Assault with a gun on an acquaintance	7.505
30	Armed holdup of a taxi driver	7.505
31	Beating up a child	7.490
32	Armed robbery of a neighborhood druggist	7.487
33	*Causing auto accident death while driving when drunk*	7.455
34	Selling secret documents to a foreign government	7.423
35	Armed street holdup stealing $200 cash	7.414
36	Killing someone in a bar room free-for-all	7.392
. . .		
49	*Selling marijuana*	6.969
50	Father-daughter incest	6.959
51	Causing the death of an employee by neglecting to repair machinery	6.918
52	Breaking and entering a bank	6.908
53	Mugging and stealing $25 in cash	6.873
54	*Selling pep pills*	6.867
. . .		
65	*Using LSD*	6.557
66	*Driving while drunk*	6.545
67	Practicing medicine without a license	6.500
. . .		
140	*Being drunk in public places*	2.849

Source: Adapted from P. H. Rossi et al., "The Seriousness of Crimes: Normative Structure and Individual Differences," *American Sociological Review* 39 (April 1974), pp. 228–229.
* Emphasis added to drug- and alcohol-related offenses.

machinery (51)? Probably not. Another survey of perceived seriousness conducted in the late 1970s by McCleary et al. (1981) found markedly lower rankings for drug-related offenses, even though the rankings for other kinds of crime were basically consistent with those reported by Rossi et al. (1974). Specifically, the crimes of selling LSD and marijuana slipped 47 and 63 points, respectively, in the seriousness rankings in less than a decade.

These survey results point to several reasons why relativistic researchers have found the drug and alcohol area to be a fascinating and fruitful site for exploring societal definitions and reactions to deviance. First, as vividly illustrated by the case of heroin in Table 11–1, drug-related forms of deviance have at various times and places been the target of *severe societal reactions* that are usually reserved for only the most heinous of crimes. Second, definitions of drug-related deviance tend to be *historically volatile,* sometimes undergoing rather dramatic changes in intensity and meaning in relatively short periods of time. This is shown not only by the recent shift in seriousness rankings discussed above but also by the fact that being drunk in public places ranked dead last in Table 11–1. Presumably, if this survey had been conducted during the Prohibition movement when the public drunk was defined as an "enemy" (Gusfield, 1967), the latter result would have been quite different. Finally, crisis reactions and other changes in societal responses to drug-related deviance can often be linked to *underlying social, political, or economic conflicts* (Lidz & Walker, 1980; Helmer, 1975). This was the essence of Gusfield's (1963) analysis of the "symbolic crusade" against alcohol, of course. In a similar vein, how would you explain the intense public and political concern with LSD, marijuana, and other drug problems in the United States during the Vietnam era, a concern that is clearly documented in Table 11–1? Why would *perceptions* of a drug crisis *diminish* throughout the 1970s while *rates of drug use* generally *increased*? One need not look only to the distant past for cases where the social control of drugs is closely tied to major political cleavages and group conflicts.

However, in the following research illustration by Morgan (1978), we will do just that. Her case study analyzes several sources of conflict between working-class whites and Chinese that motivated the legislation of anti-opium laws in 19th century California. By calling attention to both the *symbolic* (i.e., status maintenance) and *instrumental* (i.e., economic control) functions of these laws, Morgan's work has a bearing on both versions of conflict theory discussed in Chapter 10. This particular episode also exemplifies the intimate relationship between antidrug crusades and racial or ethnic conflict throughout

U.S. history. In addition to the European-alcohol connection examined by Gusfield (1963), later efforts at drug control exploited stereotypes of "cocaine crazed" blacks in the South and Mexican "marijuana addicts" in the Southwest (Helmer, 1975; Musto, 1973). Racial discrimination, in return, was often justified by attributing a drug menace to minority groups. For example, the following words were spoken on the floor of the U.S. Congress in 1943 while a complete ban of Chinese immigration to this country was being debated (quoted in Parrillo, 1980: 282):

> The Chinese are inveterate opium-smokers most of the day. They brought that hideous opium habit to this country. . . . There is no melting pot in America that can change their habits or change their mentality. . . . If there are any people who have refused to accept our standard and our education, it is the Chinese.

Morgan's analysis shows how the heavy political tool wielded by this congressman during World War II was initially forged and used against Chinese immigrants in the years following the California gold rush. You will also get a glimpse of how the sale and use of opiate drugs (later including heroin) first became defined as threatening, alien acts—definitions that are still alive and well in California, Baltimore, and elsewhere in American society over 100 years later.

RESEARCH ILLUSTRATION 11-B

The legislation of drug law: Economic crisis and social control

*Patricia A. Morgan**

This paper uses California's first opium law in 1875 to examine the process of early drug legislation, specifically the political and economic conditions leading up to the passage of the law. We explore the possibility that initial opium prohibition was simply a component of a larger process of social control aimed at securing the isolation of the Chinese in the lower rungs of the labor market. It is suggested that analyses of social control must take into account the interrelationship

---

Source: Article reprinted from *Journal of Drug Issues* 8 (Winter 1978), pp. 53–62.

* Patricia A. Morgan, Ph.D, teaches in the Field Studies Program at the University of California, Berkeley. An earlier version of this paper was presented at the Society for the Study of Social Problems, New York, August, 1976. Appreciation is expressed to Donald R. Cressey and Craig Reinarman for their help on an earlier draft.

between economic, political and ideological motivations behind any quest for prohibitive legislation.

Any close examination of legal prohibitions against drug use should include the law's historical development, those socio-economic forces which lay the foundation for legislative action. This study of the first opium laws enacted against the Chinese in 19th century California endeavors to do this. It explores the anti-opium crusade as part of the dynamics of both class conflict and symbolic/status dominance within the working class.

The case-study method employed here has often been the most appropriate way to examine the sources of drug law. Becker, Musto, and Helmer, among others, have shown that the case-study method offers the best possibility for in-depth analysis of the wide variety of conditions preceding legislative action.[1] In addition, our study has made use of the abundant historical material available to the researcher in California.[2] Although the economic and racial conditions in California were unique in the country during that time, its moral crusades and legislative action did represent later popular views linking immoral behavior with ethnic and racial minorities. This theme can be seen running through the works of Duster (1970), Becker (1963), Helmer (1975), Lindesmith (1965), and Gusfield (1964). The interpretations of these events vary, however, according to the theoretical framework adopted by the researcher. This paper addresses the issue of moral reform via Becker's idea of moral crusades (1963) and Gusfield's notion of the symbolic function of the law (1968).

In discussing Becker, we focus primarily on his notion that laws dealing with problems of moral order and deviance develop as a direct result of moral crusades waged by individuals or groups which inform the public of particular immoral conditions. Here Becker likens a crusader to a moral entrepreneur who develops through moral initiative a rule-making and selective enforcement enterprise:

> Wherever rules are created and applied, we should be alive to the possible presence of an enterprising individual or group. Their activities can properly be called moral enterprise, for what they are enterprising about is the creation of a new fragment of the moral constitution of society, its code of right and wrong (1963: 145).

There are two important questions, however, that Becker ignores. What acts as a catalyst to initiate such legal action by these moral crusaders? More importantly, how did these individuals receive the legitimation and power to affect change over other groups within the legal system? These questions will be addressed later in this paper.

Gusfield, in his work on moral reform, notes the importance of status in rule making. One function of the law is maintenance of control, a second is legitimation of a group's position in society. Gusfield terms these two functions the instrumental and the symbolic. The instrumental function lies completely with enforcement, "unenforced this function does not exist" (1969: 309). The symbolic function of the law, however, does not depend on enforcement:

> There is a dimension of meaning in symbolic behavior which is not given in its immediate and manifest significance, but in what the action connotes for the audience that views it. . . . the symbol "has acquired a meaning which is added to its immediate intrinsic significance." . . . In analyzing law as symbolic, we are oriented less to behavioral consequences as a means to a fixed end: more to meaning as an act, a decision, a gesture important in itself (1969: 309).

Gusfield's conceptualization of moral reform limits itself, for the most part, to the realm of status. The law, however, can take on symbolic meanings which in themselves have instrumental force. The symbolic force behind moral reforms can reinforce basic divisions within the working class. The passage of these laws can be seen, then, as a means of coopting a segment of the working class, providing it with mere symbolic superiority over other "immoral" and economically threatening groups. This, in effect, can prevent a collective effort of combined work class interests.

THE CHINESE IN CALIFORNIA

The first law against opium use in California was part of a general anti-Chinese crusade in the latter part of the 19th century. The Chinese population in the U.S. was growing steadily from a little over 4,000 in 1850 to over 107,000 in 1890 with the overwhelming majority residing in California.[3] Although hostility was present at the beginning of Chinese immigration, it did not develop into a full-scale crusade until after 1870. The gold rush was a frantic era of rapid development and widely fluctuating economic conditions; it attracted people from widely different social, racial and economic backgrounds. Hostility against the Chinese was, at first, sporadic and based primarily on local labor competition.[4] It was alleviated somewhat when construction began on the Central Pacific railroad employing over 9,000 Chinese workers (Coolidge, 1909: 63).

After the Civil War, the labor picture changed as new discoveries of silver and gold brought thousands west—young men uprooted from the war and immigrants from Europe drifting into California looking for work. The labor situation worsened in the 1870s when the national panic of 1973 depressed local industries, and the completion of the railroad threw thousands of Chinese on the job market. White labor groups in California started forming loose coalitions in opposition to the growing competition of Chinese workers.

The Chinese were working jobs for cheaper pay that whites felt rightfully belonged to them. They were industrious and able to live on less than their white counterparts and "as they entered one field of activity after another it was claimed that they not only drove out American laborers but also tended to monopolize the industry (Sandemeyer, 1939: 32). This claim has been documented for the cigar and shoe making industry as well as for certain types of clothing manufacture (cf. Chiu, 1963).

When the national economic depression hit the larger industries in California, the Chinese turned more toward small business and trade enterprises formerly under the control of the white middle class. Chinese competition in these areas drove thousands into the camp of organized labor. As McWilliams has noted:

> the labor movement in California . . . has included elements which are not ordinarily thought of as part of labor . . . the small shop keeping element; a large section of the rural population; and a sizeable element of what today would be called 'white collar' workers (1949: 139).

Thus, both working and middle classes began to have a stake in organized anti-Chinese activities.

In September, 1877, many of the unemployed laborers in San Francisco organized the Workingmen's Party, which had a brief, but important, impact on California labor history.[5] In a series of vacant lot meetings in the city, they denounced the Chinese as the cause rather than possible victims of capitalist prosperity. The California Workingmen's Party, like its counterparts in the Eastern part of the country, was very much aware of the evils of "big business."[6] They were therefore opposed to the large corporate and landholding monopolies which had continued longer than any other sector to encourage Chinese immigration. In their eyes, the corporations were similar to Southern plantations with the Chinese as "slave" laborers against whom no white worker could compete. This view was articulated in a Western newspaper which warned the white worker to "give California a wide berth, for the laborer is not worthy of his hire in that state, even when there is work for him to do."[7]

The Workingmen's Party was aware of the connections between labor's problems and the monopolistic control of industry and railroads in the state. Their platform dealt with many economic and social issues unrelated to the Chinese. It stated, for instance, that the "object of the new party was to unite all of the poor and laboring men into one group for defense against the encroachment of capital" (Sandemeyer, 1939: 65). But poor and laboring men did not mean Chinese, because "Chinese labor provided the emotional drive and concrete motivation necessary for uniting the working men of the state" (Sandemeyer, 1939: 65). It was also the ideological mechanism which convinced workers that the elimination of the Chinese from the labor market would result in immediate economic improvement.

Agitating for Chinese exclusionary laws, the Workingmen's Party began to receive serious attention. The presence of the Chinese "menace" considerably strengthened the power of white labor:

> It contributed more than any other one factor to the strength of the California labor movement. It is the one subject upon which . . . it has always been possible to obtain concerted action. . . . legislation prohibiting the further immigration of Oriental laborers has been the chief object of the organized activities of the working people of California for over fifty years (Eaves, 1910: 6).

In their crusade against the Chinese, the Workingmen's Party began to receive support from several different sources. First, the newspapers began to increase their campaign against the Chinese, and second, this was supported by the state legislature, which began official inquiries into every aspect of the presence of the Chinese population.

The Chinese had thus lost what little protection they had previously enjoyed. The corporate and railroad interests that had defended Chinese workers in the past now either joined the chorus of Chinese exclusionists or remained silent. The worsening economic picture and the large influx of militant unemployed white workers made the presence of Chinese labor problematic, as well, for big business in the state.

THE STATE LEGISLATURE AND THE CHINESE

After the panic of 1873, the legislature demanded more anti-Chinese reforms, and soon became a major force against the Chinese. Although earlier regional sporadic anti-Chinese sentiments had been addressed by the state legislature, they had been largely ineffective. Previous anti-Chinese legislation had focused primarily on Chinese exclusion, but those early laws did not receive much attention from the press, had almost no practical effect, and served primarily as "symbolic" reassurance that the state would not become overrun by alien Chinese.

The transition from those early Chinese exclusionary laws and later anti-opium laws is important for this analysis. Legal action that began with exclusionary measures helped to set the stage for the passage of laws which later harrassed the Chinese on many levels. By 1885, most aspects of the Chinese presence suffered under some legal sanction. Thus, the common expression, "he hasn't a Chinaman's chance" became very appropriate.

Starting in the 1850s, laws were introduced and passed by zealous legislators who wanted to limit or completely half the immigration of Orientals to California. Many of these laws were later declared unconstitutional, but were often modified and reintroduced into the state legislature as the need dictated.

Chinese exclusionary laws[8]

1855 A state law prohibited Chinese and Mongolians from entering the state; later declared unconstitutional.

1858 A state law prohibited Asiatics from entering the state except when driven ashore by stress of weather or unavoidable accident, later declared unconstitutional.

1870 A state law provided a penalty of not less than $1,000 for any person bringing an Asiatic into the state without first presenting evidence of good character. In 1876, this law was declared unconstitutional.

1879 After repeated resolutions to the federal government, Congress passed a bill limiting the number of Chinese who came to the U.S. on any one vessel to 15.

1880 The U.S. Congress ratified a treaty with China giving the United States the right to "regulate limit or suspend" Chinese immigration, but not to prohibit it.

1882 The U.S. Congress suspended Chinese immigration for 10 years.

Several other laws provided economic or political sanctions against the Chinese within the state of California:[9]

1850 The Foreign Miners Tax Act placed a monthly tax on noncitizens working the mines. This was later modified to pertain only to Orientals.

1854 The state Supreme Court included Chinese in a 1850 statute prohibiting court testimony of non-whites for or against whites.

1855 A head tax of $50 per person was levied on those who employed or brought into the country those "persons who could not become citizens." Although no legislation specifically named the Chinese, the tax was used primarily against them.

1862 A police tax required all Asians not already paying the Miners Tax and not engaged in agriculture to pay a monthly tax of $2.50.

1875 The California Supreme Court denied naturalization to a Chinese individual, thus establishing precedent denying legal citizenship to the Chinese.

These are merely examples of state legislative actions. The list does not include similar widespread local ordinances. Both state and municipal treasuries were made thousands of dollars healthier each year as a result of such tax laws.

After the economic depression of the 1870s the state legislature began inquiring into the "moral" aspects of the Chinese population. This helped to maintain an ideology, developing during this time which transferred onus from the business class as cause of economic problems to a moral attack against a race that could be perceived as the cause of a wide range of problems. Accordingly, the California legislature created several "fact-finding" committees which looked into every aspect of the Chinese lifestyle.[10] The findings of these committees served both to legitimate the prejudicial actions of past legal sanctions and to form the basis for further legislation. Thus, the one subject that began to receive a large amount of official attention was the problem of vice found in Chinese communities. For instance, statutes were enacted against gambling and lottery. Although not specifically worded directly against the Chinese, they did, in fact, allow for selective enforcement. As one journalist observed:

> The San Francisco papers recently recorded, with much satisfaction, the fact that the police had determined to suppress the Chinese gambling houses. . . . Considering the fact that the same laws which prohibit Chinese gambling prohibit monte, faro, and other sports of the superior race; and considering moreover that one faro game will do more actual harm in a month than a dozen Chinese hells would do in a year. . . . It is a matter of notoriety that there are some seven or eight old established faro banks on Montgomery Street alone. . . . The proprietors of them sport their figures on the fashionable promenades, redolent of essences and clothed in purple and fine linen. These are the men, and theirs the institutions upon which the sagacity and enterprise of the police authorities should be expended. But there is little hope for any such interference with them. They possess vested rights here and none dare meddle with them. The legislator who is asked to check their iniquitous practices looks coldly upon the petitioner, for he spent his last evening among them, and he thinks they are mighty good fellows.[11]

Thus selective enforcement of vice laws against the Chinese was used without interfering with white middle or upper class gambling habits.

Inequitable rule enforcement went hand-in-hand with anti-Chinese legislative action. The success of this trend after 1870 presented in the following statistics show that by 1900 over 80 percent of Chinese arrests in San Francisco were for crimes against "morality."

Offense	Percent of Chinese arrests[12]
1. Crimes against property	.96
2. Crimes against the person	1.03
3. Crimes against public health (includes opium)	15.95
4. Crimes against public policy and morals (includes gambling)	82.00

It seems safe to conclude that "moral reform" was an important motivation, during the last part of the 19th century, for the anti-Chinese crusade. It became an important component in exclusionary policies coming out of the state legislature.

THE CHINESE AND OPIUM

The Chinese habit of smoking opium began to attract attention after the Civil War. This is because the earliest Chinese immigrants in California did not smoke opium. In China, opium use was concentrated primarily among the working class and peasant communities. The sale and distribution of opium within China was handled by the merchant and landlord classes, which were also the first groups to arrive in California. As John Helmer has pointed out:

> The Chinese immigrants were typically the younger sons of landowners without primogeniture rights of inheritance. . . . They were not usually from laboring origins. . . . They paid for their own passages and brought capital with them to invest. . . . The number of wage laborers among the Chinese in the early period was low. As can be expected, if opium use was confined to this class, there is no record of its use among the first generation of immigrants in California. . . . Indeed, there is no mention of opium-smoking until the mid 1860s.[13]

Thus, the first anti-opium crusade in U.S. history was directed against working class Chinese brought over initially for use as cheap mass labor, a function no longer needed by 1870. Consequently, the anti-opium crusades begun in the 1870s was waged as an ideological battle in connection with the economic one to remove these workers from the labor market. It was not the use of opium itself, but the smoking, a unique Chinese habit, which became the focal point for legislative action. Most importantly, opium smoking became a special problem when white men and women in the state began to "contaminate" themselves by frequenting the dens in Chinatown.

Direct action against Chinese opium smoking was first taken in 1875 when the city of San Francisco enacted an ordinance prohibiting the co-mingling of the races in Chinatown's opium dens (Kane, 1882: 23). Although the ordinance had some success, it was soon found to be limited.

> The vice was indulged in much less openly, but none the less extensively, for although the larger smoking-houses were closed, the small dens in Chinatown were well patronized, and the vice grew surely and steadily (Kane, 1882: 25).

Finally, the San Francisco police department made an impassioned plea before the California State Senate Committee on Chinese Immigration in 1878:

> These latter places were conducted by Chinamen, and patronized by both White men and women, who visited these dens at all hours of the day and night, the habit and its deadly results becoming so extensive as to call for action on the part of the authorities. . . . The department of the police, in enforcing the law with regard to this matter, have found white women and Chinamen side by side under the effects of this drug—a humiliating sight to anyone who has anything left of manhood.[14]

The media soon became an important force behind this crusade, waging a moral battle that placed the Chinese in an ever increasingly vulnerable position. Essentially the media reinforced the idea that the Chinese were responsible for opium smoking among Caucasians. They were portrayed as sinister agents who lured young men and women into the opium dens. Newspapers in the state daily saw to it that all "moral citizens" knew the consequences of letting the Chinese remain in California. According to the San Francisco *Post*, the Chinaman "has impoverished our country, degraded our free labor and hoodlumized our children. He is now destroying our young men with opium."[15] The Sacramento *Union*, among others, fanned the fire of incensed American manhood by printing lurid accounts of what went on inside these opium houses:

> Upon a matting-covered couch lay a handsome white girl in silk and laces, sucking poison from the same stem which an hour before was against the repulsive lips and yellow teeth of a celestial. She was just

> taking the last pipeful; the eyes were heavy, the will past resistance or offense. She glanced up lazily, but was too indifferent to replace the embroidered skirts over the rounded ankles the disturbed drapery exposed.[16]

The media, however, generally overlooked the possibility that reformers were observing fake Chinatown opium dens operated by whites:

> Many of the places wherein opium was smoked, or was supposed to be smoked, were fakes, tourist shockers conducted by the professional guides to the quarter, who were licensed by the city and were organized as the Chinatown Guides Association (Asbury, 1933: 166).

However, the state legislature, in 1881, supported the media's charges against the immoral "anti-American" Chinese and enacted a law against opium smoking. Importantly, this law was aimed specifically at opium dens and opium parlors which then existed only in Chinese communities. As the law, itself, stated:

> Every person who opens or maintains, to be resorted to by other persons, any place where opium, or any of its preparations, is sold or given away to be smoked at such place; and any person who, at such place sells or gives away any opium, or its aid preparations, to be smoked . . . is guilty of a misdemeanor.[17]

In as much as the only places where opium was being smoked were in the Chinese opium parlors, the legislation was clearly anti-Chinese.

A few years after the California law, the Federal government began discriminating between the different uses of opium in various tax measures. For instance, the government decided who, in fact, would control the importation and preparation of opium for smoking in this country. In 1890, Congress passed a law which stated that only American citizens were allowed to manufacture opium for smoking although the use of such was formally outlawed in the state where almost all opium smoking occurred (Brecher, 1972: 44).

The fact that the California law remained a misdemeanor and the nature Federal tax measures concerning importation, point to serious questions concerning the actual prevalence of opium smoking among the Chinese. Helmer has estimated that no more than 6 percent of the Chinese population in California engaged in the habit regularly (1975: 28). In addition, the sketchy available records give no indication that legal enforcement of the opium law was important in ridding the state of the Chinese presence.[18] The law's importance seemed to lie in bolstering California's claim to moral as well as economic reasons for Chinese exclusion.

Consequently, California's first opium law was directed only against those who smoked opium. The vast majority of those who used the drug by other means were not affected. Yet other forms of opium use were more common than the Chinese habit of opium smoking which California had declared both illegal and immoral. The influence of the patent medicine industry alone has led Troy Duster to observe: "in proportion to the population, addiction was probably eight times more prevalent then than now, despite the large increase in the general population" (1970: 8). But these opium users were not considered deviant, falling under some morally evil influence, or anti-American. To the extent that their opium use was considered a problem at all, it was referred to as a medical and not a moral issue. This double standard remained until the passage of the Harrison Tax Act in 1914, and only later did all opiate use develop into a general moral issue.[19] Those first Federal laws relating to the manufacture and regulation of opium were not crusades against immorality. The same economic and political factors which led to the moral crusade in California were not operating in the 1914 Harrison Act.

Thus, we conclude that the first opium laws in California were not the result of a moral crusade against the drug itself. Instead, it represented a coercive action directed against a vice that was merely an appendage of the real menace—the Chinese—and not the Chinese per se, but the laboring "Chinamen" who threatened the economic security of the white working class. Moral concern here took place on two levels. The first, and more apparent level seemed to be aimed ultimately at removing the Chinese from the labor force. The moral battle could thus be seen as a supporting element to that end. However, on another more subtle level, the moral crusade against opium smoking could be viewed as an ideological mechanism diverting attention away from the real causes of the workers' problem—the economic power relationships in the state over which the white worker had little control. Those power interests were not harmed by a normative crusade which aimed hostilities back toward a segment of the working class itself.

When we try to fit Becker's idea of moral entrepreneurs into California's anti-opium crusade, a further analysis is needed. Moral crusades do not take place solely as a result of the appearance of deviant group behavior or of moral entrepreneurs. The enactment of moral reform laws are generally connected to particular historical conditions which act as catalysts to such action. Furthermore, these crusades usually receive legitimation from a source of authority within the system itself, in this case the media and the state legislature.

Similarly, Gusfield's analysis of the symbolic and instrumental functions of the law have to be broadened to include more than status maintenance alone. The motivation, which can stem from social or economic crises, behind quests for status dominance must be examined before either symbolic or instrumental functions of moral law can attain historical significance. In addition, symbolism in the law can affect groups in very instrumental ways. By agitating for normative control over Chinese moral habits, those crusading for status dominance also were in the process of instrumentally controlling the behavior of the Chinese vis a vis the labor market. By creating a diversion deflecting the more fundamental causes of the real economic issues, such drives for status maintenance also had the effect of insuring the continuance of basic power in the state—a real consequence. When this is understood, the historical significance of the first opium laws takes on a broader perspective than mere moral entrepreneurship or status maintenance alone.

Therefore, when studying the development of moral crusades leading to legal sanctions, one must look beyond the normative level of analysis to other structural processes during that period. There is a close symbiotic relationship between normative, economic, and political dimensions in any state system. One, therefore, cannot study crusades occurring on any one level without first examining the causal contributions of the others.

NOTES

1. The case study is an analytical interpretation of events and not an historical interpretation. Our aim is not to generate new facts or data; rather it is more in keeping with Gusfield's notion of research "written within the methodological perspective of the sociologist interested in moral reform (1963: 2)."
2. For example, the Bancroft Library at the University of California at Berkeley preserved every newspaper article related to the subject of the Chinese in California from 1860 to roughly 1885. These can be found in the Bancroft scraps (volume 6), along with public addresses and private documents related to the labor movements during that period.
3. The 1850 figure is based on H. H. Bancroft, *History of California* VII, San Francisco, 1887; the 1890 figure is based on the United States Census, Washington, D.C.
4. For a more complete examination of this earlier period see, Ping Chiu, *Chinese Labor in California*, Madison, University of Wisconsin Press, 1963, pp. 52–66.
5. The California Workingmen's Party started by James Kearny remained powerful in the state during the elections of 1878 and 1880. They were able to elect enough supporters to the legislature to decisively effect the new California State Constitution of 1881.
6. For more information on the Workingmen's Party both in California and on the East Coast, see Philip S. Foner, *History of the Labor Movement in the United States*, Volume 1, New York, International Publishers, 1947, pp. 452–488.
7. From the Denver *News*, as quoted in the San Francisco *Chronicle*, April 2, 1876.
8. State of California, *Statutes*, 1855, 1858, 1870, State Printing Office, Sacramento California. The 1879, 1880, and 1882 laws are taken from Thomas W. Chinn (ed) *A History of the Chinese in California*, San Francisco, Chinese Historical Society of America, 1969, pp. 24–25.

9. Quoted in Chinn, p. 25.
10. One of the principal investigations conducted by the state was the California State Senate Committee report, entitled, "Chinese Immigration, Its Social, Moral and Political Effects," released in 1878, State Printing Office, Sacramento, California.
11. The Sacramento *Record,* December ?, 1870, found in the Bancroft Scraps, V. 6., University of California, Berkeley.
12. Taken from Walter Beach, *Oriental Crime in California,* New York, AMS Publishers, 1932.
13. John Helmer, *Drugs and Minority Oppression,* New York, Seabury Press, 1975, p. 19. For further information see, H. H. Kane, *Opium Smoking in America and China,* New York: GP Putnam's, 1882, and George F. Seward, *Chinese Immigration, Its Social and Economic Aspects,* New York, Scribners, 1881.
14. Report of the California State Senate, 1878, p. 152.
15. The San Francisco *Post,* March 1, 1879.
16. The Sacramento *Union,* March ?, 1879, taken from the Bancroft Scraps, Vol. 6. University of California, Berkeley.
17. State of California, Statutes, 1881, p. 34.
18. In addition to Helmer, earlier authors on the question of Oriental crime reached essentially the same conclusion, see Beach (1932), Chin (1969) and Cooledge (1909).
19. For a more complete account of the first federal opium law see David Musto, *The American Disease,* p. 54–67. The fact that opiate use prior to 1900 was considered primarily a medical and not a moral problem see Terry and Pellens (1928).

REFERENCES

Asbury, Herbert
    1933 *The Barbary Coast.* New York: Garden City Publishers.
Beach, Walter G.
    1932 *Oriental Crime in California.* New York: AMS
Becker, Howard
    1963 *Outsiders: Studies in the Sociology of Deviance.* London: Collier McMillian.
Chin, Thomas
    1969 *A History of the Chinese in California.* San Francisco: Chinese Historical Society.
Chiu, Ping
    1963 *Chinese Labor in California.* Madison: University of Wisconsin Press.
Colledge, Mary Roberts
    1909 *Chinese Immigration.* New York; Henry Holt
Duster, Troy
    1970 *The Legislation of Morality.* New York: The Free Press.
Eaves, Lucille
    1910 *A History of California Labor Legislation.* Berkeley: University of California Press.
Gusfield, Joseph
    1963 *Symbolic Crusade.* Urbana: University of Illinois Press.
    1969 "Moral Passage: The Symbolic Process in Public Designations of Deviance" in Friedman Macaulay, *Law and the Behavioral Sciences.* New York: Bobbs-Merrill.
Helmer, John
    1975 *Drug Use and Minority Oppression,* New York: Seabury Press.
Kane, H. H.
    1882 *Opium Smoking in America and China.* New York.
Lindesmith, Alfred
    1965 *The Addict and the Law.* Bloomington: University of Indiana Press.
McWilliams, Carey
    1949 *California: The Great Exception,* New York: A. A. Wyn.

Musto, David
    1973 *The American Disease.* New Haven: Yale University Press.
Sandemeyer, E. C.
    1939 *The Anti-Chinese Movement in California.* Urbana, University of Illinois.
Terry, Charles and Mildred Pellens
    1928 *The Opium Problem.* New York: Bureau of Hygiene.

INTRODUCTORY COMMENTS ON GALLIHER AND WALKER'S RESEARCH

The early anti-opium crusade in California has received limited attention among social scientists, but the next research illustration features one of the most notorious and widely studied legal events in the historical literature on deviance (see Galliher & Pepinsky, 1978). On October 1, 1937, only a few years after the repeal of Alcohol Prohibition, a "new prohibition" was ushered in as the Marijuana Tax Act went into effect (Kaplan, 1970; Musto, 1973). Technically a revenue measure, this act effectively ended legal distribution of marijuana in the United States by making it subject to an exorbitant transfer tax. This taxation strategy, which had been used to control opiate drugs in 1914 and machine guns in 1934, avoided some sticky constitutional questions about federal authority. More important for our present purposes, the Marijuana Tax Act brought the national "marijuana problem" squarely under the jurisdiction of a branch of the Treasury Department, the Federal Bureau of Narcotics. The activities of the Commissioner of this Bureau, Harry J. Anslinger, have become almost legendary. Anslinger served as the prototype for Becker's (1963) concept of the moral entrepreneur, which was discussed above by Morgan (1978). Becker implied that Anslinger's *moral enterprise*—his personal efforts in mobilizing the support of friendly interest groups and in "using the available media of communication to develop a favorable climate of opinion"—played a major, if not determining, role in the swift passage of the Marijuana Tax Act by Congress (1963: 145–146). However, Becker's rendition of the moral crusade against marijuana during this period has become quite controversial as you will see in Galliher and Walker's (1977) attempt to untangle "The Puzzle of the Social Origins of the Marihuana Tax Act of 1937."

A major issue in research on the events surrounding the Marijuana Tax Act is whether antimarijuana propaganda disseminated by Anslinger and other sympathetic groups created a groundswell of support for federal legislation in 1937. Galliher and Walker's analysis shows how difficult it often is to establish a causal sequence using historical data. Did the Bureau's propaganda campaign come *before* or *after* the Marihuana Tax Act? If it came before the act, as Becker argued, did the publicity about the dangers of the "killer drug" actually influence congressional action? Unlike the more dramatic medieval events documented by Chambliss (1964), the episode examined by Galliher and Walker involves subtle questions of time order and causal impact that pose special difficulties for the historical analyst, even though these events occurred only a few decades ago.

RESEARCH ILLUSTRATION 11-C

The puzzle of the social origins of the Marihuana Tax Act of 1937*

John F. Galliher and Allynn Walker

Several recent studies of the origins of the Marihuana Tax Act of 1937, while analyzing the same data sources, have surprisingly come to differing conclusions. Contrary to the results of most of these studies, there is insufficient evidence to conclude that there was a major effort by the Federal Bureau of Narcotics to generate a public marihuana crisis to create pressure for this legislation. Indeed a review of newspapers as well as the Congressional Record does not demonstrate a nationwide marihuana crisis. Moreover, this legislation is not the important legislative change implied by these studies, but merely a symbolic gesture involving a Bureau promise of no increased funding required by this law's passage.

During the past few years a number of researchers have studied the origins of the first federal attempt to control marihuana in the United States, the Marihuana Tax Act of 1937. Superficially this legislation seems unnecessary; at the time of its passage all states already had laws prohibiting the sale and possession of marihuana. This law, which imposed a prohibitively high tax on the drug, was modeled after federal control of addictive drugs, and perhaps much of the interest in examining the origins of this law stems from researchers' beliefs in the irrationality of applying the same types of controls to marihuana. The implication of considerable scholarly attention is that this law represents an important legal change. Curiously, while these studies have used largely the same data, they have come to different and often contradictory conclusions. The purpose of this study is to re-examine these data as well as additional information in an attempt to integrate disparate findings.

Source: Article reprinted from *Social Problems* 24, no. 3 (February 1977), pp. 367–376.
* Thanks are due Alfred R. Lindesmith, Edward Hunvald, and James McCartney for their helpful comments on an earlier draft of this paper.

The first of these studies is by Becker (1963), who sees drug prohibition in general, and marihuana control in particular, as coinciding with three traditional American values: (1) disapproval of behavior that could cause loss of self-control; (2) disapproval of action taken solely to produce states of ecstasy; and (3) a view that concern for human welfare or humanitarianism requires the suppression of drugs.

However, Becker claims that in the early 1930s neither the public nor law enforcement officials considered the use of marihuana a serious problem. Indeed he shows that in 1930 only 16 states had passed laws prohibiting the use of marihuana, yet by 1937 all states had passed such legislation. Why this sudden turn of events? Becker's explanation is that the main force behind the law's passage was the Treasury Department's Bureau of Narcotics.

> The Bureau's efforts took two forms: cooperating in the development of state legislation affecting the use of marihuana, and providing facts and figures for journalistic accounts of the problem (Becker, 1963: 138).

Becker (1963: 141) shows that in the Reader's Guide to Periodical Literature no articles on marihuana appeared from January 1925–June 1935, but four appeared from July 1935–June 1937, and 17 from July 1937–June 1939, with a rapid decline thereafter. He claims that during the bulge period, five of the seventeen articles show explicit influence of the Bureau.

Regarding the motives of the Bureau, Becker (1963: 138) says:

> While it is, of course, difficult to know what the motives of Bureau officials were, we need assume no more than that they perceived an area of wrongdoing that properly belonged in their jurisdiction and moved to put it there. The personal interest they satisfied in pressing for marihuana legislation was one common to many officials: the interest in successfully accomplishing the task one has been assigned and in acquiring the best tools with which to accomplish it.

Dickson (1968) shows that Becker's data on publication are misleading given the time intervals used. Indeed by looking at exact publication dates rather than broad time intervals, it becomes clear that only one article appeared in the seven months before the bill was signed into law. Dickson (1968: 155) claims that, "The great bulk of Bureau-inspired publicity came after the passage of the act, not before" and that therefore the public was apathetic prior to and during the bill's passage. This post-legislative propaganda, he asserts, shows that the Bureau director, H. J. Anslinger, was not motivated by moral issues but only attempted to increase the Bureau's power and scope of operations after the bill was passed.

After considerable discussion of Anslinger's motives, Dickson (1968: 156) concludes, "It would be either naive or presumptuous to deny that some combination of both moral and bureaucratic factors exist in any given crusade." It has, in fact, become accepted practice to blame the Act on a publicity campaign waged by the Narcotics Bureau under Mr. Anslinger's leadership rather than assessing relevant social structural conditions at the time which might have influenced the bill's passage:

> This Act was the result of a publicity campaign staged by the Federal Bureau of Narcotics under Mr. Anslinger's direction and leadership (Lindesmith, 1965: 228).
>
> In its report covering 1936, the bureau *first* (emphasis added) begins its continuous presentation of the "violent addict" myth. . . . brutal murders and other violent attacks are lucidly presented which purportedly illustrate the homicidal tendencies and the general debasing effects arising from marihuana use (Reasons, 1974: 146).
>
> Largely because of public concern, primarily induced by the Bureau of Narcotics, the Marihuana Tax Act was passed in 1937 placing a prohibitively high tax on marihuana and creating a whole new class of criminals (Reasons, 1974: 146).

Reasons seems to suggest that public concern and outrage could be instantly created. Becker shows that in 1931 the Treasury Department played down the seriousness of the problem, suggesting that newspaper articles had exaggerated the problem of marihuana use.

Musto (1973: 221) suggests that in 1932 the Federal Bureau of Narcotics again minimized the importance of marihuana. The Bureau claimed that abuse of marihuana occurred mainly in settlements of Latin Americans.

> A great deal of public interest has been aroused by newspaper articles appearing from time to time on the evils of the abuse of marijuana or Indian hemp, and more attention has been focused upon specific cases reported of the abuse of the drug than would otherwise have been the case. This publicity tends to magnify the extent of the evil and lends color to an inference that there is an alarming spread of the improper use of the drug, whereas the actual increase in such use may not have been inordinately large (Musto, 1973: 221).

Indeed as late as January 1937, Anslinger was quoted as saying that marihuana control was a state problem (Musto, 1973: 221–222).

Unlike Becker, Lindesmith, and Reasons, Musto (1973: 229) suggests that "the FBN does not appear to have created the marihuana scare of the early 1930s." Musto claims that the fear of marihuana was concentrated mainly in the southwestern states where there were the greatest concentrations of Mexican immigrants, who brought with them traditions of marihuana use. While Mexicans were tolerated during the economic boom of the 1920s as a source of cheap labor, during the 1930s the hatred toward this group escalated from the competition they created for scarce jobs and their willingness to work for low wages. Predictably, as this group became economically threatening, their habits also became more threatening.

Musto recently interviewed Anslinger to explore his motives in pressing for this legislation. Anslinger states that it was political pressure generated from these states and not the ambition of those in the Federal Bureau of Narcotics that was the crucial factor in the passage of the new law.

> Southwestern police and prosecuting attorneys likewise protested constantly to the federal government about the Mexicans' use of the weed (Musto, 1973: 220).
>
> The pressure for a federal antimarihuana law was political, Anslinger states, from local police forces in affected states to the governors; from the governors to Secretary of the Treasury Henry Morgenthau, Jr.; from Morgenthau to the Treasury's General Counsel; and finally to the Commissioner of Narcotics (Musto, 1973: 223).
>
> In the summer of 1936 it therefore became obvious that there would be no law to placate the Southwest unless some federal legislation under traditional legal powers was enacted (Musto, 1973: 225).

Bonnie and Whitebread (1974), unlike Becker, Reasons, Lindesmith, and Musto, claim that there was no intense concern with marihuana in the United States at the time the marihuana bill passed Congress and that this legislation went largely unnoticed.

> All in all, neither narcotic drugs in general nor marihuana in particular were major public issues during the thirties (Bonnie and Whitebread, 1974: 115).
>
> Interest in marihuana was still regional, although transient interest had now been aroused elsewhere. Viewed nationally, apathy was the norm (1974: 117).

Yet Bonnie and Whitebread acknowledge that Anslinger exerted considerable energy prior to 1937 to convince Americans of the dangers of marihuana. Until just prior to the Marihuana Tax Act's passage, however, Anslinger's suggested remedy for this problem was uniform state laws to handle the problem, for he doubted the constitutionality of federal attempts to control a drug where no importation from foreign countries was alleged.

Although there is some agreement among these writers, this small group of studies provides all possible combinations of results. Becker, Lindesmith, and Reasons see a national marihuana panic created by

FBN propaganda which propelled the legislation through Congress. Dickson finds this panic to be a result of a FBN propaganda effort designed to increase the scope and power of the Bureau after the bill's passage. Musto finds a marihuana crisis prior to the bill's passage but one localized in the Southwest and not a result of Bureau propaganda. Bonnie and Whitebread see evidence of FBN propaganda but no national marihuana crisis.

There are three distinct issues raised by comparing the findings of these studies. One is, what in fact has been documented regarding the Federal Bureau of Narcotics activities involving the Marihuana Tax Act of 1937? After this has been determined, the next question to be raised involves the demonstrated effects of these activities. And finally, what conclusions can be drawn about the possible explanation of these Bureau activities?

METHOD AND DATA

This study is based on three types of information. One is a review of the information found in the previous studies which have been used to document the Bureau's lobbying efforts on behalf of the Act. This study also reassesses the Congressional Records involving the Marihuana Tax Act of 1937, including House and Senate floor debate and public hearings. This was done in part to document Bureau activities but also to reflect the existing sentiment at the time in the Congress. No claim is made that the use of this data source is innovative, since all the works cited above show a first-hand familiarity with these records. Yet, while they show an explicit reference to these records, they do not completely agree on their meaning and significance. A review of three metropolitan newspapers in the Southwest (*Dallas Morning News*, *Denver Post*, and *Los Angeles Times*) and New York City (*New York Times*) and Washington, D.C. (*Washington Post*) was made to assess the cultural mileau and public attitude toward marihuana in the year prior to the bill's passage (May 31, 1936–June 1, 1937). Reasons, Musto, and Becker claim that year to be of great importance in changing public opinion. These newspaper data can be used to determine if indeed there was a crisis.

RESULTS

Cited evidence of Bureau propaganda

Becker (1963: 142) cites an article in the July 1937 American Magazine, "Marihuana: assassin of youth," by H. J. Anslinger with Courtney Ryley Cooper. Becker indicates that of the 17 articles on marihuana indexed in the Reader's Guide between July 1937 and June 1939, five referred to this Bureau-inspired article. Lindesmith (1965: 228) cites no evidence for his claim that:

> This Act was the result of a publicity campaign staged by the Federal Bureau of Narcotics under Mr. Anslinger's direction and leadership.

Dickson (1968: 152) also offers no specific support for the observation that:

> It seems clear from examining periodicals, newspapers, and the Congressional Record that the Bureau was primarily responsible for the passage of the act.

Reasons (1974: 146) cites Dickson's unsupported assertion and the following unsupported claim:

> Many articles appeared in professional and policy [sic] journals which can be traced back to the Federal Bureau of Narcotics.

Reasons (1974: 146) does cite some specific sources, however:

> Anslinger personally provided information for two articles that appeared in Hygeia, published by the American Medical Association.

Bonnie and Whitebread (1974: 98) base their claims of propaganda just prior to the 1937 Act on the American Magazine article and on a 1936 speech by Anslinger on NBC.

In conclusions Lindesmith and Dickson offer no support for their claims of FBN propaganda. Bonnie and Whitebread cite one article and one radio speech. Becker cites the same article and observes that five indexed articles also cited this article. Reasons' claims are without support except for reference to Dickson's unsupported claim and to two articles published by the AMA. This yields a total of three articles and one radio speech, clearly a product of the FBN. Yet only Musto (1973: 229) finds insufficient evidence to prove a major propaganda role for the FBN. In fairness it must be noted that it may still be that the FBN played a major role in propagandizing on behalf of the law, but perhaps the contacts were largely informal and by word of mouth, and therefore not a part of the documents available from this period.

Bonnie and Whitebread (1974: 95) provide convincing evidence, however, that the Bureau instigated an "educational campaign" on the evils of marihuana in the early 1930s as part of an effort to secure uniform state prohibitions of all drugs. This campaign, however, was largely unsuccessful, although it undoubtedly contributed to the general definition of marihuana as evil and its widespread prohibition in the states.

Congressional Record: Floor debate and public hearings

There was no floor debate on the bill in the House or the Senate. Indeed the only discussion occurred during the hearings in the House and Senate. This is a clear sign that the bill was not a topic of dissent or division of opinion within the Congress.

Public hearings were held first by the House Ways and Means Committee where the bill originated, then in the Senate Finance Committee. Three types of witnesses testified at these hearings: (1) witnesses representing the hemp and birdseed industries who urged alteration of the bill as originally drafted to exempt these groups from legal controls under the Act; (2) witnesses representing government agencies who spoke on behalf of the bill (Primary witnesses in this group were H. J. Anslinger, Commissioner, Bureau of Narcotics, and the Treasury Department's assistant general counsel, Clinton M. Hester.); and (3) Dr. William C. Woodward, legislative counsel of the American Medical Association, who spoke against the bill.

The government witnesses used two main techniques during the public hearings: unverified case histories of the tragedy caused by marihuana use and newspaper editorials cited as fact. Commissioner Anslinger provided lurid case histories from a variety of regions, all outside the southwestern states, during the House and Senate hearings. The theme emerges from his testimony that the country was not only faced with a crisis but a *widespread and national* crisis recently grown to major proportions.

> It is only in the last 2 years that we had a report of seizures anywhere but in the Southwest. Last year New York State reported 195 tons seized, whereas before that I do not believe that New York could have reported 1 ton seized (U.S. Cong., House, 1937b: 20–21, April 27).

> Last year the State of Pennsylvania destroyed 200,000 pounds (U.S. Cong., House, 1937b: 25, April 27).

Mr. Anslinger (U.S. Cong., Senate, 1937: 14) also offered opinion as fact to liven up his long list of cases:

> I believe in some cases one cigarette might develop a homicidal mania, probably to kill his brother [sic].

This opinion, as well as all of his other testimony, went unquestioned by Congress.

Newspaper articles were demonstrably effective as was newspaper editorial opinion, which was used as factual evidence, by Bureau representatives as well as members of Congress. In a House report to accompany the bill (U.S. Cong., House, 1937a: 2), the sponsor, Rep. Doughton, expresses the following view:

> The seriousness of the problem is also emphasized by the fact that newspapers in over 100 cities in the country have reported the illicit use of marihuana within the communities which they serve.

And Mr. Hester during the House hearings (U.S. Cong., House, 1937b: 6, April 27) quoted from an editorial of the Washington Times which also reflects national rather than regional concern:

> The marihuana cigaret [sic] is one of the most insidious of all forms of dope, largely because of the failure of the public to understand its fatal qualities.
> The Nation is almost defenseless against it, having no Federal laws to cope with it and virtually no organized campaign for combatting it.
> The result is tragic.
> School children are the prey of peddlers who infest school neighborhoods.
> High-school boys and girls buy the destructive weed without knowledge of its capacity for harm, and conscienceless dealers sell it with impunity.
> This is a national problem, and it must have national attention.
> The fatal marihuana cigarette must be recognized as a deadly drug and American children must be protected against it.

Similar editorials are then quoted by Mr. Hester from the Washington Post and the Washington Herald.

Near the end of the House hearings, expert medical testimony was heard on the issue of the necessity and desirability of this bill. The witness was Dr. William C. Woodward, legislative counsel of the American Medical Association, who was both a physician and lawyer. He was a well-known and prestigious figure, long a familiar personality in Congress representing the powerful AMA. He and his organization opposed the bill (U.S. Cong., House, 1937b: 92, May 4):

> That there is a certain amount of narcotic addiction of an objectionable character no one will deny. The *newspapers* (emphasis added) have called attention to it so prominently that there must be some grounds for their statements. It has surprised me, however, that the facts on which these statements have been based have not been brought before this committee by *competent primary evidence. We are referred to newspaper publications concerning the prevalence of marihuana addiction. We are told that the use of marihuana causes crime* (emphasis added).

Dr. Woodward suggested a number of federal agencies which could have been called as possible sources of direct information regarding the effects of marihuana including the Bureau of Prisons, the Children's Bureau, the Office of Education, and the Public Health Service.

> The Bureau of Public Health Service has also a division of pharmacology. If you desire evidence as to the *pharmacology of Cannabis* (emphasis added), that obviously is the place where you can get direct and primary evidence, rather than the indirect hearsay evidence (U.S. Cong., House, 1937b: 92, May 4).

Dr. Woodward objected to the bill's imposition of a tax on physicians prescribing marihuana because it would not address the problem of the clandestine distribution as described by the government. Instead of new federal legislation, he recommended reliance on existing state laws. He also questioned why the medical profession had not been consulted in the drafting of the bill (U.S. Cong., House, 1937b: 116, May 4).

> No medical man would identify this bill with a medicine until he read it through, because *marihuana is not a drug* (emphasis added) (U.S. Cong., House, 1937b: 117, May 4).

Yet on the basis of other information Congress appeared to believe that his opinion of the pharmacological properties of marihuana was wrong.

> Mr. Dingell. *We know that it is a habit that is spreading, particularly among youngsters. We learn that from the pages of the newspapers.* . . . The number of victims is increasing each year (emphasis added).
>
> Dr. Woodward. There is no evidence of that (U.S. Cong., House, 1937b: 117, May 4).
>
> Mr. McCormack. There is no question but that the drug habit has been increasing rapidly in recent years.
>
> Dr. Woodward. There is no evidence to show whether or not it has been (U.S. Cong., House, 1937b: 118, May 4).
>
> Mr. McCormack. It is used, we were told, by 200,000,000 people throughout the world. *All I know is what I have read about it* (emphasis added) (U.S. Cong., House, 1937b: 118, May 4).

Against Dr. Woodward's testimony, the Chairman of the House Ways and Means Committee, Rep. Doughton, sponsor of the bill, presented two newspaper editorials from the Washington Times and Washington Post which, as indicated above, were earlier introduced into the hearings by Mr. Hester, the Treasury Department's legal counsel (U.S. Cong., House, 1937b: 120, May 4).

Finally Mr. Anslinger and Mr. Hester helped sell the bill by arguing, both in the House and Senate hearings, that no new appropriations would be required by its enactment (U.S. Cong., House, 1937b: 27, April 27; U.S. Cong., Senate, 1937: 21). Dickson (1968: 156) has shown that after the bill's passage, Mr. Anslinger continued to claim, during appropriations hearings, that no new funds were necessary to enforce the law; perhaps he did this because of parsimoniousness in the use of tax dollars. Indeed after the Act's passage in 1937 (perhaps to stay within budget constraints), Anslinger instructed his agents in a confidential memorandum to leave the massive number of small marihuana possession cases to state courts and act only in the much rarer cases of suppliers (Bonnie and Whitebread, 1974: 180–181).

We are then left with two sources of information about the activities of the Federal Bureau of Narcotics: evidence from existing studies and the Congressional Record. Existing studies provide little evidence of a Bureau lobby on behalf of the Marihuana Tax Act of 1937 but some evidence of efforts to secure passage of uniform drug laws in all states. Included was an attempt to inform the public of the dangers associated with marihuana. The other source of information regarding Bureau activities, the Congressional Record, shows several days of partisan testimony before House and Senate committees by Bureau employees.

Newspapers

The next question involves the consequences of the effort to inform the public about marihuana. A review of three newspapers in southwestern cities and one each in New York and Washington, D.C., suggests that the concern about marihuana was more diffuse than Musto claims but less intense than suggested by Reasons. These newspapers reported other news, including domestic economic depression, massive union strikes, the beginning Nazi takeover of Europe, the Spanish Civil War, and the threat of Russian communism. In the *Los Angeles Times,* for example, between May 31, 1936 and June 1, 1937, the 12-month period preceding the bill's passage, only seven articles concerning marihuana appeared; in the *Dallas Morning News* 11 such articles appeared, and in the *Denver Post,* 18. During the same time period, in the more nationally oriented *New York Times* and *Washington Post* there were 19 and 6 articles respectively. This makes an overall average in all newspapers of approximately one article per month. Aside from the limited number of articles on marihuana, their location in the newspapers is instructive. Only two appeared on the front page. Prominence was usually reserved for news involving other drugs, especially heroin or opium. The infrequency and inconspicuousness of marihuana articles is surprising, given the frequent reference to newspaper articles about marihuana in Congress. Despite little evidence of a marihuana panic as reflected in these articles, marihuana was always characterized as a dangerous narcotic. That is how it is described by Congressmen; and there is evidence that concern with marihuana had increased from earlier in the decade.[1]

SUMMARY AND CONCLUSION

The cause of the activities of Anslinger and the Bureau is difficult to assess with the information available. Yet some analysis of the causes of Anslinger's behavior and that of his subordinates is possible. Anslinger argued publicly for uniform state drug laws. It is common for federal police officials to see merit in a uniform legal structure which simplifies federal relations with state police agencies. Also, Anslinger and Hester testified before Congress on behalf of the proposed legislation. Once an administration sets its policy, (Musto, 1973: 223), it is common for federal bureau chiefs to testify in support of the policy. Anslinger's documented behavior is usual enough, and not that of a zealous, moral crusader or a power-hungry bureaucrat. Assigning major responsibility for legal change to a specific individual, as has been done in the case of the Marihuana Tax Act, leads to diverse psychological explanations, which are difficult to verify. Blaming a government official for what many, including liberals, see as a ridiculous law is not unexpected, except in sociologists trained to analyze structural conditions rather than individual characteristics.

It is probable that the Bureau campaign to secure uniform state drug laws had some influence on later definitions of marihuana. However, the evidence used by Becker, Lindesmith, Reasons, Dickson, and Bonnie and Whitebread does not support their claim of an FBN propaganda effort to secure passage of the Marihuana Tax Act of 1937. A total of three articles and one radio speech hardly constitutes a national propaganda effort. It appears that this role of the FBN has

---

[1] A review of the New York Times Index reveals the following annual tally of articles on marihuana:

Year	N
1937	13
1936	9
1935	3
1934	4
1933	1
1932	1
1931	1
1930	0

become an article of faith for many studying federal marihuana legislation.

The average of one article per month represents something less than the results of a zealous, national propaganda campaign and does not reflect a national crisis, even if it is an increase from previous years. A crisis of the time was the Nazi takeover of Europe, which accounted for at least one article a day. An energetic propaganda campaign would produce at least one news story a day, as in a national political campaign for President. Without a national crisis, assigning the responsibility for a widespread and effective propaganda campaign becomes a moot point; and there does not appear to have been a national crisis.

Becker, Dickson, and Reasons agree that prior to the Anslinger-orchestrated Bureau propaganda campaign, there was generally citizen apathy toward marihuana and that Anslinger and the Bureau were responsible for the public arousal. But this seems to give them too much credit. Long before the campaign got underway, many states had laws prohibiting sale and possession of marihuana, and prior to the first federal hearings, all states had such laws (Dickson, 1968: 154).

Not only is there no evidence of a propaganda campaign, but contrary to Anslinger's and Hester's interpretation of the newspaper editorials which they presented at the Congressional hearings, there is insufficient evidence to demonstrate a national or local marihuana crisis just prior to the bill's passage. Any concern about marihuana use was not isolated in the Southwest, as Musto claims. Certainly the review of southwestern newspapers indicates something less than a public panic; they were filled with stories of international aggression and domestic economic depression. Marihuana stories offered slight competition at such a time. Indeed Alfred Lindesmith (1975) recently recalled:

> I was engaged in studying drugs when the marihuana law was passed but I didn't even know it nor did I notice any national furor.

Throughout the hearings no one challenged or questioned Mr. Hestor's or Mr. Anslinger's unsupported testimony except, of course, Dr. Woodward. This may indicate that the members of Congress were already convinced. Editorials were given more credence than medical testimony by the members of Congress, and the seeming lack of interest of most Congressmen, including their casual dismissal of Dr. Woodward's testimony, indicate that Congress was convinced of the danger in marihuana. The fact that some Congressmen relied heavily on the few and relatively inconspicuous newspaper articles indicates that these stories fit the common sense opinion of the period and were quoted for this reason. There is no evidence that this was a new view, or that Congress was startled by Anslinger's testimony. As Bonnie and Whitebread (1974: 117) indicate, "Viewed nationally, apathy was the norm." The strong words used in the Congressional hearings by Anslinger and Hester do not prove a major propaganda effort by the FBN, contrary to Dickson, nor, of course, do these words necessarily reflect a national crisis. Anslinger could make such statements without fear of contradiction because his claims were supported by widespread but apparently low-level citizen approbation about the evil nature of marihuana, and no scientific evidence apparently existed at the time to contradict him as shown by Dr. Woodward's helplessness. It would seem that if such scientific evidence had existed, Dr. Woodward would have known of its existence and would have used it.

Finally, the symbolic properties of the Marihuana Tax Act are of great importance. Without new funding, this law clearly could not be fully implemented. It was largely a technical adjustment in federal law, duplicating existing state laws—not the important legal change implied by Becker, Dickson, Reasons, Lindesmith, and Bonnie and Whitebread. These researchers seem to have been confused by the same symbolism as Edelman remarks in other observers of legislative action. Anslinger promised no budget increases to enforce the new law and indicated an unwillingness to allow his agents to spend great amounts of time on marihuana cases. Edelman (1964) suggests that the political behavior of people is determined by whether a piece of legislation symbolically reassures them. Similarly, Gusfield (1963, 1967) has argued that national prohibition of alcohol was largely unenforced, which permitted a public affirmation of the values of prohibitionists without great inconvenience to drinkers. As in the case of the 1937 Marihuana Tax Act, necessary funds to insure the implementation of prohibition were never appropriated (Gusfield, 1963: 120).

It may be the case that pressure from law enforcement officials in the Southwest was an initial precipitating agent in the bill's passage. However, two points must be made in this regard: (1) This pressure does not appear to reflect a Mexican marihuana panic in the Southwest as Musto claims, and (2) the bill's clear sailing in Congress cannot be accounted for solely by this political pressure. Rather it must be recognized that the bill was not objectionable to most, both because it supported widespread common sense opinion of the time and because it was purely symbolic legislation. Certainly no Congressmen demanded increased appropriations to fund marihuana control.

To Anslinger, Congress did not seem very concerned and "the only information they had was what we would give them in our hearings" (Musto, 1973: 225).

It does appear that Congress was not very concerned. Apparently they recognized the public relations or symbolic nature of the Act. Also, those groups likely to be supportive of such legislation did not send representatives to the hearings in the House and Senate. The most plausible interpretation for their inactivity is that Anslinger did not feel it necessary to ask for their assistance, given the lack of Congressional opposition.

REFERENCES

Becker, Howard S.
    1963 Outsiders. New York: Free Press of Glencoe.
Bonnie, Richard J. and Charles H. Whitebread II
    1974 The Marihuana Conviction: A History of Marihuana Prohibition in the United States. Charlottesville: University Press of Virginia.
Dallas Morning News
    May 31, 1936–June 1, 1937
Denver Post
    May 31, 1936–June 1, 1937
Dickson, Donald T.
    1968 "Bureaucracy and morality: an organizational perspective on a moral crusade," Social Problems 16:143–156.
Edelman, Murray
    1964 The Symbolic Uses of Politics. Urbana: University of Illinois Press.
Gusfield, Joseph R.
    1963 Symbolic Crusade: Status Politics and the American Temperance Movement. Urbana: University of Illinois Press.
    1967 "Moral passage: the symbolic process in public designations of deviance," Social Problems 15:175–188.
Lindesmith, Alfred R.
    1965 The Addict and the Law. Bloomington: Indiana University Press.
    1975 Letter, August 21, 1975 in possession of the authors.
Los Angeles Times
    May 31, 1936–June 1, 1937
Musto, David F.
    1973 The American Disease: Origins of Narcotic Control. New Haven: Yale University Press.
New York Times
    May 31, 1936–June 1, 1937
New York Times Index
    1930–1935
Reasons, Charles E.
    1974 The Criminologist: Crime and the Criminal. Pacific Palisades, California: Goodyear.
U.S. Congress, House of Representatives
    1937a Report No. 792 to accompany H. R. 6906, "The marihuana taxing bill." Seventy-fifth Congress, First Session, May 11.
    1937b "Taxation of marihuana." Hearings before the Committee on Ways and Means. Seventy-fifth Congress, First Session on H. R. 6385, April 27, 28, 29, 30, and May 4.

U.S. Congress, Senate
  1937 "Taxation of marihuana." Hearing before a Subcommittee of the Committee on Finance. Seventy-fifth Congress, First Session on H. R. 6906, July 12.
Washington Post
  May 31, 1936–June 1, 1937

CONCLUSION

The research illustrations in this final chapter show how sociologists have taken advantage of historical changes in the law as opportunities to gain insight into deviance as a politically defined phenomenon. A concern with legal manifestations of group conflict or class domination has long been central to research in the conflict tradition. Indeed, most of the theoretical contributions discussed in Chapter 10—ranging from Gusfield's *Symbolic Crusade* (1963) to Taylor, Walton, and Young's *The New Criminology* (1973)—deal mainly with problems of crime and legal order. However, some historical researchers have begun to broaden the scope of the macro-relativistic approach by focusing on various cultural and political aspects of "therapeutic" forms of social control (see Chorover, 1979; Conrad & Schneider, 1980; Kittrie, 1971; Scull, 1977; 1981; Spector, 1981).

In our own historical overview of the field of deviance in Chapter 2, we saw how early sociologists relied upon the medical metaphor of pathology as an all-purpose label for urban problems and deviant behavior at the turn of the 20th century. We have also seen that the medical imagery of the social pathologists was strongly colored by the same system of rural American values that inspired the moral crusade for national prohibition. Other medical and biological conceptions of cultural threats to the "American way of life" during that period had more ominous implications. Immigrant groups such as the Irish, Italians, and eastern European Jews were the subjects of allegedly "scientific" inquiries into their peculiar "racial traits" (Chorover, 1979: 57–75). These "alien" groups, along with black Americans, were characterized as biologically inferior, as degenerate ethnic breeds that could taint the purity of native American stock. A deviant trait commonly attributed to these ethnic groups by scientific experts was feeblemindedness. In a study of immigrants sponsored by the U.S. Public Health Service in 1912, the famous mental tester, Henry Goddard, reported that "83 percent of the Jews, 80 percent of the Hungarians, 79 percent of the Italians, and 87 percent of the Russians seeking entry into the United States were 'feebleminded'" (Chorover, 1979: 66).

The specter of an invading mass of feebleminded aliens not only helped hasten the passage of highly restrictive immigration quotas in the 1920s but also broadened support for a more "scientific" method of controlling the spread of biological defects: "eugenic" sterilization. The American eugenic movement, which was heavily influenced by the philosophy of social Darwinism, advocated forced sterilization of the mentally and socially "unfit" as a means for improving the "racial qualities of human beings" (Kittrie, 1971: 310–333). Beginning with Indiana in 1907, a number of states passed legislation providing for involuntary sterilization of the mentally ill, the mentally deficient, and epileptics. A few states also included "habitual criminals" and "moral degenerates" on their statutory lists of biological deviants suitable for sterilization. A "model" law proposed in 1922 would have extended this coercive treatment to "inebriates, drug addicts, the tuberculous, the leprous, the blind, the deaf, the crippled . . . homeless paupers, tramps, and ne'er-do-wells" (Kittrie, 1971: 325). Although the far-reaching system of "therapeutic" control envisioned in the latter proposal was never enacted in the United States, many thousands of "mental defectives" were subjected to involuntary sterilization for the sociobiological cause of racial improvement.

The full destructive force of the political machinery that was set in motion by proponents of "racial purification" in the United States was not realized until the 1930s in Nazi Germany. Offering "praise for American work in biological reform," German eugenists drew liberally upon the earlier U.S. experience for information and justification for the development of their own program of "racial hygiene" (Chorover, 1979: 98). Within two years after Hitler rose to power in 1933, an estimated 150,000 "defective" individuals had been subjected to compulsory sterilization by Nazi "racial scientists" (Kittrie, 1971: 325). This was only the beginning. A new phase in the evolution of the Nazi system of "therapeutic" control was reached at a conference held in Berlin in 1939 (Chorover, 1979: 101–103). There, some of the leading psychiatrists in Germany played a central part in drawing up detailed plans for the mass execution of patients in mental hospitals throughout the nation, a program that was euphemistically referred to as euthanasia (mercy killing). Over a quarter of a million mental patients were eventually exterminated, each of whom had first been officially labeled by a reviewing panel of psychiatrists as a "life devoid of value." These lives—as well as the lives of millions of Jews, Slavs, Poles, gypsies, homosexuals, the physically handicapped, the mentally retarded, and countless other "deviants" from Nazi racial ideals—are haunting historical monuments to the brutal, dehumanizing power that "therapeutic" forms of control can place in the hands of the modern State.

Legal and medical reactions to deviance in Hitler's Germany pose an enormous challenge to the conceptual and theoretical frameworks we have examined throughout this book. Conventional normative or relativistic definitions of deviance seem insufficient or inappropriate when applied to a social world where mass slaughter was officially sanctioned and routinely practiced, where genocide was rationally planned and carried out, where the ordinary meanings of deviance and social control are distorted or pushed to their limits. How, for example, does one conceptualize the acts of "euthanasia" performed by German psychiatrists? Are these to be treated as instances of psychiatric labeling and reaction processes? Or, should they be analyzed as instances of intentional homicide, as deviant behavior? Does one approach this historical episode with the theoretical goal of explaining its causes or of understanding its human significance?

Perhaps the major reason why analytical choices that are usually obvious become so difficult here is because the *moral context of the study of deviance is,* in this tragic case, *turned upside down.* Becker's (1967) question—Whose side are we on?—appears unnecessary, even callous. Can any modern analyst of Nazi atrocities remain value-neutral? An open moral commitment to the victims of this brutality—the underdogs—is almost taken for granted. Identification with the official viewpoint on deviance in Nazi Germany becomes highly problematic, to say the least. Thus, the standards of the politically dominant group, the moral order from which sociologists usually take their bearings, fail in this instance to provide an orienting framework for the study of deviant phenomena. This rare reversal of moral sympathies discloses the fundamental and pervasive influence that "overdog" values have on the identification and analysis of deviance under more ordinary political circumstances.

It is no wonder that the founders of sociology were drawn to history as a vital resource for their investigations of social life. Past events provide some powerful natural experiments, as illustrated here by Chambliss' (1964) study of the consequences of the Black Death, as well as evidence of more subtle patterns of variation and continuity that escape contemporary observers. Researchers like Gusfield (1963), Morgan (1978), and Helmer (1975) have been able to detect a common theme of cultural conflict that runs through much of the early drug and alcohol legislation in this country. We have just noted a continuity between American reactions to the threat of "racial pollution" and the Nazi system of "racial hygiene" that is fully visible only from a historical perspective. In fact, the study of deviance itself is subject to political and moral forces that can only be understood through historical reflection. In returning to the classic historical methods of Marx and others, the conflict tradition has offered the field of deviance some powerful tools for *self-analysis* as well as for the analysis of deviant phenomena.

References

Adams, Reed
    1973 "Differential association and learning principles revisited." *Social Problems* 20 (Spring): 458–470.

Akers, Ronald L.
    1977 *Deviant Behavior: A Social Learning Approach* (2d ed.). Belmont, Calif.: Wadsworth.
    1968 "Problems in the sociology of deviance: Social definitions and behavior." *Social Forces* 46 (June): 455–465.

Akers, Ronald L., Marvin D. Krohn, Lonn Lanza-Kaduce and Marcia Radosevich
    1979 "Social learning and deviant behavior: A specific test of a general theory." *American Sociological Review* 44 (August): 635–655.

Anderson, Nels
    1923 *The Hobo*. Chicago: University of Chicago Press.

Aronson, Elliot and J. Merrill Carlsmith
    1968 "Experimentation in social psychology." Pp. 1–79 in Gardner Lindzey and Elliot Aronson (eds.), *The Handbook of Social Psychology* (2d ed.), Volume Two. Reading, Mass.: Addison-Wesley.

Balkan, Sheila, Ronald J. Berger and Janet Schmidt
    1980 *Crime and Deviance in America: A Critical Approach*. Belmont, Calif.: Wadsworth.

Ball, John C.
    1957 "Delinquent and non-delinquent attitudes toward the prevalence of stealing." *Journal of Criminal Law, Criminology, and Police Science* 48 (September–October): 259–274.

Bankowski, Zenon, Geoff Mungham and Peter Young
    1977 "Radical criminology or radical criminologist?" *Contemporary Crises* 1 (January): 37–52.

Bean, J. M. W.
    1963 "Plague, population and economic decline in England in the later middle ages." *The Economic History Review* (2d series) 15 (April): 423–437.

Becker, Howard S.
    1973 *Outsiders: Studies in the Sociology of Deviance* (enlarged ed.). New York: Free Press.
    1967 "Whose side are we on?" *Social Problems* 14 (Winter): 239–247.
    1964 *The Other Side: Perspectives on Deviance*. New York: Free Press.
    1963 *Outsiders: Studies in the Sociology of Deviance*. New York: Free Press.

1953 "Becoming a marihuana user." *American Journal of Sociology* 59 (November): 235–243.

Beirne, Piers
    1980 "Some more on empiricism in the study of law: A reply to Jacobs." *Social Problems* 27 (April): 471–475.
    1979 "Empiricism and the critique of Marxism on law and crime." *Social Problems* 26 (April): 373–385.

Bell, Wendell
    1957 "Anomie, social isolation, and the class structure." *Sociometry* 20: 105–116.

Bendix, Reinhard
    1960 *Max Weber: An Intellectual Portrait*. Garden City, N.Y.: Doubleday.

Berger, Alan S. and William Simon
    1974 "Black families and the Moynihan report: A research evaluation." *Social Problems* 22 (December): 145–161.

Bernstein, Ilene N., William R. Kelley and Patricia Doyle
    1977a "Societal reaction to deviants: The case of criminal defendants." *American Sociological Review* 42 (October): 743–755.

Bernstein, Ilene N., Edward Kick, Jan T. Leung and Barbara Schulz
    1977b "Charge reduction: An intermediary stage in the process of labelling criminal defendants." *Social Forces* 56 (December): 362–384.

Black, Donald J.
    1973 "The social organization of the arrest." Pp. 154–160 in Earl Rubington and Martin S. Weinberg (eds.), *Deviance: The Interactionist Perspective* (2d ed.). New York: Macmillan.
    1970 "Production of crime rates." *American Sociological Review* 35 (August): 733–748.

Black, Donald J. and Albert J. Reiss
    1970 "Police control of juveniles." *American Sociological Review* 35 (February): 63–77.

Blum, Alan F.
    1970 "The sociology of mental illness." Pp. 31–70 in Jack Douglas (ed.), *Deviance and Respectability: The Social Construction of Moral Meanings*. New York: Basic Books.

Blumer, Herbert
    1969 *Symbolic Interactionism: Perspective and Method*. Englewood Cliffs, N.J.: Prentice-Hall.

Bord, Richard
    1971 "Rejection of the mentally ill: Continuities and further developments." *Social Problems* 18 (Spring): 496–509.

Bordua, David J.
    1967 "Recent trends: Deviant behavior and social control." *The Annals of the American Academy of Political and Social Science* 369 (January): 149–163.
    1962 "Some comments on theories of group delinquency." *Sociological Inquiry* 2 (Spring): 245–260.
    1961 "Delinquent subcultures: Sociological interpretations of gang delinquency.: *The Annals* 338 (November): 119–136.
    1959 "Juvenile delinquency and 'anomie': An attempt at replication." *Social Problems* 6 (Winter): 230–238.

Braithwaite, John
    1981 "The myth of social class and criminality reconsidered." *American Sociological Review* 46 (February): 36–57.
    1979 *Inequality, Crime, and Public Policy*. London: Routledge & Kegan Paul.

Brent, Edward E. and Richard E. Sykes
    1979 "A mathematical model of symbolic interaction between police and suspects." *Behavioral Science* 24 (November): 338–402.

Briar, Scott and Irving Piliavin
    1965 "Delinquency, situational inducements, and commitment to conformity." *Social Problems* 13 (Summer): 35–45.

Brittan, Arthur
   1973 *Meanings and Situations.* London: Routledge & Kegan Paul.
Burgess, Ernest W.
   1925 "The growth of the city: An introduction to a research project." Pp. 47–62 in Robert E. Park, Ernest W. Burgess and R. D. McKenzie (eds.), *The City.* Chicago: University of Chicago Press.
Burgess, Robert L. and Ronald L. Akers
   1966 "A differential association-reinforcement theory of criminal behavior." *Social Problems* 14 (Fall): 128–147.
Campbell, Donald T. and Julian C. Stanley
   1963 *Experimental and Quasi-Experimental Designs for Research.* Chicago: Rand McNally.
Carey, James T.
   1975 *Sociology and Public Affairs: The Chicago School.* Beverly Hills: Sage.
Carter, Timothy J. and Donald Clelland
   1979 "A neo-Marxist critique, formulation and test of juvenile dispositions as a function of social class." *Social Problems* 27 (October): 96–108.
Cavan, Ruth S.
   1961 "The concepts of tolerance and contraculture as applied to delinquency." *Sociological Quarterly* 2 (October): 243–258.
Chambliss, William J.
   1973 "Functional and conflict theories of crime." New York: MSS Modular Publications, Module 17.
   1964 "A sociological analysis of the law of vagrancy." *Social Problems* 12 (Summer): 67–77.
Chauncey, Robert L.
   1975 "Comment on 'The labeling theory of mental illness.'" *American Sociological Review* 40 (April): 248–252.
Chilton, Roland J.
   1964 "Continuity in delinquency area research: A comparison of studies for Baltimore, Detroit, and Indianapolis." *American Sociological Review* 29 (February): 71–83.
Chirot, Daniel
   1976 "Introduction: Thematic controversies and new developments in the uses of historical materials by sociologists." *Social Forces* 55 (December): 232–241.
Chorover, Stephan L.
   1979 *From Genesis to Genocide: The Meaning of Human Nature and the Power of Behavior Control.* Cambridge, Mass.: MIT Press.
Cicourel, Aaron V.
   1968 *The Social Organization of Juvenile Justice.* New York: Wiley.
Clark, John P. and Eugene P. Wenninger
   1962 "Socio-economic class and area as correlates of illegal behavior among juveniles." *American Sociological Review* 27 (December): 826–834.
Clayton, Richard R. and William B. Lacy
   1982 "Interpersonal influences on male drug use and intentions to use." *International Journal of the Addictions.* In press.
Clinard, Marshall B.
   1957 *Sociology and Deviant Behavior.* New York: Rinehart.
Clinard, Marshall B. and Robert F. Meier
   1979 *Sociology of Deviant Behavior* (5th ed.). New York: Holt, Rinehart & Winston.
Cloward, Richard A.
   1959 "Illegitimate means, anomie, and deviant behavior." *American Sociological Review* 24 (April): 164–176.
Cloward, Richard A. and Lloyd E. Ohlin
   1960 *Delinquency and Opportunity: A Theory of Delinquent Gangs.* New York: Free Press.
Cohen, Albert K.
   1965 "The sociology of the deviant act: Anomie theory and beyond." *American Sociological Review* 30 (February): 5–14.

1959 "The study of social disorganization and deviant behavior." Pp. 461–484 in Robert K. Merton, Leonard Broom and Leonard S. Cottrell, Jr. (eds.), *Sociology Today: Problems and Prospects*. New York: Basic Books.
1955 *Delinquent Boys: The Culture of the Gang*. Glencoe, Ill.: Free Press.

Cohen, Albert K. and James F. Short, Jr.
1966 "Juvenile delinquency." Pp. 84–135 in Robert K. Merton and Robert A. Nisbet (eds.), *Contemporary Social Problems* (2d ed.). New York: Harcourt, Brace & World.

Cohen, Albert K., Alfred Lindsmith and Karl Schuessler (eds.)
1956 *The Sutherland Papers*. Bloomington: Indiana University Press.

Cohen, Lawrence E. and James R. Kluegel
1978 "Determinants of juvenile court dispositions: Ascriptive and achieved factors in two metropolitan courts." *American Sociological Review* 43 (April): 162–176.

Cole, Stephen and Harriet Zuckerman
1964 "Appendix: Inventory of empirical and theoretical studies of anomie." Pp. 243–289 in Marshall B. Clinard (ed.), *Anomie and Deviant Behavior*. New York: Free Press.

Conrad, Peter and Joseph W. Schneider
1980 *Deviance and Medicalization: From Badness to Sickness*. St. Louis: Mosby.

Coser, Lewis A.
1971 *Masters of Sociological Thought: Ideas in Historical and Social Context*. New York: Harcourt Brace Jovanovich.
1956 *The Functions of Social Conflict*. New York: Free Press.

Cressey, Donald R.
1962 "Role theory, differential association, and compulsive crimes," Pp. 443–467 in Arnold M. Rose (ed.), *Human Behavior and Social Processes*. Boston: Houghton Mifflin.
1960 "Epidemiology and individual conduct: A case from criminology." *Pacific Sociological Review* 3 (Fall): 47–54.

Cressey, Paul
1932 *The Taxi-Dance Hall*. Chicago: University of Chicago Press.

Dahrendorf, Ralf
1959 *Class and Class Conflict in Industrial Society*. Stanford, Calif.: Stanford University Press.

Davis, Nannette J.
1980 *Sociological Constructions of Deviance* (2d ed.). Dubuque, Iowa: Wm. C. Brown.
1972 "Labeling theory in deviance research." *Sociological Quarterly* 13 (Autumn): 447–474.

Dentler, Robert A. and Lawrence J. Monroe
1961 "Social correlates of early adolescent theft." *American Sociological Review* 26 (October): 733–743.

Dohrenwend, Bruce P. and Barbara Snell Dohrenwend
1969 *Social Status and Psychological Disorder*. New York: Wiley.

Dohrenwend, Bruce, Barbara Snell Dohrenwend, Madelyn Schwartz Gould, Bruce Lind, Richard Neugebaure and Robin Wunsch-Hitzig (eds.)
1980 *Mental Illness in the United States: Epidemiological Estimates*. New York: Praeger.

Douglas, Jack D.
1971 *American Social Order: Social Rules in a Pluralistic Society*. New York: Free Press.
1970 *Deviance and Respectability: The Social Construction of Moral Meanings*. New York: Basic Books.
1967 *The Social Meanings of Suicide*. Princeton, N.J.: Princeton University Press.

Dubin, Robert
1959 "Deviant behavior and social structure: Continuities in social theory." *American Sociological Review* 24 (April): 147–164.

Dunham, H. Warren, Patricia Phillips and Barbara Srinivasan
    1966 "A research note on diagnosed mental illness and social class." *American Sociological Review* 31 (April): 223–227.

Durkheim, Emile
    1951 *Suicide: A Study in Sociology.* New York: Free Press.
    1938 *The Rules of Sociological Method.* Chicago: University of Chicago.
    1933 *The Division of Labor in Society.* New York: Macmillan.

Eaton, William W.
    1980 *The Sociology of Mental Disorders.* New York: Praeger.

Elliott, Delbert S. and Suzanne S. Ageton
    1980 "Reconciling race and class differences in self-reported and official estimates of delinquency." *American Sociological Review* 45 (February): 95–110.

Empey, LaMar T.
    1982 *American Delinquency: Its Meaning and Construction* (2d ed.). Homewood, Ill.: Dorsey Press.

Erikson, Kai T.
    1966 *Wayward Puritans: A Study in the Sociology Deviance.* New York: Wiley.
    1962 "Notes on the sociology of deviance." *Social Problems* 9 (Spring): 307–314.

Erlanger, Howard S.
    1976 "Is there a 'subculture of violence' in the South?" *Journal of Criminal Law and Criminology* 66 (December): 483–490.

Faris, Robert E. L.
    1967 *Chicago Sociology: 1920–1932.* Chicago: University of Chicago Press.

Finestone, Harold
    1976 *Victims of Change: Juvenile Delinquents in American Society.* Westport, Conn.: Greenwood Press.

Fleischman, Paul R. et al.
    1973 "Letters." *Science* 180 (April 27): 356–369.

Freedman, Jonathan L. and Anthony N. Doob
    1968 *Deviance: The Psychology of Being Different.* New York: Academic Press.

Freidson, Eliot
    1966 "Disability as social deviance." Pp. 71–99 in Marvin B. Sussman (ed.), *Sociology and Rehabilitation.* Washington, D.C.: American Sociological Association.

Fuller, Richard C. and Richard R. Myers
    1941a "Some aspects of a theory of social problems." *American Sociological Review* 6 (February): 24–33.
    1941b "The natural history of a social problem." *American Sociological Review* 6 (June): 320–328.

Galliher, John F. and Harold E. Pepinsky
    1978 "A meta-study of social origins of substantive criminal law." Pp. 27–38 in Marvin D. Krohn and Ronald L. Akers (eds.), *Crime, Law, and Sanctions: Theoretical Perspectives.* Beverly Hills: Sage.

Galliher, John F. and Allyn Walker
    1977 "The puzzle of the social origins of the Marihuana Tax Act on 1937." *Social Problems* 24 (February): 367–376.

Gibbs, Jack P.
    1972 "Issues in defining deviant behavior." Pp. 39–68 in Robert A. Scott and Jack Douglas (eds.), *Theoretical Perspectives on Deviance.* New York: Basic Books.
    1966 "Conceptions of deviant behavior: The old and the new." *Pacific Sociological Review* 9 (Spring): 9–14.

Glaser, Daniel
    1962 "The differential-association theory of crime." Pp. 425–442 in Arnold M. Rose (ed.), *Human Behavior and Social Processes.* Boston: Houghton Mifflin.

1956 "Criminality theories and behavioral images." *American Journal of Sociology* 61 (March): 433–444.

Glynn, Thomas J.
    1981 "From family to peer: A review of transitions of influence among drug-using youth." *Journal of Youth and Adolescence* 10 (October): 363–383.

Goffman, Erving
    1961 *Asylums*. Garden City, N.Y.: Anchor Books.

Goldstein, Michael S.
    1979 "The sociology of mental health and illness." Pp. 381–409 in Alex Inkeles, James Coleman, and Ralph H. Turner (eds.), *Annual Review of Sociology, Volume 5*. Palo Alto, Calif.: Annual Reviews.

Goode, Erich
    1975 "On behalf of labeling theory." *Social Problems* 22 (June): 570–583.

Gouldner, Alvin W.
    1968 "The sociologist as partisan: Sociology and the welfare state." *The American Sociologist* 3 (May): 103–116.

Gove, Walter R.
    1980 *The Labelling of Deviance: Evaluating a Perspective* (2d ed.). Beverly Hills: Sage.
    1979 "The labeling versus the psychiatric explanation of mental illness: A debate that has become substantively irrelevant (reply to a comment by Horwitz)." *Journal of Health and Social Behavior* 20 (September): 301–304.
    1976 "Reply to Imershein and Simons and Scheff." *American Sociological Review* 41 (June): 564–567.
    1975a "Labelling and mental illness: A critique." Pp. 35–81 in Walter R. Gove (ed.), *Labelling Deviant Behavior: The Evaluation of a Perspective*. New York: Sage/Halstead.
    1975b "The labelling theory of mental illness: A reply to Scheff." *American Sociological Review* 40 (April): 242–248.
    1970 "Societal reaction as an explanation of mental illness: An evaluation." *American Sociological Review* 35 (December): 873–884.

Gove, Walter R. and Michael R. Geerken
    1977 "The effect of children and employment on the mental health of married men and women." *Social Forces* 56 (September): 66–76.

Greenley, James R.
    1979 "Familial expectations, posthospital adjustment, and the societal reaction perspective on mental illness." *Journal of Health and Social Behavior* 20 (September): 217–227.

Gusfield, Joseph R.
    1967 "Moral passage: The symbolic process in public designations of deviance." *Social Problems* 15 (Fall): 175–188.
    1963 *Symbolic Crusade: Status Politics and the American Temperance Movement*. Urbana: University of Illinois Press.

Hagan, John, John Hewitt and Duane Alwin
    1979 "Ceremonial justice: Crime and punishment in a loosely coupled system." *Social Forces* 58 (December): 506–527.

Hagan, John, Ilene H. Nagel (Bernstein) and Celesta Albonetti
    1980 "The differential sentencing of white-collar offenders in ten federal district courts." *American Sociological Review* 45 (October): 802–820.

Harary, Frank
    1966 "Merton revisited: A new classification for deviant behavior." *American Sociological Review* 31 (October): 693–697.

Hawkins, M. J.
    1979 "Continuity and change in Durkheim's theory of social solidarity." *Sociological Quarterly* 20 (Winter): 155–164.

Hawkins, Richard and Gary Tiedeman
    1975 *The Creation of Deviance: Interpersonal and Organizational Determinants*. Columbus, Ohio: Merrill.

Heider, Fritz
    1958 *The Psychology of Interpersonal Relations.* New York: Wiley.
Helmer, John
    1975 *Drug use and minority oppression.* New York: Seabury Press.
Henderson, Scott
    1980 "A development in social psychiatry: The systematic study of social bonds." *Journal of Nervous and Mental Disease* 168 (February): 63–69.
Hepburn, John R.
    1977 "Social control and the legal order: Legitimated repression in a capitalist state." *Contemporary Crises* 1 (January): 77–90.
Hindelang, Michael J.
    1981 "Variations in sex-race-age-specific incidence rates of offending." *American Sociological Review* 46 (August): 461–474.
    1978 "Race and involvement in common law personal crimes." *American Sociological Review* 43 (February): 93–109.
    1973 "Causes of delinquency: A partial replication and extension." *Social Problems* 20 (Spring): 471–487.
Hindelang, Michael J., Travis Hirschi and Joseph G. Weis
    1981 *Measuring Delinquency.* Beverly Hills: Sage.
    1979 "Correlates of delinquency: The illusion of discrepancy between self-report and official measures." *American Sociological Review* 44 (December): 995–1014.
Hinkle, Roscoe C. and Gisela J. Hinkle
    1954 *The Development of Modern Sociology.* New York: Doubleday.
Hirschi, Travis
    1969 *Causes of Delinquency.* Berkeley: University of California Press.
Hirst, Paul Q.
    1975 "Marx and Engles on law, crime and morality." Pp. 203–232 in Ian Taylor, Paul Walton and Jock Young (eds.), *Critical Criminology.* London: Routledge & Kegan Paul.
Hollingshead, August B. and Frederick C. Redlich
    1958 *Social Class and Mental Illness.* New York: Wiley.
    1953 "Social stratification and psychiatric disorders." *American Sociological Review* 18 (April): 163–169.
Holzman, Philip S. et al.
    1973 "Brief communications." *Bulletin of the Menninger Clinic* 37 (November): 629–638.
Horwitz, Allan
    1979 "Models, muddles, and mental illness labeling." *Journal of Health and Social Behavior* 20 (September): 296–300.
    1977 "Marxist theories of deviance and teleology: A critique of Spitzer." *Social Problems* 24 (February): 362–363.
Huba, G. J. and P. M. Bentler
    1980 "The role of peer and adult models for drug taking at different stages in adolescence." *Journal of Youth and Adolescence* 9 (October): 449–465.
Imershein, Allen W. and Ronald L. Simons
    1976 "Rules and examples in lay and professional psychiatry: An ethnomethodological comment on the Scheff-Gove controversy." *American Sociological Review* 41 (June): 559–563.
Inkeles, Alex
    1959 "Personality and social structure." Pp. 249–276 in Robert K. Merton, Leonard Broom and Leonard S. Cottrell, Jr. (eds.), *Sociology Today: Problems and Prospects.* New York: Basic Books.
Jacobs, David
    1980 "Marxism and the critique of empiricism: A comment on Beirne." *Social Problems* 27 (April): 467–470.
Jaquith, Susan M.
    1981 "Adolescent marijuana and alcohol use: An empirical test of differential association theory." *Criminology* 19 (August): 271–280.

Jeffery, C. Ray
    1965 "Criminal behavior and learning theory." *Journal of Criminal Law, Criminology, and Police Science* 56 (September): 294–300.

Jensen, Gary F.
    1974 "Review of *The New Criminology*." *Social Forces* 53 (December): 368–369.
    1972 "Parents, peers, and delinquent action: A test of the differential association perspective." *American Journal of Sociology* 78 (November): 562–575.

Johnson, Barclay D.
    1965 "Durkheim's one cause of suicide." *American Sociological Review* 30 (December): 875–886.

Johnson, Bruce D.
    1973 *Marihuana Users and Drug Subcultures*. New York: Wiley.

Johnson, Richard E.
    1979 *Juvenile Delinquency and Its Origins: An Integrated Theoretical Approach*. Cambridge: Cambridge University Press.

Jones, Edward E. and Keith E. Davis
    1965 "From acts to dispositions: The attribution process in person perception." Pp. 219–266 in Leonard Berkowitz (ed.), *Advances in Experimental Social Psychology:* Vol. 2. New York: Academic Press.

Jones, T. Anthony
    1981 "Durkheim, deviance and development: Opportunities lost and regained." *Social Forces* 59 (June): 1009–1024.

Kandel, Denise B.
    1980 "Drug and drinking behavior among youth." Pp. 235–285 in Alex Inkeles, Neil J. Smelser and Ralph H. Turner (eds.), *Annual Review of Sociology, Volume 6, 1980*. Palo Alto, Calif.: Annual Reviews Inc.
    1978 *Longitudinal Research on Drug Use: Empirical Findings and Methodological Issues*. Washington, D.C.: Hemisphere-Wiley.

Kaplan, John
    1970 *Marijuana—The New Prohibition*. New York: World.

Kelley, Harold H.
    1967 "Attribution theory in social psychology." Pp. 192–240 in David Levine (ed.), *Nebraska Symposium on Motivation, 1967*. Lincoln: University of Nebraska Press.

Kessler, Ronald C. and Paul D. Cleary
    1980 "Social class and psychological distress." *American Sociological Review* 45 (June): 463–478.

Kirk, Stuart
    1974 "The impact of labeling on rejection of the mentally ill: An experimental study." *Journal of Health and Social Behavior* 15 (June): 108–117.

Kitsuse, John I.
    1975 "The 'new conception of deviance' and its critics." Pp. 273–284 in Walter R. Gove (ed.), *The Labelling of Deviance: Evaluating a Perspective*. New York: Halstead Press.
    1972 "Deviance, deviant behavior, and deviants: Some conceptual problems." Pp. 233–243 in William J. Filstead (ed.), *An Introduction to Deviance: Readings in the Process of Making Deviants*. Chicago: Markham.
    1962 "Societal reaction to deviant behavior: Problems of theory and method." *Social Problems* 9 (Winter): 247–256.

Kitsuse, John I. and Aaron V. Cicourel
    1963 "A note on the use of official statistics." *Social Problems* 11 (Fall): 131–139.

Kitsuse, John I. and David C. Dietrick
    1959 "*Delinquent Boys:* A critique." *American Sociological Review* 24 (April): 208–215.

Kittrie, Nicholas N.
    1971 *The Right to Be Different: Deviance and Enforced Therapy*. Baltimore: Johns Hopkins Press.

Kleiner, Robert J. and Seymour Parker
    1963 "Goal-striving, social status, and mental disorder: A research review." *American Sociological Review* 28 (April): 189–203.

Kornhauser, Ruth Rosner
    1978 *Social Sources of Delinquency: An Appraisal of Analytic Models*. Chicago: University of Chicago Press.

Krohn, Marvin D. and Ronald L. Akers
    1977 "An alternative view of the labelling versus psychiatric perspectives on societal reaction to mental illness." *Social Forces* 56 (December): 341–362.

Kuhn, Thomas S.
    1970 *The Structure of Scientific Revolutions* (2d ed.). Chicago: University of Chicago Press.

LaFree, Gary
    1981 "Official reactions to social problems: Police decisions in sexual assault cases." *Social Problems* 28 (June): 582–594.

Lander, Bernard
    1954 *Towards an Understanding of Juvenile Delinquency*. New York: Columbia University Press.

Langner, Thomas S. and Stanley T. Michael
    1963 *Life Stress and Mental Health*. New York: Free Press.

Larkin, William E. and L. Anthony Loman
    1977 "Labeling in the family context: An experimental study." *Sociology and Social Research* 61 (January): 192–203.

Lemert, Edwin M.
    1981 "Issues in the study of deviance." *Sociological Quarterly* 22 (Spring): 285–305.
    1974 "Beyond Mead: The societal reaction to deviance." *Social Problems* 21 (April): 457–468.
    1972 *Human Deviance, Social Problems and Social Control* (2d ed.). Englewood Cliffs, N.J.: Prentice-Hall.
    1967 *Human Deviance, Social Problems and Social Control*. Englewood Cliffs, N.J.: Prentice-Hall.
    1964 "Social Structure, social control, and deviation." Pp. 57–97 in Marshall B. Clinard (ed.), *Anomie and Deviant Behavior*. New York: Free Press.
    1951 *Social Pathology*. New York: McGraw-Hill.

Liazos, Alexander
    1972 "The poverty of the sociology of deviance: Nuts, sluts, and 'preverts.'" *Social Problems* 20 (Summer): 103–120.

Lidz, Charles W. and Andrew L. Walker
    1980 *Heroin, Deviance and Morality*. Beverly Hills: Sage.

Liem, Ramsay and Joan Liem
    1978 "Social class and mental illness reconsidered: The role of economic stress and social support." *Journal of Health and Social Behavior* 19 (June): 139–156.

Lin, Nan, Ronald S. Simeone, Walter M. Ensel and Wen Kuo
    1979 "Social support, stressful life events, and illness: A model and an empirical test." *Journal of Health and Social Behavior* 20 (June): 108–119.

Link, Bruce
    1982 "Mental patient status, work, and income: An examination of the effects of a psychiatric label." *American Sociological Review* 47 (April): 202–215.

Lundman, Richard J.
    1974 "Routine police arrest practices: A commonwealth perspective." *Social Problems* 22 (October): 127–141.

Mankoff, Milton
    1971 "Societal reaction and career deviance: A critical analysis." *Sociological Quarterly* 12 (Spring): 204–218.

Manning, Peter
    1973 "On deviance." *Contemporary Sociology* 2 (March): 123–128.

Marks, Stephen R.
   1974 "Durkheim's theory of anomie." *American Journal of Sociology* 80 (September): 329–363.

Martin, Michael W. and Jane Sell
   1979 "The role of the experiment in the social sciences." *Sociological Quarterly* 20 (Autumn): 581–590.

Marx, Karl and Frederick Engels
   1969–
   1970 *Selected Works* (3 vols.). Moscow: Progress.
   1955 *The Communist Manifesto.* New York: Appleton-Century-Crofts.
   1947 *The German Ideology.* New York: International.

Matza, David
   1969 *Becoming Deviant.* Englewood Cliffs, N.J.: Prentice-Hall.
   1964 *Delinquency and Drift.* New York: Wiley.

McCaghy, Charles H.
   1976 *Deviant Behavior: Crime, Conflict, and Interest Groups.* New York: Macmillan.

McCleary, Richard, Michael J. O'Neal, Thomas Epperlein, Constance Jones and Ronald H. Gray.
   1981 "Effects of Legal Education and Work Experience on Perceptions of Crime Seriousness." *Social Problems* 28 (February): 276–289.

McCord, William and Joan McCord
   1959 *Origins of Crime: A New Evaluation of the Cambridge-Somerville Youth Study.* New York: Columbia University Press.

McCormick, Albert E.
   1977 "Rule enforcement and moral indignation: Some observations on the effects of criminal antitrust convictions upon social reaction processes." *Social Problems* 25 (October): 30–39.

McHugh, Peter
   1970 "A common-sense conception of deviance." Pp. 61–68 in Jack D. Douglas (ed.), *Deviance and Respectability: The Social Construction of Moral Meanings.* New York: Basic Books.

McNeill, William H.
   1976 *Plagues and Peoples.* Garden City, N.Y.: Anchor Press/Doubleday.

Mead, George Herbert
   1934 *Mind, Self and Society.* Chicago: University of Chicago Press.

Mercer, Jane R.
   1973 *Labeling the Retarded.* Berkeley: University of California Press.

Merton, Robert K.
   1976 "The sociology of social problems." Pp. 3–43 in Robert K. Merton and Robert Nisbet (eds.), *Contemporary Social Problems* (4th ed.). New York: Harcourt Brace Jovanovich.
   1966 "Social problems and sociological theory." Pp. 775–823 in Robert K. Merton and Robert Nisbet (eds.), *Contemporary Social Problems* (2d ed.). New York: Harcourt, Brace & World.
   1964 "Anomie, anomia, and social interaction: Contexts of deviant behavior." Pp. 213–242 in Marshall B. Clinard (ed.), *Anomie and Deviant.* New York: Free Press.
   1959 Social conformity, deviation and opportunity structure: A comment on the contributions of Dubin and Cloward." *American Sociological Review* 24 (April): 177–189.
   1957 *Social Theory and Social Structure* (rev. ed.). New York: Free Press.
   1938 "Social structure and anomie." *American Sociological Review* 3 (October): 672–682.

Miles, Agnes
   1981 *The Mentally Ill in Contemporary Society.* New York: St. Martin's.

Miller, Walter B.
   1958 "Lower class culture as a generating milieu of gang delinquency." *Journal of Social Issues* 14: 5–19.

Mills, C. Wright
   1962   *The Marxists*. New York: Dell.
   1959   *The Sociological Imagination*. New York: Oxford.
   1956   *The Power Elite*. New York: Oxford.
   1951   *White Collar: The American Middle Class*. New York: Oxford.
   1942   "The professional ideology of social pathologists." *American Journal of Sociology* 49 (September): 165–180.

Morgan, Patricia A.
   1978   "The legislation drug law: Economic crisis and social control." *Journal of Drug Issues* 8 (Winter): 53–62.

Morris, Christopher
   1977   "Plague in Britain." Pp. 37–47 in *The Plague Reconsidered: A New Look at Its Origins and Effects in Sixteenth and Seventeenth Century England, A Local Population Studies Supplement*. Cambridge: Local Population Studies.

Mueller, Daniel P.
   1980   "Social networks: A promising direction for research on the relationship of the social environment to psychiatric disorder." *Social Science and Medicine* 14A (March): 147–161.

Mugford, Stephen K.
   1974   "Marxism and criminology: A comment on the symposium review on 'The New Criminology.'" *Sociological Quarterly* 15 (Autumn): 591–596.

Murphy, Fred, Mary M. Shirley and Helen M. Witmer
   1946   "The incidence of hidden delinquency." *American Journal of Orthopsychiatry* 16 (October): 686–696.

Musto, David F.
   1973   *The American Disease: Origins of Narcotic Control*. New Haven: Yale University Press.

Myers, Martha A.
   1979   "Offended parties and official reactions: Victims and the sentencing of criminal defendants." *Sociological Quarterly* 20 (Autumn): 529–540.

Neff, James A. and James D. Orcutt
   1978   "Deviance and definitional processes: A conceptual and empirical analysis." *Sociological Quarterly* 19 (Summer): 376–385.

Nettler, Gwynn
   1982   *Criminal Careers, Volume One: Explaining Criminals*. Cincinnati: Anderson.
   1978   *Explaining Crime* (2d ed.). New York: McGraw-Hill.

Newman, Graeme
   1976   *Comparative Deviance: Perception and Law in Six Cultures*. New York: Elsevier.

Nisbet, Robert A.
   1965   *Emile Durkheim*. Englewood Cliffs, N.J.: Prentice-Hall.

Nye, F. Ivan
   1958   *Family Relationships and Delinquent Behavior*. New York: Wiley.

Nye, F. Ivan, James F. Short, Jr. and Virgil J. Olson
   1958   "Socio-economic status and delinquent behavior." *American Journal of Sociology* 63 (January): 381–389.

Orcutt, James D.
   1975   "Deviance as a situated phenomenon: Variations in the social interpretation of marijuana and alcohol use." *Social Problems* 22 (February): 346–356.
   1973   "Societal reaction and the response to deviation in small groups." *Social Forces* 52 (December): 259–267.

Park, Robert E.
   1952   *Human Communities: The Collected Papers*. Glencoe, Ill.: Free Press.

Park, Robert E. and Ernest W. Burgess
   1921   *Introduction to the Science of Sociology*. Chicago: University of Chicago Press.

Parrillo, Vincent N.
    1980   *Strangers to these Shores: Race and Ethnic Relations in the United States.* Boston: Houghton Mifflin.

Parsons, Talcott
    1951   *The Social System.* New York: Free Press.
    1937   *The Structure of Social Action.* New York: McGraw-Hill.

Petrunik, Michael
    1980   "The rise and fall of 'labelling theory': The construction and destruction of a sociological strawman." *Canadian Journal of Sociology* 5 (Summer): 213–233.

Piliavin, Irving and Scott Briar
    1964   "Police encounters with juveniles." *American Journal of Sociology* 63 (January): 381–389.

Platt, Anthony M.
    1975   "Prospects for a radical criminology in the USA." Pp. 95–112 in Ian Taylor, Paul Walton and Jock Young (eds.), *Critical Criminology.* London: Routledge & Kegan Paul.
    1969   *The Child Savers: The Invention of Delinquency.* Chicago: University of Chicago Press.

Pope, Whitney
    1976   *Durkheim's "Suicide": A Classic Analyzed.* Chicago: University of Chicago Press.
    1973   "Classic on a classic: Parsons' interpretation of Durkheim." *American Sociological Review* 38 (August): 399–415.

Porterfield, Austin
    1943   "Delinquency and its outcome in court and college." *American Journal of Sociology* 49 (November): 199–208.

Prus, Robert C.
    1975   "Labeling theory: A Reconceptualization and a propositional statement on typing." *Sociological Focus* 8 (January): 79–96.

Quinney, Richard
    1979   *Criminology* (2d ed.). Boston: Little, Brown.
    1977   *Class, State, and Crime: On the Theory and Practice of Criminal Justice.* New York: McKay.
    1975   *Criminology: Analysis and Critique of Crime in America.* Boston: Little, Brown.
    1974   *Critique of Legal Order: Crime Control in Capitalist Society.* Boston: Little, Brown.
    1973   "Review of *The New Criminology.*" *Sociological Quarterly* 14 (Autumn): 589–594.
    1972   "From repression to liberation: Social theory in a radical age." Pp. 317–341 in Robert A. Scott and Jack D. Douglas (eds.), *Theoretical Perspectives on Deviance.* New York: Basic Books.
    1970   *The Social Reality of Crime.* Boston: Little, Brown.
    1964   "Crime in political perspective." *The American Behavioral Scientist* 8 (December): 19–22.

Radosevich, Marcia, Lonn Lanza-Kaduce, Ronald L. Akers and Marvin D. Krohn
    1980   "The sociology of adolescent drug and drinking behavior: A review of the state of the field: Part II." *Deviant Behavior* 1 (January–March): 145–169.
    1979   "The sociology of adolescent drug and drinking behavior: A review of the state of the field: Part I." *Deviant Behavior* 1 (October–December): 15–35.

Rains, Prudence
    1975   "Imputations of deviance: A Retrospective essay on the labeling perspective." *Social Problems* 23 (October): 1–11.

Reasons, Charles E.
    1975   "Social thought and social structure: Competing paradigms in criminology." *Criminology* 13 (November): 332–365.

Reckless, Walter C.
    1961a *The Crime Problem* (3d ed.). New York: Appleton-Century-Crofts.

1961b "A new theory of delinquency and crime." *Federal Probation* 25 (December): 42–46.
Reiss, Albert J., Jr.
    1971 *The Police and the Public*. New Haven: Yale University Press.
    1951 "Delinquency as the failure of personal and social controls." *American Sociological Review* 16 (April): 196–207.
Reiss, Albert J. and A. Lewis Rhodes
    1961 The distribution of juvenile delinquency in the social class structure." *American Sociological Review* 26 (October): 720–732.
Roman, Paul M. and Harrison M. Trice
    1968 "The sick role, labelling theory and the deviant drinker." *International Journal of Social Psychiatry* 12: 245–251.
Rose, Arnold M. and Holger R. Staub
    1955 "Summary studies on the incidence of mental disorders." Pp. 87–116 in Arnold M. Rose (ed.), *Mental Health and Mental Disorder*. New York: Norton.
Rosenhan, David L.
    1973 "On being sane in insane places." *Science* 179 (January 19): 250–258.
Rossi, Peter H., Emily Waite, Cristine E. Bose and Richard E. Berk
    1974 "The seriousness of crimes: Normative structure and individual differences." *American Sociological Review* 39 (April): 224–237.
Rubington, Earl and Martin S. Weinberg (eds.)
    1981 *The Study of Social Problems*. (3d ed.). New York: Oxford University Press.
    1978 *Deviance: The Interactionist Perspective* (3d ed.). New York: Macmillan.
Rushing, William A. and Jack Esco
    1977 "Status resources and behavioral deviance as contingencies of societal reaction." *Social Forces* 56 (September): 132–147.
Scheff, Thomas J.
    1979 "Reply to comment by Horwitz." *Journal of Health and Social Behavior* 20 (September): 305–306.
    1976 "Reply to Imershein and Simons." *American Sociological Review* 41 (June): 563–564.
    1975 "Reply to Chauncey and Gove." *American Sociological Review* 40 (April): 252–257.
    1974 "The labeling theory of mental illness." *American Sociological Review* 39 (June): 444–452.
    1966 *Being Mentally Ill: A Sociological Theory*. Chicago: Aldine.
Schervish, Paul G.
    1973 "The labeling perspective: Its bias and potential in the study of political deviance." *The American Sociologist* 8 (May): 47–57.
Schur, Edwin M.
    1971 *Labeling Deviant Behavior: Its Sociological Implications*. New York: Harper & Row.
    1969 "Reactions to deviance: A critical assessment." *American Journal of Sociology* 75 (November): 309–322.
    1965 *Crimes Without Victims*. Englewood Cliffs, N.J.: Prentice-Hall.
Schwab, John J. and Mary E. Schwab
    1978 *Sociocultural Roots of Mental Illness: An Epidemiologic Survey*. New York: Plenum Medical.
Scott, Robert A.
    1969 *The Making of Blind Men*. New York: Russell Sage.
Scull, Andrew T.
    1981 *Madhouses, Mad-Doctors, and Madmen: The Social History of Psychiatry in the Victorian Era*. Philadelphia: University of Pennsylvania Press.
    1977 *Decarceration: Community Treatment and the Deviant—A Radical View*. Englewood Cliffs, N.J.: Prentice-Hall.
Sellin, Thorsten
    1938 *Culture Conflict and Crime*. New York: Social Science Research Council, Bulletin 41.
Shaw, Clifford R.
    1930 *The Jack-Roller*. Chicago: University of Chicago Press.

Shaw, Clifford R. and Henry D. McKay
    1942   *Juvenile Delinquency and Urban Areas*. Chicago: University of Chicago Press.

Shaw, Clifford R., Fredrick Zorbaugh, Henry D. McKay and Leonard S. Cottrell
    1929   *Delinquency Areas*. Chicago: University of Chicago Press.

Short, James F., Jr.
    1958   "Differential association with delinquent friends and delinquent behavior." *Pacific Sociological Review* 1 (Spring): 20–25.
    1957   "Differential association with delinquency." *Social Problems* 4 (January): 233–239.

Short, James F. and Robert F. Meier
    1981   "Criminology and the study of deviance." *American Behavioral Scientist* 24 (January–February): 462–478.

Short, James F., Jr. and F. Ivan Nye
    1957–   "Reported behavior as a criterion of deviant behavior." *Social Problems* 5
    1958   (Winter): 207–213.

Short, James F., Jr. and Fred L. Strodtbeck
    1965   *Group Process and Gang Delinquency*. Chicago: University of Chicago Press.
    1963   "The response of gang leaders to status threats: An observation on group process and delinquent behavior." *American Journal of Sociology* 68 (March): 571–579.

Shrewsbury, J. F. D.
    1970   *A History of Bubonic Plague in the British Isles*. Cambridge: Cambridge University Press.

Simmel, Georg
    1955   *Conflict and the Web of Group-Affiliations*. New York: Free Press.

Simmons, J. L.
    1965   "Public stereotypes of deviants." *Social Problems* 13 (Fall): 223–232.

Simon, William and John H. Gagnon
    1976   "The anomie of affluence: A post-Mertonian conception." *American Journal of Sociology* 82 (September): 356–378.

Skinner, B. F.
    1953   *Science and Human Behavior*. New York: Macmillan

Smith, Douglas A. and Christy A. Visher
    1981   "Street level justice: Situational determinants of police arrest practices." *Social Problems* 29 (December): 167–177.

Spector, Malcolm
    1981   "Beyond crime: Seven methods to control troublesome rascals." Pp. 127–156 in H. Laurence Ross (ed.), *Law and Deviance*. Beverly Hills: Sage.

Spector, Malcolm and John I. Kitsuse
    1977   *Constructing Social Problems*. Menlo Park, Calif.: Cummings.

Spitzer, Steven
    1977   "On the Marxian theory of social control: A reply to Horwitz." *Social Problems* 24 (February): 364–365.
    1975   "Toward a Marxian theory of deviance." *Social Problems* 22 (June): 638–651.

Srole, Leo
    1975   "Measurements and classifications in socio-psychiatric epidemiology: Midtown Manhattan Study I (1954) and Midtown Manhattan Restudy II (1974)." *Journal of Health and Social Behavior* 16 (December): 347–364.
    1956   "Social integration and certain corollaries: An exploratory study." *American Sociological Review* 21 (December): 709–716.

Srole, Leo, Thomas S. Langner, Stanley T. Michael, Price Kirkpatrick, Marvin K. Opler and Thomas A. C. Rennie
    1978   *Mental Health in the Metropolis: The Midtown Manhattan Study* (rev. ed.). New York: New York University Press.

Srole, Leo, Thomas S. Langner, Stanley T. Michael, Marvin K. Opler and Thomas A. C. Rennie
    1962 *Mental Health in the Metropolis: The Midtown Manhattan Study.* New York: McGraw-Hill.
Stafford, Mark C. and Sheldon Ekland-Olson
    1982 "On social learning and deviant behavior: A reappraisal of the findings." *American Sociological Review* 47 (February): 167–169.
Stark, Rodney
    1975 *Social Problems.* New York: Random House.
Steffensmeier, Darrell J. and Robert M. Terry
    1975 *Examining Deviance Experimentally: Selected Readings.* Port Washington, N.Y.: Alfred.
    1973 "Deviance and respectability: An observational study of reactions to shoplifting." *Social Forces* 51 (June): 417–426.
Strickland, Donald E.
    1982 " 'Social learning and deviant behavior: A specific test of a general theory': A comment and critique." *American Sociological Review* 47 (February): 162–167.
Sudnow, David
    1965 "Normal crimes: Sociological features of the penal code in a public defense office." *Social Problems* 12 (Winter): 255–276.
Sutherland, Edwin H.
    1956a "Development of the theory." Pp. 13–29 in Albert Cohen, Alfred Lindesmith, and Karl Schuessler (eds.), *The Sutherland Papers.* Bloomington: Indiana University Press.
    1956b "Critique of the theory." Pp. 30–41 in Albert Cohen, Alfred Lindesmith and Karl Schuessler (eds.), *The Sutherland Papers.* Bloomington: Indiana University Press.
    1956c "Crime and the conflict process." In Albert Cohen, Alfred Lindesmith, and Karl Schuessler (eds.), *The Sutherland Papers.* Bloomington: Indiana University Press.
    1949 *White Collar Crime.* New York: Holt, Rinehart & Winston.
    1947 *Principles of Criminology* (4th ed.). Philadelphia: Lippincott.
    1939 *Principles of Criminology* (3d ed.). Philadelphia: Lippincott.
Sutherland, Edwin H. and Donald R. Cressey
    1974 *Criminology* (9th ed.). Philadelphia: Lippincott.
Sykes, Richard E.
    1977 "Techniques of data collection and reduction in systematic field observation." *Behavior Research Methods and Instrumentation* 9: 407–417.
Sykes, Richard E. and John P. Clark
    1975 "A theory of deference exchange in police-civilian encounters." *American Journal of Sociology* 81 (November): 584–600.
Sykes, Gresham M. and David Matza
    1957 "Techniques of neutralization: A theory of delinquency." *American Sociological Review* 22 (December): 644–670.
Szasz, Thomas S.
    1961 *The Myth of Mental Illness.* New York: Hoeber-Harper.
    1960 "The myth of mental illness." *American Psychologist* 15 (February): 113–118.
Tannenbaum, Frank
    1938 *Crime and the Community.* Boston: Ginn.
Taylor, Ian, Paul Walton and Jock Young
    1975 *Critical Criminology.* London: Routledge & Kegan Paul.
    1973 *The New Criminology: For a Social Theory of Deviance.* New York: Harper & Row.
Thielbar, Gerald W. and Saul D. Feldman
    1978 "Images of deviants and their behavior: Stereotypes and social context." Pp. 265–280 in Saul D. Feldman (ed.), *Deciphering Deviance.* Boston: Little, Brown.

Thio, Alex
    1973 "Class bias in the sociology of deviance." *The American Sociologist* 8 (February): 1–12.

Thoits, Peggy and Michael Hannan
    1979 "Income and psychological distress: The impact of an income-maintenance experiment." *Journal of Health and Social Behavior* 20 (June): 120–138.

Timasheff, Nicholas S. and George A. Theodorson
    1976 *Sociological Theory: Its Nature and Growth* (4th ed.). New York: Random House.

Tittle, Charles R.
    1980 *Sanctions and Social Deviance: The Question of Deterrence*. New York: Praeger.

Tittle, Charles R., Wayne J. Villemez and Douglas A. Smith
    1978 "The myth of social class and criminality: An empirical assessment of the empirical evidence." *American Sociological Review* 43 (October): 643–656.

Toby, Jackson
    1957 "Social disorganization and stake in conformity: Complementary factors in the predatory behavior of hoodlums." *Journal of Criminal Law, Criminology and Police Science* 48 (May–June): 12–17.

Traub, Stuart H. and Craig B. Little (eds.)
    1980 *Theories of Deviance* (2d ed.). Itasca, Ill.: Peacock.

Tuchman, Barbara W.
    1978 *A Distant Mirror: The Calamitous 14th Century*. New York: Knopf.

Turk, Austin T.
    1976a "Law as a weapon in social conflict." *Social Problems* 23 (February): 276–291.
    1976b "Law, conflict, and order: From theorizing toward theories." *Canadian Review of Sociology and Anthropology* 13 (August): 282–294.
    1974 "Review of *The New Criminology*." *Contemporary Sociology* 3 (May): 217–219.
    1969 *Criminality and Legal Order*. Chicago: Rand McNally.
    1966 "Conflict and criminality." *American Sociological Review* 31 (June): 338–352.
    1964a "Prospects for theories of criminal behavior." *Journal of Criminal Law, Criminology and Police Science* 55 (December): 454–461.
    1964b "Toward construction of a theory of delinquency." *Journal of Criminal Law, Criminology and Police Science* 55 (June): 215–229.

Turner, R. Jay
    1981 "Social support as a contingency in psychological well-being." *Journal of Health and Social Behavior* 22 (December): 357–367.

Turner, R. Jay and John W. Gartrell
    1978 "Social factors in psychiatric outcome: Toward the resolution of interpretive controversies." *American Sociological Review* 43 (June): 368–382.

Turner, R. Jay and Morton O. Wagenfeld
    1967 "Occupational mobility and schizophrenia: An assessment of the social causation and social selection hypotheses." *American Sociological Review* 32 (February): 104–113.

Vold, George B.
    1958 *Theoretical Criminology*. New York: Oxford.

Voss, Harwin L.
    1966 "Socio-economic status and reported delinquent behavior." *Social Problems* 13 (Winter): 314–324.

Waller, Willard
    1936 "Social problems and the mores." *American Sociological Review* 1 (December): 924–933.

Weber, Max
    1958 *The Protestant Ethic and the Spirit of Capitalism*. New York: Scribner's.

Webster, William H.
    1977 *Crime in the United States,* 1977. Washington, D.C.: U.S. Department of Justice.

Wheaton, Blair
    1980 "The sociogenesis of psychological disorder: An attributional theory." *Journal of Health and Social Behavior* 21 (June): 100–124.
    1978 "The sociogenesis of psychological disorder: Reexamining the causal issues with longitudinal data." *American Sociological Review* 43 (June): 383–403.

Wiedeman, George H. et al.
    1973 "Brief communications." *Bulletin of the Menninger Clinic* 37 (September): 519–530.

Williams, Ann W., John E. Ware, Jr. and Cathy A. Donald
    1981 "A model of mental health, life events, and social supports applicable to general populations." *Journal of Health and Social Behavior* 22 (December): 324–336.

Williams, Franklin Pruitt
    1976 *On the Question of Differential Justice: A Look at a Criminal Justice System.* Unpublished doctoral dissertation. Tallahassee: Florida State University.

Wilson, Thomas P.
    1970 "Conceptions of interaction and forms of sociological explanation." *American Sociological Review* 35 (August): 697–710.

Winslow, Robert W.
    1970 *Society in Transition: A Social Approach to Deviancy.* New York: Free Press.

Wolff, Kurt H. (ed.)
    1950 *The Sociology of Georg Simmel.* New York: Free Press.

Wolfgang, Marvin E. and Franco Ferracuti
    1967 *The Subculture of Violence: Toward an Integrated Theory in Criminology.* London: Tavistock.

Wuebben, Paul L., Bruce C. Straits and Gary I. Schulman (eds.)
    1974 *The Experiment as a Social Occasion.* Berkeley: Glendessary Press.

Yinger, J. Milton
    1960 "Contraculture and subculture." *American Sociological Review* 25 (October): 625–635.

Name index

A

Adams, Reed, 156, 158
Ageton, Suzanne S., 148
Akers, Ronald L., 60–61, 62, 68, 156–57, 158, 168, 195, 203, 207, 221, 311, 339
Albonetti, Celesta, 308
Alvarez, R., 304, 305
Alwin, Duane, 308
Anderson, Nels, 37
Andrew, F. M., 210, 219
Andrews, F., 138
Andrews, Kenneth H., 202, 203
Anslinger, Harry J., 371, 373–78, 380–85
Aronson, Elliot, 291
Asbury, Herbert, 367
Asch, S. E., 269, 304, 305
Ash, P., 268
Astrachan, B., 219, 220

B

Bahr, S., 208, 219
Baker, R., 134
Bales, Robert F., 294, 306
Balkan, Sheila, 51
Ball, D. W., 293, 305
Ball, John C., 48
Ball, S., 134
Ball-Rokeach, 133
Bancroft, H. H., 369, 370
Bankowski, Zenon, 333
Barry, A., 268
Bartels, Robert, 268
Bayley, David H., 273, 287
Beach, Walter, 370
Bean, J. M. W., 339
Beccaria, Cesare, 323
Beck, A. T., 268

Becker, Howard S., 20, 22–23, 25, 49, 50, 53, 60, 61, 62, 63–65, 108, 126, 162, 184–92, 197, 199–203, 224, 227, 230–38, 241, 242, 246, 249, 268, 289, 304, 305, 327, 338, 359, 368, 370, 371–77, 382–85, 388
Beirne, Piers, 334
Belknap, I., 268
Bell, Wendell, 48
Benedict, R., 268
Bentham, Jeremy, 323
Bentler, P. M., 221
Berger, Alan S., 220, 221
Berger, Ronald J., 51
Berk, Richard E., 355–57
Bernard, Jessie, 208, 219
Bernstein, Ilene N., 308
Bickman, L., 293, 305
Birnbaum, J., 208, 219
Bittner, Egon, 273, 275, 277, 286, 287
Black, Donald J., 58, 270, 273, 275, 277, 278, 279, 281, 282, 286, 287, 292, 305
Blackstone, William, 105, 126
Blake, R. R., 292, 293, 306
Blalock, Hubert M., Jr., 275, 287
Blau, Peter M., 272, 287
Bloch, Herbert A., 173
Blum, Alan F., 240
Blumenthal, M., 138
Blumer, Herbert, 60, 225, 226
Bohr, R. H., 268
Bonger, Willem, 107, 126
Bonnie, Richard J., 375–77, 381, 382, 384, 385
Bord, Richard, 307
Bordua, David J., 64, 75, 83
Bose, Cristine E., 355–57
Bowers, R. V., 92
Braatoy, Trygve, 91
Bradshaw, F., 343, 346
Braginsky, B. M., 268

407

NAME INDEX

Braginsky, D. D., 268
Braithwaite, John, 148
Brecher, Edward M., 367
Brent, Edward E., 271
Briar, Scott, 18, 58, 158, 162, 270, 275, 279, 281, 282, 286, 288, 292, 306
Britt, David W., 203
Brittan, Arthur, 152
Brody, E. B., 268
Bruner, J. S., 269
Burgess, Ernest W., 37, 38–39, 40
Burgess, Robert L., 60, 61, 68, 156, 157, 315
Burkett, Steven R., 201, 203

C

Cameron, Mary O., 293, 306
Campbell, A., 209, 219
Campbell, Donald T., 289
Campbell, Ernest Q., 203
Carey, James T., 36, 293, 306
Carlsmith, J. Merril, 291
Carter, Timothy J., 58
Caudill, W., 268
Cavan, Ruth S., 83
Chambliss, William J., 60, 107, 108, 110, 124, 126, 127, 277, 285, 287, 319, 338–55, 372, 388
Chandler, P. J., 292, 306
Chapman, Dennis, 108, 123
Chauncey, Robert L., 307
Chin, Thomas W., 369, 370
Chirot, Daniel, 340
Chisolm, L., 208, 219
Chisolm, Roderick M., 92
Chilton, Roland J., 75
Chiu, Ping, 361, 369, 370
Chorover, Stephan L., 386, 387
Cicouvel, Aaron V., 26, 49, 58, 240, 292, 306
Clark, John P., 58, 271, 273, 274, 287, 288, 309
Clark, Robert E., 92
Clayton, Richard R., 221
Cleary, Paul D., 147
Clelland, Donald, 58
Clinard, Marshall B., 9, 41, 43
Cloward, Richard A., 46, 47, 68, 74, 75, 79–82, 83, 106, 124, 126, 127, 153, 155, 173, 183, 184
Cohen, Albert K., 45, 46, 47, 68, 75, 77–79, 81, 82, 83, 125, 127, 151, 153, 158, 169, 171, 195, 201, 203, 226
Cohen, Lawrence E., 308
Cole, Stephen, 75
Comte, Auguste, 33, 34
Conrad, Peter, 386
Cooley, Charles H., 225
Coolidge, Mary Roberts, 360, 370
Cooper, Courtney Ryley, 376

Cooper, Marcia, 92
Coser, Lewis A., 33, 48, 315, 316
Crain, R., 138
Cressey, Donald R., 14, 15, 45, 59, 153, 155, 174, 189, 203, 204, 221, 226, 358
Cressey, Paul, 37
Crowne, D., 136
Cumming, E., 208, 219, 268
Cumming, J., 268
Curtis, Lynn, 109, 125, 127, 128
Cutter, Henry S. G., 182

D

Dahrendorf, Ralf, 48, 316
Darley, D. M., 292, 297, 306
Davie, Maurice R., 94
Davis, Keith E., 240
Davis, Kingsley, 92
Davis, Nannette, J., 33, 51, 56, 60, 239, 329
Denis, G., 219, 220
Denner, B., 292, 297, 306
Dentler, Robert A., 49
Deutscher, Irwin, 352
Dickson, Donald T., 373, 374, 376, 377, 380–85
Dietrick, David C., 83
Dohrenwend, Barbara Snell, 147, 205
Dohrenwend, Bruce P., 147, 205
Doleschal, E., 120, 127
Dollard, John, 92
Donald, Cathay A., 221
Doob, Anthony N., 291
Douglas, Jack D., 71, 239, 292, 293, 306
Doyle, Patricia, 308
Draguns, J. G., 268
Dubin, Robert, 75
Dunham, H. Warren, 92, 147
Durkheim, Emile, 68–71, 72, 73, 76, 84, 87, 152, 158, 159, 160, 205–207, 235, 312, 322–24, 337–39
Duster, Troy, 359, 368, 370

E

Eaton, William W., 9, 147, 207
Eaves, Lucille, 362, 370
Eckhard, Kenneth W., 272
Edelman, Murray, 384, 385
Ekland-Olson, Sheldon, 221
Elliot, Delbert S., 148
Emerson, Robert M., 292, 306
Empey, LaMar T., 148, 220
Engels, Friedrich, 312, 313, 330, 337
Ennis, P., 135
Ensel, Walter M., 221
Epperlein, Thomas, 357

NAME INDEX

Erikson, Kai T., 22, 49, 50, 53, 54, 108, 127, 223, 224, 227, 231, 232, 234–35, 236–37, 238, 241, 338
Erlanger, Howard S., 88, 129, 130, 131, 132–46, 147, 148, 204, 220
Esco, Jack, 307

F

Farina, A., 269
Faris, Robert E. L., 36, 92
Feld, Sheila, 208, 209, 219
Feldman, H., 209, 220
Felix, R. H., 92
Ferracuti, Franco, 68, 82, 106, 124, 125, 126, 128, 129, 133, 140, 142, 145
Figlio, Robert, 109, 128
Finestone, Harold, 36, 183
Fleischman, Paul R., 248
Fonda, C. P., 268
Foner, Philip S., 369
Foote, Caleb, 344, 351, 352
Fox, James C., 272
Freed, A., 292, 306
Freedman, Jonathan L., 291
Freeman, H. E., 269
Freidson, Elliot, 239
Friedman, N., 354
Freudenberg, R. K., 269
Fuller, Richard C., 50, 226, 316

G

Gagnon, John H., 76
Galle, Omar, 209, 219
Galliher, John R., 185, 203, 338, 371–86
Gartrell, John W., 147
Gastil, Raymond D., 132, 133, 137, 145
Geerken, Michael, 168, 205, 206, 207–20, 221
Geertz, Hildred S., 182
Geis, Gilbert, 341
Gerard, Donald L., 91
Gibbs, Jack P., 54, 55, 62
Gilmore, H. R., 268
Ginsberg, Irving J., 201, 202, 203
Glaser, Daniel, 60, 155, 156, 157, 226
Glynn, Thomas J., 221
Goffman, Erving, 108, 127, 174, 238, 268, 293, 294, 306
Gold, Martin, 110, 111, 120, 127, 128
Goldkamp, John, 106, 127
Goldman, A. R., 268
Goldman, Nathan, 279, 286
Goldstein, Michael S., 221
Goode, Erich, 195, 203, 238
Gottfredson, Michael, 117, 127
Gould, Leroy, 110, 120, 127
Gould, Madelyn Schwartz, 147, 205

Gouldner, Alvin W., 64, 242, 327, 328
Gove, Walter, 168, 205, 206, 207–20, 221, 238, 307, 308
Graham, H., 132
Gray, Ronald H., 357
Green, H. W., 92
Greenley, James R., 201, 202, 203, 307
Griffin, Brenda S., 201, 203
Griffin, Charles T., 201, 203
Gurin, Gerald, 219
Gurr, T., 132
Gusfield, Joseph R., 312, 316–19, 335, 337, 338, 357–60, 368–70, 384, 385, 386, 388

H

Hackney, Sheldon, 132, 133
Hagan, John, 308
Hall, Jerome, 340, 353, 354
Halsbury, Earl of, 350, 351
Hannan, Michael, 147
Harary, Frank, 75
Hartley, Eugene S., 174
Haven, H., 146
Hawkins, M. J., 71
Hawkins, Richard, 235, 237, 240
Head, K., 138
Heider, Fritz, 240
Heise, David, 203
Helmer, John, 358, 359, 365, 367, 370, 388
Henderson, Scott, 221
Hepburn, John R., 329
Hester, Clinton M., 378–80, 382–84
Hewitt, John, 308
Hindelang, Michael J., 88, 102, 103, 104–28, 147, 148, 158, 204, 206
Hinkle, Gisela J., 32, 33, 35, 42
Hinkle, Roscoe C., 32, 33, 35, 42
Hirschi, Travis, 68, 110, 127, 148, 158–61, 162, 167, 204, 206, 207, 220, 221
Hirst, Paul Q., 333
Hoffman, Lois W., 219
Hollander, E. P., 304, 306
Hollingshead, August B., 48, 88, 89, 90, 91–102, 147, 204, 205, 269
Holzman, Philip S., 248
Homans, George, 173, 304, 306
Horwitz, Allan, 307, 339
Huba, G. J., 221
Hughes, E. C., 293, 306
Hughes, M., 209, 219
Humphreys, Land, 292, 306
Hyde, Robert W., 91

I–J

Imershein, Allen W., 307
Inkeles, Alex, 71, 152

Jacobs, David, 334
Jacobson, L., 269
Jansyn, Leon, 174
Jaquith, Susan M., 221
Jeffery, C. Ray, 60, 68, 156
Jensen, Eric L., 201, 203
Jensen, Gary F., 168, 333
Johnson, Barclay D., 71
Johnson, Bruce D., 195, 201, 202, 203, 204
Johnson, Richard E., 221
Jones, Constance, 357
Jones, Edward E., 240

K

Kahn, R., 138
Kandel, Denis B., 168, 195, 201, 202, 203, 204, 221
Kane, H. H., 366, 370
Kaplan, John, 268, 371
Kassebaum, Gene, 294, 306
Kelley, Clarence, 116, 121, 127
Kelley, Harold H., 240
Kelley, William R., 308
Kennedy, Ruby J. R., 94
Kessler, Ronald C., 147
Kick, Edward, 308
Kingsley, Lowell V., 91
Kirk, Stuart, 307
Kirkpatrick, Price, 205
Kitsuse, John I., 17, 18, 22, 26, 49, 50, 53, 54, 57, 58, 62, 83, 108, 127, 224, 227, 230, 231, 232, 233–34, 235, 237, 238, 239, 241, 247, 289, 292, 293, 306, 308, 316, 321
Kittrie, Nicholas N., 386, 387
Klein, Viola, 208, 220
Kleiner, Robert J., 147
Kluckhohn, Clyde, 92
Kluegel, James R., 308
Kobrin, Solomon, 183
Kohn, Martin, 174
Kohout, Frank J., 300, 306
Kornhauser, Ruth Rosner, 220
Kreitman, N., 268
Krohn, Marvin D., 158, 168, 195, 201, 203, 204, 221
Kuhn, Thomas S., 238
Kuo, Wen, 221

L

Lacey, Forrest W., 352
Lachapelle, R., 219, 220
Lacy, William B., 221
LaFree, Gary, 308
Lander, Bernard, 75
Lane, Roger, 286, 287
Langner, Thomas S., 147, 205, 208, 219

Lanza-Kaduce, Lonn, 158, 168, 195, 203, 221
Larkin, William E., 307
Latane, B., 292, 297, 306
Lazer, C., 208, 219
Lefkowitz, M., 292, 293, 306
LeMasters, E. E., 219, 220
Lemert, Edwin M., 22, 49, 50, 53, 55, 62, 64, 108, 128, 223, 226–31, 232, 235, 236, 237, 238, 239, 241, 293, 306, 308
Lemkau, Paul, 92, 268
Leung, Jan T., 308
Liazos, Alexander, 50, 55, 56, 239, 242, 286, 287, 328
Liell, John T., 285, 287
Liem, Joan, 147, 205
Liem, Ramsay, 147, 205
Lin, Nan, 221
Lind, Bruce, 147, 205
Lindesmith, Alfred, 195, 201, 203, 340, 359, 370, 374, 375, 377, 382–85
Lindzey, G., 269
Link, Bruce, 308
Linsky, A. S., 269
Lippitt, Ronald, 174
Little, Craig B., 36
Lofland, John, 293, 304, 306
Loftin, Colin, 133, 137, 146
Loman, L. Anthony, 307
Lopata, Helena, 208, 220
Lundman, Richard J., 246, 269–88, 289, 307, 308
Luton, Frank H., 92

M

Maccoby, Eleanor, 174
MacMillan A., 219, 220
Malamud, Irene, 92
Malamud, William, 92
Malzberg, B., 92
Mancuso, J. C., 269
Mandel, Rudolf, 182
Mankoff, Milton, 239
Manning, Peter, 238
Marden, Charles F., 285, 287
Marks, Stephen R., 71
Marlowe, D., 136
Martin, J. C., 294, 306
Martin, Michael W., 291
Marx, Karl, 60, 311–14, 325–27, 330, 331, 333, 337, 338, 340
Matza, David, 37, 41, 42, 46, 47, 60, 68, 83, 158, 162, 163, 190, 204, 224
McCaghy, Charles H., 320, 321
McCleary, Richard, 357
McConnell, John W., 94
McCord, Joan, 291
McCord, William, 291

McCormick, Albert E., 21
McEvoy, James, 135
McFarland, Paul T., 272
McHugh, Peter, 240
McKay, Henry D., 41, 43, 45, 79
McNeill, William H., 339
McWilliams, Carey, 361, 370
Mead, George Herbert, 225, 226
Mechanic, David, 275, 287
Megargee, Edwin I., 146
Meier, Robert F., 9, 41, 309
Mendelsohn, Harold, 273, 287
Mensh, I. N., 269
Mercer, Jane R., 239
Merton, Robert K., 12–13, 14, 15, 31–32, 43–45, 46, 48, 50, 53, 59, 68, 71–77, 78, 79–80, 81, 83, 84, 106, 124, 126, 128, 146, 147, 148, 153, 158, 159, 163, 324
Meyer, Gladys, 285, 287
Michael, Stanley T., 147, 205
Miles, Agnes, 147
Milewski, Maureen, 273, 275, 287
Miller, Neal, 92
Miller, Walter B., 46, 47–48, 68, 82, 169, 182, 316
Mills, C. Wright, 32, 35, 327, 328
Mischel, W., 258, 269
Monroe, Lawrence J., 49
Morgan, J. N., 210, 219
Morgan, Patricia A., 338, 358–71, 388
Morris, Christopher, 339
Morrisey, J., 268
Mouton, J. S., 292, 293, 306
Mueller, Daniel P., 221
Mugford, Stephen K., 333
Mulvihill, D., 109, 125, 128
Mungham, Geoff, 333
Murdock, G. P., 94
Murphy, Fred, 48
Murray, Henry A., 92
Musto, David F., 348, 349, 370, 371, 374, 375, 381–85
Myers, J., 219, 220
Myers, Jerome K., 94
Myers, Martha A., 308
Myers, Richard R., 50, 226, 316
Myrdal, Alva, 208, 220

N

Nagasawa, Richard, 110, 126
Neff, James A., 309
Nettler, Gwynn, 120, 126, 128, 148, 204
Neugebaure, Richard, 147, 205
Newcomb, Theodore M., 174
Newman, Graeme, 335
Nisbet, Robert A., 71
Nunnally, J. C., 269

Nye, F. Ivan, 48, 49, 68, 158, 161, 167, 206, 208, 217, 219, 220

O

Ohlin, Lloyd E., 46, 47, 68, 74, 75, 79–82, 83, 106, 124, 126, 127, 153, 155, 169, 173, 183, 184
O'Neal, Michael J., 357
Opler, Marvin K., 205
Orcutt, James D., 185–204, 239, 240, 309
Orne, E., 269

P

Park, Robert E., 37, 38, 315
Parker, Seymour, 147
Parrillo, Vincent N., 358
Parsons, Talcott, 71, 75, 92, 235, 294, 306
Pearlin, L., 208, 220
Pellens, Mildren, 370, 371
Pepinsky, Harold E., 371
Petersen, David M., 201, 277, 280, 286, 287
Petrullo, L., 269
Petrunik, Michael, 309
Pettigrew, Thomas F., 132
Pfautz, Harold W., 183
Phillips, D. L., 294, 306
Phillips, L., 258, 268, 269
Phillips, Patricia, 147
Piliavin, Irving, 18, 58, 158, 162, 270, 275, 279, 280, 281, 282, 286, 288, 292, 306
Platt, Anthony M., 319
Polansky, Norman, 174
Pollak, Otto, 294, 306
Polsky, Howard, 174
Pope, Whitney, 71
Porterfield, Austin, 48
Prus, Robert C., 240

Q–R

Quinney, Richard, 22, 23–26, 51, 62, 107, 124, 128, 280, 286, 288, 314, 320, 321, 329–34
Radloff, L., 208, 209, 220
Radosevich, Marcia, 158, 168, 195, 203, 221
Rains, Prudence, 50, 227, 230
Reasons, Charles E., 11, 374–77, 381–85
Reckless, Walter C., 158, 161, 294, 306
Redl, Fritz, 174
Redlich, Frederick C., 48, 88, 89, 90, 91–102, 147, 204, 205, 268, 269
Reed, J., 133, 138, 144, 145
Reimer, David, 110, 111, 120, 127
Reinarman, Craig, 358
Reiss, Albert J., Jr., 58, 68, 117, 120, 128, 158, 162, 270, 275, 278, 279, 281, 286, 287, 288, 305

Remington, Frank J., 273, 288
Rennie, Thomas A. C., 205
Reynolds, H. T., 194, 204
Rheinstein, M., 354
Rhoades, Larry, 291
Rhodes, A. Lewis, 58
Ring, K., 268, 269
Robertson, J. P., 269
Rollins, B., 209, 220
Roman, Paul M., 239
Rosanoff, A. J., 91
Rose, Arnold M., 9, 208, 220, 341
Rosen, Sidney, 174
Rosenberg, Morris, 275, 288
Rosenblum, Victor G., 273, 288
Rosenhan, David L., 246-69, 307, 309
Rosenhan, M. S., 269
Rosenthal, R., 269
Rossi, Peter H., 355-57
Roth, William F., 92
Rubington, Earl, 17, 31, 34, 43, 224, 238
Ruesch, Jurgen, 92
Rushing, William A., 307

S

Sainsburg, P., 268
Sandemeyer, E. C., 361, 362, 371
Sarbin, T. R., 269
Scarpitti, Frank R., 272
Scheff, Thomas J., 238, 268, 293, 306, 307-8
Schervish, Paul G., 56
Schmidt, Janet, 51
Schmitt, H. O., 268
Schneider, Joseph W., 386
Schrivener J., 268
Schuessler, Karl, 195, 201, 203, 300, 306
Schulman, Gary I., 291
Schulz, Barbara, 308
Schur, Edwin M., 61, 62, 227, 238, 239, 294, 306
Schwab, John J., 147, 204, 205
Schwab, Mary E., 147, 204, 205
Schwartz, C., 219, 220
Schwartz, M. S., 269
Scott, Robert A., 239
Scott, W. Richard, 272, 287
Scoville, S. E., 269
Scull, Andrew T., 386
Seeman, W., 268
Seiler, L., 219, 220
Sell, Jane, 291
Sellin, Thorsten, 43, 45, 109, 110, 128, 315
Seward, George F., 370
Shapiro, D., 269
Sharp, L., 208, 220
Shaw, Clifford R., 37, 40, 41, 43, 45, 79

Short, James F., Jr., 48, 49, 83, 158, 168-85, 220, 309
Shrewsbury, J. F. D., 339, 340
Siedman, Robert, 107, 108, 124, 127
Siegel, Joseph, 91
Silver, Allan, 280, 286, 288
Simeone, Ronald S., 221
Simmel, Georg, 315
Simmons, J. L., 3, 4, 6, 7, 16, 293, 306
Simmons, O. G., 269
Simon, William, 76, 220, 221
Simons, Ronald L., 307
Single, Eric, 202, 204
Skinner, B. F., 157
Skolnick, Jerome H., 274, 280, 286, 288
Smith, Douglas A., 147, 148, 204, 308
Somers, Robert H., 194, 204
Sonquist, J. A., 210, 219
Spector, Malcolm, 316, 321, 386
Spencer, Herbert, 33, 34
Spier, Rosalind Barclay, 132
Spitzer, Steven, 60, 329-34
Spradley, James P., 275, 280, 285, 286, 288
Srinivasan, Barbara, 147
Srole, Leo, 48, 75, 147, 205
Stafford, Mark C., 221
Stanley, Julian C., 289
Stanton, A. H., 269
Stark, Rodney, 135, 161
Staub, Holger R., 9
Steffensmeier, Darrel J., 246, 288-307, 338
Steffensmeier, Renee, 291
Steinberg, T. A., 268
Stern, Ludwig, 91
Stone, G. P., 293, 306
Straits, Bruce C., 291
Strickland, Donald E., 221
Strodtbeck, Fred L., 83, 168-85, 220
Sudnow, David, 240, 273, 288, 293, 306
Sutherland, Edwin H., 12, 14-15, 32, 43-45, 48, 50, 59, 60, 61, 68, 79, 80, 82, 151, 153-58, 167, 168, 186, 189, 190, 192, 195, 197, 199, 200-202, 204, 221, 315, 316
Sutherland, J. F., 91
Sykes, Gresham M., 46, 47, 68, 83, 163
Sykes, Richard E., 271, 274, 288, 309
Szasz, Thomas, 238

T

Tagiuri, R., 269
Tannenbaum, Frank, 22, 49, 108, 128, 226, 235-36
Taylor, Ian, 50, 56, 60, 61, 62, 64, 67, 157, 311, 314, 323-26, 329, 333, 334, 338, 386
Terry, Charles, 370, 371
Terry, Robert M., 246, 288-307, 338

NAME INDEX

Theodorson, George A., 327
Thio, Alex, 20, 50, 56, 242, 286, 288, 328, 329
Thoits, Peggy, 147
Thomas, Charles W., 201
Thomas, W. I., 36, 37, 225
Tiedeman, Gary, 235, 237, 240
Tietze, C., 92
Timasheft, Nicholas S., 327
Tittle, Charles R., 147, 148, 167, 204, 221
Toby, Jackson, 158
Tousignant, M., 219, 220
Towers, J., 268
Traub, Stuart H., 36
Trice, Harrison M., 239
Tuchman, Barbara W., 339
Tumin, M., 109, 125, 128
Turk, Austin T., 321, 322, 333
Turner, R., Jay, 147, 221

V

Veroff, Joseph, 219
Villemez, Wayne J., 147, 148, 204
Visher, Christy A., 308
Vold, George B., 48, 315, 316
Voss, Harwin L., 220

W

Wagenfeld, Morton O., 147
Walker, Allyn, 185, 203, 338, 371–86
Waller, Willard, 50, 226, 316
Walton, Paul, 50, 56, 60, 61, 62, 64, 67, 157, 311, 314, 323–26, 329, 333, 334, 338, 386
Ward, David A., 294, 306
Ware, John E., Jr., 221
Warner, W. L., 92
Weber, Max, 337, 338, 340, 354
Webster, William H., 270
Weinberg, Martin S., 17, 31, 34, 43, 224, 238
Weis, Joseph G., 148, 204
Weisman, C., 138
Wenninger, Eugene P., 58
Werthman, Carl, 280, 288
Westie, F. R., 294, 306
Wexler, D. B., 269
Whatley, C. D., 294, 306
Wheaton, Blair, 147
Wheeler, S., 292, 306
White, William A., 91
White, William Foote, 173, 178
Whitebread, Charles H., II, 375–77, 381, 382, 384, 385
Whitney, Fraine, 288
Wiedeman, George H., 248
Wieder, D. Lawrence, 203, 204
Wilkins, Leslie, 120, 127
Williams, Ann W., 221
Williams, Franklin Pruitt, 58
Williams, Jay, 110, 120, 128
Williams, Robin M., Jr., 294, 306
Wilson, James Q., 279, 286, 288
Wilson, Orlando W., 285, 288
Wilson, Thomas P., 60
Winslow, Robert W., 36
Wiseman, Jacqueline P., 275, 288
Wishner, J., 269
Wolff, Kurt H., 315
Wolfgang, Marvin E., 68, 82, 106, 109, 110, 120, 124, 125, 126, 128, 129, 133, 140, 142, 145
Woodward, William C., 378–80
Wuebben, Paul L., 291
Wunsch-Hitzig, Robin, 147, 205

Y–Z

Yablonsky, Lewis, 183
Yinger, J. Milton, 83
Young, Jock, 50, 56, 60, 61, 62, 64, 67, 157, 311, 314, 323–27, 329, 333, 334, 338, 386
Young, Peter, 333
Zigler, E., 258, 269
Zimmerman, Don H., 203, 204
Zingraff, Matthew T., 201
Znaniecki, Florian, 36, 37
Zubin, J., 268
Zuckerman, Harriet, 75

Subject index

A–B

Anomia, 75–76
Anomie
  of affluence, 76
  and social structure, 71–75
  and suicide rates, 69–71
  theory, 12–13, 44
Attribution theory, 240–41
Black Death, 339–40, 342–44
Blue laws, 354

C

Capitalist society, 313–14
Chicago School of sociology, 35–42
Chinese immigration, 360–65
Class
  bias in arrest, 280, 284
  conflict, 313–14
  and delinquency, 170–71
  variations in
    crime, 48–49
    mental disorder, 89, 91–102
Concentric zone model, 38–40
Conflict theory, 21, 23–26, 107, 311–12, 333–35
Conformity, explanation of, 158–59
Control tradition, 158–63
Crime
  perceived seriousness, 355–57
  and social class, 48–49, 58–59, 147–48
Criminalization, 321–22
Critical criminology; see Neo-Marxist theory
Culture conflict, 45, 315

D

Delinquency
  and control theory, 161
  and drift, 163

Delinquency—*Cont.*
  and subcultural theory, 77
Delinquent gangs, 169–84
Detached workers program, 169, 174
Deviance
  public definitions of, 3–4
  sociological definitions of, 5–7, 26–27, 53–56
Deviant
  behavior, 43–45
  career, 22–23, 230, 232, 236
Dialectical analysis, 323
Differential association
  and determinism, 60–61, 157
  and marijuana use, 188–90
  theory, 14–15, 44–45, 153–55
Differential association-reinforcement theory, 60–61, 156–58
Differential identification theory, 155–56
Drug-related crime, 355–58

E

Ecological research, 37–40
Egoism and suicide, 159–60
Employment and mental health, 207–20
Ethnomethodology, 239–40
Eugenic movement, 387
Experimental research, 289–91, 298–99
Explanation of deviant behavior
  and determinism, 59–62
  and normative perspective, 10–12
  sociological versus psychological, 151–52, 157–58

H–I

Historical research, 337–40, 371–72
Homicide rate, 132
Illegitimate opportunity, 79–82, 124–25, 155

415

SUBJECT INDEX

Interactionist social psychology; *see* Symbolic interactionism
Interest group conflict, 319–22
Interpretive theory, 60–62, 225–26

L

Labeling theory, 20, 22–23, 230–42, 292–93, 307–9, 327–29
Levels of analysis, 11–12
Longitudinal research, 202
Lower-class culture, 82
Lumpenproletariat, 314, 330

M

Macro-normative approach, 12–13
Macro-relativistic approach, 21, 23–26
Marijuana
  effects, 187–88
  legislation, 371–85
  use, 185–204
Mental disorder,
  epidemiology, 88–89
  labeling of, 238, 246–47, 250, 255–58, 307–8
  and marital status, 208–9
  and social class, 91–102, 147
  untreated prevalence, 204–5
Micro-normative approach, 14–15, 151–52
Micro-relativistic approach, 20, 22–23
Moral
  boundary, 234
  entrepreneur, 232, 359, 371
Motivation of deviant behavior, 220–21

N

Nazi Germany, 387–88
Neo-Marxist theory, 322–33
Norm
  types, 7–8
  violations, 53–54, 227–28
Normative
  period, 31, 43–49
  perspective on deviance, 7–12, 43, 67–68

O–P

Observational research, 245–46, 270–72
Opium control, 358–69
Police
  arrest practices, 274–86
  reactions, 18, 270–72, 308
Political economy, 329–30
Positivism, 33
Primary deviation, 229
Prohibition movement, 316–19
Psychiatric
  hospitalization, 251–55, 258–63

Psychiatric—*Cont.*
  symptoms, 204–5, 214–16
Public drunkenness, 270, 275–85

R–S

Race
  and crime rates, 104–28
  and police discrimination, 279–80, 283
Relativistic
  period, 31, 49–51
  perspective on deviance, 15–22, 49–50, 223
Secondary deviation, 229–30, 235–37
Self-concept, 161, 229
Self-report survey, 48–49, 110, 129, 191–92
Sex differences
  in arrest, 279
  in labeling, 293–94, 301–3
  in psychiatric disorder, 207–9
Shoplifting, reactions to, 290–305
Social
  audience, 223
  bonding
    and mental disorder, 205–7, 221
    theory of delinquency, 159–61
  control, 235–36, 245, 331–32
  disorganization
    concept, 36
    period, 31, 35–43
  learning tradition, 153–58
  pathology
    concept, 34
    period, 31, 32–35
Societal reaction, 224, 228–30; *see also* Labeling theory
Status politics, 316–19
Sterilization, 387
Subculture
  content, 82
  formation, 81
  theory, 46–47, 77–84
  of violence, 82, 106, 125, 133
Symbolic interactionism, 224–26, 230

T–V

Therapeutic control, 386–87
Uniform Crime Reports, 103, 109
Vagrancy laws, 340–55
Value-free science
  criticism of, 20–21, 63–65, 241
  and normative perspective, 19, 61–62
Victimization survey, 103, 111–13
Violence
  approval of, 138–40
  gang, 182–84
  regional variations, 129–46
  self-reported, 135–40

PAROLES
CAROL SPIRO   SAT

Mod. conflict
uzo pko.

Functional	Conflict
tending consistently to support the existing social systems or status quo	Sees society as in a continuous state of flux & emphasizes the source of change
Overemphasizes societal harmony & thereby minimizes the imp. of conflict & change	looks at how some groups acquire power & maintain dominance over other groups
conflict pay too little attention to the ques. what holds society together	little use of modern research methods, stat. evidence & comp Anal.
Dur. = social order	

little